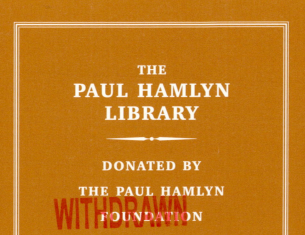

Archaeology at Aksum, Ethiopia, 1993-7

Volume I

MEMOIRS OF THE BRITISH INSTITUTE IN EASTERN AFRICA: NUMBER 17

REPORT 65 , RESEARCH COMMITTEE OF THE SOCIETY OF ANTIQUARIES OF LONDON

ARCHAEOLOGY AT AKSUM, ETHIOPIA, 1993-7

by

DAVID W. PHILLIPSON

with the principal assistance of

JACKE PHILLIPS

and contributions by

Ayele Tarekegn, Sheila Boardman,
Chester R. Cain, Helen Cook, Ann Feuerbach,
Niall Finneran, Jennifer P. Ford, Rowena Gale, Michael Harlow,
Graham C. Morgan, Paul Pettitt, Jillian B. Phillips,
Laurel Phillipson, Andrew Reynolds, Roger Schneider,
Klara Spandl, Tekle Hagos, Jess Tipper,
Martin Watts and David Williams

in two volumes

VOLUME I

LONDON
2000

The British Institute in
Eastern Africa

The Society of Antiquaries
of London

Published by

The British Institute in Eastern Africa,
c/o The British Academy,
10, Carlton House Terrace,
London SW1Y 5AH

and

The Society of Antiquaries of London,
Burlington House,
Piccadilly,
London W1V 0HS

Distributed by

Oxbow Books,
Park End Place,
Oxford OX1 1HN

ISBN 1 872566 13 8

(c) The British Institute in Eastern Africa 2000

Designed by David W. Phillipson

Filmset by Gary Reynolds Typesetting Services, Cambridge

Printed and bound in England by Short Run Press, Exeter

PREFACE

This work offers an account of archaeological research undertaken at Aksum in Ethiopia under the auspices of the British Institute in Eastern Africa between 1993 and 1997. From lowly antecedents, Aksum rapidly gained importance during the first centuries AD as the capital of one of the most prosperous states in sub-Saharan Africa, exploiting local agricultural resources and raw materials - including ivory and gold - which were fed into the Red Sea trade network linking the Roman Empire with regions as far distant as India. Today, the site is renowned for its ancient monuments, most notably its monolithic stelae. In view of these impressive monuments and in recognition of its prime importance in the history of Ethiopia and the potential for further archaeological research, Aksum has been designated a World Heritage Site by UNESCO.

The years since 1991 have seen a rapid increase in tourism at Aksum, both Ethiopian and foreign. Visitors come primarily to see the Cathedral and the archaeological sites, including the Museum. None of these attractions is yet being conserved or developed in a manner which is commensurate with the growth of tourism. This, and the control of visitors, present a major challenge which the ecclesiastical and governmental authorities have yet to face. The archaeological research here described was throughout undertaken with a view to the long-term conservation and presentation of the sites investigated, as will be noted in the following chapters. However, the authorities have taken the wise decision to postpone admission of visitors to recently excavated monuments until such time as adequate infrastructure is in place to ensure their protection in perpetuity.

The research was designed to illuminate aspects of Aksumite society which had not been emphasised in previous investigations: the domestic economy as well as long-distance trade, the living-conditions and burial customs of commoners in addition to the tombs and palaces of the élite, local crafts and industries in comparison with imported luxuries. The aim has been to produce a more rounded picture of ancient Aksum than has been available hitherto.

Investigation of the processes whereby the Aksumite polity arose was not a prime focus of the research here described, but has been conducted in the vicinity of Aksum by a separate project directed by Drs Rodolfo Fattovich and Kathryn Bard, the results of which are being published elsewhere. An important Pre-Aksumite settlement was, however, located and investigated; an account is included in the present work.

Every effort has been made to present our research results promptly and in a form accessible to most users. Stratigraphical minutiae and details of many individual artefacts have been omitted here, but may in due course be consulted in the Archive by arrangement with the Centre for Research and Conservation of the Cultural Heritage (CRCCH) in Addis Ababa or with the British Institute in Eastern Africa in London. Likewise, the present work contains relatively little broad historical synthesis or conclusions other than those arising directly from the sites and artefacts investigated in 1993-7. A preliminary overview has already appeared (D.W.Phillipson 1998) and further works are in course of preparation. Prompt publication - sadly, a rare occurrence in Aksumite archaeology - places the primary evidence in the public domain.

A prominent and much appreciated feature of the research here described has been the full collaboration both of the Ethiopian government in Addis Ababa and of the Tigray authorities. Although research sponsors and colleagues are acknowledged in Chapter 1, it is appropriate here to record with gratitude the interest and support of successive Ministers of Culture in Addis Ababa, His Excellency Ato Leule-Selassie Temamo and His Excellency Ato Woldemichael Chemu. At CRCCH, Dr Kassaye Begashaw was succeeded as Head by Ato Jara Haile Mariam, with the Archaeology and Anthropology section under Dr Yonas

Beyene: all have done much to facilitate the research. In Tigray, the President, Ato Gebru Asrat, took a personal interest in the work, as did Dr Solomon Iqbal and successive Heads of the Culture Bureau, Ato Messele Zeleke, Ato Hailu Habtu and Ato Atakilti Hagege, and their colleagues in Aksum. It is appropriate also to record our indebtedness to the ecclesiastical authorities of the Ethiopian Orthodox Tewahedo Church, especially to His Holiness the Patriarch and to the Nebured of Aksum.

Special appreciation is due to the people of Aksum, whose interest and co-operation was by no means limited to those who were formally employed by the Project.

Professor Merid Wolde Aregay and Professor Taddesse Tamrat of the History Department at Addis Ababa University have provided invaluable advice as, at the Institute of Ethiopian Studies, have Dr Bahru Zewde and Dr Abdussamad Ahmad. The interest and support of Her Britannic Majesty's successive Ambassadors to Ethiopia, Mr James Glaze, Mr Robin Christopher and Mr Gordon Wetherell, their wives and staff, have been greatly appreciated. Finally, it is a pleasure to record our gratitude to the staff of the British Council in Addis Ababa, especially to the former Director Mr Michael Sargent and Mrs Patsy Sargent, and to Ato Tadesse Terfa.

It is hoped that the Project whose work is reported here will prove to have made a lasting contribution to Ethiopian archaeology, not only in terms of academic knowledge, but in popular understanding both Ethiopian and foreign, as well as in training of local personnel and in preparing for sustainable and sympathetic tourism.

David W. Phillipson

Gonville & Caius College,
Cambridge.
20 September 2000

CONTENTS

VOLUME I

Chapter 1   Background to the Project *(D.W.P.)*   p.   1

Chapter 2   The Prehistoric Antecedents of Aksum   p.   17

        Early and Middle Stone Ages *(Laurel Phillipson)*   p.   17

        Late Stone Age *(Niall Finneran)*   p.   22

        Overview *(Laurel Phillipson)*   p.   26

Chapter 3   The Central Stelae Area *(D.W.P.)*   p.   27

Chapter 4   The Tomb of the Brick Arches   p.   31

        Structure and stratigraphy *(Jess Tipper)*   p.   31

        Artefacts

            Pottery and other clay objects *(Jacke Phillips)*   p.   57

            Glass and beads *(Michael Harlow)*   p.   77

            Metal *(D.W.P.)*   p.   86

            Ivory *(D.W.P.)*   p. 116

            Stone *(D.W.P.)*   p. 124

        Human skeletal remains *(Helen Cook)*   p. 126

        Archaeobotany *(Sheila Boardman)*   p. 127

        Overview *(D.W.P.)*   p. 128

        Conservation *(D.W.P.)*   p. 132

Chapter 5   Stela 3 *(D.W.P.)*   p. 135

Chapter 6   The Stela-2 site   p. 139

        Introduction *(D.W.P.)*   p. 139

        Preliminary investigations, 1993-4 *(D.W.P.)*   p. 139

        The 1997 excavation *(Martin Watts)*   p. 141

        Artefacts from the 1994 and 1997 excavations *(D.W.P.*

                         and Martin Watts)   p. 154

        Archaeobotany *(Sheila Boardman)*   p. 156

        Overview *(D.W.P. and Martin Watts)*   p. 156

Chapter 7   The Complex of Monuments associated with Stela 1   p. 157

The present configuration of the Stela-1 complex *(D.W.P.)*   p. 157

Stela 1 *(D.W.P.)*   p. 161

The Mausoleum

Structure *(Michael Harlow and D.W.P.)*   p. 165

Excavations within the Mausoleum *(Michael Harlow and Jacke Phillips)*   p. 179

External excavations *(Michael Harlow and Jacke Phillips)*   p. 183

Artefacts from primary contexts

Pottery *(Jacke Phillips)*   p. 194

Glass and beads *(Michael Harlow)*   p. 197

Metal *(D.W.P.)*   p. 200

Shell *(D.W.P.)*   p. 204

Lithics *(Laurel Phillipson)*   p. 205

Artefacts from later contexts

Pottery and other clay objects *(Jacke Phillips)*   p. 205

Glass and beads *(Michael Harlow)*   p. 212

Metal *(D.W.P.)*   p. 215

Shell *(D.W.P.)*   p. 215

Stone *(D.W.P.)*   p. 215

Lithics *(Laurel Phillipson)*   p. 216

Human skeletal remains *(Helen Cook)*   p. 216

Archaeobotany *(Sheila Boardman)*   p. 217

Archaeozoology *(Chester R. Cain)*   p. 218

The East Tomb

Structure and excavation *(D.W.P.)*   p. 218

Artefacts *(Jacke Phillips and D.W.P.)*   p. 220

Overview *(D.W.P.)*   p. 220

Conservation *(D.W.P. and Michael Harlow)*   p. 223

Chapter 8   The Gudit Stelae Field *(Ayele Tarekegn and D.W.P.)*   p. 225

Chapter 9   Quarries, Stone Working and Stela Erection   p. 229

The Aksumite quarries at Gobedra Hill and Adi Tsehafi *(Jillian B. Phillips and Jennifer P. Ford)*   p. 229

Transport and stela-erection *(D.W.P. and Laurel Phillipson)*   p. 247

Stone dressing *(Laurel Phillipson)*   p. 254

Overview *(D.W.P.)*   p. 266

VOLUME II

Chapter 10   The D Site at Kidane Mehret   p. 267

                    The site and its sequence (D.W.P. and Jacke Phillips)   p. 267

                    Structures and stratigraphy (Jacke Phillips, Andrew
                                    Reynolds and Klara Spandl)   p. 280

                Artefacts

                        Pottery and clay objects (Jacke Phillips)   p. 303

                        Glass, beads and pendants (Michael Harlow)   p. 337

                        Metal (D.W.P.)   p. 342

                        Ivory and bone (D.W.P.)   p. 345

                        Textiles (Sheila Boardman)   p. 345

                        Ground and carved stone (D.W.P. and Laurel
                                    Phillipson)   p. 346

                        Seals (D.W.P.)   p. 350

                        Lithics (Laurel Phillipson)   p. 352

                    Human skeletal remains (Helen Cook)   p. 363

                    Archaeobotany (Sheila Boardman)   p. 363

                    Archaeozoology (Chester R. Cain)   p. 369

                    Overview (D.W.P.)   p. 372

Chapter 11   The K site in Maleke Aksum   p. 381

                    Excavation and stratigraphy (Michael Harlow and Jacke
                                    Phillips)   p. 381

                Artefacts

                        Pottery and clay objects (Jacke Phillips)   p. 389

                        Glass and beads (Michael Harlow)   p. 400

                        Metal (D.W.P.)   p. 404

                        Ivory, horn, bone and shell (D.W.P.)   p. 407

                        Stone and brick (D.W.P.)   p. 408

                        Lithics (Laurel Phillipson)   p. 408

                    Human skeletal remains (Helen Cook)   p. 411

                    Archaeobotany (Sheila Boardman)   p. 412

                    Archaeozoology (Chester R. Cain)   p. 414

                    Overview (D.W.P.)   p. 417

Chapter 12   Other Sites and Monuments   p. 419

                    P, H and X sites *(D.W.P.)*   p. 419

                    L site *(Tekle Hagos and D.W.P.)*   p. 420

                    Mestaha Werki *(Laurel Phillipson)*   p. 421

                    Inscriptions and engravings at Adi Tsehafi *(Laurel Phillipson)* p. 423

                    The Tomb of Bazen, the Tomb of the False Door and the

                        Tombs of Kaleb and Gabra Maskal

                        (D.W.P.)   p. 425

Chapter 13   Surface collections of Aksumite lithic industries *(Laurel Phillipson)*   p. 433

Chapter 14   Syntheses   p. 449

                    Lithic industries *(Laurel Phillipson)*   p. 449

                    Overview of pottery development *(Jacke Phillips)*   p. 453

                    Glass and beads *(Michael Harlow)*   p. 458

                    Ivory-working techniques *(Laurel Phillipson)*   p. 460

                    Archaeobotany *(Sheila Boardman and D.W.P.)*   p. 468

                    Distribution of Aksumite materials and settlement

                        (Laurel Phillipson)   p. 470

Chapter 15   Concluding discussion *(D.W.P.)*   p. 473

        Appendices   p. 489

            I   The 1992 Research Design *(D.W.P.)*   p. 489

            II   Classical Aksumite pottery: surface treatment and decoration

                        (Jacke Phillips)   p. 491

            III   Petrology of imported amphorae *(David Williams)*   p. 494

            IV   Metallurgical examination and analysis *(Ann Feuerbach)*   p. 497

            V   Excavated Aksumite coins *(D.W.P.)*   p. 500

            VI   Radiocarbon dates *(D.W.P., Paul Pettitt , Sheila Boardman

                        and Rowena Gale)*   p. 504

            VII   Archaeobotanical methodology *(Sheila Boardman and

                        Rowena Gale)*   p. 507

            VIII   Archaeozoological methodology *(Chester R. Cain)*   p. 510

            IX   Inscriptions *(Roger Schneider)*   p. 512

            X   A sample of render from the Mausoleum

                        (Graham C. Morgan)   p. 515

            XI   Magnetic susceptibility readings *(Jillian B. Phillips

                        and Jennifer P. Ford)*   p. 516

            XII   Recent use of the Stelae Park area *(Jacke Phillips)*   p. 519

            XIII   Inventory numbers of illustrated artefacts *(D.W.P.)*   p. 521

        Bibliographic references   p. 525

        Index   p. 537

ILLUSTRATIONS IN VOLUME I

Fig. 1	Location map of Aksum relative to Northeast Africa and the Red Sea.	p. 2
Fig. 2	Contour map of the Aksum vicinity.	pp. 4-5
Fig. 3	Air photograph of the area covered by Fig. 2.	p. 6
Fig. 4	Photographic panorama of Aksum, taken from Mai Qoho.	p. 7
Fig. 5	The Old Cathedral at Aksum, seen from the bell-tower.	p. 8
Fig. 6	Detailed air photograph of central Aksum, naming the principal features.	p. 9
Fig. 7	Plan of Aksum town, showing central sites.	p. 10
Fig. 8	Ecclesiastical visitors to the excavation.	p. 11
Fig. 9	List of sites excavated.	p. 12
Fig. 10	The 1994 excavation team.	p. 14
Fig. 11	Time-chart for the archaeology of the Aksum area.	p. 17
Fig. 12	Map of the survey area showing sites and find-spots.	p. 18
Fig. 13	Acheulian-type bifaces, surface finds.	p. 19
Fig. 14	Large prepared-core artefacts, surface finds.	p. 20
Fig. 15	Middle Stone Age type artefacts, surface finds.	p. 21
Fig. 16	Views of Anqqer Baahti and Baahti Nebait rockshelters.	p. 23
Fig. 17	Plans of Anqqer Baahti and Baahti Nebait.	p. 24
Fig. 18	Artefacts from Baahti Nebait.	p. 25
Fig. 19	The Stelae Park seen from the dome of the New Cathedral.	p. 27
Fig. 20	Plan of the Stelae Park and west-east section.	p. 28
Fig. 21	North-south cross-sections of the Stelae Park.	p. 29
Fig. 22	General plan, Tomb of the Brick Arches.	p. 32
Fig. 23	Section of the adit, Tomb of the Brick Arches.	p. 33
Fig. 24	Structural sections within the Tomb of the Brick Arches.	p. 34
Fig. 25	Tomb of the Brick Arches: the adit.	p. 35
Fig. 26	Tomb of the Brick Arches: Arch I.	p. 36
Fig. 27	Views inside the Tomb of the Brick Arches.	p. 37
Fig. 28	Tomb of the Brick Arches: artefacts as exposed by excavation.	p. 38
Fig. 29	Plan of the Tomb of the Brick Arches, showing excavation subdivisions.	p. 38
Fig. 30	Stratigraphic correlation chart, Tomb of the Brick Arches.	pp. 40-3
Fig. 31	The pit in the floor of Chamber A, Tomb of the Brick Arches.	p. 44
Fig. 32	The heap of extracted artefacts outside Loculus E, Tomb of the Brick Arches.	p. 45

Fig. 33   Tomb of the Brick Arches: composite plan of Robbing 2.   p. 46

Fig. 34   Section through Passage G, Tomb of the Brick Arches.   p. 47

Fig. 35   Tomb of the Brick Arches: distribution of fragments from individual artefacts.   p. 48

Fig. 36   Tomb of the Brick Arches: Loculus E on termination of excavation.   p. 49

Fig. 37   Tomb of the Brick Arches: sections of Loculus E and Passage G.   p. 50

Fig. 38   Tomb of the Brick Arches: distribution of fragments from the bird-shaped vessel.   p. 50

Fig. 39   Chamber D, with Loculi H and J, Tomb of the Brick Arches.   p. 51

Fig. 40   Excavation in progress in Loculus H, Tomb of the Brick Arches.   p. 52

Fig. 41   Sections across Loculi H and J, Tomb of the Brick Arches.   p. 53

Fig. 42   Plan of copper alloy plates and mirrors in Loculus J, Tomb of the Brick Arches.   p. 55

Fig. 43   Pottery beakers and bowls from the Tomb of the Brick Arches.   p. 58

Fig. 44   Pottery bowls and basins from the Tomb of the Brick Arches.   p. 61

Fig. 45   Painted and other pottery from the Tomb of the Brick Arches.   p. 62

Fig. 46   Animal-model basins from the Tomb of the Brick Arches.   p. 63

Fig. 47   Pottery basins and jars from the Tomb of the Brick Arches.   p. 65

Fig. 48   Pottery jar from the Tomb of the Brick Arches.   p. 66

Fig. 49   Pottery jars from the Tomb of the Brick Arches.   p. 67

Fig. 50   Pottery jars from the Tomb of the Brick Arches.   p. 69

Fig. 51   Pottery jar and spouted strainer vessel from the Tomb of the Brick Arches.   p. 70

Fig. 52   Pottery face-jars from the Tomb of the Brick Arches.   p. 71

Fig. 53   Pottery face-jars from the Tomb of the Brick Arches.   p. 73

Fig. 54   Miscellaneous pottery from the Tomb of the Brick Arches.   p. 74

Fig. 55   Pottery stove or brazier from the Tomb of the Brick Arches.   p. 75

Fig. 56   Bird-shaped pottery vessel from the Tomb of the Brick Arches.   p. 76

Fig. 57   Summary of glass from the Tomb of the Brick Arches.   p. 78

Fig. 58   Glass vessels from the Tomb of the Brick Arches.   p. 79

Fig. 59   Glass objects from the Tomb of the Brick Arches.   p. 80

Fig. 60   Glass goblet and sphere from the Tomb of the Brick Arches.   p. 81

Fig. 61   Glass fragments from the Tomb of the Brick Arches.   p. 82

Fig. 62   Beads from the Tomb of the Brick Arches.   p. 83

Fig. 63   Summary of beads from the Tomb of the Brick Arches.   p. 84

Fig. 64   Beads from the Tomb of the Brick Arches.   p. 85

Fig. 65   Beads from the Tomb of the Brick Arches.   p. 86

Fig. 66   Gold and silver artefacts from the Tomb of the Brick Arches.   p. 87

Fig. 67   Copper alloy nails, tacks, shank, strips etc. from the Tomb of the Brick Arches.   p. 88

Fig. 68   Distribution of copper alloy nails, tacks etc from the Tomb of the Brick Arches.   p. 89

Fig. 69   Copper alloy bars, spoon, washers etc from the Tomb of the Brick Arches.   p. 89

Fig. 70   Copper alloy knives, hinges and cotter pins from the Tomb of the Brick Arches.   p. 90

Fig. 71   Copper alloy hinges, cotter-pin and strips from the Tomb of the Brick Arches.   p. 91

Fig. 72   Copper alloy box-fittings from Loculus J, Tomb of the Brick Arches.   p. 92

Fig. 73   Copper alloy box fittings from Chamber B and mirrors from Loculus J   p. 93

Fig. 74   Copper alloy mirrors from the Tomb of the Brick Arches.   p. 94

Fig. 75   The 'block' of cuprous scrap from Chamber A , Tomb of the Brick Arches.   p. 95

Fig. 76   Tomb of the Brick Arches: the 'cover' as re-assembled.   p. 96

Fig. 77   Tomb of the Brick Arches: the 'cover' as reconstructed.   p. 97

Fig. 78   Tomb of the Brick Arches: the 'trough'.   p. 98

Fig. 79   Tomb of the Brick Arches: the rondel as re-assembled.   p. 99

Fig. 80   Tomb of the Brick Arches: the rondel as reconstructed.   p. 100

Fig. 81   Tomb of the Brick Arches: cuprous fragments from the 'block'.   p. 101

Fig. 82   Tomb of the Brick Arches: grille fragments and reconstruction.   p. 102

Fig. 83   Tomb of the Brick Arches: artefacts from the 'block'.   p. 102

Fig. 84   Tomb of the Brick Arches: plates, glass inserts and reconstructions.   p. 103

Fig. 85   Tomb of the Brick Arches: bars and nails from the 'block'.   p. 104

Fig. 86   Tomb of the Brick Arches: bimetallic plaques in situ .   p. 105

Fig. 87   Types of bimetallic plaques from the Tomb of the Brick Arches.   p. 106

Fig. 88   Details of bimetallic plaques from the Tomb of the Brick Arches.   p. 107

Fig. 89   Bimetallic objects in iron and copper alloy from the Tomb of the Brick Arches.   p. 109

Fig. 90   Iron knives from the Tomb of the Brick Arches.   p. 110

Fig. 91   Iron knives from the Tomb of the Brick Arches.   p. 111

Fig. 92   Iron cramps, latches, flanged objects and spearheads, Tomb of the Brick Arches.   p. 112

Fig. 93   Large iron spearhead from the Tomb of the Brick Arches.   p. 113

Fig. 94   Iron nails, eyelet spike, strip, bars, rods and 'fitting',Tomb of the Brick Arches.   p. 114

Fig. 95   Iron and silver object from the Tomb of the Brick Arches.   p. 115

Fig. 96   X-ray and detail of iron and silver object from the Tomb of the Brick Arches.   p. 116

Fig. 97   Ivory furniture components from the Tomb of the Brick Arches: panels.   p. 117

Fig. 98   Ivory furniture components from the Tomb of the Brick Arches: panel details.   p. 118

Fig. 99   Ivory furniture components from the Tomb of the Brick Arches: finial.   p. 119

Fig. 100   Ivory furniture components from the Tomb of the Brick Arches: slats and finial.   p. 120

Fig. 101   Tomb of the Brick Arches: ivory plaques as block-lifted.   p. 121

Fig. 102   Ivory plaques from the Tomb of the Brick Arches.   p. 121

Fig. 103   Details of ivory plaques from the Tomb of the Brick Arches.   p. 122

Fig. 104   Turned cylindrical ivory boxes from the Tomb of the Brick Arches.   p. 123

Fig. 105   Ivory figurine from the Tomb of the Brick Arches.   p. 124

Fig. 106   Miscellaneous ivory artefacts from the Tomb of the Brick Arches.   p. 125

Fig. 107   Lower grindstone from the Tomb of the Brick Arches.   p. 126

Fig. 108   Human bones from the Tomb of the Brick Arches.   p. 127

Fig. 109   Radiocarbon dates from the Tomb of the Brick Arches.   p. 129

Fig. 110   Conservation measures at the Tomb of the Brick Arches.   p. 132

Fig. 111   Stela 3 from the southeast.   p. 135

Fig. 112   Details of Stela 3.   p. 136

Fig. 113   Present inclination of Stela 3.   p. 137

Fig. 114   Stelae 3 and 21 in 1906 and 1992.   p. 138

Fig. 115   Exploratory excavation in 1994 on the site of Stela 2.   p. 140

Fig. 116   The 1997 excavation on the site of Stela 2.   p. 142

Fig. 117   Sections of the 1997 excavation on the site of Stela 2.   p. 144
Fig. 118   Plan of the 1997 excavation on the site of Stela 2: Aksumite features.   p. 145
Fig. 119   The east wall of the shaft to the northeast of Stela 2.   p. 145
Fig. 120   The Stela-2 substructure.   p. 146
Fig. 121   How Stela 2 was toppled.   p. 148
Fig. 122   Plan of the 1997 excavation on the site of Stela 2: Post-Aksumite features.   p. 149
Fig. 123   The recent round house exposed in the 1997 excavation on the site of Stela 2.   p. 150
Fig. 124   Fragments of Stela 2 recovered during the 1997 excavations.   p. 154
Fig. 125   Artefacts from the excavation on the site of Stela 2.   p. 155
Fig. 126   Plan of the Stela-1 area including Nefas Mawcha.   p. 157
Fig. 127   Stela 1 and Nefas Mawcha.   p. 158
Fig. 128   The lowered area west of Stela 1.   p. 159
Fig. 129   Stela 1 from the west, showing fractures.   p. 160
Fig. 130   Section along Stela 1.   p. 160
Fig. 131   The base of Stela 1, seen from the east.   p. 161
Fig. 132   The view southward along the top of the fallen Stela 1, towards Nefas Mawcha.   p. 162
Fig. 133   Cross-section of Stela 1.   p. 162
Fig. 134   The lower (formerly southern) false door of Stela 1.   p. 163
Fig. 135   The upper false door of Stela 1 and the scar where its handle has been removed.   p. 164
Fig. 136   Plan and section of the Mausoleum and East Tomb.   p. 165
Fig. 137   The eastern portal of the Mausoleum.   p. 166
Fig. 138   Photogrammetry of the Mausoleum's eastern portal.   p. 167
Fig. 139   A view westwards along the central passage of the Mausoleum.   p. 167
Fig. 140   Inner faces of the Mausoleum entrances.   p. 168
Fig. 141   Photogrammetry of the Mausoleum's central passage.   facing p. 168
Fig. 142   Photogrammetry of Mausoleum sidechambers D and E.   facing p. 169
Fig. 143   Views inside the Mausoleum.   p. 169
Fig. 144   Mausoleum sidechambers D, F and K.   p. 171
Fig. 145   Photogrammetry of Mausoleum sidechamber F.   p. 172
Fig. 146   Photogrammetry of Mausoleum sidechamber K.   p. 173
Fig. 147   Plan of paving surviving in the Mausoleum.   p. 174
Fig. 148   Excavation below the Mausoleum floor.   p. 174
Fig. 149   The western arch of the Mausoleum, open.   p. 175
Fig. 150   The western entrance to the Mausoleum.   p. 176
Fig. 151   Render inside the Mausoleum.   p. 177
Fig. 152   The inscribed letter on the roof of Mausoleum sidechamber E.   p. 177
Fig. 153   The Mausoleum roof shafts seen from below.   p. 178
Fig. 154   The slab from the central shaft of the Mausoleum, now erected vertically.   p. 179
Fig. 155   Plan of the Mausoleum showing excavation divisions.   p. 180
Fig. 156   Sections of deposits within the Mausoleum.   p. 181
Fig. 157   Deposits at entrances to Mausoleum sidechambers.   p. 182
Fig. 158   Excavated contexts within the Mausoleum attributed to phases.   p. 183

Fig. 159   Plan of trenches external to the Mausoleum.   p. 184

Fig. 160   Trenches M4 and M5: sections and plan.   p. 185

Fig. 161   Trench M6 from the southwest, showing the tunnel dug into sidechamber K.   p. 186

Fig. 162   Plan and photogrammetry of walls outside the west end of the Mausoleum.   p. 187

Fig. 163   Trench M7: west section.   p. 188

Fig. 164   Trench M8: west section and plan.   p. 189

Fig. 165   Trench M8: the upper side of the Mausoleum roof-slabs.   p. 190

Fig. 166   Excavated contexts in the Mausoleum external trenches, attributed to phases.   p. 191

Fig. 167   Correlation of phases inside and outside the Mausoleum.   p. 192

Fig. 168   Plan of phase-5 house walls in trenches M5 and M6.   p. 193

Fig. 169   Pottery bowls, basin, jar and pedestal from phase I within the Mausoleum.   p. 195

Fig. 170   Pottery jar, pots and African Red Slip bowl, phase I within the Mausoleum.   p. 196

Fig. 171   Potsherds from phase I within the Mausoleum.   p. 197

Fig. 172   Summary of Mausoleum phase-I glass.   p. 197

Fig. 173   Glass from phase I within the Mausoleum.   p. 198

Fig. 174   Glass inlay from Mausoleum phase I.   p. 199

Fig. 175   Summary of Mausoleum phase-I beads.   p. 200

Fig. 176   Beads from phase I within the Mausoleum.   p. 200

Fig. 177   Gold and gilded artefacts from phase I within the Mausoleum.   p. 201

Fig. 178   Mausoleum phase-I artefacts of gold, silver etc.   p. 202

Fig. 179   Copper alloy artefacts from phase-I contexts within the Mausoleum.   p. 202

Fig. 180   Iron artefacts from phase-I contexts within the Mausoleum.   p. 203

Fig. 181   Shell plaques from phase I within the Mausoleum.   p. 204

Fig. 182   Lithics from phase-I contexts within the Mausoleum.   p. 205

Fig. 183   Glazed pottery from Mausoleum post-Aksumite and recent contexts.   p. 205

Fig. 184   Pottery bowls, jar and lid from later contexts inside the Mausoleum.   p. 206

Fig. 185   Post-Aksumite jar from within the Mausoleum.   p. 207

Fig. 186   Post-Aksumite jar from the Mausoleum trenches.   p. 208

Fig. 187   Post-Aksumite pots from the Mausoleum trenches.   p. 209

Fig. 188   Pottery bowls, jars, pot and lid from the Mausoleum trenches.   p. 210

Fig. 189   Mausoleum clay objects.   p. 211

Fig. 190   Summary of glass from later Mausoleum contexts.   p. 212

Fig. 191   Glass from later Mausoleum contexts.   p. 213

Fig. 192   Beads from later Mausoleum contexts.   p. 213

Fig. 193   Summary of beads from later Mausoleum contexts.   p. 214

Fig. 194   Beads from later Mausoleum contexts.   p. 214

Fig. 195   Copper alloy artefacts from later Mausoleum contexts.   p. 215

Fig. 196   Iron knives from later Mausoleum contexts.   p. 215

Fig. 197   Slate disc and inscribed burnisher, from the Mausoleum.   p. 216

Fig. 198   Likanos flake from the Mausoleum.   p. 216

Fig. 199   Human remains from the Mausoleum.   p. 217

Fig. 200   Photogrammetry of the East Tomb entrance.   p. 218

Fig. 201   The East Tomb.   p. 219

Fig. 202   Reconstructed bird's eye view of the Stela-1 complex.   p. 221

Fig. 203   Conservation measures undertaken at the Stela-1 complex.   p. 224

Fig. 204   View of the Gudit Stelae Field.   p. 225

Fig. 205   Map of the Gudit Stelae Field.   p. 226

Fig. 206   Excavations at the Gudit Stelae Field, and a re-used stela baseplate at Dungur. p. 227

Fig. 207   Map of Gobedra Hill, showing location of quarries.   p. 230

Fig. 208   Definitions of terms used in descriptions of quarries.   p. 231

Fig. 209   Plan of Gobedra Quarry I.   p. 232

Fig. 210   Gobedra Quarry I.   p. 233

Fig. 211   Plans of Gobedra Quarries II and III.   p. 234

Fig. 212   Gobedra Quarry II.   p. 235

Fig. 213   Gobedra Quarry III and slipway, from the air.   p. 236

Fig. 214   Basalt pounder from Gobedra Quarry III.   p. 236

Fig. 215   Gobedra Quarry III.   p. 237

Fig. 216   Slipway at Gobedra Quarry III.   p. 238

Fig. 217   Gobedra Quarry IV.   p. 239

Fig. 218   Plans of Gobedra Quarry V.   p. 241

Fig. 219   Gobedra Quarry V.   p. 242

Fig. 220   Adi Tsehafi quarry.   p. 244

Fig. 221   Adi Tsehafi quarry.   p. 245

Fig. 222   Contour map of the area between Gobedra and Aksum.   p. 248

Fig. 223   Sections across the proposed stela-route.   p. 249

Fig. 224   Photo-panorama of probable stela-route.   p. 250

Fig. 225   Reconstruction of transport and erection of stelae, by Berhane Meskel Ftsah.   p. 252

Fig. 226   Possible methods of stela-erection.   p. 253

Fig. 227   Modern mason's tools.   p. 255

Fig. 228   Internal impressions of stone-dressing marks.   p. 256

Fig. 229   Stone-dressing: Tomb of the Brick Arches and Nefas Mawcha.   p. 258

Fig. 230   Stone-dressing: Tomb of the False Door.   p. 260

Fig. 231   Rubbings of dressed stones at the Tomb of the False Door and the Mausoleum.   p. 261

Fig. 232   Rubbings of Stela 2 and associated dressed stonework.   p. 262

Fig. 233   Stone-dressing: Stelae 1, 3 and 19.   p. 263

Fig. 234   The south face of Stela 3.   p. 264

Fig. 235   Rubbings of Stelae 19 and 21.   p. 265

Chapter 1

BACKGROUND TO THE PROJECT
(D.W.P.)

Previous research

This is not the place to repeat details of the archaeological research that was undertaken at Aksum prior to the 1970s. Summaries, with bibliographic references, have been published by Munro-Hay (1989: 27-31) and by Negussie (1993, 1994). Noteworthy and reprehensible is the substantial amount of excavation which has been undertaken but never fully published; this irresponsibility causes serious difficulty to all subsequent researchers and deprives the Ethiopian public and international scholarship of information to which they are entitled.

The foundation for all subsequent studies laid by the Deutsche Aksum-Expedition (DAE) of 1906 (Littmann *et al.* 1913) has long been acknowledged and the details are now more readily available to English-readers, especially within Ethiopia, since the recent publication of an annotated translation (D.W.Phillipson 1997). The value of the DAE record is all the greater because so much of the field evidence therein described is no longer extant. It is unfortunate that the subsequent processes of destruction, resiting and (often inaccurate) restoration have, with few exceptions, gone unrecorded.

Prior to the 1970s, numerous scholars added to the DAE foundation, but little emphasis was, so far as the published accounts indicate, placed on such matters as detailed chronological sequences or economic base. As the present writer observed at the Institute of Ethiopian Studies at Addis Ababa University in 1989: 'Archaeology at Aksum has so far concentrated its attention on monumental architecture and on artefacts of foreign origin. ... What we have at present is an archaeology of the Aksumite élite, represented by the residences and tombs of the rich and powerful who had access to luxury goods imported from the Mediterranean world. By contrast, we know very little about the lives and homes of the common people who must have comprised the vast majority of Aksum's inhabitants and subjects. ... Aksum ... is generally seen as the centre of a great trading state which gathered together the products of the interior and exported them *via* the Red Sea coast in exchange for luxury items originating in various parts of the Roman and Byzantine Empires. Because at present archaeologists know far more about the products of these empires, it is this

aspect of the trade - Aksum's imports rather than the exports - that have been emphasised in the archaeological literature. ... Yet it was ... Aksum's control over sources of supply ... which was of paramount importance in her rise to power and prosperity. One has only to look at the map to see that this was so. ... Aksum arose on the plateau ..., not on its eastern side with short (albeit arduous) access to the Red Sea coast and the overseas markets, but near the plateau's western edge several days' extra journey from the main port at Adulis. It was this access to the interior ... that was the prime factor in determining the location of Aksum. So far, very little has been done to illustrate archaeologically how and where Aksum's primary wealth was obtained - the wealth that attracted the external trading contacts which later developed. ... The food-producing economy of the Aksumite state must have been both efficient and well organised, if only to support the large population of craftsmen and labourers who must have been involved in the construction of the capital's monuments and its long-distance trade. We cannot be looking here at the food-producing capacity of the immediate area of Aksum itself, but at that of a much wider region' (D.W.Phillipson 1990: 55-7). This paper may be regarded as a manifesto for the research described in the present work.

Some at least of these considerations had been in the mind of Dr Neville Chittick when, on behalf of the British Institute in Eastern Africa, he planned the archaeological campaign at Aksum that began under his direction in 1972, with large-scale field seasons in 1973 and 1974. Chittick understandably began his work with an effort to establish a chronological sequence for the main stelae field. As the posthumous report (Munro-Hay 1989) makes clear, this had been the principal area investigated when research was curtailed at short notice by deteriorating security conditions accompanying the Ethiopian revolution of 1974. Other research efforts at the same time were beginning to focus on allied problems but shared a similar fate. Joseph Michels started a detailed archaeological survey of the area between Aksum and Yeha; the results, never fully published (cf. Michels 1990, 1994), show the ultimate potential of such studies, even though reservations may be expressed over Michels' methodology and his chronological framework. Between 1974

1

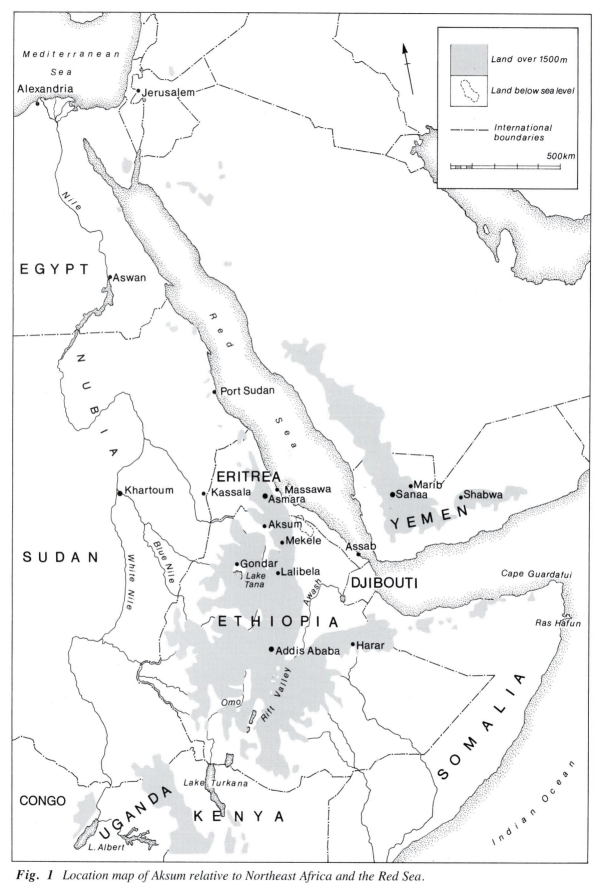

Fig. 1 *Location map of Aksum relative to Northeast Africa and the Red Sea.*

and 1991, it was not practicable for archaeologists, Ethiopian or foreign, to undertake fieldwork in Tigray. The paper cited above (D.W.Phillipson 1990) may be taken as a statement of the knowledge and research priorities seen as that period drew to a close.

Planning

With the return of peaceful conditions to Tigray in 1991, consideration could be given to the resumption of archaeological research in and around Aksum. Two groups rose to the challenge. Italian and American interests co-operated, under the direction of Drs Rodolfo Fattovich and Kathryn Bard, to undertake fieldwork on Beta Giyorgis hill, northwest of Aksum, where burial and settlement sites evidently covered a long period of time, extending back to a period earlier than the occupation of the central area but also continuing into Late Aksumite times. The present writer, on behalf of the British Institute in Eastern Africa, began a five-year campaign at Aksum itself and in its immediate vicinity. It is with the latter operation that this work is concerned. Preliminary reports on the Beta Giyorgis research have appeared regularly (*e.g.* Bard *et al.* 1997; Fattovich 1994; Fattovich and Bard 1993, 1995, 1996, 1997a, 1997b, 1998; Fattovich *et al.* 2000). No attempt is made in the present work to offer any detailed integration of the two investigations, the foci of which are largely complementary.

The research here described has been to some extent a continuation of that which the British Institute in Eastern Africa undertook under Dr Neville Chittick's direction in 1972-4. As noted above, this work was cut short and never completed. Other investigations which Chittick had planned were never begun. A preliminary report (Chittick 1974) provides a clear indication of the large scale on which excavation was undertaken and of its intended future direction. By the time of Chittick's lamented death in 1984, he had not been able to return to Aksum; and he had not felt it appropriate to prepare a definitive report on research which he regarded as unfinished (Oliver 1997: 367). In 1985, the Institute's Governing Council, recognising that resumption of fieldwork might be long delayed and that new investigations might be significantly different in outlook from those that would have been envisaged by Chittick, requested Dr Stuart Munro-Hay to prepare an account of the 1972-4 research for publication in the Institute's *Memoir* series.

Preparation of an archaeological report after the death of the director is always difficult; in this case the problem was exacerbated by the fact that it was not possible for Dr Munro-Hay or any of his collaborators to visit Aksum in order to check details on site or to examine excavated artefacts stored there. Certain facets of the research, such as the animal bones, thus had to

be excluded from the publication. Despite these shortcomings, the resultant *Memoir* (Munro-Hay 1989) provides a comprehensive account of the unfinished research, with valuable descriptions of the pottery and other artefacts that were recovered. The chapters on the artefacts are far more detailed than any that had been published previously, even though their chronology and associations are not always completely clear. The present volume, it is hoped, goes some way towards rectifying these deficiencies.

Although no archaeological excavations were conducted at Aksum between 1974 and 1993, the ancient monuments were well cared for and, with very few exceptions, suffered remarkably little damage during the civil war which occupied the greater part of that time. When a stone inscription of the fourth century AD was discovered by chance during cultivation on the northern edge of Aksum in 1982, it was admirably protected *in situ* and its transcription and historical interpretation promptly published (Bernand 1982). A comprehensive corpus of pre-Aksumite and Aksumite inscriptions in Ethiopia subsequently appeared but offered little new interpretation (Bernand *et al.* 1991). The pioneering synthesis by Sergew (1972), which attempted to integrate archaeological and historical materials, has been only partly superseded by the works of Anfray (1990), Munro-Hay (1991, 1997) and D.W.Phillipson (1998).

In 1989 a conference on Aksum was organised by the Institute of Ethiopian Studies at Addis Ababa University to mark the publication of the definitive account of Dr Chittick's excavations (Munro-Hay 1989). Several of the papers presented on that occasion were subsequently published in volume 23 of the *Journal of Ethiopian Studies*. The participants from the British Institute in Eastern Africa took the opportunity of holding talks with the then Minister for Culture and emphasising the Institute's willingness to resume fieldwork at Aksum, were this the wish of the relevant Ethiopian authorities, as soon as security and political conditions were appropriate. Although in 1989 the central government was not in control of the Aksum area, the Institute was left in no doubt that there was wide Ethiopian support for continued fieldwork (Oliver 1997: 406).

Some two years later peace was re-established under a new government and the Institute began to plan its return to Aksum. A Research Strategy was prepared, based largely on the paper 'Aksum in Africa' which the present writer had presented at the 1989 Addis Ababa conference and from which excerpts have been quoted above (D.W.Phillipson 1990). From the beginning, five annual field seasons were planned. Professors Taddesse Tamrat and Merid Wolde Aregay of Addis Ababa University contributed greatly to the

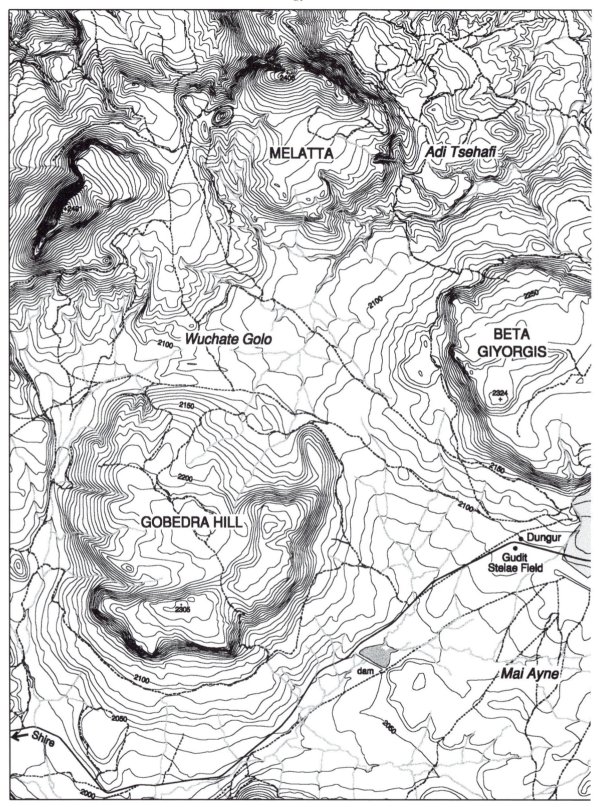

Fig. 2 *Contour map of the Aksum vicinity.*

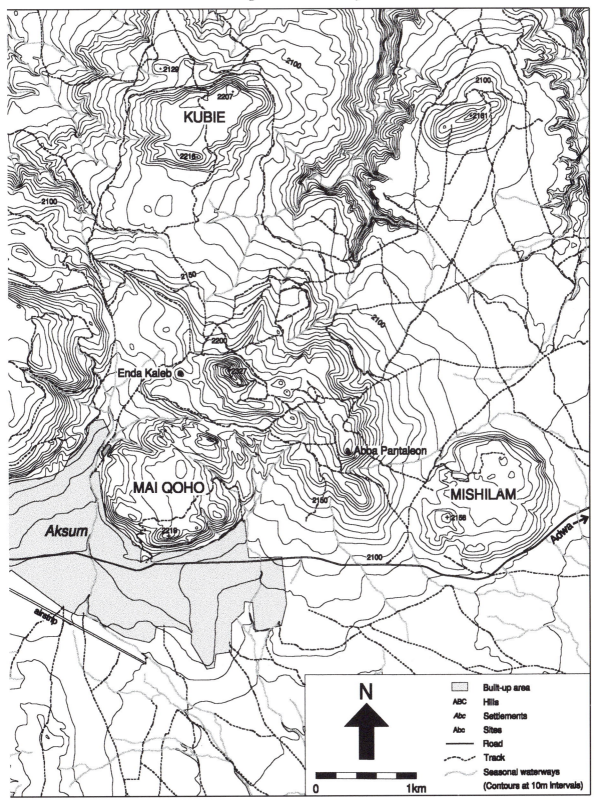

Fig. 2 *continued*.

Fig. 3 *Air photograph of the area covered by Fig. 2.*

developing research strategy and ensured its relevance to Ethiopian needs and aspirations.[1] It was envisaged that the Project would seek to provide archaeological training and experience for Ethiopian students and personnel, and that it would offer to assist the relevant authorities in the fields of monument conservation and museum development. Chittick's successor as the Institute's Director, Dr J. E. G. Sutton, and the writer visited Addis Ababa and Aksum for discussions with the relevant authorities in December 1992. It was clear from these meetings that the formal approval of the Centre for Research and Conservation of the Cultural Heritage (CRCCH) would in due course be forthcoming. The Institute was thus able to proceed with seeking to raise financial support for a five-year research project.

The Research Strategy (reproduced in Appendix I) was first submitted to the Society of Antiquaries of London, which adopted the investigation of Aksum as a major research project, its previous initiative at the Anglo-Saxon burial site of Sutton Hoo being then drawn to a close. This accolade greatly assisted the Institute in obtaining additional promises of financial

support from the British Academy and its Humanities Research Board, the McDonald Institute for Archaeological Research in the University of Cambridge, and the British Museum. The 1995 season had the additional benefit of a grant from the National Geographic Society. Graduate student involvement was supported by grants from Gonville & Caius College at Cambridge, the Swan Fund of the University of Oxford, and the L. S. B. Leakey Foundation. Specific aspects of the research were financed by the Natural Environment Research Council in 1997 and 1998. Despite these contributions, well over half of the total cost of the Aksum Project was borne by the Institute itself. Dr Jacke Phillips, employed as Research Assistant for the five-year duration of the Project, was based in office accommodation generously provided by the McDonald Institute. All other non-Ethiopian personnel gave their services voluntarily, in most cases in return for modest honoraria. The achievements of the Project are very largely due to the generosity and diligence of these participants, whose names are recorded below.

The financial viability of the Project having been assured, Dr Kassaye Begashaw (who was at that time the Head of CRCCH) was able to confirm his organisation's formal approval for the proposed investigation, subject to the usual terms and conditions for

---

[1] Despite this University involvement, it unfortunately did not prove possible for students to accept the Project's invitations to participate in fieldwork. Trainees were, however, enrolled from Mekelle and Aksum.

foreign-based archaeological research projects working in Ethiopia. As part of the detailed planning and consultation process, the writer was present at a symposium organised in Aksum by CRCCH in September 1993 and attended by a wide range of people representing local Aksum interests as well as other, predominantly Ethiopian, organisations concerned with development in the region. This meeting provided a useful opportunity for discussing the aims of the proposed archaeological work.

The general approval of CRCCH having been confirmed, a detailed permit was requested, and granted, each year. This allowed excavation within clearly defined areas, together with archaeological reconnaissance of the area within a 10-km radius of Aksum.

Geographical background

Before summarising the season-by-season implementation of the Research Strategy, it will be helpful to provide the reader with a view of the geographical background (Figs 1, 2, 3). Aksum, in the Tigray Region of northern Ethiopia, lies at a general altitude of 2200 m overlooking the broad and fertile Hatsebo Plain. It lies close to the Mareb / Takezze watershed on a ridge of high ground which extends westwards from the principal highlands of eastern Tigray, themselves facing the great escarpment which forms the western edge of the rift filled by the Red Sea and Danakil lowlands. In the immediate vicinity of Aksum is a series of rounded hills, from west to east Gobedra, Beta Giyorgis, Mai Qoho and Mishilam, from the summits of which, on a clear day, the view extends southwards across the Takezze Gorge to the Simien Mountains, and northwards across the Mareb to the distant mountains of Eritrea. Aksum itself lies between and to the south of Beta Giyorgis and Mai Qoho, centred on the widening valley of the Mai Hejja stream which rises in the narrow watershed between the two hills. The locale is here illustrated by a map (Fig. 2), and photographically from the air (Fig. 3) and as a panorama (Fig. 4).

Today, Aksum is the administrative centre for the Central Region of Tigray. It is a place of great importance and sanctity to the Ethiopian Orthodox Church, its Cathedral of St Mary of Zion (Fig. 5) being regarded as housing the Ark of the Covenant. The monuments of central Aksum (Figs 6, 7) bring tourists to the town from all parts of the world.

Research, 1993-9

Against the background outlined above, a summary of the five years' research activity may now be given. Logistical arrangements in each year followed a similar pattern. The Project negotiated exclusive use of the Kaleb Hotel in Aksum, where most team-members

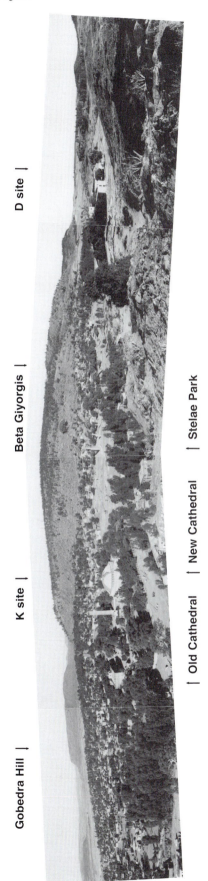

Fig. 4 Photographic panorama of Aksum, taken from Mai Qoho.

Fig. 5 *The Old Cathedral at Aksum, seen from the bell tower.*

were accommodated and where laboratories and storage facilities were established for the duration of each field season. Motor vehicles were obtained through the good offices of the British Council in Addis Ababa and, in 1993, of Addis Ababa University.

It was considered advisable for the first field season to be on a comparatively small scale and to concentrate its attentions on monuments within the Stelae Park which had been partially investigated by Dr Chittick in 1972-4. The 1993 season was preceded by a visit to Mekelle in order to discuss the plans with the Tigray regional authorities, including the President of Tigray Ato Gebru Asrat. The team comprised seven overseas personnel, accompanied by representatives of CRCCH and the Tigray Culture Bureau; the names of the team-members during this and subsequent seasons are presented below. Much effort was, in this initial season, devoted to building confidence and explaining the Project's work to the people of Aksum. The need for this should occasion no surprise, for foreigners other than military personnel had been very rare in Aksum for the previous nineteen years, tourism had barely been re-established, and archaeological research

had been far from people's concerns for almost an entire generation.

In 1993, the Tomb of the Brick Arches was re-opened and the collapsed west wall of its adit reconstructed; clearance of the antechamber, begun in 1974, was completed and the second chamber largely excavated. The recovery of finely carved ivory provided an insight into both the richness of the tomb and the conservation problems that would have to be faced. At the Stela 1 complex, the Mausoleum was entered and its central passage completely excavated. The East Tomb was likewise entered, but because of its poor structural condition excavation was not continued. The entrances to all these monuments were roofed and sealed in order to secure their protection. The Project was honoured to receive a number of distinguished visitors, including Ato Gebru Asrat, His Holiness the Patriarch, and Dr Kassaye Begashaw. The interest and support of these dignitaries helped considerably to enhance the Project's standing within Aksum.

Work in 1994 achieved further progress in the Mausoleum and at the Tomb of the Brick Arches, architectural evaluations being made of the stability and conservation requirements of both monuments. In addition, an exploratory excavation was made in the intervening area in order to establish the former position of the second-largest stela, which had been taken to Rome in 1937. Test trenches were also made in what seemed to be an area of domestic occupation at Kidane Mehret (D site) on the northern side of Aksum. A photographic record was made of archaeological remains in the Cathedral Precinct. An architectural survey of the Old Cathedral was made at the request of the ecclesiastical authorities. Excavation was also begun in the Gudit Stelae Field, an apparently middle- or lower-status burial ground to the west of Aksum.

Expansion in 1995 included large-scale excavation at Kidane Mehret and an initial foot-survey for prehistoric sites in the Aksum vicinity. Recovery of archaeobotanical materials by wet-sieving of bulk soil samples was initiated, concentrating on the deposits at Kidane Mehret. Excavation of the Mausoleum was completed and those in the Tomb of the Brick Arches and at the Gudit Stelae Field continued. At the conclusion of the excavation season, some members of the team remained in Aksum for a further four weeks to continue work on the artefacts that had been recovered.

The 1996 season saw excavation completed at the Tomb of the Brick Arches and continued for a final season at Kidane Mehret and at the Gudit Stelae Field. Within the built-up area of Maleke Aksum a second area of domestic occupation (K site) was investigated by means of test trenches. Further field survey was conducted and a detailed study of Aksumite lithic artefacts was begun. Small-scale excavation was undertaken at the rockshelter of Anqqer Baahti, located some 5 km east of Aksum. Archaeobotanical research continued and, for the first time, an archaeozoologist joined the team.

Early in 1997, funds were obtained from the Natural Environment Research Council which made it possible for Sheila Boardman, the Project's archaeobotanist, to continue her work on the Aksum material at the Royal Botanic Gardens, Kew, and at the McDonald Institute in Cambridge.

The final field season, in 1997, was largely devoted to work on the artefacts and to survey. Excavations were conducted at Baahti Nebait rockshelter, west of Aksum; and a record was made of the ancient quarries on Gobedra Hill. As a separate undertaking, at the request of and with support from CRCCH following negotiations for the second-largest stela to be returned to Ethiopia, substantial excavations were undertaken in order to help evaluate a suggestion that the monument might be re-erected on its original site.

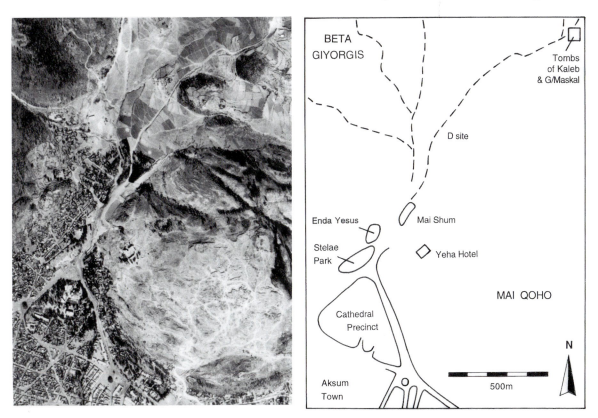

Fig. 6 *Detailed air photograph of central Aksum, with key naming the principal features.*

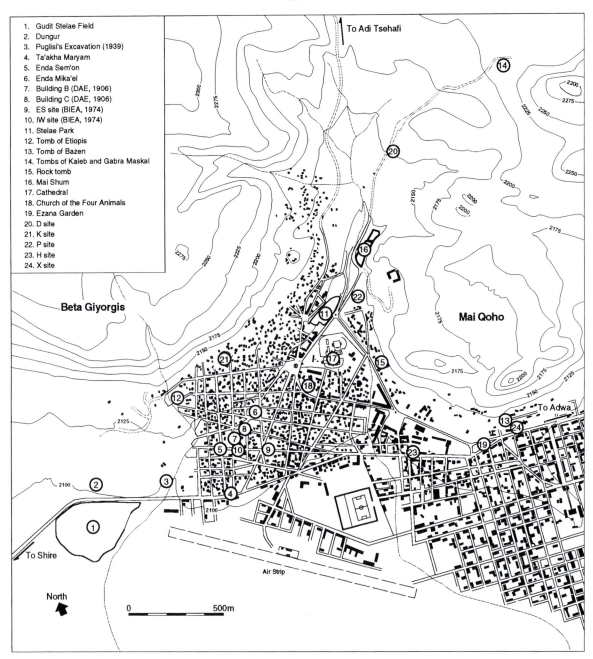

1. Gudit Stelae Field
2. Dungur
3. Puglisi's Excavation (1939)
4. Ta'akha Maryam
5. Enda Sem'on
6. Enda Mika'el
7. Building B (DAE, 1906)
8. Building C (DAE, 1906)
9. ES site (BIEA, 1974)
10. IW site (BIEA, 1974)
11. Stelae Park
12. Tomb of Etiopis
13. Tomb of Bazen
14. Tombs of Kaleb and Gabra Maskal
15. Rock tomb
16. Mai Shum
17. Cathedral
18. Church of the Four Animals
19. Ezana Garden
20. D site
21. K site
22. P site
23. H site
24. X site

Fig. 7 *Plan of Aksum town, showing central sites.*

After fieldwork at Aksum had been completed, Sheila Boardman continued her study in Addis Ababa of the plant materials that had been recovered.

Post-excavation work continued throughout the period of research in the field, between seasons, and for almost three years following the last field season. Excavation recording was the responsibility of the individual supervisors; recording of pottery and other artefacts was co-ordinated by Jacke Phillips and artefact conservation by Noël Siver. Most of the photography in Aksum was the work of Laurel and David Phillipson. The names of others who contributed their knowledge and skills are recorded below.

Investigation of artefacts was severely hampered by the extreme reluctance of the Ethiopian authorities to grant permission for the temporary export of archaeological material for study purposes. Such permissions as were eventually granted are greatly appreciated and resulted in important information which is recorded in this report; all the specimens so exported

Fig. 8 *Ecclesiastical visitors to the excavation.*

(other than samples for destructive analysis) have already been returned to Ethiopia. Many comparisons and analyses could not be undertaken in Ethiopia, and the Project's inability to export the relevant items for specialist examination has caused serious lacunae in the research here reported. Further conservation work, especially on the ivory, could also have been undertaken had temporary export of the relevant items been permitted.

The radiocarbon analyses reported in Appendix VI were undertaken at the Radiocarbon Accelerator Unit at the University of Oxford, supported by a grant from the Natural Environment Research Council.

Public relations and publication

Throughout the period of fieldwork, considerable effort was made to develop local interest in the research. Visits to the excavation were encouraged, bulletins and press releases were issued. The excavations were visited by Cabinet Ministers, Ambassadors and ecclesiastical dignitaries (Fig. 8), as well as by local residents and groups of school children. In each of the last three field seasons a formal dinner was held in Aksum, providing an opportunity for the Project team to entertain those with particular interest in or support for the research: guests included the Nebured of Aksum, the British Ambassador to Ethiopia, the Head of CRCCH, and the Director of the British Council office in Ethiopia.

The five years of research that were originally proposed have now been completed and the results are set out here. Meanwhile, every effort has been made to provide full and prompt information about the Project's work, both within Ethiopia and internationally. Lectures and/or Press Conferences were held in Aksum after each field-season (with a running translation into Tigrinya), Mekelle and Addis Ababa. Academic and popular presentations have been given in Britain, Canada, Germany, South Africa, the United States of America and Zambia. Papers have been read at international conferences in Britain, Ethiopia, Germany, Poland, Portugal, the United States and Zimbabwe. Interim reports have been published through the Project's various sponsors: in the *Cambridge Archaeological Journal* (D.W.Phillipson 1994a), in the *Antiquaries Journal* (D.W.Phillipson 1995a) and in *Azania* (D.W.Phillipson, Reynolds *et al.* 1996). Less detailed preliminary reports have been published regularly (D.W.Phillipson 1994b, c, 1995b, 1996a, b), while particular aspects of the research have been described by Ayele (1996), Boardman (1999), Cain (1999), Finneran (1998), J.S.Phillips (1996, 1998), D.W.Phillipson (2000), and L.Phillipson (2000a, b). Where discrepancies occur between preliminary reports and the present work, it is the latter which should be regarded as authoritative. Two unpublished Cambridge doctoral dissertations (Ayele 1997; Finneran 1999) are based on research conducted as part of the Project. An account

of the first four seasons has appeared in the *Journal of Ethiopian Studies* (D.W.Phillipson and Phillips 1998). A one-day symposium on Aksum, largely devoted to the Project's work, was held at the Society of Antiquaries of London in April 1998. An overview of the whole project was presented to the British Academy by David Phillipson as the Albert Reckitt Archaeological Lecture in February 2000, and will be published in *Proceedings of the British Academy*.

The present report

The account which follows is ordered by the individual sites which were excavated or otherwise investigated. Artefacts are described in the context of the site from which they were recovered, rather than being grouped typologically as has previously been customary in analogous reports. To aid comparisons, drawings are wherever possible reproduced at a common scale for each class of artefact, as follows:

- pottery: 35%
- iron objects: 40%
- lithics: 40% or 80%
- other clay objects and glass: 50%
- copper alloy objects: 70% (other than large castings which are at 40%)
- gold, silver etc: 135%
- beads: 150%.

Photographc illustrations are, of necessity, at various scales, always clearly indicated.

It is appropriate to record the designations of the various excavations and their subdivisions, as used

Designation	Site	Season/s	Chapter in this report
A	Anqqer Baahti rockshelter	AX96	2
B	Tomb of the Brick Arches	AX93, AX94, AX95, AX96	4
D	D site at Kidane Mehret	AX94, AX95, AX96	10
E	East Tomb	AX93	7
G	Gudit Stelae Field	AX94, AX95, AX96	8
H	Opposite Ghenet Hotel	AX95	12
K	K site in Maleke Aksum	AX96	11
L	Mai Lahlaha bridge near Tomb of Etiopis	AX97	12
M	Mausoleum and adjacent area	AX93, AX94, AX95	7
N	Baahti Nebait rockshelter	AX97	2
P	Below Yeha Hotel	AX94	12
R	Stela-2 site	AX97	6
S	Exploratory excavation at Stela-2 site	AX94	6
X	Near Tomb of Bazen	AX95	12

Fig. 9 Sites excavated. Details of surface collections are provided in Chapters 2 and 14.

in the field and in this report. Each excavation season was designated AX93, AX94 *etc.*, and the areas excavated were differentiated by a single capital letter, as listed in Fig. 9.

Within an excavation, subdivisions of structures, such as chambers of a tomb, were designated by a second capital letter, so that BD, for example, indicates Chamber D within the Tomb of the Brick Arches. An Arabic numeral indicates either an excavated trench or a horizontal subdivision of the area concerned: thus M6 indicates trench 6 in the Mausoleum area, while ME42 represents area 42 within Mausoleum Chamber E. These general principles were applied uniformly throughout all five seasons; variations and refinements are noted in the relevant chapters below. Stratigraphic layers and contexts were recorded in the field as encircled Arabic numbers and are presented here between rounded brackets, thus: (5). During excavation and subsequently artefacts of particular interest were inventoried and given sequential numbers preceded by the excavation site-prefix; these numbers are distinguished by containment within a triangle, so that D/97\ signifies inventoried artefact no. 97 from D site; its full stratigraphic provenance is recorded as AX94D7(8), meaning that it was recovered in the 1994 season at Aksum, at D site, in trench 7, context (8). Inventory numbers are, for simplicity, not extensively cited in the present report except where this is necessary for cross-reference purposes. The inventory numbers of all illustrated artefacts are, however, listed in Appendix XIII. Artefacts that were not separately inventoried were also studied and assessed, details being included in the following chapters.

The chronological scheme adopted in this report is discussed in Chapters 14b and 15; it is summarised below in Fig. 415.

Personnel

The Project whose results are reported here has depended on the willing and able assistance of an estimated 200 people, including professionals, students, trainees and a team of locally employed workers. Without their various contributions achievement of the Project's objectives would have been impossible.

Dr Jacke Phillips was employed as the Project's full-time Research Assistant from July 1993 until September 1998. She was assisted from time to time by Ms Laura Basell, Ms Yun-Shun Chung, Ms Dorothee Lotz, Ms Clare Vellacott and Ms Victoria Wallace.

In the field, the professional staff of the Project comprised Ato Ayele Tarekegn (Trainee Supervisor 1993 and Excavation Supervisor 1994-6), Ms Sheila Boardman (Archaeobotanist 1995-7), Ms Rebecca Bridgman (Graduate Student 1996), Mr Chester R. Cain (Archaeozoologist 1996-7), Ms Helen Cook (Pottery Assistant and Osteologist 1997), Ato Getu Degefa (Trainee Supervisor 1993-4 and Assistant Supervisor 1997), Mr Niall Finneran (Graduate Student 1995 and Excavation Supervisor 1996-7), Ms Jennifer P. Ford (Quarries Specialist 1997), Mr Ronnie Gibbs (Assistant Object Conservator 1994), W/t Gidey Gebre Yohannes (Pottery Assistant 1997), Mr Michael Harlow (Excavation Supervisor 1993-6 and Glass/Beads Specialist 1997), Mr Douglas Hobbs (Surveyor 1993), Ms Odile Hoogzaad (Registrar 1996), Mr Alistair Jackson (Surveyor 1994-5), Ms Jenny Jones (Excavation Supervisor 1994), Ms Sophie Julien (Assistant Object Conservator 1997), Mr Michael Mallinson (Conservation Architect 1994), Ms Maria Mertzani (Assistant Object Conservator 1995), Mr Sunil Nandha (Finds Assistant 1994), Dr Jacke Phillips (Research Assistant and Ceramicist 1993-7), Ms Jillian B. Phillips (Quarries Specialist 1997), Dr Laurel Phillipson (Lithics Specialist and Photographer 1996-7), Mr Tom Pollard (Surveyor 1996-7), Mr Graham Reed (Draftsman 1997), Mr Gavin Rees (Excavation Supervisor 1993), Mr Andrew Reynolds (Excavation Supervisor 1995), Mr Eric Robson (Draftsman 1996), Ms Sarah Semple (Draftswoman 1994-5), Ms Noël Siver (Object Conservator 1993-7), Ms Klara Spandl (Excavation Supervisor 1996), Ms Rachael Sparks (Registrar 1997), Ato Tekle Hagos (Trainee Supervisor 1995 and Assistant Supervisor 1997), Mr Jess Tipper (Excavation Supervisor 1993-6), Ms Stephanie Ward (Assistant Object Conservator 1996-7) and Mr Martin Watts (Excavation Supervisor 1997).

The following staff from the Tigray Bureau of Culture, Information and Tourism were attached to the Project: Ato Gebre Kidan Wolde Hawariat (1994-7), Ato Gigar Tesfaye (1993), Ato Girma Elias (1994-5), Ato Haile-Selassie Berhe (1993-4), Ato Makonnen Tadesse (1995), Ato Tekle Berhe (1994) and Ato Tekle Hagos (1993).

The Centre for Research and Conservation of the Cultural Heritage (CRCCH), Addis Ababa, was formally represented by Ato Gigar Tesfaye (1995-6), Ato Tamrat Wedajo (1993) and W/o Tsehay Eshetie (1994, 1997). Members of CRCCH staff who also worked with the Project were Ato Asamerew Dessie (1997), Ato Gigar Tesfaye (1997), W/t Kalemwa Araya (1997), Ato Tesfaye Hailu (1995) and W/o Tsehay Eshetie (1996).

Trainees contributed to the work in many ways: W/t Desta Abbay (1995-7), Ato Fitsum Alemseged (1996), W/t Gidey Gebre Yohannes (1994-5), Ato Haile Ayalneh (1994-6), Ato Iyasu Gebre Abzghi (1996-7), Ato Kebede Zeru (1997), W/t Lekyelesh Kebede (1994), Ato Mehari Abraha (1994), W/t Mesrak

Kenfe (1995), W/t Mezan Solomon (1995), Ato Teferi Tesfai (1995), Ato Tesfaye Berhane (1996-7) and Ato Tsigemeskel Wondimhunegn (1994-6).

Ato Girma Mamo was employed for all five seasons as driver/mechanic. Ato Fisseha Zibelo (1996), Ato Kiros Abbay (1995-7), Ato Taddesse Kasahun (1997), and Ato Takasta Gebre Kidan (1993-4) were foremen in charge of the labour force.

The maximum strength of the locally employed workforce was 65 in 1993, 84 in 1994, 91 in 1995, 107 in 1996, and 70 in 1997.

A group photograph of the 1994 Project team is reproduced as Fig. 10.

Post-excavation research outside Ethiopia has, in addition to many of those named above, has involved or been advised by the following:

- Drs Raymond and Bridget Allchin (Ancient India and Iran Trust, Cambridge)
- Dr Gina Barnes (University of Durham)
- Dr Robert H. Brill (Corning Museum of Glass)
- Mr David Buckton (British Museum)
- Mrs Keren Butler (University of Cambridge)
- Dr Dilip Chakrabarti (University of Cambridge)
- Dr J. A. Charles (St John's College, Cambridge)
- Mr Mark Clarke (University of Cambridge)
- Ms Julie Dawson (Fitzwilliam Museum, Cambridge)
- Professor Rodolfo Fattovich (Istituto Orientale, Naples)
- Ms Ann Feuerbach (University College, London)
- Dr Adrian Friday (University of Cambridge)
- Dr Rowena Gale
- Dr Ian Glover
- Professor Philip Grierson (Gonville & Caius College, Cambridge)
- Professor Wolfgang Hahn (University of Vienna)

Fig. 10 *The 1994 excavation team.*

- Dr Elizabeth Harper (Gonville & Caius College, Cambridge)
- Ms J. Harrison-Hall (British Museum)
- Dr Martin Henig (University of Oxford)
- Professor Charles Higham (University of Otago)
- Dr Bent Juel-Jensen
- Dr Carl Knappett (Christ's College, Cambridge)
- Dr Marta Lahr (University of Cambridge)
- Professor Michael Loewe (University of Cambridge)
- Professor David McMullen (University of Cambridge)
- Dr Jianjun Mei (University of Cambridge)
- Dr Graham C. Morgan (University of Leicester)
- Ms Helen Morrison
- PDS Ltd
- Ms Cinzia Perlingieri (Istituto Orientale, Naples)
- Dr Paul Pettitt (University of Oxford)
- Dr Jessica Rawson (Merton College, Oxford)
- Dr Roger Schneider (Addis Ababa University)
- Dr Colin Shell (University of Cambridge)
- Dr St John Simpson (British Museum)
- Ms V. Tatton-Brown (British Museum)
- Dr Roberta Tomber (Museum of London)
- Dr David Whitehouse (Corning Museum of Glass)
- Dr David Williams (Southampton University)
- Dr Rachel Wood (Gonville & Caius College, Cambridge).

The processing of photographs reproduced in this book has depended on the skill of Mr Gwil Owen, Mr Neal Maskell and Ms Lydia Bourn. Other artwork has been produced by Dr Niall Finneran, Ms Jane Goddard, Dr Laurel Phillipson, Mr Graham Reed, Ms Joanna Richards, Mr Eric Robson, Ms Sarah Semple, Ms Sarah Sherlock, Dr Katherine Spence, Mr David Williams and Ms Stephanie Wynne-Jones. Computer-generated graphics and tabulations have been prepared for publication by Ms Jennifer Bedlow, Mr Hugh Conway Morris, Mr Douglas Hobbs, Miss Tacye Phillipson and Mr Tom Pollard.

As noted on the title-page and elsewhere, many of those named above have also contributed to the present report. Contributions appear under the names of those primarily responsible for them, but most incorporate material provided by others and all have been edited by David Phillipson who is responsible for the overall content. Laurel Phillipson has given much advice and assistance throughout.

Chapter 2

THE PREHISTORIC ANTECEDENTS
OF AKSUM

In comparison with other regions of eastern Africa and the Horn, the prehistoric sequence of the north Ethiopian and Eritrean highlands is poorly known. In the Aksum area the only relevant published records prior to 1993 related to lithic artefacts of Middle Stone Age type as noted by Puglisi (1941): blades and putative flake-scrapers at four localities including Gobedra and 'Enda Georgis', and the excavation of a small rockshelter on Gobedra Hill (D.W.Phillipson 1977). Although prehistory was not the main focus of the Project, the opportunity was taken of making surveys and limited surface collections. This work was undertaken by Niall Finneran in 1995 and by Laurel Phillipson in 1996 and 1997. In 1996 and 1997, Finneran conducted excavations in two rockshelters near Aksum: although the results of this work form the basis of his doctoral dissertation (Finneran 1999) at the University of Cambridge and will be published separately, a brief outline is included here.

Survey was restricted to the area within a 10-km radius of Aksum, as delineated by the permit issued by the Ethiopian authorities. In practice, most work was done in the western, central and northern parts of this area, excluding the top of Beta Giyorgis hill where separate archaeological investigations were being undertaken (Bard *et al.* 1997; Fattovich and Bard 1997b; Fattovich *et al.* 2000). Recording was not restricted to prehistoric material, occurrences of later date being noted when they were encountered: they are, however, discussed separately in Chapters 12 and 13, below. Our very incomplete knowledge of prehistory in the Aksum area is best summarised in a chronological chart (Fig. 11). The principal archaeological occurrences observed in the course of survey are shown on the accompanying map (Fig. 12).

Early and Middle Stone Ages
(Laurel Phillipson)

Early Stone Age artefacts including Acheulian type bifaces and a few large Levallois type flakes with multifaceted striking platforms were recovered from four

sites in the vicinity of Aksum. These pieces, all much abraded and obviously redeposited, are of basalt or highly silicified silt / sandstone (Figs 13, 14).

A very heavily abraded handaxe (Fig. 13d) and two radial- and one parallel-scarred flakes (Figs 14c - e) with maximum dimensions between 95 and 101 mm from prepared cores were found on the surface at D site. Intensive search in the surrounding area revealed no particular locale from which these pieces might

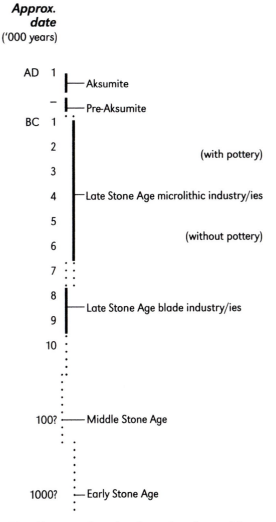

Fig. 11 Time-chart for the archaeology of the Aksum area.

17

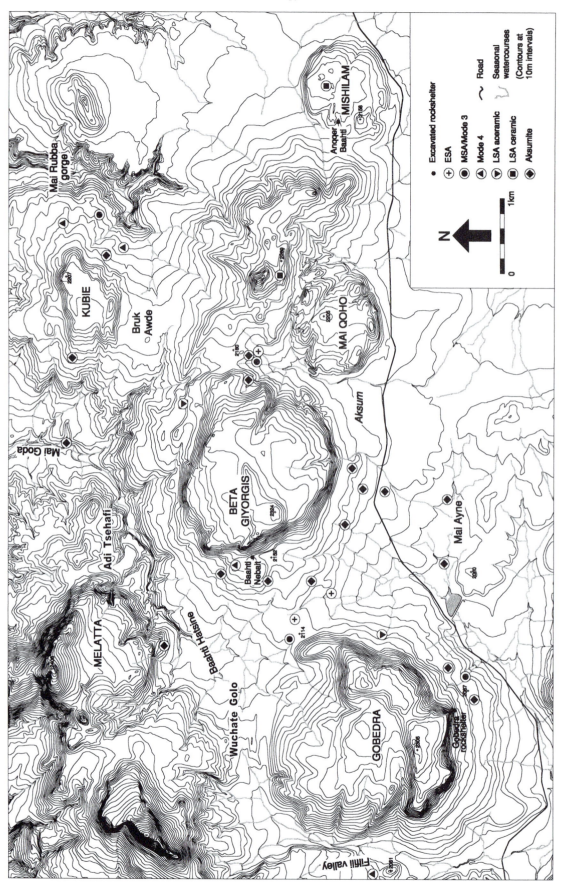

Fig. 12 Map of the survey area showing sites and find-spots.

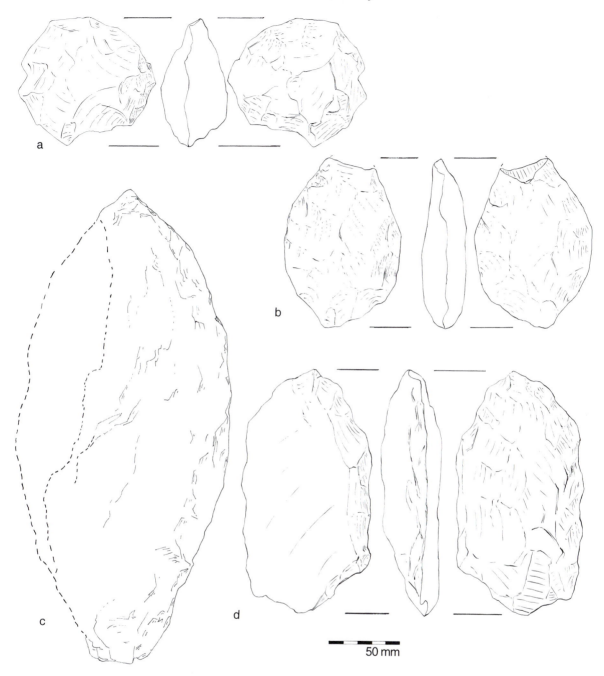

Fig. 13 *Acheulian-type bifaces, surface finds: **a** - from the southern foot of Gobedra Hill (basalt);*
*   **b, c** *- from c. 0.5 km east-southeast of Wuchate Golo (sandstone);* **d** *- from the D-site area,*
*   bifacially trimmed with an area of more recent damage (basalt).*

have been derived. However, a radial prepared core 105 by 80 by 23 mm and a broken radial-scarred flake >65 by 81 by 19 mm with multifaceted striking platform, both heavily abraded, were recovered from the west slope of Likanos Hill, overlooking D site.

   More abundant material of Early Stone Age type was located on an eroding land surface about 0.5 km east-southeast of Wuchate Golo, near the foot of Gobedra Hill. A moderately dense surface scatter of re-deposited lithic material was noted in this area, of which only a few sample pieces were collected. These included a partially bifacial sandstone side-chopper made on a large radial-scarred prepared-core flake (Fig. 13c), a fully bifacial, heavily abraded handaxe (Fig. 13b), and a parallel-scarred prepared-core flake 105 by 62 by 24 mm with a trifaceted striking platform.

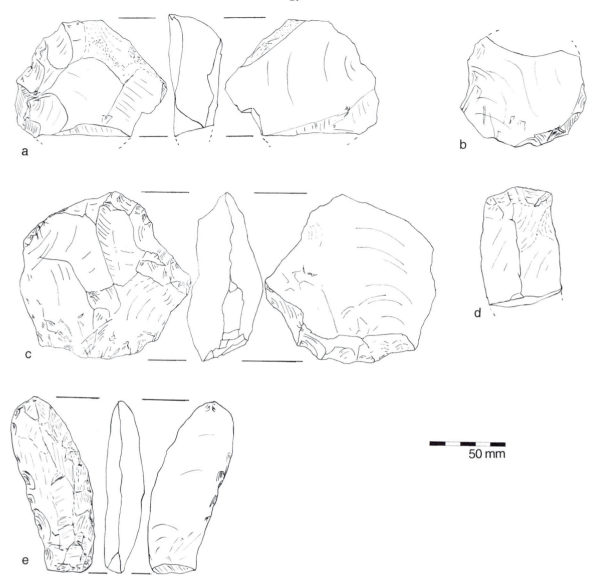

50 mm

Fig. 14 *Large prepared-core artefacts, surface finds:* ***a*** *- core from Surface Collection F (sandstone);*
b *- flake from Surface Collection F (sandstone);* ***c*** *- flake from the D-site area (sandstone);*
d, e *- flakes from the D-site area (basalt).*

Another much abraded bifacial tool or core (Fig. 13a) was found at the foot of the southern slope of Gobedra Hill.

Taken together, these few Early Stone Age artefacts suffice to indicate human occupation of the northern Ethiopian highlands at a very early time, perhaps 500,000 or more years ago. While they are all heavily weathered and obviously redeposited, the local topography is such that they are unlikely to have been transported more than short distances from their original places of deposition. It is possible that excavation into the talus slopes of Gobedra Hill would recover a larger sample of this early material. Until more information is available, there is no reason to suppose that these artefacts can be attributed to a single period or phase within a vast prehistoric time span.

Middle Stone Age type artefacts from surface occurrences are somewhat more abundant than those of Early Stone Age type, though all are weathered and re-deposited pieces from dispersed contexts. The Middle Stone Age type material is sparse, ill represented and insufficient to define an industry or industries (Fig. 15). Judging primarily from the varying degrees of weathering on different pieces, it seems likely that this material does not all belong to a single phase or temporal period.

Most commonly found are basalt, mudstone and chert flake-blades and radial-scarred flakes with

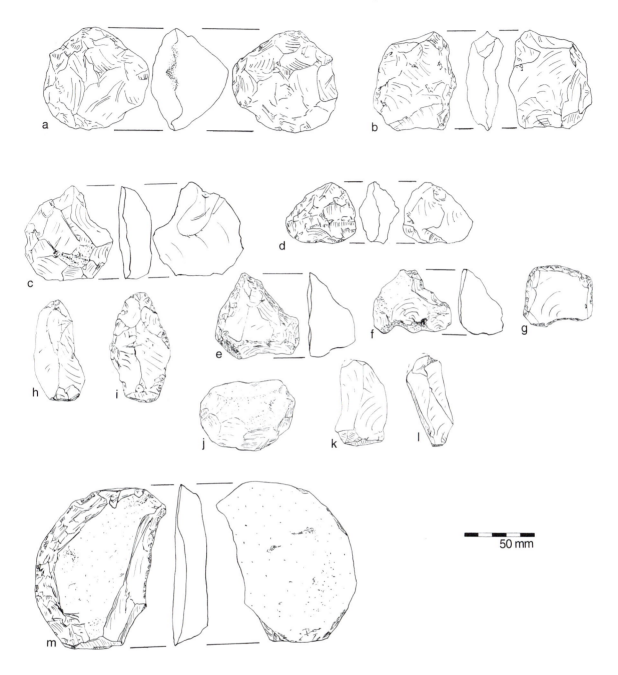

50 mm

Fig. 15 *Middle Stone Age type artefacts, surface finds: **a-d** - radial cores from the D-site area (a and b sandstone, c mudstone, d chert); **e** - convergent scraper from Surface Collection F (sandstone); **f** - denticulate scraper from Surface Collection F (yellow chert); **g** - scraper on flake with multifaceted striking platform from Surface Collection M (chert); **h** - flake from c. 0.5 km east-southeast of Wuchate Golo (sandstone); **i** - flake from c. 300 m west-southwest of the Tomb of Menelik (sandstone); **j** - flake from Surface Collection M (mudstone); **k, l** - flakes with multifaceted striking platforms, Surface Collection M (chert); **m** - tabular scraper from c. 0.5 km east-southeast of Wuchate Golo (chert).*

maximum dimensions between 90 and 40 mm (Figs 15h-l). While many appear to have been trimmed into the form of sub-triangular, convergent or sub-rectangular side-scrapers (Figs 15e-g), subsequent accidental damage cannot generally be distinguished from original deliberate retouch. Several biconvex and plano-convex radial cores (Figs 15a-d) with diameters between about 70 and 50 mm and two ovate chert bifaces or cores, 76 by 58 by 28 mm and 45 by 38 by 25 mm, were also collected. This Middle Stone Age type material, 25 artefacts in all, has been recovered from all areas in which surface collections were made. A slight concentration of Middle Stone Age type flakes was noted eroding from a soil horizon near a place called Enda Kolankul, to the west of and slightly lower in elevation than the Tomb of Menelik (Surface Collection F on Fig. 384, below). What was probably this same sloping horizon was also exposed in the vicinity of Surface Collection M (Fig 384), where the smaller of the two radial cores or bifaces noted above, a mudstone and two chert flake-blades 45 to 68 mm long, two chert radial-scarred flakes with multifaceted platforms, 59 and 37 mm long, and a mudstone flake-scraper were collected.

An apparently unique, possibly Middle Stone Age, artefact found near Wuchate Golo is a steeply trimmed semi-circular scraper, 113 by 77 by 25 mm, made on a spall of tabular yellow chert (Fig. 15m). Another unique piece is an otherwise insignificant chert flake, 47 by 40 by 26 mm, from the surface at D site, with a distinctive 'desert varnish' patina. This surface gloss occurs naturally on chert and similar stones which have been exposed for long periods to quite specific climatic conditions (Dorn 1994). As a similar patina was observed on no other artefactual or natural lithics in the area, it may be assumed that it was imported to the site.

Judging on purely stylistic grounds, most of the Middle Stone Age type artefacts found as surface occurrences, with the possible exception of those comprising Surface Collection M, appear to predate the mudstone blade assemblages from the lower levels of nearby excavated rockshelters, though some individual artefacts may have been contemporaneous with them. In all cases, the sample sizes are too small to permit meaningful statistical comparisons.

Much of the broad valley between Gobedra and Beta Giyorgis has been lowered to its present level by post-Aksumite erosion, but where earlier levels have been preserved on the flanks of the surrounding hills there are sufficient archaeological remains from which can be reconstructed an outline cultural sequence possibly spanning some 500,000 years. On the northeast flank of Gobedra, about 0.5 km east of Wuchate Golo, in the area of the watershed is exposed the remnants of an east-facing, gently sloping land surface on which late Acheulian type bifaces occur together with occasional relatively large flakes and other artefacts which may probably be attributed to a late Acheulian or early Middle Stone Age type of industry. That the several bifaces which have been recovered are all heavily weathered is a clear indication that major episodes of soil erosion in the area greatly predate the inception

of agriculture, forestry and cattle keeping. Despite their heavy weathering, the lie of the land is such that these bifaces cannot have travelled far from their original places of deposition, which may have been on the higher slopes of Gobedra Hill. Some of the Middle Stone Age type artefacts, which need not all be attributed to a single period or phase, are less heavily abraded.

The chief significance of this material is as an indicator of early human occupation in the highlands of northern Ethiopia, an area for which such evidence was previously lacking. Surface finds of similar apparently Acheulian material, including bifaces and a large radial core, have also been made on the south flank of Gobedra Hill and at D site on the southwestern flank of Likanos Hill, which is itself a northern extension of Mai Qoho. What are perhaps Middle Stone Age or late Acheulian type flakes also occur sparsely in a much eroded area west of the Aksumite Tomb of Menelik on the western flank of Beta Giyorgis. Less weathered, somewhat smaller and perhaps more recent Middle Stone Age artefacts can be recovered in small quantities at a slightly higher altitude in the same area, where they are associated with the shallow soil deposits on whose surface the Aksumite collections H - N were made. Surface Collection M represents this material.

Late Stone Age
(Niall Finneran)

The primary goal of the 1995 survey was the location of Late Stone Age lithic occurrences and of rockshelters the excavation of which might amplify the Gobedra sequence and provide additional associations of floral and faunal remains. Three large landscape zones were defined and each was investigated on foot for one week, archaeological remains, modern land-use patterns and general landscape morphology being noted. Maps at a scale of 1:60,000 were available and aerial photographs, obtained from the Ethiopian Mapping Agency, were subsequently used as the basis for the detailed mapping here reproduced.

The western survey zone encompassed the Gobedra environs and the Filfili Valley. The latter area was studied in some detail since part of it was due to be inundated by a new reservoir. Scatters of quartz microliths were noted around the southern flanks of Gobedra Hill, occasionally in apparent association with recognisably Pre-Aksumite or Aksumite pottery (cf. Chapter 13, below). Small rockshelters and enclosed areas were noted in the vicinity of the Gobedra rockshelter previously excavated, and also along the southeastern flank of the hill northeast of the lioness

Fig. 16 *Views of excavated rockshelters: **a** - Anqqer Baahti from the east with, at the left, the church of Abba Pantaleon on its rock pinnacle; **b** - Baahti Nebait from the west.*

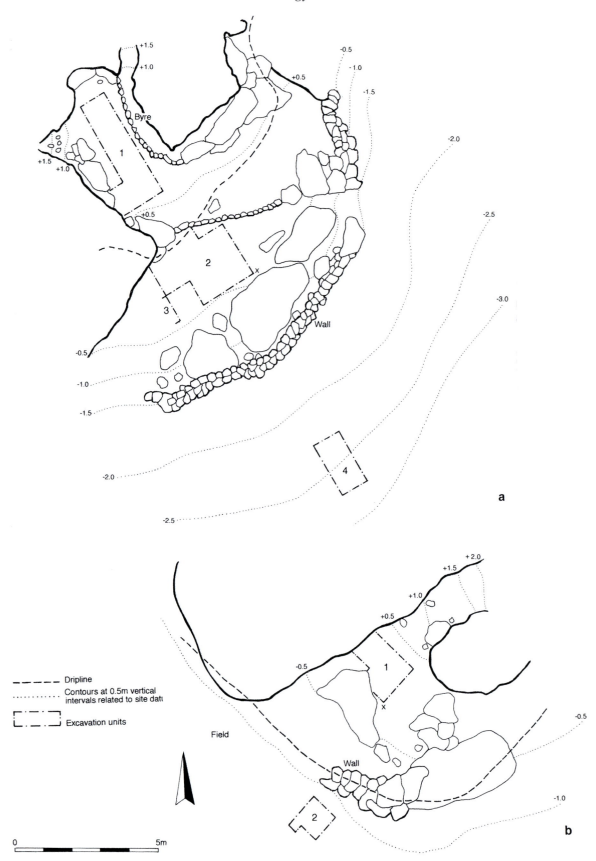

Fig. 17 *Plans of excavated rockshelters:* ***a*** *- Anqqer Baahti;* ***b*** *- Baahti Nebait.*

carving (D.W.Phillipson 1997: 160-1). Along the western crest of the Filfili Valley were observed isolated scatters including blades in mudstone and fine-grained sandstone analogous to those from the lowest levels of the Gobedra rockshelter excavation, together with waste derived from their production.

The northern zone extended from Beta Giyorgis, across the flat farmland of Bruk Awde towards the low hill called Kubie. A rockshelter (Baahti Nebait) was located close to the track which leads around the western flank of Beta Giyorgis, some 4 km northwest of Aksum: this was excavated in 1997, as noted below. Occurrences of blades and production-waste were seen on the southeastern slopes of Kubie, overlooking the Mai Rubba Gorge.

Within the eastern survey zone, extending from Mishilam Hill to the Mai Rubba Gorge, a similar pattern was noted. Blade industries were located around the lips of the gorge and its tributaries, while microlithic material (sometimes associated with pottery) occurred mainly on the south- and west-facing hill-flanks, offering some shelter from the prevailing rain-bearing northeasterly winds. Very few hill-flank sites were discovered on exposed north-or east-facing slopes, even in areas that have suffered comparatively little erosion. The rockshelter known as Anqqer Baahti was located in this zone, in a small valley beneath a sandstone dome in the western flank of Mishilam Hill: it was excavated in 1996.

Anqqer Baahti excavation

Anqqer Baahti rockshelter (Fig. 16a) consists of a main chamber, used recently as a byre, and a series of outer terraces. Three major excavation units were defined (Fig. 17a): unit 1 sampled the main-chamber deposits, unit 2 the main outer terrace, and unit 4 the talus deposits. (Unit 3 took the form of a witness-section through a recent porcupine den, and proved to be

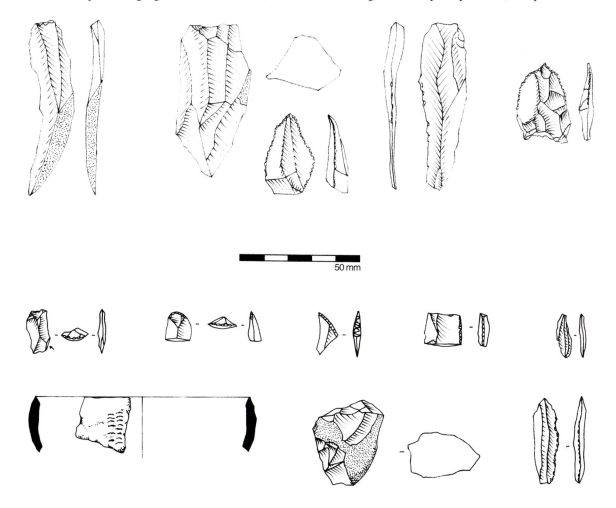

50 mm

Fig. 18 *Artefacts from Baahti Nebait: those above the scale are from the basal blade industry, those below are from the microlithic industry.*

uninformative.) Each unit was excavated using strict single-context recording, and samples of deposit were taken from each context for wet-sieving and flotation.

Much vertical displacement was noted in the unit-1 deposits and the small lithic assemblage consequently proved uninformative; the potsherds included a number of recognisable Pre-Aksumite and Aksumite types. Unit 2 yielded a better concentration of lithic material, and it was here that the broad sequence was defined. The lowest stratum produced a blade industry in mudstone. This was overlain by a quartz microlithic industry with occasional backed forms. At the top of the sequence this stone industry was associated with pottery: a thin coarse ware decorated with horizontal bands of thumbnail impressions. A similar sequence and typology had been observed at Gobedra (D.W.Phillipson 1977). On a smaller scale, this sequence was reflected in unit 4. The faunal remains were largely dominated by mature and neonatal burrowing insectivore / small carnivore remains and a few fragments of bovid bones. Plant material was abundant in units 1 and 2, representing a wide range of cultivated crops; it appears however that most of this was likewise was intrusive, as is confirmed by the results of radiocarbon analyses summarised in Appendix VI.

Baahti Nebait excavation

This small rockshelter (Fig. 16b) is located under a prominent rock outcrop on the western flank of Beta Giyorgis, and encloses a small narrow chamber some 15 sq. m in area. Two excavation units were opened (Fig. 17b): unit 1 sampled the chamber deposits and the smaller unit 2 the heavy clay vertisols outside. Unit 1 proved to be highly productive, the lithic sequence mirroring those at Anqqer Baahti and Gobedra.

The deposits in unit 1 consisted of a series of superimposed clays. The basal contexts contained the blade-industry, here made from fine-grained sandstone as well as from the mudstone seen at the other excavated rockshelters. Charcoal from this horizon yielded two radiocarbon age determinations in the tenth millennium bp (OxA-8359, OxA-8384). Above this is an aceramic microlithic industry, again in quartz. These

layers are sealed by compact clay, virtually sterile, in turn overlain by microlithic material associated with pottery, notably thin coarse ware occasionally decorated with thumbnail impressions (Fig. 18). Unit 2 did not prove archaeologically informative.

Preservation of organic materials at Baahti Nebait proved to be exceptionally good. Large quantities of burned bovid fragments were recovered from the lower contexts in unit 1. With the appearance of the microlithic industry, the proportion of smaller animals increased. Plant remains were also recovered from unit 1, although results of radiocarbon dating (Appendix VI) indicate that much of it is intrusive to the horizons from which it was recovered. Detailed accounts of the excavations at Anqqer Baahti and Baahti Nebait, including Sheila Boardman's reports on the botanical remains, are being prepared for publication elsewhere.

Overview
(Laurel Phillipson)

While it is now incontrovertible that there is some Early Stone Age, Acheulian type lithic material dating to perhaps about a half a million years ago to be found in the Aksum area along with a moderate scatter of Middle Stone Age type flakes, cores and scrapers and a limited number of discrete Late Stone Age occupation sites, human occupation of this part of the Ethiopian highlands appears to have been sparse and probably intermittent until, most probably, some time in the second or first millennium BC. As noted above, a continuity of microlithic tool types, with a gradual reduction in artefact size and refinement of retouch, suggests a fundamental continuity of population from final Late Stone Age times through the introduction of farming economies and into Classical and Late Aksumite times. The actual picture was probably more complex than that for which we have evidence, with some, perhaps limited, population movement accompanying the introduction and development of new cultural elements and economic patterns.

Chapter 3

THE CENTRAL STELAE AREA
(D.W.P.)

NOTE: Throughout Chapters 3-7, following the practice adopted by the excavators, compass-points are for clarity and simplicity based on the assumptions that the main terrace wall of the Stelae Park is aligned from east to west and that Stela 3 faces south. Maps and plans accompanying these chapters all show the 'Excavation North' on which this convention is based, as well as Magnetic North.

The principal stelae of Aksum occupy a prominent position overlooking the town from relatively flat ground at the foot of Beta Giyorgis hill (Fig. 19). Their location is shown on the map at Fig. 7.

The stelae were numbered by the 1906 Deutsche Aksum-Expedition (Littmann *et al*. 1913). This scheme has been followed by subsequent researchers who have expanded it to include stelae discovered during more recent investigations, notably those of 1972-4 (Munro-Hay 1989: 340-6). The stelae carved in imitation of buildings, generally referred to as storeyed stelae, are numbered from 1 to 6 in decreasing order of size (D.W.Phillip- son 1997: 11-43; Munro-Hay 1989: figs 4.1-4). Stela 1 is the largest storeyed stela, originally 32.6 m long, which now lies broken, its apex shattered through impact with the structure known as Nefas Mawcha. Stela 2, likewise fallen and broken, was taken to Rome in 1937 during the Italian occupation of Ethiopia and re-erected in the Piazza di Porta Capena; its return is under discussion at the

Fig. 19 *The Stelae Park seen from the dome of the New Cathedral. Stela 1 is on the extreme left, with excavations on the site of Stela 2 in the centre.*

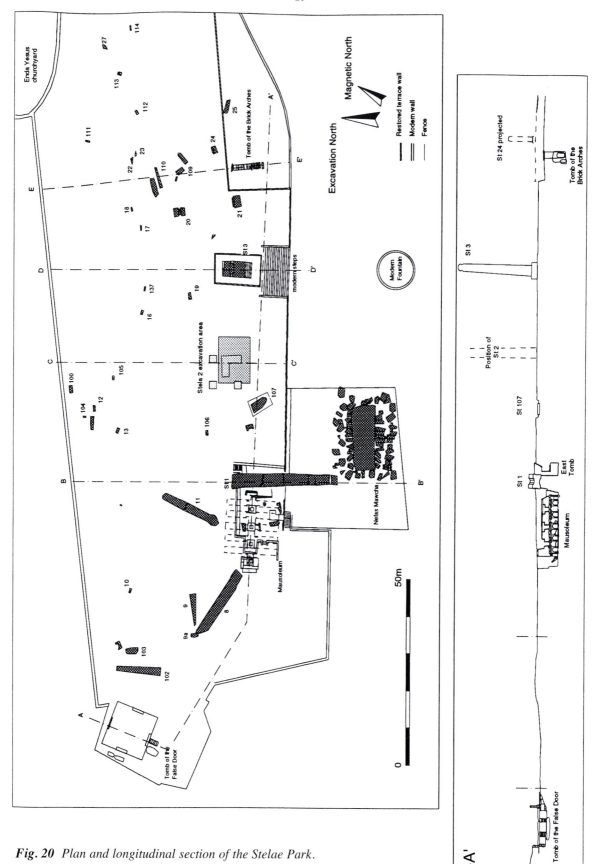

Fig. 20 *Plan and longitudinal section of the Stelae Park.*

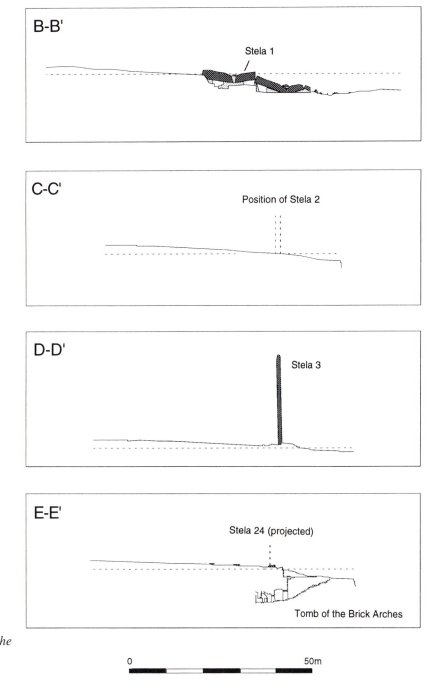

Fig. 21 *Cross-sections of the Stelae Park: for positions, see Fig. 20.*

0   50m

time of writing. Stela 3 still stands at Aksum. Stelae 4, 5 and 6, all fallen and broken, are not discussed here. There are numerous additional stelae, carved less elaborately or not at all (Munro-Hay 1989: 340-6; D.W.Phillipson 1998: 96-8). Research on the quarrying, transport, dressing and erection of the stelae is described in Chapter 9, below.

The function and significance of the Aksumite stelae have long been subjects of enquiry. Although it has generally been accepted for many years that they were essentially funerary in origin, more precise information has only recently come to light. The excavations of 1972-4 demonstrated that the central stelae area had been used for funerary purposes since at least the first or second centuries AD (Munro-Hay 1989: 150-7). During this time, the area was gradually built up by the construction of a series of terraces and platforms supporting stelae, beneath which were subterranean tombs. The stelae and other features which are visible on the surface today mostly date from a period some hundreds of years after the area's initial use.

The area surrounding the three largest stelae is currently laid out as a park. During the first half of the present century, the area supported a number of houses, gardens and associated structures which are shown on numerous old photographs and were documented in some detail by the DAE; traces of them have been revealed during subsequent excavations. In the early 1960s, at the instigation of Ras Mengesha Seyoum, then Governor-General of Tigray, the area was cleared, levelled, walled and adorned with hedges and flowering shrubs to form the present Stelae Park. Several leaning stelae were straightened and consolidated at this time (D.W.Phillipson 1997: 11-59), and some masonry blocks were resited. Today, the Stelae Park comprises a walled open space of some 1.3 ha, sloping gently downwards to the south (Figs 20, 21).

The Project of 1993-7 investigated several areas, care being taken at all times to ensure minimal visible impact on the Stelae Park. The investigations are described here in the following order:

- Chapter 4: The Tomb of the Brick Arches, located some 25 m east of the standing Stela 3;
- Chapter 5: Stela 3, which was examined in detail, although no excavations were undertaken in its vicinity;
- Chapter 6: The site where Stela 2 formerly stood;
- Chapter 7: The complex of monuments associated with Stela 1.

Some overall conclusions on the use and significance of the Stelae Park are summarised in Chapter 15, below, while an account of the more recent use of the area will be found in Appendix XII.

Chapter 4

THE TOMB OF THE BRICK ARCHES

SUMMARY: The Tomb of the Brick Arches,
located near the southeastern margin of the Stelae Park,
comprises four interconnecting underground chambers reached by a stepped adit.
Although disturbed by robbers, a wide range of artefacts was preserved,
including pottery, glass, beads, metalwork and finely carved ivory.
It had been used for the interment of three or, possibly, four individuals
and probably dates to the fourth century AD.

STRUCTURE AND STRATIGRAPHY
(Jess Tipper)

The Tomb of the Brick Arches (Figs 22-4) is located some 25 m east of Stela 3, and does not itself appear to have been associated with any particular stela now extant. No indication of the presence of a tomb was visible on the surface until excavations directed by Jean Doresse in 1954 revealed the upper part of the adit (Leclant 1959). This was further explored under Neville Chittick's direction in 1974, when the tomb was entered, its general plan recorded and the first of its four chambers largely excavated (Munro-Hay 1989: 55-60). Its date was then estimated as falling in the late third or early fourth century AD. Chittick's excavation of the Tomb of the Brick Arches was designated by him DA I. In the following account all stratigraphic references including this rubric refer to the 1974 research. The tomb was re-opened in 1993, a portable generator was installed to provide electric light, and excavation continued in four subsequent seasons under the supervision of Jess Tipper, assisted in 1993 and 1994 by Getu Degefa. These excavations were designated by the prefix B. (For simplicity, the prefix is not cited in the present chapter, other than in references to the artefact inventory.) The superstructure and surroundings of the tomb (Munro-Hay 1989: 55-6) were not further investigated.

The tomb is approached by means of an adit (Figs 23, 25) extending downwards to the north, with eighteen surviving stone steps. There are two further steps under the entrance arch (Arch I) itself, making twenty in all. The steps comprise minimally dressed slabs with risers built of small undressed stones akin to those in the adit walls. The heights of individual steps vary between 0.22 and 0.28 m. Counting downwards from the top, the third, tenth and sixteenth steps

are deeper than the others, forming miniature landings. The adit, 12.2 m long by between 1.4 and 1.5 m wide, attains a depth of 6.2 m. It is walled with small undressed stones set in mud mortar and was originally roofed with about twenty horizontal rough stone lintels, of which eight (Figs 25a, b) now survive *in situ*. An additional lintel was found lying in the adit during the 1974 excavation (Munro-Hay 1989: 55). On the east side of the adit the original Aksumite stone wall survives to its full height in a remarkably fine state of preservation; the western wall had collapsed. At the foot of the steps, which are likewise well preserved, a horseshoe-shaped brick arch, designated Arch I (Fig. 26), gives access to the tomb, the aperture being between 1.00 and 1.30 m wide and 2.57 m in total height. The arch, 1.00 m deep, is constructed of mould-made, fired, red-brown clay bricks set in lime mortar; they average 200 by 200 by 70 mm in size. A detailed drawing of Arch I has been published by Chittick (1974: fig. 8; see also Munro-Hay 1989: fig. 6.2). The brickwork is set at each side upon horizontal stone slabs (cf. Fig. 229a; p. 259, below). A similar but much larger slab forms a lintel over the arch. It is clear from the butt-joints that the wall incorporating Arch I was constructed before the side-walls of the adit, brick fragments from the former being incorporated with the stonework of the latter.

When the upper steps of the adit were cleared by Doresse in 1954, many human bones were found under the surviving lintels, probably recent in date (Leclant 1959: 10-12; Munro-Hay 1989: 55; see also Appendix XII, below). The adit was completely excavated in 1974, the upper levels being designated DA I(2), with an arbitrary change to DA I(3) at the level of the stone lintel over Arch I.

The tomb itself comprises four chambers cut from the soft sandstone bedrock, their floor being between 9.5 and 10.0 m below the modern surface. The

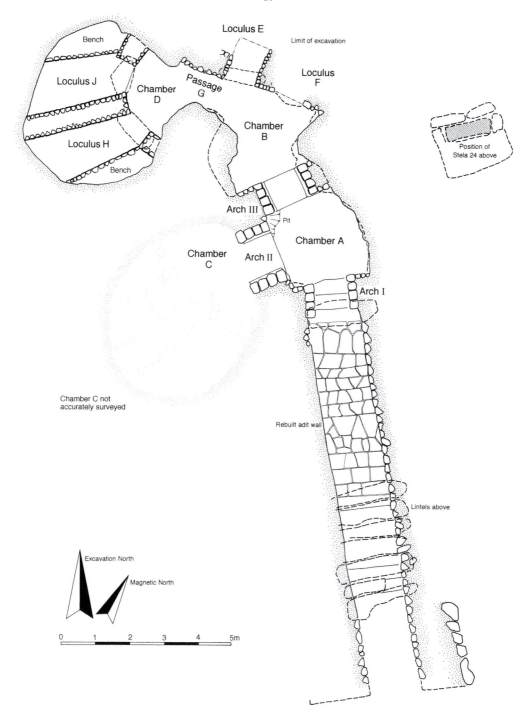

Fig. 22 *General plan, Tomb of the Brick Arches.*

complex seems to have been roughly carved out as a whole, covering an irregular area some 14 m by 12 m overall, with an original maximum height of less than 2.3 m. It was then subdivided by the insertion of stone cross-walls containing brick arches or lintelled apertures (Fig. 27). The stones were set in mud, although the bricks, used exclusively in the construction of

arches, were set in lime mortar.[2] Three chambers each contain two burial loculi, of which only those in the innermost chamber (D) have been fully excavated. The

---

[2] See Appendix X for an analysis by Dr Graham Morgan of lime mortar from the Mausoleum. Although the mortar in the Tomb of the Brick Arches was similar in superficial appearance, it has not been demonstrated that its composition was identical.

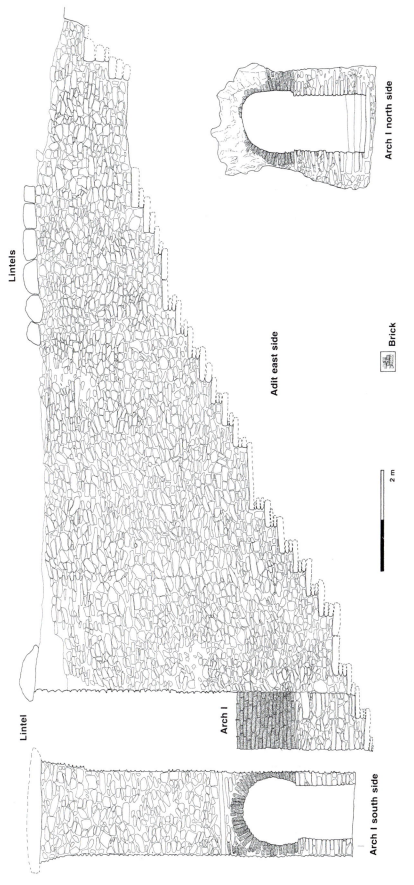

Lintels

Adit east side

Arch I north side

2 m

Brick

Lintel

Arch I

Arch I south side

Fig. 23 *Section of the adit, Tomb of the Brick Arches.*

plan (Fig. 22, above) shows the designations of individual chambers, loculi and brick arches.

Three of the four rock-cut chambers were investigated in 1993-6, continuing work begun in 1974. Excavation in Chambers A and B was completed, and Chamber D was fully excavated, including its component Loculi H and J. On the northern side of Chamber B, excavation of Loculi E and F, whence many of the objects found on the floor of that chamber probably derived, was abandoned as dangerous owing to the collapse of the roof. Chamber C, which had been investigated preliminarily in 1974, was not reopened at the request of the Tigray authorities who were concerned that its excavation might affect the stability of the nearby Stela 3. The chambers and loculi are discussed below in order of excavation northwards and then

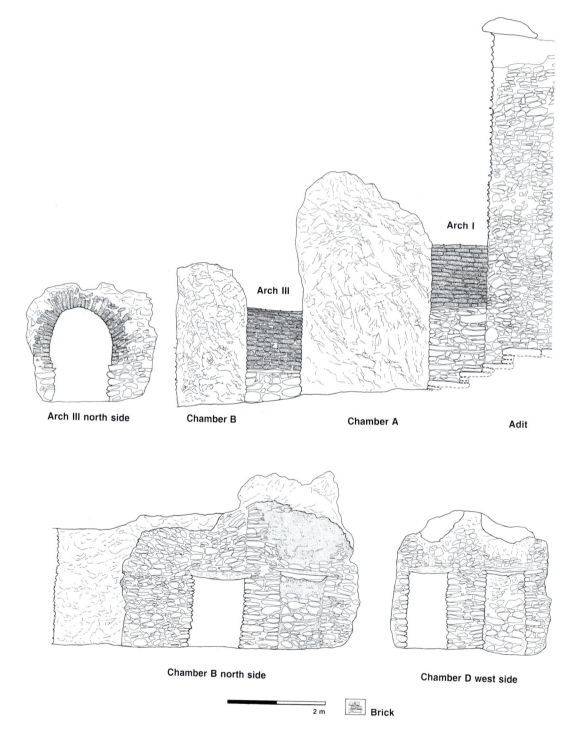

Fig. 24 *Detailed structural sections within the Tomb of the Brick Arches.*

Fig. 25 *The adit, Tomb of the Brick Arches: **a, b -** excavation in progress showing lintels over the adit; **c** - general view down the adit; **d** - view up the adit. Scales: 0.5 m.*

westwards, following the layout of the tomb from its entrance to the innermost loculi.

When the tomb was first opened in 1974, it was noted that the deposits were damp and preservation good, items of leather and wood being recovered (Chittick 1974: 173-4). Unfortunately, since that time, even though the adit was back-filled, the deposits within the tomb have largely dried out and contracted, leaving voids up to 0.16 m wide adjacent to the rock-cut walls (cf. Fig. 41b, below); preservation of certain types of artefact was thus markedly poorer in 1993-6 than it had been two decades previously.

Excavation revealed masses of artefacts throughout the tomb (Fig. 28), necessitating meticulous excavation and complex recording. A 0.5-m grid was established within Chamber B and subsequently extended and modified to provide horizontal control for planning purposes (Fig. 29), the resultant squares being designated by lower-case letters. All material was excavated in spits, artefacts being planned *in situ*

at a scale of 1:10. Most artefacts were individually inventoried. Samples, including the contents of most of the intact pottery vessels, were examined for archaeobotanical remains, but very few were found (pp. 127-8, below). The soil from the artefact-bearing deposits was sieved through 1-mm mesh. This allowed a detailed analysis to be undertaken of the fragmentation and distribution of objects, illustrating both their original placement and their subsequent disturbance. Certain objects must have been taken from the tomb by robbers, others were removed during the 1974 excavation, and yet others remain in unexcavated areas. It has however proved possible to reconstruct many vessels which had been dumped and broken on the floor and to plot the distribution of related artefacts in order to illustrate the effect of robber activity.

Four phases of robbing could be traced throughout Passage G, Chamber D, and its loculi H and J. In the present work, these phases are designated Robbing 1 to Robbing 4 in chronological order (Fig.

a   b

Fig. 26 *The Tomb of the Brick Arches: **a** - general view of Arch I, from the adit; **b** - the eastern part of Arch I, seen from the adit. Scales: 0.5 m.*

*Fig. 27 a - The view inside the Tomb of the Brick Arches , from Chamber B through Arch III into Chamber A, with the north side of Arch I and the foot of the adit visible in the background; **b** - the lintels over Loculi E (before partial excavation) and F. Scales: 0.5 m.*

30). Only the lower levels of robbing could be defined in Chamber B, as the upper deposits had been removed in 1974. Although all these robbing episodes resulted in disturbance, it seems likely that the removal of particularly valuable objects was largely restricted to the first phase, Robbing 1. With very few possible exceptions (pp. 57, 77, below), it seems unlikely that robbers introduced artefacts into the tomb.

Chamber A

The antechamber (Chamber A) measures *c*. 2.5 m square. Its present height from floor to roof is *c*. 2.0 m, but the original height was probably closer to 1.5

m before it was increased by partial collapse of the roof. The irregular rock-cut floor slopes down towards two further brick arches, III and II, respectively leading northward into Chamber B and westward into Chamber C (Munro-Hay 1989: pl. 6.2). The deposits within Chamber A were almost entirely excavated in 1974 when a series of inwash layers, DA I(8), was defined below the fifteenth step of the adit, underlying DA I(3), continuing into the tomb. A human skull was found lying on the surface of DA I(8), along with a small quantity of pottery and glass, which must have been taken out of the tomb during the final phases of robbing.   Within Chamber A these layers were sealed

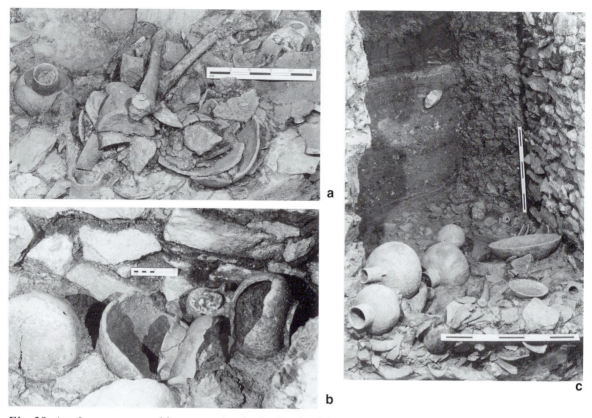

Fig. 28 *Artefacts as exposed by excavation in the Tomb of the Brick Arches: **a, c** - in Passage G;*
***b** - in Chamber D.*

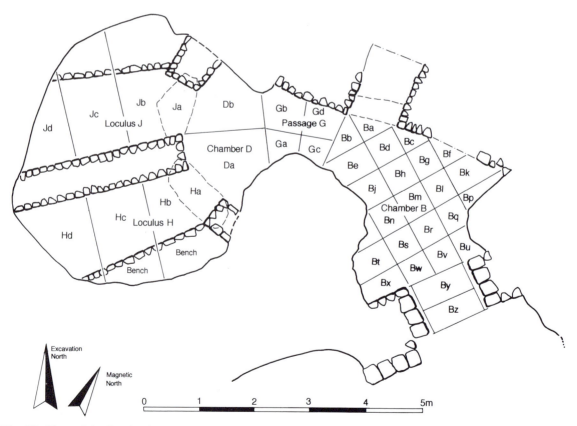

Fig. 29 *Plan of the Tomb of the Brick Arches, showing excavation subdivisions.*

by DA I(9), comprising water-borne clay deposits and fallen rock from the roof. Grave goods do not appear to have been placed within this chamber, and the small quantity of fragmentary artefacts appears to have been dropped by later robbers, including a pottery lamp found below Arch I in DA I(8) which may have been introduced secondarily for use by the robbers (Munro-Hay 1989: fig. 16.330).

The compact basal layer in Chamber A, DA I(10), was incompletely excavated in 1974. Completion of this in 1993 revealed a triangular-shaped pit, 0.92 by 0.68 m overall and 0.30 m deep, cut into the floor in the northwest corner between Arches II and III (Fig. 31). The pit contained a 38-kg mass of copper-alloy fragments so tightly packed together that they may originally have been held in some form of organic container (see below, pp. 95-105, 131). The pit extended across the entrance to Chamber B, under Brick Arch III, forming a rough step-down of *c.* 0.30 m between the chambers; it is not certain, however, that it had been dug and filled before Arch III was constructed. The excavators were able to remove the block of metal intact, without damage to Arch III. When the block was dismantled in the Project's field laboratory, fragments of charcoal were recovered from its interior. Two of these have been subjected to radiocarbon analysis, yielding dates of 1705 bp ± 45 (OxA-8340) and 1655 bp ± 40 (OxA-8341). The dated fragments were identified by Rowena Gale respectively as mixed *Ficus* and *Rhus* and as *Acokanthera*. The significance of these age-determinations is discussed below (pp. 128-30) and further details of the individual analyses are provided in Appendix VI.

Brick Arches II and III had originally been sealed by rough stone blocking, as recorded during the 1974 excavation, although both had been broken open during Robbing 1, allowing robbers to crawl through (Munro-Hay 1989: 57, pl. 6.2). There was, however, no evidence from the 1974 excavation to indicate that Brick Arch I, the entrance arch, had ever been sealed.

Chamber B

Investigation of Chamber B was complicated by the partial excavation that had taken place in 1974, when *c.* 1.05 m of the deposit was removed and designated DA I(13). The total depth of the deposits in this chamber proved to be approximately 1.80 m. The previous excavation meant that the sequence of later robbing levels could not be established. The 1974 records do not permit the levels excavated in that year to be correlated with those in Passage G, although they presumably included material from Robbing episodes 3 and 4. Furthermore, in contrast with Passage G and Chamber D where the sequence was clear, several layers were hard to interpret because of mixing and

churning that had taken place during the various robbing episodes.

Chamber B is an irregularly shaped rock-cut chamber, *c.* 2.95 m long from Brick Arch III to the entrance into Loculus E, *c.* 2.4 m in maximum width, and *c.* 2.3 m high. The northern side of the chamber is partitioned by a mud-bonded stone wall incorporating the entrances to two loculi, E and F (Fig. 27b, above), while Passage G continues northwestwards and opens out into Chamber D. An arbitrary northern section, in line with the entrance to Loculus E and cut in 1974 after the removal of the overlying deposits, was taken to mark the division between Chamber B and Passage G; the artefact deposit was, however, continuous.

Robbing 1 was defined above the lowest layer in Chamber B, which consisted of deposits B(15) and B(16), levelling the irregular rock-cut floor. A sample of burned bone from B(15) has yielded a radiocarbon date of 1925 bp ± 50 (OxA8984; see Appendix VI). Numerous ivory plaques and a very large iron spear- or lance-head (Figs 101 and 93, below) were discovered in layer B(14), representing Robbing 1. These were mixed with a large quantity of rubble, probably derived from the unblocking of Brick Arch III and the entrances to Loculi E and F.

Over 100 intact or fragmentary ivory plaques with lathe-turned concentric ridges were found during the excavation, most coming from this deposit (see pp. 119-22, below). Although they could have been pulled from either Loculus E or F, it seems equally plausible that they or the object/s of which they formed part were originally placed within Chamber B, in front of the loculi entrances. There were three concentrations: layer B(13) in squares j, m, n, r, s; layer B(14) in e, d, h, j; and B(14) in l, m, q, r. There may thus have been several objects of which these plaques formed part or, alternatively, a single object may have been broken and its components separated.

The tomb had evidently been closed prior to Robbing 1; its opening by robbers was followed by deposition of the first of several water-borne layers, B(13) which, with its counterpart in other chambers, sealed the Robbing-1 deposit on the floor of the chamber. This layer, comprising fine bands of pale grey water-borne clay resulting from periodic and very gradual deposition, had accumulated to a thickness of *c.* 0.15 m when Robbing 2 took place. The Robbing-1 deposit in Chamber B was disturbed by wall collapse during Robbing 2.

The stratigraphy of the lower layers remaining in Chamber B after the 1974 excavations was unclear, probably because of the large amount of robber activity which had taken place there. A large spread of rubble, layer B(11), was embedded within and above B(13), below the artefact deposit B(9). Some of this

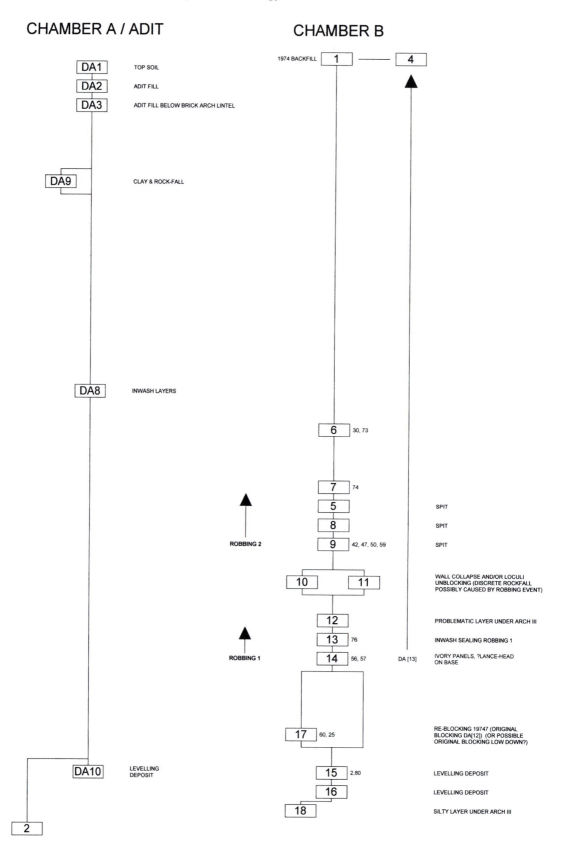

CHAMBER A / ADIT

DA1 — TOP SOIL

DA2 — ADIT FILL

DA3 — ADIT FILL BELOW BRICK ARCH LINTEL

DA9 — CLAY & ROCK-FALL

DA8 — INWASH LAYERS

ROBBING 2

ROBBING 1

DA10 — LEVELLING DEPOSIT

2

CHAMBER B

1974 BACKFILL — 1 — 4

6 — 30, 73

7 — 74

5 — SPIT

8 — SPIT

9 — 42, 47, 50, 59 — SPIT

10 — 11 — WALL COLLAPSE AND/OR LOCULI UNBLOCKING (DISCRETE ROCKFALL POSSIBLY CAUSED BY ROBBING EVENT)

12 — PROBLEMATIC LAYER UNDER ARCH III

13 — 76 — INWASH SEALING ROBBING 1

14 — 56, 57 — DA [13] — IVORY PANELS, ?LANCE-HEAD ON BASE

17 — 60, 25 — RE-BLOCKING 19747 (ORIGINAL BLOCKING DA[12]) (OR POSSIBLE ORIGINAL BLOCKING LOW DOWN?)

15 — 2,80 — LEVELLING DEPOSIT

16 — LEVELLING DEPOSIT

18 — SILTY LAYER UNDER ARCH III

Fig. 30 *Stratigraphic correlation chart, Tomb of the Brick Arches: Adit, Chambers A and B.*

40

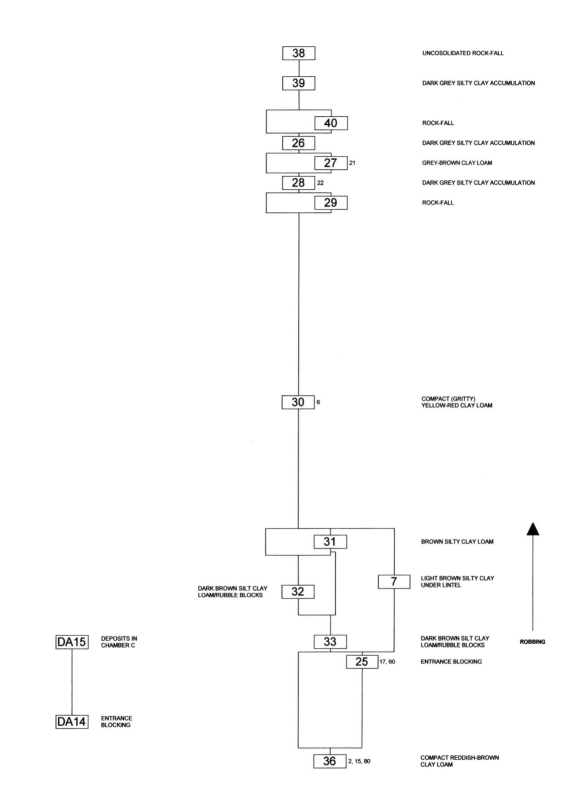

CHAMBER C   **LOCULUS E**

38	UNCOSOLIDATED ROCK-FALL
39	DARK GREY SILTY CLAY ACCUMULATION
40	ROCK-FALL
26	DARK GREY SILTY CLAY ACCUMULATION
27 21	GREY-BROWN CLAY LOAM
28 22	DARK GREY SILTY CLAY ACCUMULATION
29	ROCK-FALL
30 6	COMPACT (GRITTY) YELLOW-RED CLAY LOAM
31	BROWN SILTY CLAY LOAM
7	LIGHT BROWN SILTY CLAY UNDER LINTEL
32	DARK BROWN SILT CLAY LOAM/RUBBLE BLOCKS
DA15	DEPOSITS IN CHAMBER C
33	DARK BROWN SILT CLAY LOAM/RUBBLE BLOCKS
25 17, 60	ENTRANCE BLOCKING
DA14	ENTRANCE BLOCKING
36 2, 15, 80	COMPACT REDDISH-BROWN CLAY LOAM

ROBBING

Fig. 30 continued Stratigraphic correlation chart, Tomb of the Brick Arches: Loculus J.

PASSAGE G AND CHAMBER D   LOCULUS H

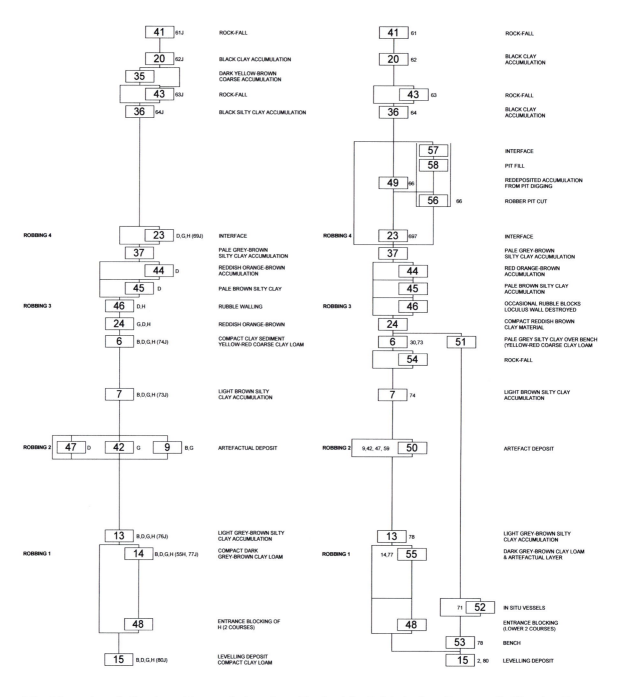

Fig. 30 continued *Stratigraphic correlation chart, Tomb of the Brick Arches: Passage G, Chamber D and Loculus H.*

LOCULUS J

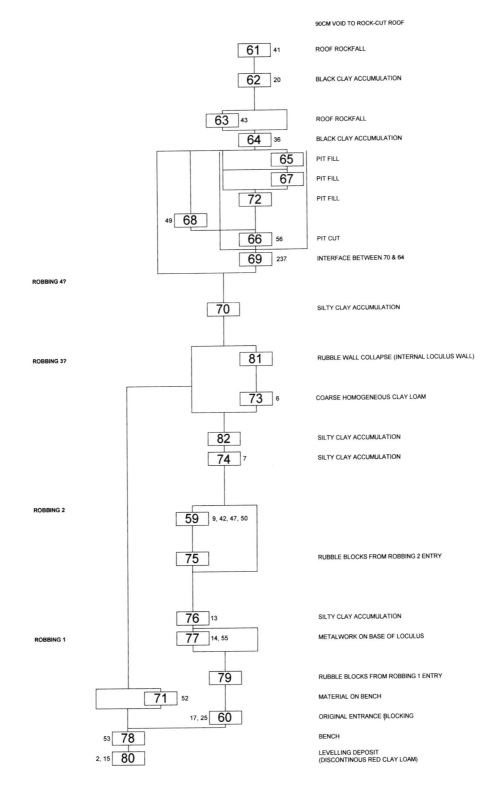

90CM VOID TO ROCK-CUT ROOF

61 41   ROOF ROCKFALL

62 20   BLACK CLAY ACCUMULATION

63 43   ROOF ROCKFALL

64 36   BLACK CLAY ACCUMULATION

65   PIT FILL

67   PIT FILL

72   PIT FILL

49 68

66 56   PIT CUT

69 237   INTERFACE BETWEEN 70 & 64

ROBBING 4?

70   SILTY CLAY ACCUMULATION

ROBBING 3?

81   RUBBLE WALL COLLAPSE (INTERNAL LOCULUS WALL)

73 6   COARSE HOMOGENEOUS CLAY LOAM

82   SILTY CLAY ACCUMULATION

74 7   SILTY CLAY ACCUMULATION

ROBBING 2

59 9, 42, 47, 50

75   RUBBLE BLOCKS FROM ROBBING 2 ENTRY

76 13   SILTY CLAY ACCUMULATION

ROBBING 1   77 14, 55   METALWORK ON BASE OF LOCULUS

79   RUBBLE BLOCKS FROM ROBBING 1 ENTRY

71 52   MATERIAL ON BENCH

17, 25 60   ORIGINAL ENTRANCE BLOCKING

53 78   BENCH

2, 15 80   LEVELLING DEPOSIT
(DISCONTINOUS RED CLAY LOAM)

Fig. 30 continued *Stratigraphic correlation chart, Tomb of the Brick Arches: Loculus J.*

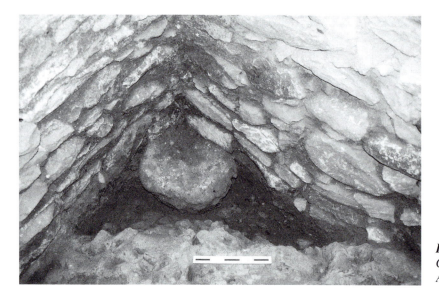

Fig. 31 *The pit in the floor of Chamber A, Tomb of the Brick Arches. Scale: 0.25 m.*

rubble could have derived from the removal of blocking at the entrances to the loculi, but the majority must have come from collapse of the wall above the entrance to Loculus F. There was also a large concentration of rubble in layer B(9), especially below the collapsed wall in front of Loculus F, which must have been dragged down during Robbing 2; another substantial deposit of wall rubble had been defined in this position in 1974. The wall above Loculus E was, however, still intact (Fig. 32). The wall above the entrance to Loculus F could have collapsed naturally, the rock-cut roof at this point being very unstable with inwash supporting large fragments of collapsed roof; it seems more likely that it was pulled down during the comprehensive Robbing 2 episode, which may be traced throughout the tomb (Fig. 33).[3]

Apparently a single event, Robbing 2 involved the large-scale extraction of grave goods from Loculi E and F into Chamber B, resulting in the creation of a heap *c.* 0.45 m in maximum depth on the floor of the chamber which, at that point, was the surface of inwash layer B(13) (Figs 32, 34). This heap in front of Arch III had been partly removed in 1974 as part of DA I(13). The artefacts extracted from the loculi were strewn across the entire base of Chamber B but concentrated in front of the two entrances, especially that of Loculus E, indicating that they had been pulled straight out into the chamber. This deposit, a mass of artefacts in varying states of preservation, was

excavated in three successive horizontal spits B(5), B(8) and B(9). It yielded a human skull and other disarticulated bones, the remains of two large ivory panels and some 42 pottery vessels, including beakers, bowls and jars, all apparently raked out of the loculi by robbers. Although the heap probably suffered from later robbing disturbance, the distribution of material on the floor of Chamber B may reflect the order in which objects were removed from the loculi. The lowest material was presumably the first to be thrown onto the floor and, by implication, came from the front of the loculi; it may have suffered less subsequent disturbance than that which overlay it.

Close study of the fragmentation and distribution of artefacts has demonstrated the extent of disturbance and dispersal of material within the tomb. Eighty-one inventoried objects (mainly pottery and glass) were shown to have actual sherd joins across grid squares and/or between chambers. Only seven of these had no fragments in Chamber B, although fragmentation of material was greater in Chamber B than elsewhere, and more sherd joins should be expected within this chamber. Sherds of a single glass vessel (Fig. 58a, below) were recovered from ten grid squares in Chamber B and Passage G; this is indicative of the substantial movement and disturbance which had taken place (Fig. 35a). Thirty-one of the objects in Chamber B have joining sherds across two grid squares, and sixteen have joins across five or more grid squares.

Fragments of individual artefacts were scattered between chambers. Three jars, one bowl and one pot-stand were shown to have joining sherds between Chambers B and D (Figs 35b-f). Their distribution is particularly revealing: all of them cluster in squares j, m and n of Chamber B, perhaps indicating that these

---

[3] The evidence in Chamber D was clearer, showing that the entrances to Loculi H and J had been unblocked during Robbing 1. The walls above the lintels had been deliberately pulled out, but not until Robbing 3 or 4, by which time water-borne layers had already reached the level of the loculi lintels.

vessels formerly stood close to each other and/or were dispersed in the same act. Moreover, four of the vessels are represented in Chamber B by sherds in Robbing-2 deposits but in Chamber D and/or Passage G by sherds from levels attributed to Robbing 4. Sherds of the pot-stand were recovered from the Robbing-2 deposit in Chambers B, layer B(8), and D, layers D(42) and D(47). In Passage G, fragments of the same vessel were found in layer G(24) which relates to Robbing 3, and in layer G(43) which overlies Robbing 4. This evidence strongly suggests that at least one further robbing episode must have taken place after Robbing 4 in Chamber B, although it could not be defined elsewhere.

Loculus E

An attempt was made in 1995 to excavate this loculus from which, as noted above, much of the artefact deposit within Chamber B probably derived. Excavation proceeded only 0.5 m into the loculus before it was

halted as no solid roof could be defined and the unstable deposits prevented further work (Figs 36, 37a).

The entrance blocking E(25) survived to a height of *c*. 0.6 m, approximately half of it having been removed during the robbing events. A deposit of rubble, E(31), E(32) and E(33), *c*. 0.6 m deep and including a large lintel/capping stone *c*. 0.75 m long, lay directly on the floor of the loculus behind the entrance blocking. The wall above the lintel was still intact, so this rubble could be the remains of a collapsed inner wall or of a bench located on the north side of the loculus against the rock-cut wall, as in Loculus H.

Although safety considerations prevented the configuration of Loculi E and F being confirmed by excavation, it is possible that they were similar to Loculi H and J, described below (pp. 54-6). On this basis, it seems likely that artefacts were placed on benches within the loculi, since otherwise they would have been buried by the inwash which followed Robbing 1. The fact that few artefacts were found in

Fig. 32 Tomb of the Brick Arches: the heap of extracted artefacts outside Loculus E, the unexcavated entrance to which may be seen on the right. Deposits filling Passage G are seen in section. Scale: 0.5 m.

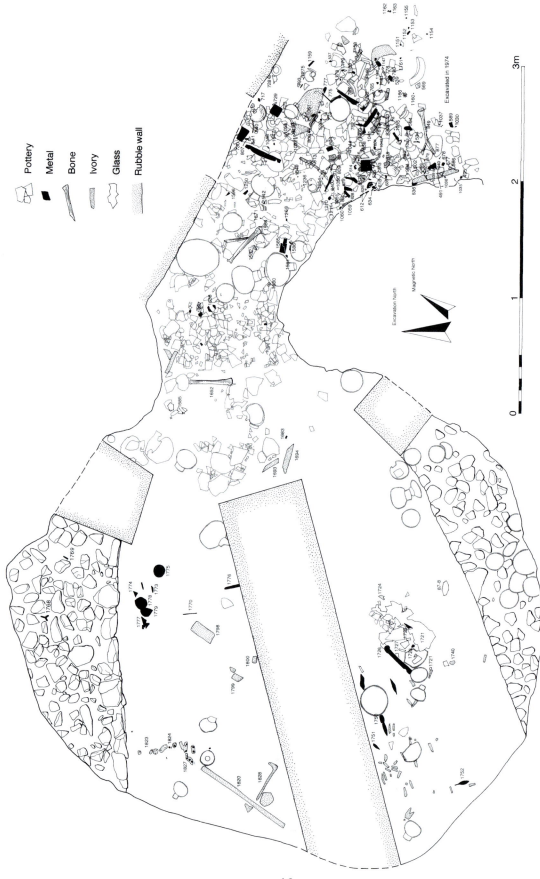

Fig. 33 Composite plan of the Tomb of the Brick Arches at the Robbing-2 phase.

Loculus E does not indicate its overall content since excavation was restricted to the entrance area and, as noted above, much of the material recovered in Chamber B may have been extracted from Loculi E and F.

A substantial rock-fall deposit E(29), consisting of unconsolidated fragments from the roof, had built up *c*. 0.55 m in depth against the wall dividing the two loculi, indicating that the soft sandstone roof has been unstable since antiquity. Overlying the rock-fall were gradually accumulated water-borne deposits, layers E(28), E(27), E(26) and E(39), interspersed with rock-fall lenses E(40) and E(38). In contrast with the other chambers, there was no void between the sterile inwash layers and the roof of the loculus, the fractured and unconsolidated rock being supported by the water-borne clay.

Robbing episodes 3 and 4 could not be clearly defined within the loculus. Evidence from the remaining stratigraphy in Chamber B, excavated in 1993, indicated that Loculus E may have been entered during Robbing 4, though this could not be defined in the excavation of the loculus itself. Within Chamber B, a water-borne clay layer B(6) was shown to plunge down *c*. 0.35 m immediately in front of the loculus entrance, perhaps as a result of robbers digging in order to gain access to the loculus.

Loculus F

Loculus F, to the east of Loculus E, was left unexcavated. A large piece of rock fractured from the roof, *c*. 0.4 m thick and extending across the width of the loculus, was supported by water-borne clay deposits. The possibility of supporting this material by inserting steel lintels, in order to rebuild the collapsed wall before excavation of the loculus, was discussed, but it was concluded that this might destabilise the roof of the chamber. A large section of walling above the entrance to the loculus appears to have been pulled out during Robbing 2, as suggested by the large quantity of rubble blocks B(11) found immediately below the extracted artefacts in B(9). The entrance blocking itself was intact to a height of *c*. 1.0 m, only the uppermost 0.4 m having been removed during robbing (Figs 24, 27b above).

Passage G

Passage G, *c*. 1.5 m long, 1.25 m wide and 2.3 m high, links Chambers B and D, extending from the entrance of Loculus E through into Chamber D (Fig. 37b). It was divided into four quadrants during excavation in order to facilitate plotting the distribution of artefacts (see Fig. 29, above). It may, however, be more appropriate to regard squares Gc and Gd as part of Chamber B and squares Ge and Gf as part of Chamber D. The rock-cut walls narrow to form a clear constriction, 1.1 m wide, before opening out into Chamber D.

A sample of *Maytenus* charcoal, identified by Rowena Gale, from the basal layer G(15) yielded a radiocarbon date of 1725 bp ± 35 (OxA-8363).

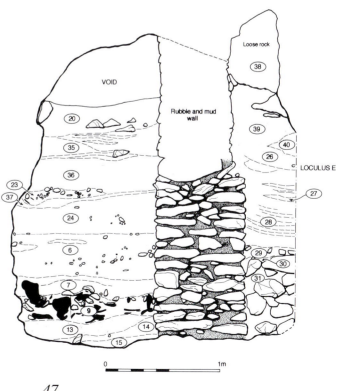

Fig. 34 *Tomb of the Brick Arches: section through deposits at the south end of Passage G (cf. Fig. 32) and extending into Loculus E (see Fig. 29).*

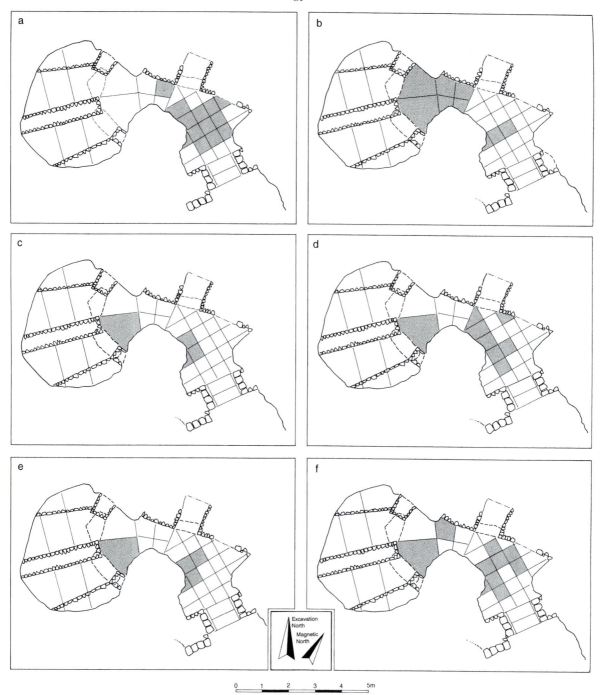

Fig. 35 *Distribution of fragments from individual artefacts in the Tomb of the Brick Arches: **a** - glass goblet B/22\; **b** - potstand B/1916\; **c** - jar B/991\; **d** - jar B/1899\; **e** - bowl B/890\; **f** - jar B/533\.*

Passage G provided the 1993-7 Project with its first opportunity to excavate the tomb's complete stratigraphic sequence, the upper deposits within Chamber B having been removed in 1974. Three separate robbing episodes were clearly defined. Three of the lathe-turned ivory plaques were preserved on the rock-cut floor in layer G(14), representing Robbing 1,

but the mass strewn across the base of Chamber B did not continue in Passage G. Layer G(14) was sealed by G(13), *c*. 0.2 m thick.

The disturbed artefact deposit excavated in Chamber B continued with varying density through Passage G into Chamber D. Artefacts were almost entirely restricted to layer G(9) in grid squares Gc and

Gd, being clearly a continuation of the mass of material found dumped on the north side of Chamber B and derived from the robbing of Loculi E and F. This layer contained a large quantity of material, including complete and semi-complete pottery vessels, disarticulated human bone, and a setting of eight bimetallic plaques mounted on wood, thrown flat on the floor (see Fig. 86, below). The location of three human-headed pottery vessels on the base of the deposit suggests that they may have been placed next to each other at the front of Loculus E and were the first objects to be pulled out. Three complete jars, found together on the west side of the passage and facing the same direction, may also have once stood next to each other. Two samples of charcoal from this deposit have been dated to 1725 bp ± 40 (OxA-8364) and 1750 bp ± 35 (OxA-8365). The samples were identified by Rowena Gale as probable *Ficus* and as *Olea*, respectively.

This deposit did not extend beyond the narrowing of Passage G. A trampled layer of artefacts, G(42), represented Robbing 2 in squares Ge and Gf, being contemporary with layers B(5), B(8), B(9), D(47), H(50) and J(59). As the robbers moved through the chambers sherds were trampled flat, broken into smaller fragments and embedded horizontally on the surface of layers B(13), G(13), D(13), H(13) and J(76).

Robbing 3 was not clearly distinguished during the excavation of Passage G due to the lack of artefacts or evidence of disturbance, even though the interface between layers G(45) and G(24) was clearly defined *c*. 0.7 m above Robbing 2. There was no counterpart to layer D(46).

Fig. 36 *Tomb of the Brick Arches: Loculus E on termination of excavation. Scale: 0.5 m.*

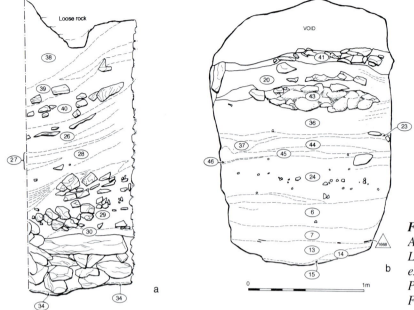

Fig. 37 *Tomb of the Brick Arches:* **a** *- north (end) section of Loculus E on termination of excavation;* **b** *- section across Passage G at its mid-point (see Fig. 29).*

Water-borne deposits *c.* 0.7 m in total thickness, comprising layers G(6), G(7), G(24) and G(37), accumulated before the final phase of robbing occurred. Robbing 4 took place after *c.* 0.2 m of further accumulation above the Robbing 3 horizon, to which it may have been relatively close in time. Layer G(23) represents Robbing 4, including further rubble from the loculi walls of Chamber D and fragments of the bird-shaped vessel illustrated in Fig. 56, below.

Fragments of this distinctive and readily identifiable bird-shaped vessel were found strewn horizontally and vertically through the deposits in Passage G, Chamber D and Loculus J, clearly demonstrating the extent of disturbance and movement of material within the tomb. Fragments were recovered from two different robbing episodes, separated by undisturbed water-borne layers in Passage G and Chamber D. The head and a leg came from Robbing 2, layer G(9), while the body was found 0.8 m higher, within Robbing 4, layer G(23); the upper right body came from G(23)b; left rear leg from G(9)c; head/neck from G(9)e; lower right body from D(23)b; base and front leg from J(72)c (Fig. 38). It would appear from this distribution that the vessel was first broken during Robbing 2, and at that stage must have been strewn across the base of the tomb between Passage G and Loculus J. During Robbing 4, a robber pit J(66) was cut down for *c.* 0.7 m through the overburden in Loculus J and, by chance, located fragments of this vessel sealed in a Robbing-2 deposit. One fragment of the vessel was actually found within the lower fill of this robber pit, layer J(72). Additional fragments were then redeposited

at the same level (23) in Chamber D and Passage G. Similar sequences are apparent for other vessels.

After the final Robbing-4 disturbance, black clay water-borne deposits gradually accumulated to a maximum thickness of 0.7 m, perhaps the result of periodic flooding down the adit or seepage from the surface, combined with intermittent roof collapse. This black clay accumulated throughout Passage G, Chamber D and its associated loculi in layers designated (20), (35), (36) and (41), as well as in Chamber B where it had been removed in 1974. There is a distinct change from pale grey-brown silty clay layers to this overlying black clay, which formed only after the final robbing episode and may suggest a change in the nature of the material washing down into the tomb.

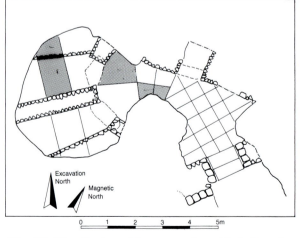

Fig. 38 *Distribution of fragments from bird-shaped vessel B/1670\.*

Fig. 39 *Chamber D in the Tomb of the Brick Arches, showing Loculi H and J:* **a** *- with loculi blocked;* **b** *- with loculi excavated;* **c** *- from Loculus J, showing bench in foreground, looking through Passage G into Chamber B where the entrance to Loculus E is visible. Scales: 0.5 m.*

Fig. 40 *Excavation of Loculus H, Tomb of the Brick Arches:* **a** *- excavation in progress, showing the bench and smashed artefacts thrown from it during Robbing 2 (scale: 0.5 m);* **b** *- bowls in situ on the bench (scale: 0.25 m).*

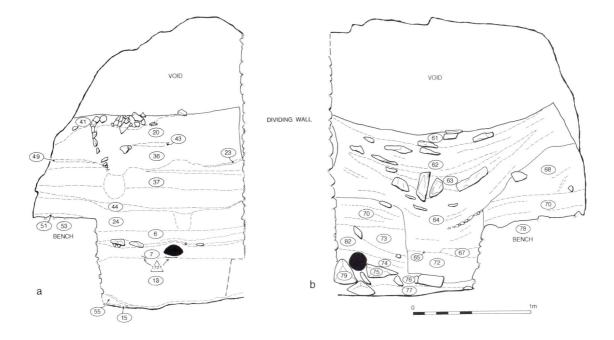

Fig. 41 *Sections across Loculi H (left) and J (right),Tomb of the Brick Arches.*

Chamber D

Chamber D is located to the west of Chamber B, opening out as the rock-cut Passage G swings westwards; this innermost chamber of the tomb is not visible from the entrance (Arch I). Chamber D widens out from *c*. 1.5 m to 2.5 m at the entrance to Loculi H and J, each of which, as described below, contains a stone-built bench. If, as suggested above, squares Ge and Gf are regarded as part of Chamber D, this chamber would have an overall length of 1.75 m, its maximum height being 2.4 m. The chamber was divided by a wall of rubble and mud to form Loculi H and J, comparable with the configuration of Chamber B with its Loculi E and F. This wall is angled inwards, creating a foyer in front of the entrances to the loculi (Figs 22, 24, 39).

Four robbing phases were clearly defined in Chamber D. Robbing 1 was represented by rubble blocks, layer D(14), strewn on the rock-cut floor in front of Loculus J and representing the unblocking of the loculi entrances, particularly H which was completely unblocked. No artefacts were found on the floor of Chamber D, indicating that material had neither been placed there originally nor thrown out of the loculi during Robbing 1.

The water-borne deposit D(13) accumulated to a depth of *c*. 0.3 m before the chamber was re-entered and comprehensively ransacked in Robbing 2. Artefacts were strewn across the base of the chamber and must have been raked off the benches in the two loculi

and out into Chamber D. The resultant deposit D(47) was concentrated in front of Loculus J in the north and central parts of the chamber. It is also possible that some of these artefacts came originally from Chamber B: as noted above (p. 44) five separate vessels had joining sherds distributed between Chambers B and D.

The quantity of artefacts in Chamber D and in Loculi H and J was very markedly less than that found in Chamber B and the incompletely excavated Loculi E and F. This seems to reflect a real difference in the quantities originally placed in these areas. The objects in Chamber B were, however, more fragmentary than those in Chamber D and its associated loculi. Based on the inventoried pottery from the tomb, and excluding that from Loculus E which was incompletely excavated, 81% of items (71 vessels in 1974, 223 in 1993-6) came from Chamber B, in comparison with 11% (40 vessels) from Chamber D and Loculi H and J combined. The pattern is similar for uninventoried pottery, which was quantified by weight: 80% (78 kg excluding 1974 pottery) from Chamber B and 6% (6 kg)[4] from Chamber D and its associated loculi.

A period of inwash accumulation, layers D(7), D(6) and D(24), followed Robbing 2. It was interrupted by Robbing 3, marked by a rubble layer D(46) in front of both Loculi H and J, *c*. 0.5 m above Robbing 2 and less than 0.3 m below the loculi lintels, representing the remains of the walls above the lintels which the robbers simply pulled down. By the

[4] This figure is skewed because most vessels in Loculi H and J were complete and received inventory numbers.

time this third robber disturbance took place, the grave goods were already sealed beneath *c.* 0.7 m of water-borne deposits.

There was a further *c.* 0.2 m of accumulation, layers D(45), D(44) and D(37), before Robbing 4. This was marked by layer D(23), consisting of rubble from further collapse of the loculi walls and a few sherds of pottery including a fragment of the bird-shaped vessel, presumably derived from the digging of two robber pits noted within the loculi. This final phase of robbing was followed by *c.* 0.7 m of black clay accumulation and intermittent roof collapse, layers D(36), D(43), D(35), D(20) and D(41), leaving a void of *c.* 0.4 m below the rock-cut roof of the chamber.

Loculus H

Loculi H and J, within the innermost chamber D, were both fully excavated. For spatial control, the restricted spaces within the loculi were excavated in 1.0 m segments, designated a, b, c and d (Fig. 29, above). The stratigraphic sequences defined in both loculi are similar to those recognised elsewhere in the tomb: four phases of robbing, separated by water-borne deposits, although it is possible that further robbing episodes have left little substantive archaeological evidence.

The southern loculus, H, measures *c.* 3.1 m long, 1.9 m wide and 2.3 m in maximum height, with a sloping rock-cut floor which reaches 0.22 m below that of Chamber B. A bench, H(53), 2.5 m long, 0.75 m wide and up to 0.75 m high, had been constructed of rubble and mud along the rock-cut south side of the loculus after the dividing wall with Chamber D had been built. In the absence of capping stones, objects were placed directly on its mud-and-rubble upper surface (Fig. 40).

The entrance to Loculus H was almost completely unblocked during Robbing 1, in contrast to Loculi J, E and F which were unblocked only to the minimum level needed to allow a robber to crawl through. Only the lower two courses of the entrance blocking H(48) remained in place, but this was enough to show that this loculus also had originally been closed. Layer H(13) sealed the remaining blocking. As robbers entered the loculus, rubble blocking-material from the entrance was strewn on the floor of Chamber D to the side and in front of Loculus J, forming layer D(14).

Objects of iron and copper alloy were found in layer H(55) on the floor of the loculus: in H(55)c was a concentration of metalwork, especially copper alloy strips with mineralised wood adhering. This was sealed by *c.* 0.4 m of inwash deposits, H(13), before Robbing 2 took place (Fig. 41a). Although some metalwork had been deposited on the rock-cut floor during

or before Robbing 1, pottery and glass remained on the bench or were only pulled off during Robbing 2, either onto the floor of the loculus or out into Chamber D. Two distinct clusters of bowls were defined on the bench. Three complete examples, immediately behind the chamber dividing wall, had been slightly disturbed, but two of them, although on their sides, were still stacked together. A second group of eight vessels was defined on the bench, forming layer H(52)c (Fig. 40b). Two bowls were stacked together; five more were on their sides, with one upside down. The location of these objects *in situ* on the bench and the lack of skeletal material within the loculus is strong evidence that this bench was used for the emplacement of grave goods and not for laying out a corpse.

Other vessels had been removed from the bench during Robbing 2 and strewn on the floor as layer H(50), while others were probably dumped in Chamber D as layer D(47). Anything of value to the robbers was presumably removed from the tomb altogether. Five complete jars were located immediately below the bench, along with five bowls, one pedestal bowl and fragments of a globe in very thin burgundy-red glass (see p. 80, Figs 59d, 60b, below). These objects could not have stood originally on the rock-cut floor, which was completely sealed by layer H(13), the *c.* 0.35 m of undisturbed water-borne accumulation separating Robbing 1 and Robbing 2.

Robbing 3 saw the destruction of the upper part of the wall dividing Loculus H from Chamber D forming layer D(46), little evidence for this event being recovered in Loculus H itself. Successive water-borne layers H(7), H(54), H(6) and H(24), *c.* 0.37 m in total thickness, lay above H(50) and below H(46). Further silting layers H(44) and H(37), *c.* 0.3 m in total thickness, separated the Robbing-3 H(46) from the Robbing-4 H(23).

During Robbing 4 a steep-sided sub-rectangular pit H(56), 1.5 by 0.8 m and 0.9 m deep, was dug against the innermost rock-cut wall as the robbers reached the back of the loculus. This pit cut down through the water-borne deposits and below the level of the bench to layer H(50) which marks Robbing 2; the robbers would thus have found previously disturbed material. The material thrown up from the digging of this pit forms layer H(49), 0.26 m in maximum thickness, dumped to the side against the rock-cut wall of the loculus, being directly comparable with layer J(68) in Loculus J (see below).

Water-borne black clay layers H(36) and H(21) sealed the Robbing-4 deposit, interrupted by collapsed roof material H(43) and H(41), the total deposit being *c.* 0.55 m thick. The deposits in Loculus H were *c.* 1.75 m in total depth, sloping down towards the back, there being a void of *c.* 0.6 m between the top of the deposits and the rock-cut roof of the loculus.

Loculus J

Loculus J is *c*. 2.9 m long and 2.05 m wide. Its maximum height is 2.2 m, and its irregular sloping floor is a maximum of 0.2 m lower than that of Chamber B. The deposits within the loculus were 1.3 m thick, there being a void of 0.9 m below the rock-cut roof. The layers could be traced through from Chamber D, but not as clearly as in Loculus H, from which the entrance blocking had been removed.

A rubble-and-mud bench, J(78), had been inserted along the northern side of the curving rock-cut wall after the construction of the dividing wall with Chamber D, opposite and paralleling that in Loculus H. The complete bench, which is not parallel to the central dividing wall, measures *c*. 2.2 m long, 0.85 m wide and 0.55 m in maximum height (Fig. 39c). A few stones had been dislodged from its edge, presumably during the digging of robber pit J(66). A 0.6-m-wide section was excavated through the bench in order to illustrate its construction, to search for possible dating evidence and to confirm that it was not a burial cist. It was found to be composed of small undressed stones set in mud mortar containing a few fragments of glass. After recording, the bench was reconstructed.

In contrast with Loculus H, the entrance blocking of this loculus, J(60), had been only partially pulled out and two thirds of it was still intact, to a maximum height of 1.05 m. Rubble had been pulled back into Chamber D, comprising layer D(48), while numerous other stones had been pushed into the loculus as J(79).

Nine thin triangular or star-shaped plates of copper alloy (Fig. 72, below), along with eight disc

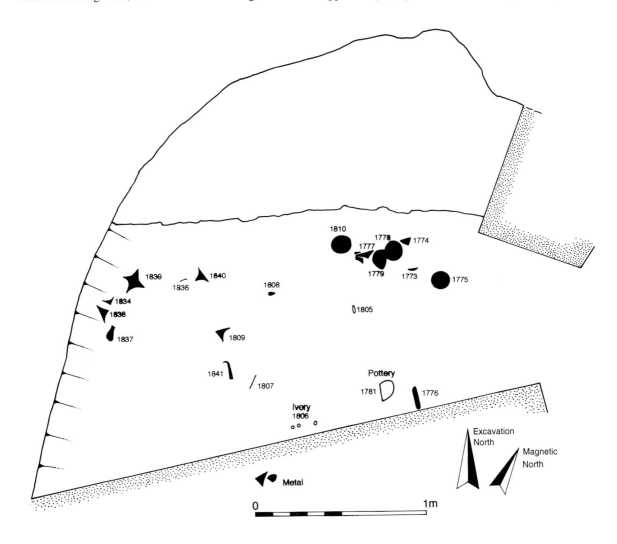

Fig. 42 *Plan showing positions of shaped copper alloy plates and mirrors in Loculus J.*

mirrors, were found strewn in layer J(77) on the floor of the loculus, belonging to Robbing 1 (Fig. 42). This deposit was sealed by *c.* 0.18 m of water-borne accumulation, comprising layers B(13), G(13), D(13), H(13) and J(76), before the loculus was re-entered and thoroughly robbed (Robbing 2). These second robbers enlarged the entrance slightly by pushing more rubble blocks down into the loculus to form J(75).

A concentration J(71) of wood remains and copper alloy tacks and nails with wood adhering to their shanks was found on the bench in an area *c.* 1.5 by 0.9 m, and on the floor beside the bench in layer J(59), where material had been displaced during Robbing 2. One hundred and ninety-nine nails and tacks were recovered from this loculus, in comparison with six in Chamber D and none in Loculus H (see p. 87 and Fig. 68, below). No patterning was discerned in the positioning of these nails. These, and the copper alloy fittings disturbed during Robbing 1, indicate the location of a substantial object constructed of wood, which may already have collapsed before the robbing took place. The impression of a wooden slat, 900 mm long by 50 mm wide, might give some indication of the original size of this object (Fig. 33, above), but no indication of any contents could be detected.

Fragments of a human skull in the robber pit J(66) (see pp. 126-7, below), and pieces of a femur from the spoil redeposited above the bench, layer J(68), must have been found strewn on the base of the loculus during the digging of the Robbing-2 pit. It is possible that a wooden bier or coffin containing a body had been placed on the bench; no bone was found on the rock-cut floor of the loculus to suggest that a body could have been laid beside the bench. As no bone was found in Loculus H and the vessels found on its bench were apparently *in situ*, it is possible to suggest an arrangement whereby one loculus, J, was used to lay out a corpse and the other, H, for the placement of grave goods. A similar pattern was observed elsewhere in the tomb, as is discussed in greater detail below (p. 130).

It seems significant that, as with Loculus H, only metalwork had been strewn on the floor during Robbing 1. Pottery was not pulled off the bench until Robbing 2. Four jars were recovered from the floor of Loculus J, one of which had been dropped on the entrance blocking; and none remained *in situ* on the bench.

In Loculus J it proved difficult to separate Robbing 3 and 4. By this stage, water-borne deposits had accumulated in the loculus to a depth of up to *c.* 0.8 m above the original floor. Robbers entered the loculus over the lintel, having pulled the dividing wall outwards into Chamber D. It is possible that a hole measuring *c.* 0.95 by 0.3 m in the internal dividing

wall between the two loculi, resulting in layer J(81), was made during Robbing 3.

A sub-rectangular robber pit, J(66) noted above, 1.6 by 0.75 m in area and 0.59 m deep with a straight-sided U-shaped profile, was dug by robbers who entered the loculus through the hole above the entrance lintel. It was located against the inside of the entrance blocking J(60) and extended back into the loculus alongside the bench which forms one side of the pit (Fig. 41b), and was probably contemporary with pit H(56) in Loculus H, attributed to Robbing 4. Fragments of a single large jar were represented both in Robbing 2, layer J(59), and in the later Robbing-3 pit J(66). The largest fragments, however, came from the disturbed inwash material J(68), cut through during the digging of the pit and redeposited above the bench and against the rock-cut wall. A sequence of events can therefore be reconstructed for the vessel which must originally have been placed on the bench, then pulled off onto the floor during Robbing 2. The later cutting of pit J(66) through layer J(59) redeposited large sherds of this vessel back above the bench, which at that stage was sealed by layers J(82) and J(70), thus reversing the original stratigraphy. Other fragments of the vessel remained within, or fell back into, the pit. This final phase of robbing in Loculus J was sealed below *c.* 0.6 m of undisturbed black water-borne clay, layers J(62) and J(64), interspersed by roof rock-fall J(61) and J(63).

Chamber C

Chamber C, located beyond Brick Arch II on the west side of Chamber A, had been broken open in antiquity, some of the bricks being damaged when the blocking was pulled out. In 1974 it was entered, examined with minimal excavation, DA I(15), and reblocked. It was not re-opened in 1993-6, and the following account, included here for completeness, is based entirely on the 1974 records (Munro-Hay 1989: 55-9). The chamber has a similar configuration to Chamber D, with a foyer *c.* 3.3 by 1.9 m in size separated from two loculi by a rubble and mud wall. The maximum dimensions of each loculus are roughly 3.8 by 1.6 m. A charcoal sample recovered in 1974 from a location described as in the 'outer part of Chamber C, against the step' yielded a radiocarbon date of 1680 bp ± 80 (P-2314, cited by Munro-Hay 1989: 26).

Chamber C differs from the others in having at least two paved steps down into the chamber from Arch II, and its northern loculus roofed with flat lintels, akin to the roofing of the adit. A possible fallen lintel was also encountered in Loculus E (p. 45, above). The southern loculus does not appear to have this arrangement, but resembles Loculi H and J. The 1974 excavation notebook shows that the walls above the lintels to both loculi had collapsed outwards into the chamber, the resultant rubble being sealed by black clay and roof rock-fall, as in Chamber D. Presumably the walls had been deliberately pulled down during one of the robbing episodes.

COMMENTARY

Comprehensive recording during the excavation of the Tomb of the Brick Arches, detailed above, has permitted significant conclusions to be drawn concerning the deposition of artefacts within the tomb and their subsequent disturbance during the four robbing episodes that have been recognised.

Metalwork was almost exclusively found in deposits on the floor of the tomb dating from Robbing 1, although in Chamber B there was also a large quantity of ivory in this position. The copper alloy and iron objects on the floor of the tomb were presumably left behind by the robbers, but other material - perhaps of precious metal - may have been removed. Excavation revealed an almost complete absence of gold and silver, but hints of its former presence were found; eight tiny fragments of gold and eight pieces of silver being recovered during the present excavation (pp. 86-7, below) and a few in 1974, including a small gold nail (Munro-Hay 1989: fig. 15.2) and a silver amulet case which was found lying against the blocking of Arch III and may have been dropped as the robbers left the tomb (*ibid.*: fig. 15.12). This suggests that the first robbing episode involved primarily the search for and removal of valuable objects, with minimal disturbance to other material. Certain items of high intrinsic value had presumably been removed from the tomb during Robbing 1, which might explain the more thorough disturbance of the deposits by robbers searching for further valuable items during Robbing 2. Robbing 3 and 4 took place subsequently, when substantial inwash deposits had accumulated, and involved extensive disturbance since there would then have been little visible indication of the location of artefacts.

It is apparent that all activity in the tomb subsequent to its initial use involved the search for and removal of valuables. Very few if any artefacts had evidently been introduced to the tomb during these robbing episodes.

ARTEFACTS

In the following sections the artefacts from the Tomb of the Brick Arches are treated as a single assemblage.

As the above discussion has made clear all the artefacts (with a very few possible exceptions which are individually noted) appear to have been placed in the tomb at the same time, despite the fact that many of them were recovered from disturbed contexts which are attributed to four successive episodes of robbing. Part of the assemblage was excavated in 1974 and has already been published elsewhere.[5] Where appropriate and possible, the following discussion takes account of the earlier discoveries so that the present volume, read in conjunction with that by Munro-Hay (1989), provides a coherent account of the materials that have so far been recovered from the Tomb of the Brick Arches. All specimens illustrated here were recovered during the excavations of 1993-6.

Pottery and other clay objects
(Jacke Phillips)

The large quantity of pottery excavated in the Tomb of the Brick Arches makes it difficult to provide a comprehensive account of the whole. This study is based on 351 inventoried vessels (71 from the 1974 excavations and 280 from those of 1993-6). In addition, between 90 and 100 kg[6] of uninventoried potsherds was recovered in 1993-6, but the weight of 1974 uninventoried pottery was not recorded. Although a detailed catalogue of the tomb's pottery contents cannot be attempted, it was clearly substantial in quantity and remarkably limited and repetitive in scope.

In comparison with most other assemblages of Aksumite pottery, that from the Tomb of the Brick Arches is elaborate; it is here attributed to the Classical Aksumite style, the significance and affinities of which are discussed on pp. 456-7, below.

Many of the forms and decorations were recorded in 1974 by Richard Wilding (in Munro-Hay 1989: 235-316). The present report cites this material when appropriate, but emphasises additions and corrections rather than repeating previously published information. There is no need, for example, to amplify or modify Wilding's comments on pottery manufacture and technology, except for additional comments regarding the painted vessels. The terminology and classification here adopted to describe Classical Aksumite

---

[5] Inventoried specimens from 1974, some of which were examined in the course of the present Project, are housed at the Museum in Aksum. Uninventoried 1974 material, not studied in detail by Chittick and his collaborators, has not been re-examined; this has restricted our view of the artefact assemblage, particularly the pottery.

[6] The weight of uninventoried pottery from 1993-6 is approximate, as some weighed sherds were subsequently inventoried.

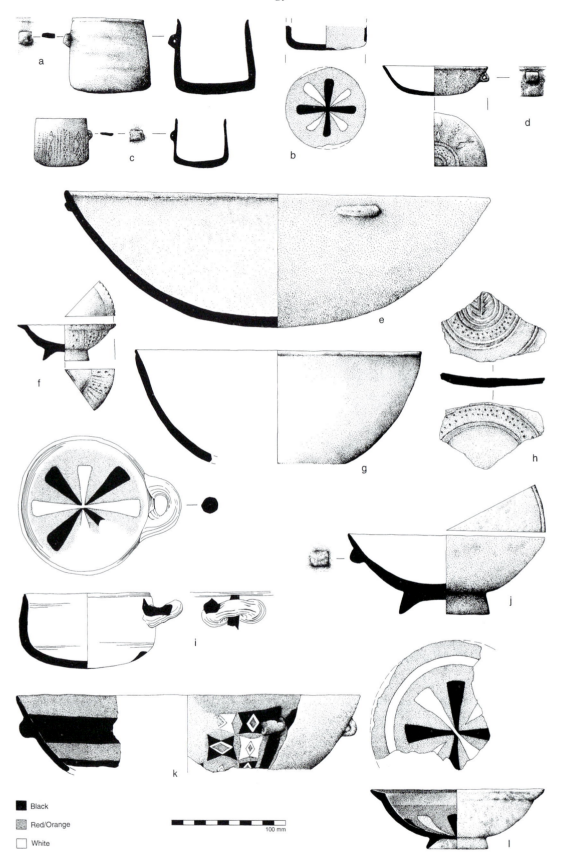

Fig. 43 *Pottery beakers and bowls from the Tomb of the Brick Arches.*

■ Black

▨ Red/Orange

□ White

100 mm

pottery embellishment and decoration is presented in Appendix II, to which the reader is referred for explanation of the terms and abbreviations used in this and subsequent chapters. Designations in square brackets are explained in Appendix II.

Beakers

The walls of these vessels taper inwards to a generally rounded rim, the rounded base is flattened and occasionally has a central dimple. Sometimes the rim has a slight exterior lip with a horizontal groove immediately below it. Characteristically, a single 'bias balance' handle is located about two thirds of the way up the body, comprising either a short horizontal lug, sometimes horizontally pierced, or a vertical flat strap of similar appearance. Rim diameters range between 35 and 88 mm, and heights from 41 to 88 mm, although two large incomplete examples have rim diameters of 120 and 160 mm. It is estimated that a total of approximately 35 beakers, including fragmented examples not studied in detail, have been recovered from the tomb. Eleven of these have rim diameters less than 50 mm, falling within Wilding's (Munro-Hay 1989: 243) definition of miniatures, including virtually all those with the most elaborate incised surface designs described below. No clear bimodality of size separates the miniatures from the other beakers. There are three basic decorative types:

- plain with smooth surface, with only a horizontal groove below the exterior rim (*e.g.* Fig. 43a; Munro-Hay 1989: figs 16.22-3);
- smooth surface, but with overall fugitive painted decoration including patterns of diamonds and superimposed crosses (*e.g.* Munro-Hay 1989: fig. 16.17); and
- having incised decoration in a variety of vertical combinations [2], [3], [5], [6] with a horizontal corrugation [A] below the rim and usually a horizontal band of ovoid walk punctates (OWP) [b], [c] near the bottom edge but occasionally without [g] (*e.g.* Munro-Hay 1989: figs 16.41-5).

No examples having only vertical corrugation [1] were recovered from the tomb. One beaker, with exterior incised decoration, has a moulded medallion design on the interior bottom. Another (Munro-Hay 1989: fig. 16.30), otherwise plain, is recorded with decoration [b], but the surface is badly preserved and it may originally have had vertical decoration in addition. Painted decoration is not common but two examples (Figs 43b, 45a; Munro-Hay 1989: fig. 16.17) have superimposed black and white crosses on the underside and, in the latter case, alternating diamonds on the exterior wall.

Bowls

Bowls, as noted by Wilding (Munro-Hay 1989: 244), have a considerable range of shape and size; in total approximately 250 have now been recovered from the tomb. The distinction made here between round- and ring-based bowls is only apparent when the base itself is preserved, so incomplete examples cannot be differentiated. Unless there is clear evidence for a foot-ring, bowls are here placed in the round-bottomed class.

Round-bottomed bowls with plain rim: All decorative embellishments are found in this vessel class, with undecorated shallow examples having only a groove below the interior rim (Figs 43e, g). They have one handle, often an unpierced vertical strap loop. Rim diameters range between 170 and 320 mm, with heights one-quarter to one-third the diameter. All designs are vertical [2], [3], with OWP band bottoms [b]-[d] or not [g]. Painted examples, with wide horizontal bands in black and/or red, square black and white panels around diamond-shaped centres (*e.g.* Fig. 43k) or white vertical highlighting, tend to be between 170 and 190 mm in diameter, while vessels with incised exterior and moulded interior [3] fall between 280 and 320 mm (Fig. 43h). In addition, there is a group of smaller examples, about 90 mm in diameter (although one is twice that), with a smooth interior and only incuse decoration on the exterior (Fig. 43d).

One-handled bowl or cup: A small shallow bowl with one horizontal coil handle on the upper body was recovered intact (Fig. 43i). It was painted with superimposed black and red crosses on the interior base and a white horizontal band just below the rim. No parallels can be cited although the painted design is very similar to that illustrated in Fig. 43l.

Foot-ring bowls with plain rim: These vessels have a decorative range similar to that of the round-bottomed bowls. Many are undecorated except for a shallow interior groove below the rim. Handles, when present, are of the solid lug type. Eleven examples were recovered *in situ* on the bench in Loculus H. Rim diameters of the undecorated examples (*e.g.* Fig. 43j) range from 150 to 180 mm, base diameters from 60 to 86 mm, although one bowl is 232 mm at the rim and 92 mm at the base. Heights range from 47 to 81 mm. Other, less numerous, bowls of this type have exterior incised decoration [2], [3], although some also boast interior moulded relief [3] with a central medallion. Where preserved, all handles but one are unpierced vertical straps below the rim; the exception is a lug handle. One vessel has an OWP band [b] just above the foot. All incised examples have a further incised design underfoot, all but one of the same type (*e.g.* Fig. 44a; Munro-Hay 1989: fig. 16.93); the exception, also with a lug handle, has a debased swastika instead. These decorated examples fall into two size-categories, ranging in rim diameter from 73 to 89 mm and from 144 to 155 mm. A specimen recovered in 1974 but unpublished bears on the interior base superimposed painted patée crosses akin to those shown in Fig. 43i.

Foot-ring bowls with ledge or everted rim:
These bowls have three decorative arrangements. Otherwise undecorated examples have a dentilated rim edge and a groove around the inner edge of the rim top (Munro-Hay 1989: fig. 16.119), possibly inspired by Roman examples.[7] Incised decoration [1], [2] is confined to the body exterior, but the rim edge is similarly dentilated and the underfoot also usually embellished (Fig. 43f with a rough cross; see Munro-Hay 1989: fig. 16.114 for the other pattern recovered); that with decoration [1] has no underfoot embellishment. Painted examples are not dentilated around the rim; one (Figs 43i, 45b) has an internal design of superimposed patée crosses in black and white on a red ground; another (Figs 44b, 45c) bears black and white diamonds on the exterior, black and white stars inside and a cross-motif of red and white triangles on the underside of the foot.

Foot-ring bowls with broad ledge-rim: One special category of ledge-rim foot-ring bowls was deliberately fired in a reduced atmosphere. All have a very broad ledge rim, possibly derived ultimately from imported Roman forms. Some rims are unembellished, but on others the top is scalloped or has a shallow groove near one or both edges (*e.g.* Fig. 44f); Munro-Hay 1989: fig. 16.118). They are quite uniform, ranging from 172 to 200 mm in rim diameter, with rim breadths between 21 and 34 mm. One example may have had a rounded bottom, but otherwise all with preserved lower body have a foot-ring.

Bowls with applied rim embellishment:
These large, shallow bowls have an everted or narrow ledge-rim with discontinuous plastic additions. When well enough preserved, they are seen to have either a round bottom or a pedestal base. This is a fairly homogeneous group. Rim diameters mostly range between 220 and 280 mm, with some larger examples between 340 and 360 mm. A variety of applied embellishments to the rim is found. One is a smooth swelled thickening of the rim edge, often with an incised dentilated or triangular-scalloped edge; this latter often employed a rough punctate to shape the triangular protuberances, and in some cases up to seven triangles were individually and separately applied. There seems to be a logical progression from the unadorned swelling through dentilated and scalloped (Fig. 44d) versions to the individual applied triangles. These

forms may derive from discontinuous notched rim embellishment on wheel-made Roman bowls of African Red Slip ware.[8] A further development of this rim embellishment involves different applied features. Stylised birds with short beak and fan-tail (*e.g.* Munro-Hay 1989: figs 16.144-5) appear, as do a variety of coil-loop handles. Both can be embellished with multiple incised lines, the former on the upper tail, the latter at the junction to the vessel rim. Some handles are double-looped, sometimes with a scallop in between. One bowl has omega-shaped strap handles on the rim top. Some vessels are well enough preserved to show that these features occurred in groups of four around the rim, either as individual motifs (Fig. 44d) or alternating: scallops and birds are found on the same bowl (Fig. 45f), as are birds and single coil handles, and scallops and multi-loop coil handles. These vessels were often painted, as with star or paired-triangle motifs in black, white and red (Fig. 44c), or a horizontal band at the rim. Others bear incised exterior decoration [2] and/or moulded relief interiors [2], [3] with a central medallion. One has an OWP band on the rim top and one is rough-wiped.

Pedestal bowls: The pedestals can rarely be associated with the vessels from which they had become detached but, in both cases where a connection can be demonstrated, they are bowls with applied embellishment on their rims, and it is likely that some of the bowl sherds discussed above come from pedestalled vessels; at least twenty different pedestal bases were noted. The pedestal is subconical, straight-walled and slightly in-tapering to the bowl, with a splayed thickened flat bottom between 170 and 190 mm in diameter, although two measure 260 mm. The exterior base is smoothed and burnished, but the underfoot is often rough-wiped. Apart from one incised and moulded example, pedestals are rough in manufacture and any decoration. A number are fenestrated with two rows of rough oval to triangular apertures, usually with crudely incised triangular or diamond-shaped designs between them (Fig. 44j). At least one has elaborate painted star or paired-triangle designs in alternating black and red with white trim, and another has highlighted decoration of white bands on the bowl exterior. The weak point of base/body junction is strengthened with a thick clay coil with drag-punctated vertical lines which bind the two parts together.

Handled bowl or ladle: This shallow bowl, 151 mm in diameter by 80 mm deep, has a single elongated vertical wide strap handle extending from the rim. Heavy and over 10 mm thick throughout, it has a self-slipped and smoothed surface. This vessel has no relationship to the specimens from elsewhere at Aksum published by Wilding (Munro-Hay 1989: fig.

---

[7] Hayes 1972: *passim*, but especially forms 44 (late third century and 71 (late fourth century). No imported pottery was found in the tomb.

[8] Hayes' (1972) forms 71, 73-73A, see also form 76.

The Tomb of the Brick Arches

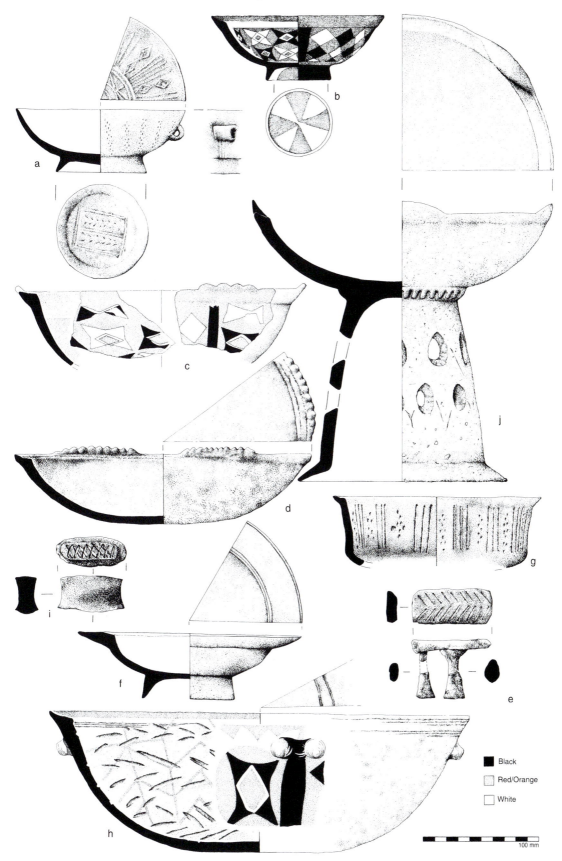

Fig. 44 *Pottery bowls and basins from the Tomb of the Brick Arches.*

61

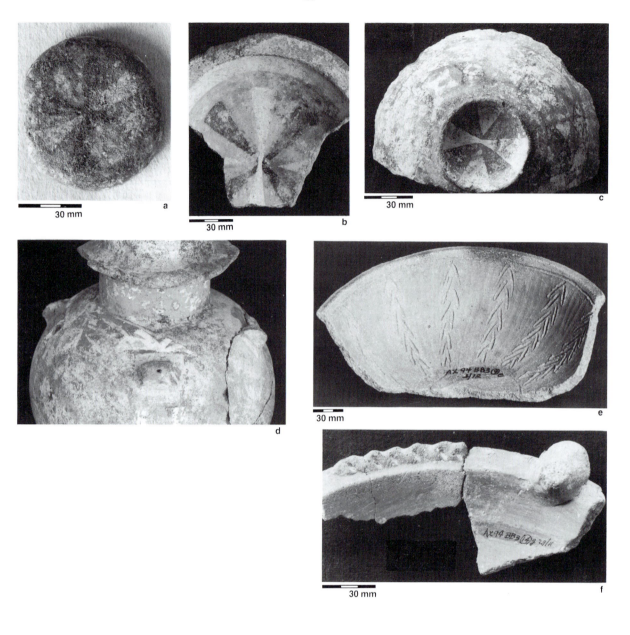

Fig. 45 *Painted and other pottery from the Tomb of the Brick Arches.*

16.231) which, as he suggests (*ibid.*: 268), are more likely to be lamps.

Basins

The designation basin, as opposed to bowl, is only applied to examples which are very large and deep, in contrast to the generally wide and shallow bowl profile, or which have interior features indicating a different purpose.[9] On this basis, there are three basic forms, and two further specialised types.

Basins with deeply incised interior: These large open vessels, with out-turned or everted ledge-rims, were deeply scored before firing over much of the interior surface in different patterns: alternating diagonals, herringbone (Fig. 45e), low festoon with vertical dividers, alternating vertical corrugation and deeply incised dashes (Fig. 44h). The interior bottom is unembellished, and delineated by a blank medallion with rough one- or two-line incised border or other decoration [f]. The most complete example (Fig. 44h) has four double-boss ledge-handles around the body. Only one has exterior decoration [1]. All are painted, although only one (Fig. 44h) retains more than the

---

[9] In Late Aksumite assemblages, as described on pp. 312-17 and 389-92 below, a clear size-difference between bowls and basins is apparent.

white undercoat on the exterior, having traces of a vertical band, large black star or paired-triangle motif and a large red circle. Rim diameters range from 305 to 360 mm.

Basins with ledge-rim: These are deep vessels with a slightly flaring ledge-rim and an angled profile to their flattened rounded bottom. Smooth-walled and unembellished on both interior and exterior, they have double- or, sometimes, triple-boss ledge-handles on the body, presumably four altogether, although none is sufficiently complete for certainty.

Broad-ledge-rim basins with splaying foot-ring and interior lip: Wilding's (Munro-Hay 1989: 257, 264) distinction between ledge-rim basins and potstands is unclear; the former term is here preferred. Two fragmentary examples were found in the tomb, one of which was rough-wiped and painted. Both are about 340 mm in rim diameter. A vessel recovered in 1974 (Munro-Hay 1989: fig. 16.164), of which a further sherd has now been found, is best classified as a miniature ledge-rim bowl despite its wide base. It has incised decoration [2] on its exterior and 110-mm-diameter rim top.

'Footwasher' basins: Three such basins, two with a ledge-rim, have been recovered. The putative footrest of one is published (Munro-Hay 1989: fig. 16.200). The two recovered in 1993-6 are miniatures, 180 mm in rim diameter. One (Fig. 44e), with exterior incised decoration [3], has one 'footrest' with a tripod support and incised herringbone pattern on the top. The other, with both interior and exterior incised decoration [2], has one small solid 'footrest' (Fig. 44i) with incised cross-hatches on top.

Animal model basins: Four of these specialised basin forms, usually with a ledge rim, having a stylised pair of yoked oxen attached to the interior bottom

50 mm

a

Fig. 46 *Animal-model basins from the Tomb of the Brick Arches.*

50 mm

b

were found in the tomb, one already published (Munro-Hay 1989: fig. 16.159) with incised decoration (3) on both interior and exterior. Another similar to this was recovered (Figs 46b, 47h), but so decorated only on the exterior and painted. The third (Fig. 46a), substantially complete, has exterior incised decoration [1] with the yoke having incised lines on its upper surface. The fourth preserves only the oxen and attached base, all surfaces being painted. In all cases the oxen stood higher than the rim. As noted by Wilding (Munro-Hay 1989: 240), the oxen represented are short-horned and unhumped. Two sizes of basin are indicated, two being about 260 mm and two only 120 mm in rim diameter. During Chittick's 1972-4 excavations at Aksum, basins of this and the previous type were only recovered in cemetery areas or surface contexts (Munro-Hay 1989: 261, 264).

Pots

These are distinguished from jars by their wide open mouth and restricted body shape, such as would be suitable for containing and pouring dry goods. The diameter at the mouth is well over half of, and often almost equal to, the maximum body diameter.

'Cauldrons': Wilding's terminology (Munro-Hay 1989: 268) is retained, with reservations, for round-bottomed bag-shaped pots with ledge-rims and multiple horizontal coil handles on the upper shoulders. Three have been recovered, all between 100 and 130 mm in rim diameter: one was painted inside and out and has two handles, one (Munro-Hay 1989: fig. 16.222) four, and the third (Fig. 47a) has two on the shoulder alternating with two attached to the rim; the second and third have incised lines on the handles and dragged punctates at their junctions. Strong burning marks are present on the two unpainted examples at the mouth, bottom and handles: these and the brazier noted below appear to be the only vessels from the tomb found in used condition (see pp. 72 and 130-1, below).

Foot-ring pots with ledge-rim: Wilding discusses and illustrates both those found in 1974 (Munro-Hay 1989: figs 16.228-9; the top view of the latter shows the handle as preserved) and no further examples have been recovered. One has a smooth surface with three deeply incised ticks at the upper handle junction, the other has decoration [3] on the body. Wilding called these 'twin-handled foot-ring cups', but they are better considered a pot form. The 'tailed' handles do not occur on other vessels in the tomb, but are a feature of later pottery decoration.

Foot-ring pots with collar: Wilding illustrates one of two found in 1974 (Munro-Hay 1989: fig. 16.295); the only variation of the second is the use of incised decoration [3C] instead of [2C]. No further

examples have been recovered. Designation as a pot form is preferred to Wilding's 'medium cylinder-necked jars with foot-ring'.

Pots with rebated profile: The only example of this type noted by Wilding was unstratified, in 'Brown Aksumite' ware with one handle (Munro-Hay 1989: fig. 16.383). Six specimens are now recognised from the Tomb of the Brick Arches; all have a tall wide neck, squat body and rounded bottom. Two varieties are noted, with a tapering or ledge-rim. Two pots (*e.g.* Fig. 47g) preserve paired handles formed by horizontal coils attached to the rebate. Five have incised decoration, horizontally [B], [E] on the neck and vertically [2], [3], [5] on the body, with bottom border [b] and on one example a row of OWP on the shoulder. Ledge-rims are dentilated and, in one case each, the rim top is incised with chevrons (Fig. 47b) or OWP. The sixth example is painted on its smooth surface. All vessels are small, with rim diameters between 140 and 180 mm, with two miniature examples at 90 mm.

Jars

Jars are distinguished from pots by their restricted mouths which never exceed half of the maximum body diameter, more suitable for liquid than dry contents. Jars as a group are the most common vessel type, approximately 300 having been recovered. They generally have a globular body, rounded bottom and cylindrical neck. A few have traces of painted highlights. Almost all fall into two basic types, with the bias balance handle on the lower shoulder only or linking the lower neck and upper shoulder. These are discussed separately before other, less common, types.

Jars with handle on shoulder only: Both smooth-surface and incised examples are found and were discussed by Wilding (Munro-Hay 1989: 270-8). The former present a fairly uniform appearance, with a horizontal squared lug handle on the shoulder and tapering rim (Fig. 47c; Munro-Hay 1989: figs 16.252-3). The only decoration, inconsistently applied, is a shallow groove below the exterior rim. The body is generally squat and the rounded bottom somewhat flattened. Necks tend to be wide, although there are some medium examples. Nine survive intact, with a well-burnished red-slipped surface. Rim diameters range from 45 to 80 mm, neck heights from 40 to 65 mm, and total heights from 120 to 155 mm. Similar jars with incised decoration have a more globular body profile, and the handle is a pierced flat vertical strap type situated at the lower end of the horizontal shoulder decoration. Necks are all of medium diameter and horizontally corrugated (Fig. 47e). Wilding illustrated four examples from the tomb (Munro-Hay 1989: figs 16.259-60, 265, 281), including one miniature. One has a medallion on the interior bottom, presumably

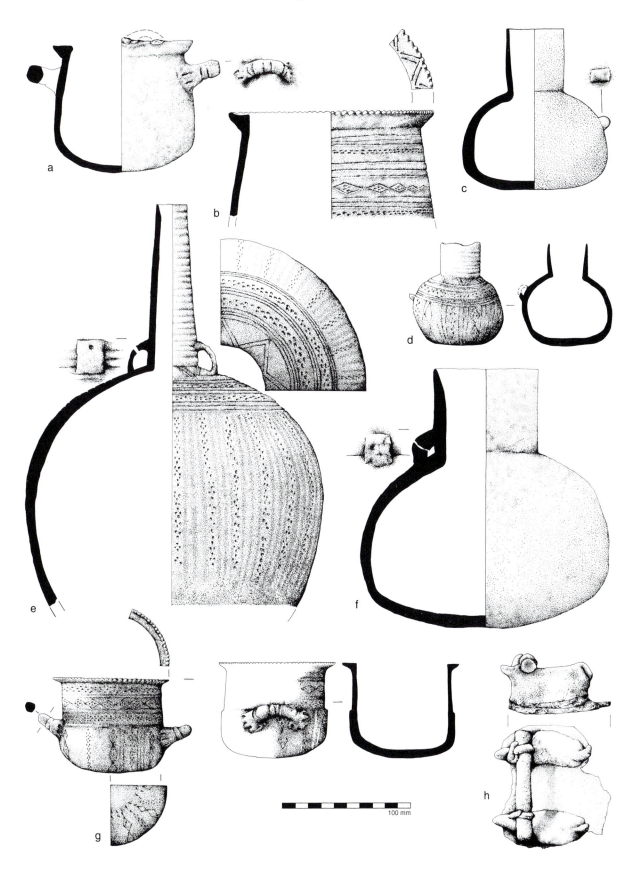

Fig. 47 *Pottery basins and jars from the Tomb of the Brick Arches.*

100 mm

Fig. 48 *Pottery jar from the*
Tomb of the Brick Arches.

moulded before the upper body was added; no other example of this was recovered in the present excavations.
Recorded incised decoration consisted only of [2C], except for miniature examples with [3C] and [2g]
(Munro-Hay 1989: fig. 16.281); only decoration [g] is
recorded at the bottom. The total heights range between 135 and 145 mm, with miniatures between 70
and 77 mm.

Jars with one horizontal and one vertical
handle on the shoulder: Two examples of this
type were recovered in the tomb, of which only one
(Fig. 48) was reconstructable. This is a broad-necked
form with incised decoration [2C] and a preserved
height of 200 mm. The vertical handle is a typical
pierced flat strap in the usual position, and opposite is
a thicker horizontal strap handle slightly lower on the
shoulder decorated with three pairs of vertical incised
lines and drag-punctated at the junctions. The other example preserves only the shoulder with incised decoration [C] having an infilled diamond on the horizontal
handle. A frequent explanation for this combination of
handles is for ease of pouring heavy contents, to gain
better purchase and avoid twisting the hands and wrists
when resting the vessel against a support; such an interpretation, however, seems unlikely in the case of
these comparatively small jars.

Jars with handle from lower neck to upper
shoulder: This appears to be the most common
type of jar, represented by both smooth-surfaced examples and vessels with incised decoration. Generally,

they are larger than those with handles only on the
shoulder. Vessel shapes, however, are usually the
same. Two smooth-surface examples from the tomb
were illustrated by Wilding (Munro-Hay 1989: figs
16.244, 247).[10] The burnished, red-slipped surface has
generally survived well. Many of these jars were recovered intact (*e.g.* Fig. 47f). The roughly produced
handle is a flat vertical strap. Necks are medium to
wide, occasionally with a horizontal groove below the
exterior rim. Rim diameters range from 70 to 90 mm,
neck heights from 60 to 90 mm and total heights from
180 to 300 mm. Similar jars with incised decoration
have a similar body profile and handle. Necks, horizontally corrugated on the exterior, are generally narrower and taller than on the smooth-surface vessels.
Wilding illustrated medium-necked examples (Munro-
Hay 1989: figs 16.258, 261) with rim diameter and
neck height being about the same (40 by 45 to 100 by
70 mm), and narrow-necked ones (*ibid.*: figs 16.268-
71) which are much narrower and taller (20 by 60 to
25 by 120 mm). This distinction may represent a typological development or different functions. Handles
are flat, vertical straps, all preserved examples being
pierced. Both medium- and narrow-necked versions
have incised decoration [2], [3]. The other pattern recovered [4] is far less common and found only on medium-necked vessels. Virtually all these jars show only
horizontal decoration [C], although [2H] (Fig. 47d)

[10] Both drawings are incorrect: the first has only one
handle, and the second a pierced handle.

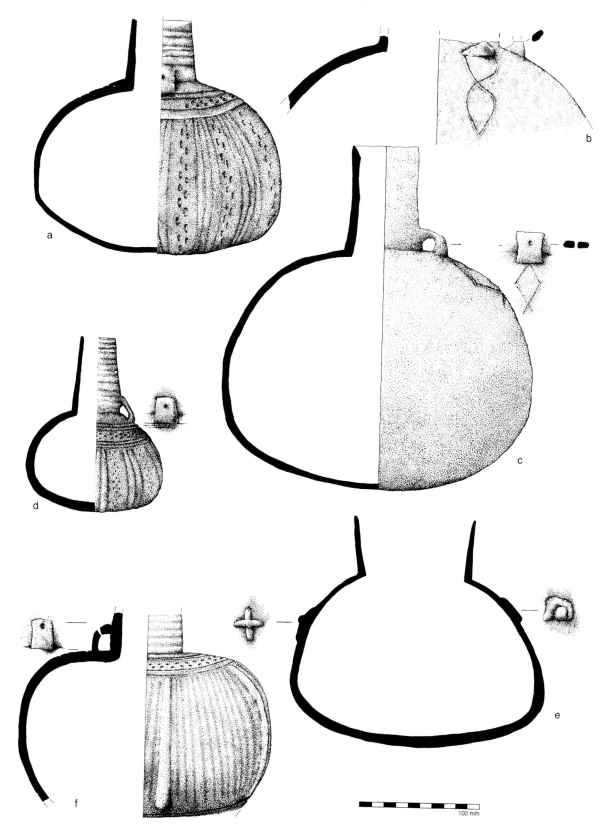

Fig. 49 *Pottery jars from the Tomb of the Brick Arches.*

and [2G] (Figs 49a, d) also appear. Occasionally decoration [a], but more often [g], is found at the bottom. Total heights cluster between 140 and 190 mm or around 290 mm.

Other single-handled jars: Several single-handled jars do not fit into the repertoire described above. All have pierced flat strap handles at the neck/shoulder junction. Three are smooth-walled and unembellished except for just below the lower handle join, where one has an incised appliqué (Munro-Hay 1989: fig. 16.248),[11] and two have incised decoration only. Fig. 49c shows an elongated diamond, and Fig. 49b a very casual figure-8 form. A unique jar (Fig. 49f) is embellished with four applied vertical ridges evenly spaced around the body, the four quarters filled with grooved vertical lines similar to corrugation; on the shoulder is a single horizontal OWP band below handle level, while the neck is horizontally corrugated.

Broad-necked handleless jars with applied decoration: Some uncommon jars lack handles but otherwise occur in a variety of types similar to those described above. Some have a pair of holes close together on the upper half of the neck, slightly diagonal to each other (*e.g.* Fig. 50b). Hole diameters range between 3 and 5 mm, but this is apparently unrelated to the vessel size. Although unworn, they may have been intended to attach a string for hanging, cf. the hole-mouth jar discussed below. Broad-necked jars, with a rim diameter significantly greater than the neck height,[12] were not found in the Tomb of the Brick Arches, except for a handleless type with applied decoration on the shoulder, of which four examples were recovered in 1974. Wilding illustrated three of them (Munro-Hay 1989: figs 16.249-51), each with an applied crescent-and-disc symbol on one shoulder, although in one case the crescent is replaced by a horizontal beaded line (*ibid.*: fig. 16.251). The opposite shoulder has an applied vertical cross, but in one case (*ibid.*: fig. 16.249) another crescent-and-disc occurs in its place. Five similar vessels were recovered in 1993-6, making a total of nine: six from Chamber B, two from Chamber D and one from Loculus H. Two (*e.g.* Fig. 49e) include the same cross and crescent-and-disc combination, two others have only one appliqué, the crescent-and-disc, while a further shoulder fragment preserves only the cross. Only this last is rough-wiped and painted on the exterior neck with wide vertical bands in red and white.

Other handleless jars: Several other vessels were sufficiently well preserved to show that, although they were otherwise similar to the handled jars, no handle had ever been applied. The collection includes examples with a smooth surface and exterior rim

groove, painted, with two depressed bosses on the shoulder (Fig. 50a), and incised (Fig. 50c; Munro-Hay 1989: fig. 16.262); all are medium-necked and between 250 and 300 mm high, except for one miniature at 143 mm. The incised decoration includes [3D] (Munro-Hay 1989: fig. 16.262) and [4F]; a particularly casually incised jar (Fig. 50c) has an uncorrugated neck with [4J] decoration. Occasionally decoration [a] but more often [g] is present at the bottom.

Hole-mouth jar: This unique object was published by Wilding (Munro-Hay 1989: fig. 16.221), seemingly the body of a jar with a squat globular body and two holes near the orifice, perhaps to facilitate hanging, but with no apparent sign of post-firing abrasion or drilling.

Ledge-rim globular jars: Numerous examples of this type have been recovered in the tomb.[13] Most have a globular, round-bottomed body, with short wide cylinder neck and ledge-rim, and two horizontal coil handles on the shoulder. The rim top is grooved at both edges, the handles incised and their junctions deeply drag-punctated, and the body either incised [2C], red-slipped and burnished (Fig. 51a), or painted with black and red vertical bands. The neck is not corrugated. Rim diameters are between 130 and 160 mm, neck diameters between 95 and 120 mm and neck heights from rim to shoulder between 35 and 50 mm; the full height of the only complete example is 265 mm. The profile generally corresponds to that of the human-headed jars (see below), without the plastic embellishment.

Human-headed jars: At least seventeen human-headed jars have been recovered in the tomb, of which five were illustrated by Wilding (Munro-Hay 1989: figs 16.285-7, 291-2). Although the heads may be recognised from small fragments, heads and bodies are hard to match in the absence of joins. All elaborately fugitive-painted on the exterior, they fall into four basic groups: large, medium and miniature plus large or medium examples with an overly-long neck and incised hair. All are essentially similar, although individually modelled, with an opening between 19 and 36 mm in diameter at the top of the head. Two smaller pre-firing holes, 3 to 5 mm in diameter, immediately behind this opening (*e.g.* Fig. 53f) were presumably for attachment of a string to secure a lid or to hang the vessel, although none show any sign of wear. Arms were not modelled, but sometimes indicated in paint. The large human-headed jars (Figs 52a, b, 53a) attain 275 mm in height and are footed, with a horizontal strap handle on the shoulder on either side and a small pierced vertical flat strap handle at the back. The medium jars (Fig. 53b; Munro-Hay 1989: figs 16.285-7)

---

[11] This illustration incorrectly shows two handles.

[12] This was the only type of jar recovered in the GT II tomb in the Gudit Stelae Field (Munro-Hay 1989: 278).

[13] It was not specifically noted by Wilding, although one example, from cleaning around the 1958 Cathedral excavations, was illustrated (Munro-Hay 1989: fig. 16.267).

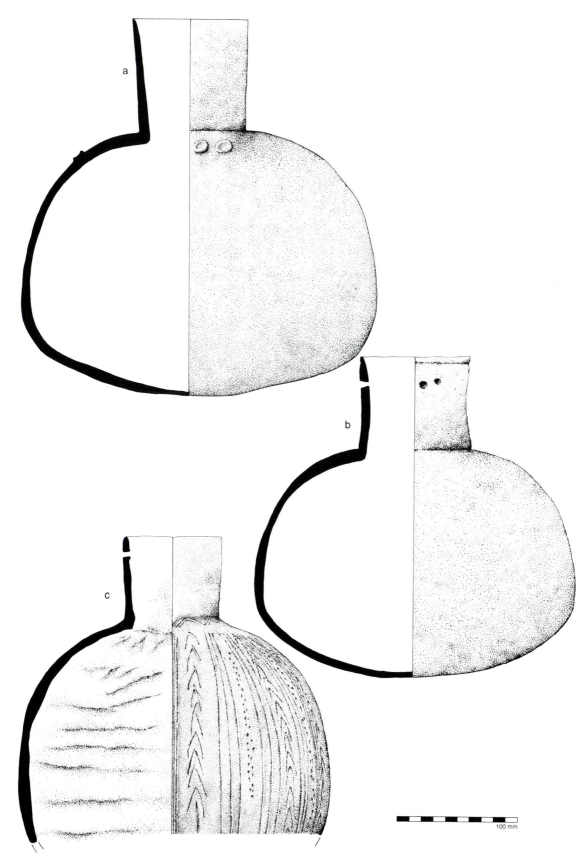

Fig. 50 *Pottery jars from the Tomb of the Brick Arches.*

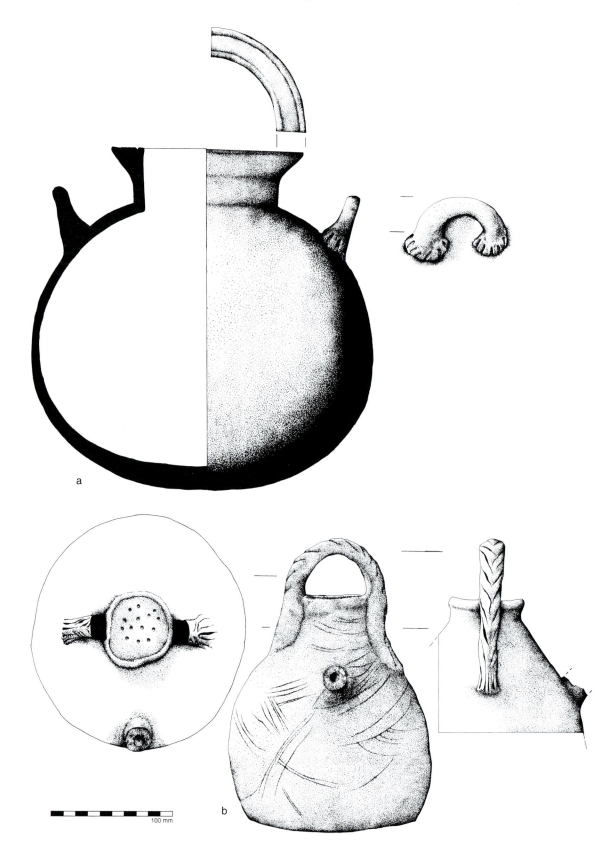

Fig. 51 *Pottery jar and spouted strainer vessel from the Tomb of the Brick Arches.*

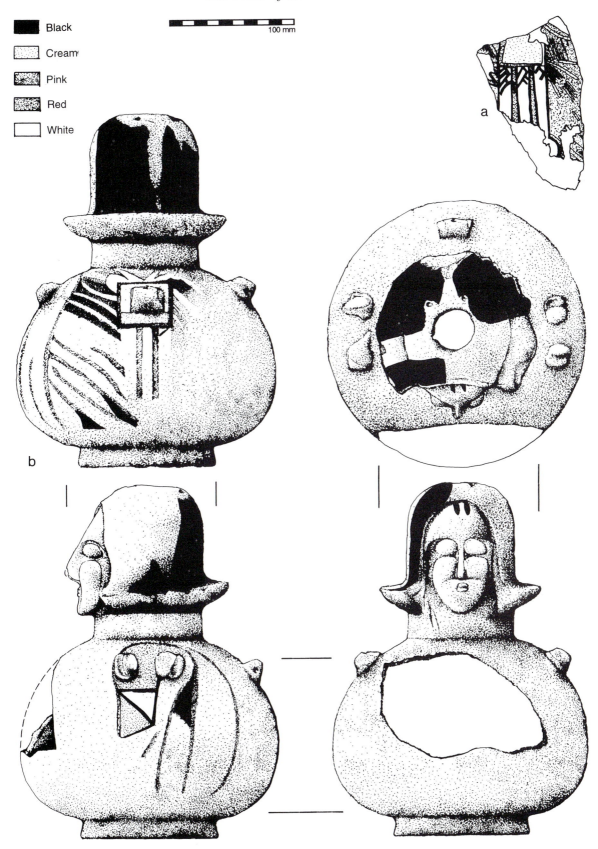

Black
Cream
Pink
Red
White

100 mm

a

b

Fig. 52 *Pottery face-jars from the Tomb of the Brick Arches.*

are round-bottomed and lack handles; the only fully preserved example is 153 mm tall. Only the head and neck of those having incised hair and long neck (Fig. 53c; *ibid.*: figs 16.291-2) are preserved, so no comments on overall size can be made. Only one miniature example, again preserving only the head and neck, was recovered. Employing only one feature as definitive of scale is hazardous, but effective comparison can be made in length of face from hairline to chin. This ranges between 90 and 95 mm on the large specimens, 65 and 75 mm on the medium ones and 26 mm on the miniature. The elongated neck examples have a medium face, but inclusion of the neck makes the scale comparable with the large examples. Some medium heads and all those with incised hair indicate a beret or cap, and sometimes also large ball earrings; earrings are not depicted without the beret. The miniature example has both, but the large examples have neither. Those figures which lack the beret have small but prominent vertical ridges on the forehead suggestive of scarification. The hairstyle, still popular in Tigray today, strongly suggests that these figures represent women (Munro-Hay 1989: 278). Painted decoration varies considerably. One (Fig. 53e) is yellow on the face and neck, with black and white eyes and black hair. On another (Fig. 53a; cf. also Munro-Hay 1989: fig. 16.286) the face and neck are again yellow, the hair is black with three vertical white bands and a black band at one eye. The head illustrated in Fig. 53b has black hair and earrings, yellowish pink face and neck, the eye outlined in orange-red. The most elaborate colouring is shown in Figs 52b and 53d: black for the hair and vertical forehead appliqués, yellow for the face and neck, white for the eyes and three vertical bands down the hair; the body bears an elaborate design of vertical and diagonal white and pink lines, with a square panel and three pendant lines in white, all over a red background and with red and black elaborations;[14] the vertical and horizontal handles are painted white and yellow respectively.

Footed storage jar: This jar has a short cylindrical neck and rounded rim, with two grooved strap handles from neck to shoulder and an incised sign (Fig. 54a), presumably on the shoulder or immediately below one of the handles. Recovered in numerous fragments, it was not possible fully to reconstruct the sign or the vessel. Both vessel shape and sign have general parallels in later material excavated in 1974 near the Tomb of Kaleb (Munro-Hay 1989: 284, fig. 16.307).

Squat jar: One jar (Fig. 54b) with a narrow cylindrical neck and pierced flat strap handle on the shoulder has a body so squat that it must be considered a distinct form; the body and neck are almost equal in height. The vessel has a smooth red-slipped and burnished surface.

Rectangular 'stove' or 'brazier'

Three specimens of this flat-based type have been recovered, one complete example described but not illustrated by Wilding (Munro-Hay 1989: 284), and two fragmentary ones in 1993-6. All have rough-wiped surfaces. Each is individual and, where preserved, about 150 mm in height. That shown in Fig. 55 is about one-quarter preserved including one corner, three interior buttresses and a deep sill at the front. If the buttresses were central, the vessel would be about 280 mm square, similar to the 1974 example, but with the sill extending beyond the front around to part of the sides.[15] The upper part of the interior and buttresses are marked by fire, but the remainder is not, a most unusual use-wear for a brazier suggesting that the designation may be a misnomer. The other example appears to be similar, but with two applied bosses near an exterior edge and without buttresses.

Spouted strainer vessel

This strange vessel (Fig. 51b), with a concave filter neck, narrow shoulder spout and basket-like strap handle, has a pear-shaped body with flattened bottom. The handle is roughly incised in a dashed pattern; the vessel is otherwise undecorated with a lightly rough-wiped unslipped surface. The tripod jar with strainer and spout from the main GT II tomb in the Gudit Stelae Field, published by Wilding (Munro-Hay 1989: fig. 16.304), has many similar characteristics, and was found to contain ten solid clay balls. As the vessel from the Tomb of the Brick Arches was found intact, its clearly heavy contents could not be investigated. Its precise purpose is unknown: it might have been some kind of rattle, but this would not explain the presence of the spout. An alternative possibility is that a liquid of some description was poured in through the filter-neck and slowly out through the spout, clay balls helping the filtering process.

Lid

One ovoid flat lid with inset underside was published by Wilding (Munro-Hay 1989: fig. 16.323). It is difficult to suggest a vessel to which this lid could have belonged, as no ovoid rims were recovered in either excavation.

Bird-shaped 'vessel'

This three-legged object (Fig. 56) may not be a vessel at all, as both orifices - at the mouth and immediately under the tail - may be firing holes. Its purpose is unknown. Perhaps originally deposited in Loculus J, its

---

[14] Similar body decoration is present on the fragment illustrated in Fig. 52a.

[15] A similar example was recovered in 1974 in Stelae Park trench ST XXIII (Munro-Hay 1989: fig. 16.308).

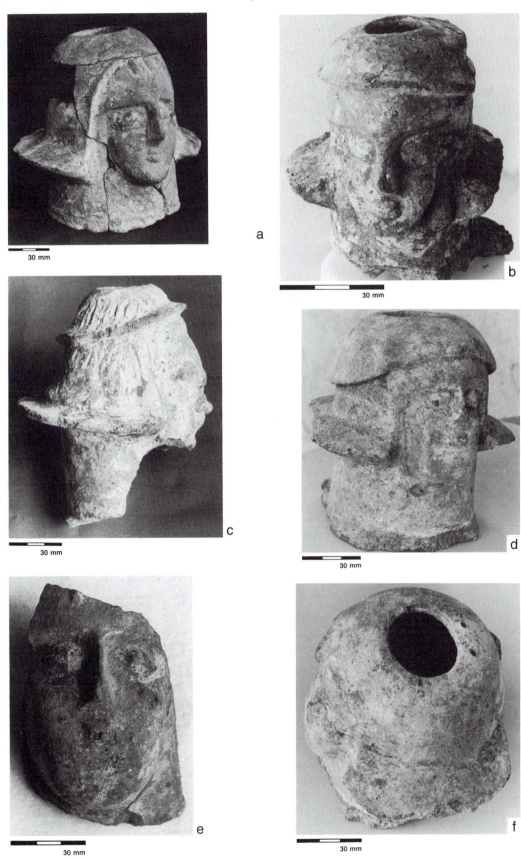

Fig. 53 *Pottery face-jars from the Tomb of the Brick Arches.*

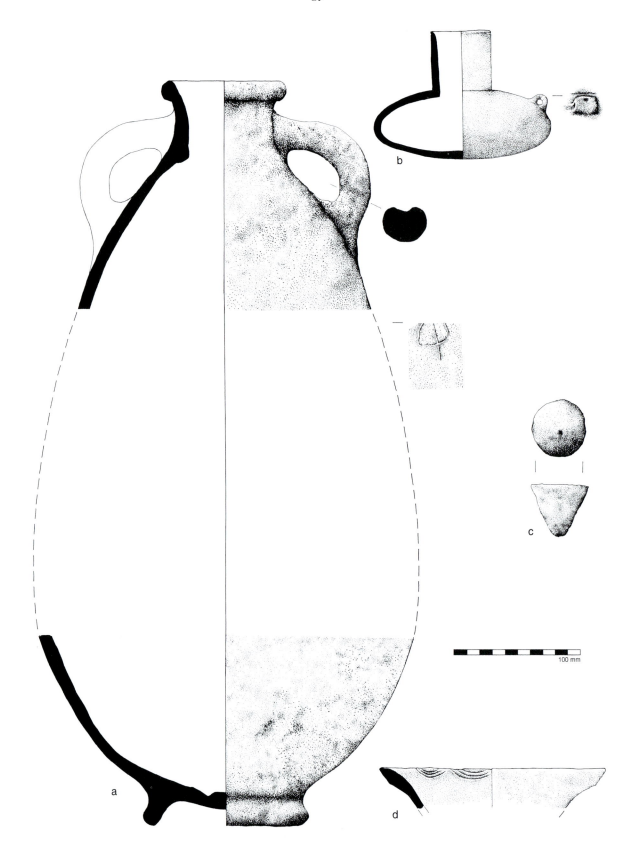

Fig. 54 *Miscellaneous pottery vessels and clay cone from the Tomb of the Brick Arches.*

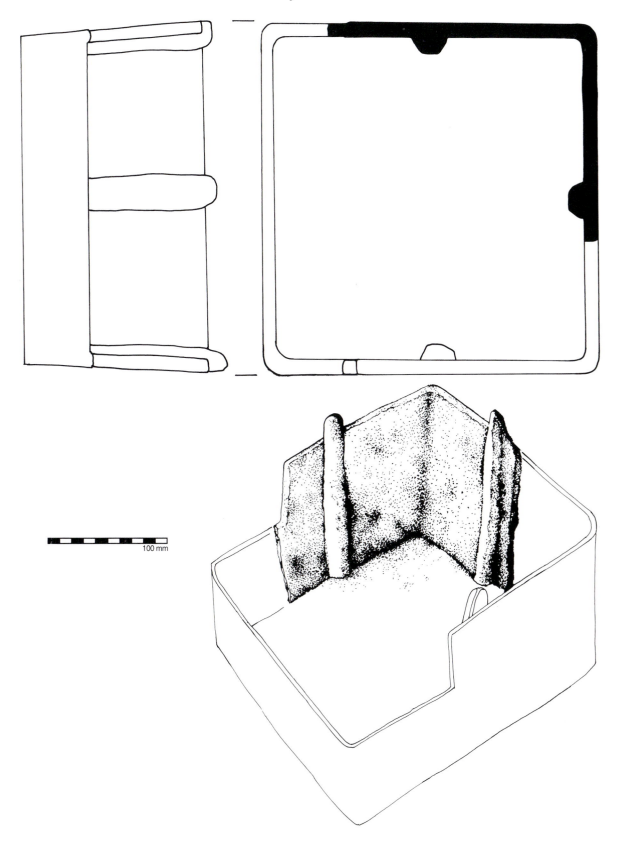

Fig. 55 *Pottery stove or brazier from the Tomb of the Brick Arches.*

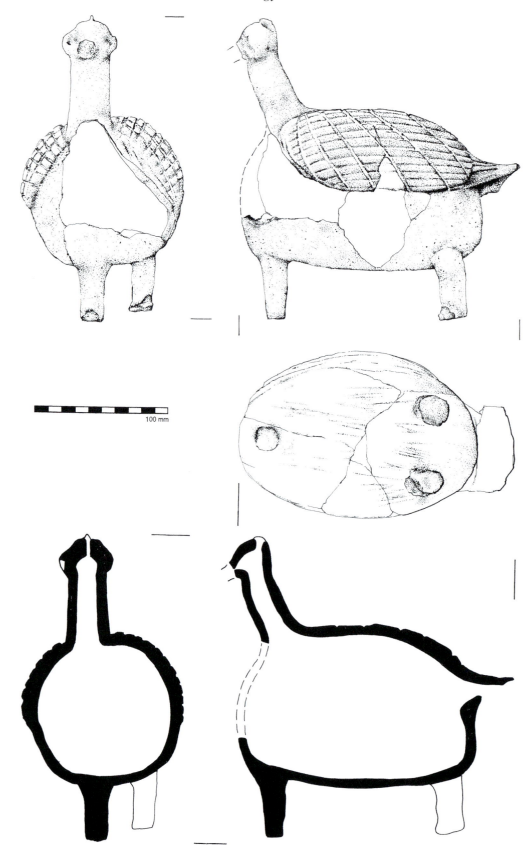

Fig. 56 *Pottery bird-shaped vessel from the Tomb of the Brick Arches.*

subsequent disturbance has been discussed above (p. 50). Crudely made but naively attractive and 212 mm tall, its only decoration consists of broadly cross-hatched wings and upper tail, with traces of yellow paint on the underside. Although a tripod bird-shaped jar was recovered from the Gudit Stelae Field in 1974 (Munro-Hay 1989: fig. 16.302), the nearest parallel for the present specimen is a head recovered in 1973 Stelae Park trench ST XIIE (*ibid*.: fig. 16.303) which, however, does have a handle; this provides a model for restoring the rather battered head of the specimen from the Tomb of the Brick Arches.

Possibly intrusive ceramics

The only lamp from the tomb is that published by Wilding (Munro-Hay 1989: fig. 16.330). Its find-spot, in DA I(8) below Arch I, suggests that it may have been brought from elsewhere by intruders. Two other vessels seem distinct from the overall repertoire, and may have been intrusive, possibly brought into the tomb by the second group of plunderers. One, unpublished, was found in Chamber B in 1974; it is an unevenly made plain miniature vessel (possibly a bowl) in a coarse brown ware. The base was not recovered, but the bowl survives to a height of 30 mm in height and is 46 mm in rim diameter. The second, represented by three fragments, all likewise in the main Robbing-2 layer of Chamber B, is a deep open bowl with exterior thickened flaring rim (Fig. 54d) about 160 mm in diameter in a dark fabric with many organic inclusions quite unlike the rest of the pottery from the tomb. Its interior rim is incised with a band of triple festooning.

Other clay objects

Cones: Two were recovered, being among the largest known at Aksum. One, 30 mm in height, 38 mm in diameter and pierced from top to bottom, is of the type commonly designated spindle whorl or loomweight. The other (Fig. 54c), 41 mm in height and 46 mm in diameter, solid and unpierced, may have been intended as a jar-stopper although no use-wear is apparent.

Plaque: One subrectangular plaque, 82 by 32 mm, with incised decoration [2] was found in the 1974 Chamber B excavations and published by Wilding (Munro-Hay 1989: fig. 16.315); no others have been recovered. There is no recorded sign of reuse or edge-abrasion, so it was probably purpose-made.

Hollow triangular object: This apparently corner element of a tapering hollow object or possibly vessel with a convex profile and flat base was entirely painted inside and out.

Commentary

The restricted repertoire of the Classical Aksumite pottery from the Tomb of the Brick Arches is striking, as is the almost complete lack of evidence that any of it had been used. It may be suggested that many of the vessels, with the exception of the cauldrons and possibly the brazier noted above, were made specifically as funerary goods.

The limited range of decorative motifs represented presumably reflects funerary fashion current at the time. In contrast with pottery from the GT II tomb in the Gudit Stelae Field (Munro-Hay 1989), very few vessels from the Tomb of the Brick Arches are decorated with overall vertical corrugation [1] or with incision on the rim tops. The latter decoration is limited to the OWP pattern only, with virtually no chevron patterns, although a few of the distinctive broad-ledge-rim bowls had straight or arcaded grooved lines. There are extremely few buttons, ringed or elaborately looped coil handles associated with smooth or vertically corrugated vessels, and no jars with incised pairs of vertical or diagonal lines (cf. Munro-Hay 1989: figs 16.242, 255, 297), no applied crossed lines (*ibid*.: figs 16.296, 298, 301) and very few applied vertical lines. Likewise, there are no examples of moulded exterior surfaces including the plain or incised bean pattern (*ibid*.: figs 16.77-9, 117, 171), although moulded interior surfaces are found. There are no painted crosses of the types shown in Munro-Hay's figs 16.15-16, 72, or small horizontal applied ridges, either plain or diagonally ticked. The repertoire of vessel types is likewise restricted, with no tripod vessels other than the bird-shaped specimen, and no round braziers. Other types, such as the human-headed jars, seem largely restricted to funerary contexts. The significance of these observations is discussed below (pp. 130-1, 457).

Glass and beads
(Michael Harlow)

GLASS

Glass from the 1993-6 excavations in the Tomb of the Brick Arches comprised 1445 inventoried fragments varying in size from 3 mm to 120 mm, plus a large number of very tiny pieces most of which demonstrably came from the same objects as the larger fragments. Most of the inventoried fragments were not readily diagnostic of the vessels and other objects from which they were derived, but it was possible to reconstruct a number of vessels. An attempt has also been made to ascertain the original placements of individual glass vessels within the tomb, prior to disturbance by robbers. Glass beads are described separately.

The accompanying table (Fig. 57) sets out the numbers of glass fragments found in the various contexts in the tomb and identifies those that provided

Chamber/ Loculus	Episode	pale burgundy red	dark burgundy red	cobalt blue	medium blue	blue/colourless cased	colourless	yellow-tinged colourless	green-tinged colourless	green	turquoise	other	Total
A	Primary	-	-	-	-	-	-	-	-	-	36*	22	58*
B	Primary	-	-	-	-	-	-	-	-	-	2	-	
	Robbing 1	-	-	6	3	-	-	-	2	-	-	-	1244
	Robbing 2	14	51	311	28	396	25	319	29	14	23	21	
D	Robbing 2	59	-	-	-	-	-	-	-	-	1	-	60
G	Primary	-	1	-	-	1	1	6	-	-	7	-	
	Robbing 2	-	-	11	-	-	2	-	-	-	-	-	29
H	Robbing 2	21	5	17	-	-	-	-	-	-	-	*	43*
J	Primary	-	-	-	-	-	-	-	-	-	2	-	2
Totals		94	57	345	31	397	28	325	31	14	71*	43*	1436*

* = plus tiny fragments not included in totals

Fig. 57 *Summary of glass from the Tomb of the Brick Arches.*

evidence of vessel forms. It is immediately apparent that most specimens came from Chamber B and, particularly, from contexts in its central and western areas which are assigned to Robbing 2.

The range and distribution of colours has also been examined. The main colours were blue, especially cobalt blue, colourless with a yellowish tinge and burgundy red; but each of these was present in varying degrees of hue, value (lightness) and chroma (relation to neutral). A few fragments of other colours such as green, turquoise (bluish green), yellow, orange, pink, black and white were observed. The frequent occurrence of cased cobalt blue and colourless translucent glass with a yellowish tinge is noteworthy; they were usually accompanied by very small, angular fragments of cobalt blue or yellow-tinged colourless glass which may have resulted from the disintegration of cased glass vessels (cf. Morrison in Munro-Hay 1989: 201).

Vessels

Fluted 'tankard': Numerous fragments of cobalt blue and medium blue glass, many with external vertical fluting, some joining rim and handle pieces and an almost complete solid rounded stem and foot, were recovered from the Robbing-2 horizon in Chamber B. The reconstruction of these fragments (Fig. 58a)

suggests a waisted cylindrical beaker with stem and fire-rounded base and at least one handle. The rim is slightly everted and the lower body is narrowed. Unfortunately, joining fragments to provide absolutely certain links between the rim, body, handle and stemmed base were missing, but the colour and thickness of the glass and traces of fluting on the rim and shoulder as well as on body fragments provide clear evidence that they belonged together. The vessel was probably formed by mould-blowing. It seems likely that some similar fragments of slightly thinner blue glass may come from a second vessel of the same type, but these were not sufficient to permit reconstruction.

Goblet: A stemmed goblet of opaque dark red glass with fire-rounded base was recovered in 1974 (Morrison's type Ia in Munro-Hay 1989: fig. 14.1).[16] Additional joining fragments from equivalent 1993-6 contexts permit a fuller reconstruction (Figs 58b, 60a) of an imposing vessel 260 mm in height. There are three horizontal parallel threads of trail just below the everted rim, the central one being slightly closer to the bottom one than to the top one. The trail is in the same glass as the rest of the goblet. A further fragment decorated in the same way may belong to the same goblet. Although no precise parallels for this

[16] The scale in this illustration is incorrect (Mrs Helen Morrison, *pers. comm.*).

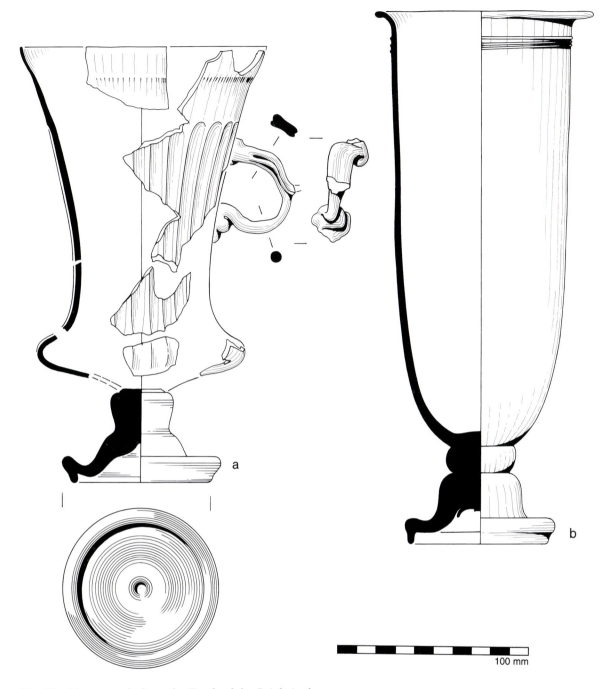

Fig. 58 *Glass vessels from the Tomb of the Brick Arches.*

vessel may be cited, it displays striking similarities with examples from Sudanese Nubia, as further discussed below (p. 459).

Shallow engraved bowl: A fragment of pale green glass engraved externally with a plant-like design of ovoids linked by stem-like lines (Fig. 61a) certainly comes from the shallow inscribed bowl of type IVc illustrated by Munro-Hay (1989: fig. 14.71). The new fragment does not join those found in 1974 and bears no further part of the inscription.

Flask: Three joining curved fragments of thin pale burgundy or purplish red glass decorated with multiple curved trails of opaque white probably come from a type-VIIa flask (cf. Munro-Hay 1989: fig. 14.91).

Narrow necked flask or bottle: The narrow neck of a vessel (Fig. 59a)[17] in pale yellowish green glass has an intricately folded diagonally sloping rim and an unusual folded and slightly upward sloping ledge between the constriction at the bottom of the

[17] This illustration shows reconstruction subsequent to the photograph of D.W.Phillipson 1995a: fig. 17.2.

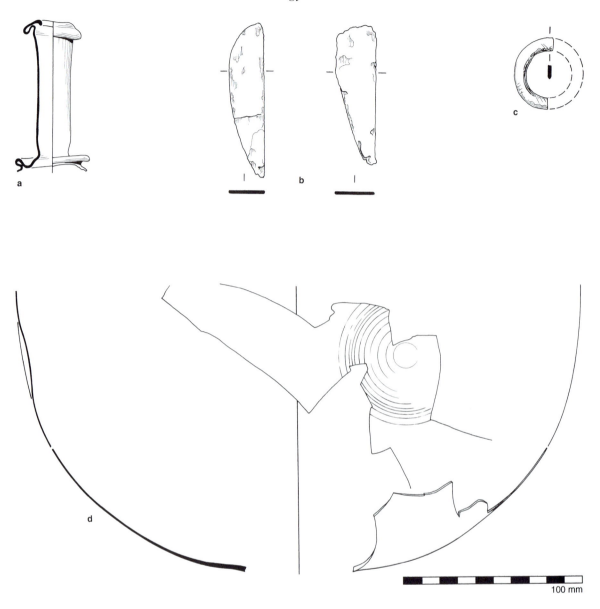

Fig. 59 *Glass objects from the Tomb of the Brick Arches.*

neck and the beginnings of the body. The remains of the body provide no clear indication of its form, but the length and narrow internal diameter of the neck, together with the fact that no handle was attached to it, suggests that the vessel might have been an unguent bottle rather than a flask.

Globe: A very unusual form in extremely thin (0.4-0.5 mm) and bubbly burgundy-red glass appears to be a large sphere between 240 and 300 mm in diameter, for which no parallels can be proposed. Despite the large number of fragments recovered and careful planning of their main concentration in loculus H, it proved impossible to reconstruct more than large arcs (Figs 59d, 60b). One area of pronounced thickening with a pontil mark was noted, but no rim fragments were recovered. It seems possible that the object represents some kind of funerary lamp, but the colour is too dark for it to have provided useful illumination. The object seems to have fallen from the stone bench in Loculus H below which the main collection of fragments was found (Fig. 40a, above); additional pieces were recovered elsewhere in the same loculus and in Chamber D and Passage G, all in contexts relating to Robbing 2.

Cased glass vessel/s: The extremely shattered nature of the cased or laminated cobalt blue on colourless glass has defeated efforts to identify the form of vessel from which it came, as had been the case in

80

100 mm

Fig. 60 *Glass goblet and sphere from the Tomb of the Brick Arches.*

1974 (Munro-Hay 1989: 201). Attempts to hold the shattered fragments together were unsuccessful but enough was preserved to see that at least one vessel had a

thick gently curved base extending fairly sharply upwards to form a beaker or cup. Most of the laminated sherds had the blue translucent glass on top of the colourless glass, but in some cases the reverse was the case. Cased vessels with two contrasting layers of translucent glass, usually with colourless glass on the inside, were produced in Europe during the fourth century, but cased glass with a translucent outer layer and a contrasting, often opaque white inner layer, is found there in first-century Roman contexts (Whitehouse 1990, 1997: 41; Price and Cottam 1998: 30). It may be of chronological significance that the cased glass in the Tomb of the Brick Arches includes none of the latter type.

Mould-blown hemispherical decorated fragments: Six fragments of sparkling colourless mould-blown glass, recovered from the Robbing-2 contexts in Chamber B, resemble those attributed to a type-Xd 'grape cluster' flask (Munro-Hay 1989: 201). The fragments (Fig. 61b) bear no evidence of mould joins. A vessel of this type from the Slade Collection in the British Museum (DBH 1224) may be of eastern origin attributable to the second or third century AD (Ms V. Tatton-Brown, *pers. comm.*; Hayes 1975: 50).

Undiagnostic decorated fragments: Most of the glass fragments from the tomb do not show any kind of decoration apart from colour or casing. Four exceptions not noted above are:
- a dark blue Y-shaped trail on the exterior of a very small fragment of colourless glass;
- two tiny convex fragments of colourless glass with traces of gilding on the exterior;
- an engraved band on the outer surface of a very thin pale burgundy body fragment; and
- an applied trail of opaque white glass marvered to the exterior surface of two fragments of pale translucent burgundy glass.

Inlay etc.

Small inlay: The 84 leaf-shaped flat cold-chipped inlay pieces all came from the hoard of metal scrap buried in the floor of Chamber A (Figs 84c-e and pp. 102-3, below, where they are discussed in greater detail). They are distinct from any other glass in the Tomb of the Brick Arches, but closely resemble specimens from Nefas Mawcha (Munro-Hay 1989: figs 14.208-14) and from primary contexts in the Mausoleum (p. 198-9, below).

Large inlay: A different form of inlay to that noted above was recovered from area (d) in Loculus H, comprising nineteen large and many small fragments of what appeared to be decayed pale turquoise glass or glass paste.[18] All were extremely fragile and friable.

---

[18] It was not, unfortunately, possible to obtain analyses of this material, which may be residue from some other substance.

a

30 mm

b

Fig. 61 *Glass fragments from the Tomb of the Brick Arches.*

The most complete specimens (Fig. 59b) were flat elongated forms, 83 to 95 mm long by 20 to 25 mm in maximum width with one long edge straight and the other curved, pointed at one end and rounded at the other. Some were found grouped in threes with their rounded ends close together and the points radiating outwards. Nothing remained of any material to which they may once have been attached.

The glass paste inlay in white, red and blue found on the bimetallic plaques from Chamber B (p. 105-8, below), should be noted in this context.

Flat ring: This object (Fig. 59c) of translucent burgundy red glass is about 1 mm thick and 20 mm in overall diameter with a central hole of about 13 mm. Faint straight striations are visible on its flat surfaces. It is not the broken-off rim of a vessel and is more likely to have been a pendant than a bead. It came from a Robbing-2 context in Chamber B and has parallels in the Mausoleum and at K site (pp. 198 and 402, below).

Commentary

Most of the glass from the Tomb of the Brick Arches was found in Chamber B in the pile of artefacts apparently removed from Loculi E and F during Robbing 2. Some glass in Loculi H and J was also disturbed during this episode, including both the burgundy-red globe and the large friable turquoise-coloured inlay. The only other fragments recovered from Loculus H were some small pieces of flat white opaque glass - possibly inlay - and two groups of small translucent fragments of cobalt blue glass. Loculus J yielded a number of vessel fragments of turquoise glass and some clear ones; these and the glass inlay from the block buried in the floor of Chamber A were the only fragments from undisturbed contexts.

BEADS

1139 beads were recovered from the Tomb of the Brick Arches during the 1993-6 excavations, a far larger number than from any other site investigated by the

Project. Almost all (98%) came from contexts associated with the Robbing-2 episode and 83% came from Chamber B, especially its west and central parts. Division of the Chamber into 0.5-m squares permitted demonstration that certain similar beads probably belonged to the same necklaces or strings (Figs 62a, b). The most striking beads from these contexts were the biconical, hexagonally faceted ones which are characteristic of this tomb and other sites at Aksum. The 197 beads which did not come from Chamber B were almost all (182) from a Robbing-2 context in Passage G. As only one came from Chamber D and one from Loculus H , it seems likely that almost all the beads originated in Chamber B and/or Loculi E and F.

The colours of the glass beads from the tomb were predominantly green, with a high proportion of turquoise but relatively few yellowish green examples. Translucent and opaque glass beads were found in most of the colours present but opaque glass was most common for the frequent drawn mid-green beads. Other common colours were cobalt blue (usually translucent), medium red (usually opaque), and a few of opaque white, opaque yellow, black and opaque pink. Colourless or lightly tinted glass beads were rare. This and the paucity of yellowish green or yellowish-tinted

colourless glass beads marks a major difference from the much smaller assemblages recovered at D and K sites. There are nine gold-in-colourless glass beads. Decoration of contrasting colour was rare but mainly found on opaque red striped or banded beads. The accompanying tables (Fig. 63) shows the numbers and forms of translucent and opaque glass beads found in the main colour groups; more detailed tabulations may be consulted in the Project Archive. The only stone beads recovered are twelve spherical or ovoid orange or orange-red carnelian specimens, discussed below.

Many of the beads exhibit substantial wear from rubbing against one another and the string on which they had been threaded. This suggests that the beads may have been personal possessions of the deceased, rather than newly acquired grave goods.

Forms of glass beads
Type-numbers are from Munro-Hay (1989: 168-78).
Biconical faceted beads (type IIc): As noted above, hexagonally faceted beads of this type are characteristic of this tomb and several other sites at Aksum. The 163 examples from the Tomb of the Brick Arches include beads of opaque dark turquoise, pale translucent turquoise, opaque red (often in a poor

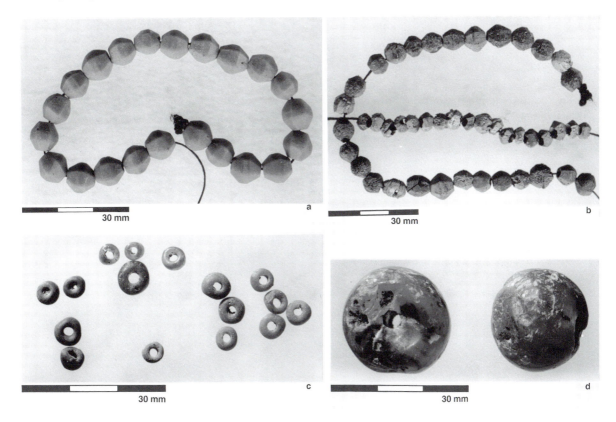

Fig. 62 *Beads from the Tomb of the Brick Arches.*

Chamber/Loculus	Episode	black O	black T	cobalt blue O	cobalt blue T	blue O	blue T	colourless T	gold in colourless T	green O	green T	turquoise O	turquoise T	red O	red T	red striped O	yellow O	yellow T	white O	white T	other glass	carnelian	Total
B	Robbing 1	–	–	1	–	–	–	–	–	–	1	3	–	–	–	–	3	–	–	–	1	–	942
B	Robbing 2	25	2	5	20	4	1	21	9	183	49	38	180	281	2	43	28	5	17	8	3	9	
D		–	–	–	1	–	–	–	–	–	–	–	–	–	–	–	–	–	–	–	–	–	1
G	Primary	–	–	–	–	–	1	–	–	2	–	–	–	1	–	–	–	–	–	–	–	–	195
G	Robbing 1	–	–	–	–	–	4	–	–	2	–	–	–	2	–	–	1	–	–	–	–	–	
G	Robbing 2	1	–	–	4	1	6	2	1	67	11	5	44	18	1	1	13	1	–	–	3	3	
H	Robbing 2	–	–	–	–	–	–	–	–	–	–	–	1	–	–	–	–	–	–	–	–	–	1
Totals		26	2	6	25	5	12	23	10	254	61	46	225	302	3	44	45	6	17	8	7	12	1139

Chamber/Loculus	Episode	I/II	III	IVa	V	VI	XIII	XIXa	XX	other glass	carnelian	Total
B	Robbing 1	–	–	–	–	1	–	7	–	1	–	942
B	Robbing 2	146	18	5	7	719	4	9	8	8	9	
D		–	–	–	–	–	–	–	–	1	–	1
G	Primary	–	–	–	1	3	–	–	–	–	–	195
G	Robbing 1	–	–	–	–	9	–	–	–	–	–	
G	Robbing 2	17	–	3	2	150	–	5	1	1	3	
H	Robbing 2	–	–	–	–	1	–	–	–	–	–	1
Totals		163	18	8	10	883	4	21	9	11	12	1139

Fig. 63 Summary of beads from the Tomb of the Brick Arches. (O = opaque, T = translucent).

state of preservation), and more rarely of dark cobalt blue glass. A collection of such beads found close together in the centre and west side of Chamber B is illustrated (Figs 62a, b; see also Fig. 65e, f). Two size ranges are represented: 9 to 11 mm (Figs 64a-d) and 4 to 7 mm (Fig. 64e). In contrast with beads in other colours, the opaque red ones commonly had larger perforations relative to their size (cf. Figs 64d, e). Another noteworthy feature is the presence (*e.g.* Figs 64a-c) or absence (*e.g.* Figs 64d, e) of a band of facets around the middle of the beads in addition to those around the cones at each end. These differences are not particular to individual colours but medial facets are much less frequent on the opaque red beads. The facets also vary considerably in size and shape from bead to bead, some being almost square and others diamond-

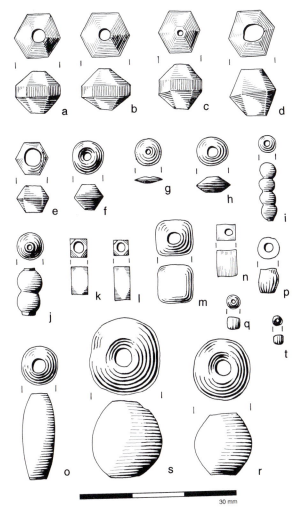

Fig. 64 Beads from the Tomb of the Brick Arches.

shaped, although most are rectangular. Close examination suggests that the facets were produced by grinding rather than in moulds, as proposed by Morrison (Munro-Hay 1989: 169). Morrison (*ibid.*) has cited parallels with beads from Gheyta in Egypt and from Firkwa dated to the fifth and sixth centuries AD. It is possible that these hexagonally faceted bicone beads came from Indian bead-making centres such as Arikamedu and Cambay, using techniques developed for making stone beads, especially some drawn beads found in this tomb may have originated in India, as discussed below.

Biconical non-faceted beads (type IIa): Four biconical beads without faceting were also recovered. They are usually smaller than the faceted variety and vary from 'standard' beads (whose length along the perforation is approximately the same as their maximum diameter, as defined by Beck (1927: 4) such as the opaque red one illustrated in Fig. 64f to the much shorter translucent dark blue 'lentoid' bicones shown in Figs 64g, h.

Drawn beads (type VI): By far the most common beads found in the tomb are drawn beads, of which there were 883 examples. Most fall into two main size ranges, although there are many variations including some very tiny examples. The largest drawn beads were circular in cross-section and barrel-shaped either short or standard. Most of these were of opaque mid-green glass, fairly regular and rounded, the largest being about 2.7 mm long and 3.6 mm in diameter. The smaller range was more irregular and variable, being between 0.8 and 1.6 mm in length and between 1.3 and 2.3 mm in diameter (Figs 62c, 64q, t, 65a). Morrison (Munro-Hay 1989: 170) cites parallels from Virampatnam in India and from Souttoukeny dated from the first and second centuries AD as well as from Faras in the second/third century. The drawn bead-making technique was known in India from at least 200 BC onwards, as at Arikamedu and Brahmapuri (Dubin 1987: 195; Stern 1991).

Rectangular beads (type XIII): Four large rectangular beads with a square cross-section and chamfered corners were recovered from Chamber B (Figs 64k, l). They are of opaque red glass, 5.7 and 5.5 mm long. As noted by Morrison (Munro-Hay 1989: 172) this type of bead is found in a wide range of Roman and Near Eastern sites.

Long and standard cubes: Two beads of this form, which was not recorded by Morrison, are illustrated. That in Figs 64n and 65c differs from those described by Morrison, being of opaque dark blue glass, 5 mm long by 4 mm wide with the perforation off-centre. The ends are flat with fairly sharp corners. The bead at Fig. 64m is discussed further below, under 'gold-in-glass' beads.

Fig. 65 *Beads from the Tomb of the Brick Arches.*

Large long cylindrical bead (cf. type VIIa):
One example of this type, in opaque dark turquoise glass, came from a Robbing-1 context in Chamber B (Fig. 64o). It is 16 mm long and 7.6 mm in diameter at the widest point. The ends are flat and the perforation is 2.5 mm in diameter. It resembles Morrison's 'ellipsoids with small diameter' (Munro-Hay 1989: 170) although it is has a rather larger diameter and is a different colour.

Standard barrel with circular cross-section (cf. type IVa): Eight of these beads were recovered, one of the largest being illustrated at Fig. 64p. It is made of opaque red glass and has longitudinal stripes of darker opaque red all around the exterior surface. These beads resemble Morrison's type IVa (Munro-Hay 1989: 169), but are different in colour and seem to be drawn rather than moulded.

Gold-in-glass beads (type XX): Nine of these large and very distinctive beads were recovered from the tomb, all but one from Chamber B. They are spherical or ovoid, except for one cuboid with rounded corners (Fig. 64m) which was 7.3 mm long and 7.2 mm wide, with a slight collar at one end. The spherical beads are larger, those illustrated at Figs 64r, s being 12.4 to 13.2 mm long by 11.1 to 11.3 mm in maximum diameter. The beads were clearly layered and when in a poor state of preservation tend to fragment along the concentric lines of the layers. Morrison (Munro-Hay 1989: 173) notes the wide distribution of these beads in the Near East, including Egypt, and in India, from Hellenistic times until the fourth century AD, after which they became rare. Dubin (1987: 70, quoting Eisen 1927: 550-649), notes their manufacture

in Constantinople during the fourth and fifth centuries. ***Segmented beads (type IX):*** Only two examples of this type of bead were recovered, both from Chamber B, with four and two linked segments respectively in opaque white and translucent colourless glass. They are illustrated in Figs 64i, j and 65d. Morrison notes that segmented beads were common throughout the Roman Empire (Munro-Hay 1989: 170-2).

Carnelian beads
Twelve of these spherical stone beads were found in the tomb, their perforations being bored from small saucer-shaped chips removed from each end (Figs 62d, 65b). They range from *c*. 9 mm to 11 mm in maximum diameter. Previous discoveries at Aksum are described by Morrison (Munro-Hay 1989: 176), noting their presence at Nile-Valley sites and at Shabwa as well as the Indian bead-making centres such as Arikamedu. Although India is recognised as having been a centre of stone bead-making since the second millennium BC (Dubin 1987: 194), it cannot be assumed that all such beads are of Indian origin (cf. Aston *et al.* 2000: 26-7, 65).

Metal
(D.W.P.)

Gold
Five fragments of gold foil were recovered from Chamber B. None exceeds 6 mm in maximum dimension and none provides any indication of the nature of the object to which it was formerly attached.

The tomb also yielded three tiny loops of gold strip. The largest (Fig. 66a) comes from Loculus E and measures 7 mm long by 2.8 mm wide. The others (Figs. 66c, d) from Chamber B are only 2.8 and 3.9 mm long by 0.8 and 1.1 mm wide respectively.

Silver
Bodkin: The specimen illustrated in Fig. 66e, from Chamber B, is a 21-mm length of round-sectioned rod, flattened and pierced at one end but broken at the other. The pierced head is 4.3 mm in diameter and the silver is worn very thin at one side of the hole, suggesting long use or suspension.

Cotter-pin: Chamber B yielded a silver cotter-pin preserved to a length of 77 mm, its splayed ends firmly driven into a piece of elephant ivory, from which the 10-mm loop protrudes (Fig. 106a, below). The ivory seems to have been a slightly tapering rod or cylinder, perhaps a handle, at least 26 mm in diameter and surviving to a maximum length of 85 mm.

Boss: Also from Chamber B is a pyramidal cap or boss of base-silver sheet (Fig. 66b), 8.5 mm square

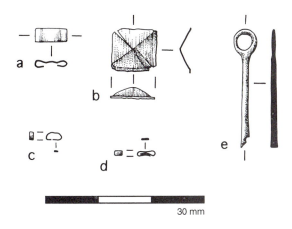

30 mm

Fig. 66 *Gold (**a, c, d**) and silver (**b, e**) artefacts from the Tomb of the Brick Arches.*

and 2 mm high.[19] It retains no sign of attachment to another object or material but, in view of its fragility, must presumably have served a decorative function. A second fragment, bent and 15 mm across, came from Loculus J.

Foil: Four tiny fragments of silver foil were recovered in Passage G.

Rivet: A silver rivet embedded in an iron object is described below (p. 114-5).

Copper alloy

N.B. Facilities were not available in Aksum to differentiate between pure copper and its various alloys. Ann Feuerbach's subsequent work on a small number of exported samples (Appendix IV) has demonstrated that some artefacts were of copper, others alloyed with silver, tin (making bronze or speculum) or zinc (making brass). The results of these analyses are noted where appropriate below, but in most cases the simple term copper alloy must suffice.

Nails and tacks: These comprise the largest category of identifiable copper alloy artefacts, with a total of 550 examples (Figs 67a-e). They show considerable typological variation although precise attribution is usually possible only in the case of relatively complete examples. The category has been divided arbitrarily between tacks (where the diameter of the head is 15 mm or more), and nails (where it is less than 15 mm), but it is not implied that this distinction has any technological significance. Where the head has not survived, the object is classed as a shank (*q.v.*), together with objects which may be sections of rods, tangs or even thick wire. A notable number of tacks and, less frequently, nails, occur paired as double examples, but it seems likely that this resulted from their use in

[19] The scale accompanying the drawing of this specimen previously published was incorrect (D.W.Phillipson 1995a: fig. 19).

close proximity so that they corroded together; the larger heads would explain why tacks were conjoined more frequently than nails. The distribution of the broad categories between different sections of the tomb is shown in Fig. 68. Single tacks clearly dominate the assemblage in all areas, but represent a significantly higher proportion in Loculus J (79%) than in Chamber B (49%). Double tacks, like double nails, are more common in Chamber B. If the double tacks are regarded as two tacks rather than as a separate category, the distinction virtually disappears. Either objects deposited in Chamber B made greater use of paired tacks, or conditions in Loculus J were less conducive to contiguous specimens corroding together. Tacks are more than three times as common as nails in all sections of the tomb. On both nails and tacks, round shanks are twice as frequent as squared ones. On very few examples, however, is the shank intact. Overall, 21% of the specimens have traces of wood adhering to them.

Shanks: a total of 338 was recorded, distributed as follows:

Chamber B	267
Chamber D	6
Passage G	36
Loculus J	29.

Comparison with the intact copper alloy artefacts from the tomb supports the view that the shanks are mostly headless fragments of nails and tacks (Fig. 67f). This is further supported by the observation that many shanks retain traces of wood.

Rivet: the single loose example, from Loculus J, comprises a 4-mm length of round-sectioned rod, 4.2 mm in diameter (Fig. 67g). Both ends are flat but not quite parallel; they retain no visible trace of hammering. A large group of similar artefacts from the block of metal pieces recovered from the pit in Chamber A is discussed below (p. 103).

Pins/needles: Two fragments come from Chamber B; only one preserves the head, which is pierced. From Loculus J come two examples, one a headless fragment, the other a complete pin 63 mm long with a round cross-section, slightly thickened at the flat head.

Rods and bars: Two similar examples, both from Chamber B, each broken at one end, are preserved to lengths of 133 and 107 mm (Figs 67h, i). They are round in section and 3 mm in diameter for most of their lengths, becoming flat or square at one pointed end. From Loculus J comes a bent or curved 36-mm fragment of slightly tapering bar with rectangular cross-section 5.7 to 7.4 by 4.8 to 5.5 mm. It may be connected with one (Fig. 69a) from the same context which comprises two longer (62 mm) pieces of similar-sized bar twisted and possibly hammered together at one end, separating at the other at *c*. 90 degrees, traces of wood being preserved in the angle.

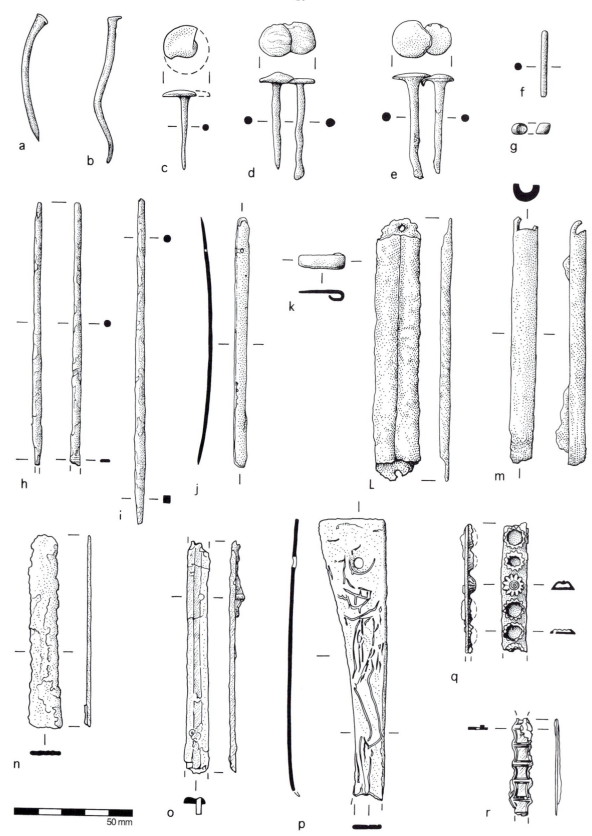

Fig. 67 *Copper alloy nails, tacks, shank, rivet, strips and rods from the Tomb of the Brick Arches.*

	Chamber B	Chamber D	Loculus G	Loculus J	Total
Tacks	154	5	20	156	335
Double tacks	80	–	4	6	90
Nails	74	1	4	37	116
Double nails	9	–	–	–	9
Total	317	6	28	199	550

Fig. 68 Distribution of copper-alloy nails, tacks etc in the Tomb of the Brick Arches.

Plain strips: There are five specimens from Chamber B (*e.g.* Fig. 67n) and one from Loculus J (Fig. 67j), being miscellaneous fragments of copper alloy strip. Invariably broken, the surviving pieces range from 11 to 102 mm in length.

Looped strips: An apparently complete specimen of unknown purpose from Chamber B is 19 mm long by 5.8 mm wide, looped over at one end (Fig. 67k).

Grooved strips: There are nine specimens of grooved copper alloy strip akin to that linking the two bimetallic plaques illustrated in Fig. 87c (see p. 108, below). All but one are between 16 and 18 mm wide (cf. Munro-Hay 1989; fig. 15.68); the only complete example (Figs 67l, 71h) is 106 mm long, perforated at each end. Seven come from Chamber B, one from Passage G. The exception, from Chamber B, (Fig. 67o; cf. also Munro-Hay 1989: fig. 15.67) is 10 mm wide, surviving to a length of 94 mm.

Semi-circular strips: Three specimens from Chamber B are 7.5 to 11.0 mm wide, with domed cross-section and hollow underside (Figs 67m, 71g; cf. Munro-Hay 1989: fig. 15.92).

Engraved strip: A single specimen from Chamber B is a tapering strip, 113 mm long and 28 mm in maximum width, engraved with a human figure (Fig. 67p; cf. Munro-Hay 1989: fig. 15.59).

Bubbled strip: A 51-mm length of copper-alloy strip 9.4 mm wide from Loculus H has a regular series of six raised hollow 'bubbles' on its surface (Fig. 67q). It has not been possible to ascertain how this effect was achieved.

Scalloped-edge strip: Four examples, all from Chamber B, resemble that illustrated by Munro-Hay (1989: fig. 15.69), being lengths of narrow (8.0 to 9.5 mm wide) strip with scalloped edges, engraved with a repeating hour-glass design (Figs 67r, 71e). One is perforated and one retains traces of wood on the reverse, so they probably decorated some wooden object.

Spoon: A fragile and fragmentary object from Chamber B is interpreted as a small spoon (Fig. 69b). The handle, preserved to a length of 35 mm, is 8 mm in maximum width and pierced at one end. Found with it but not demonstrably joining are eight fragments of curved sheet which may represent the bowl of the spoon, if such it be.

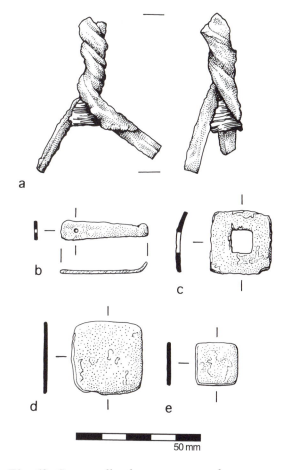

Fig. 69 Copper-alloy bars, spoon, washers etc. from the Tomb of the Brick Arches.

89

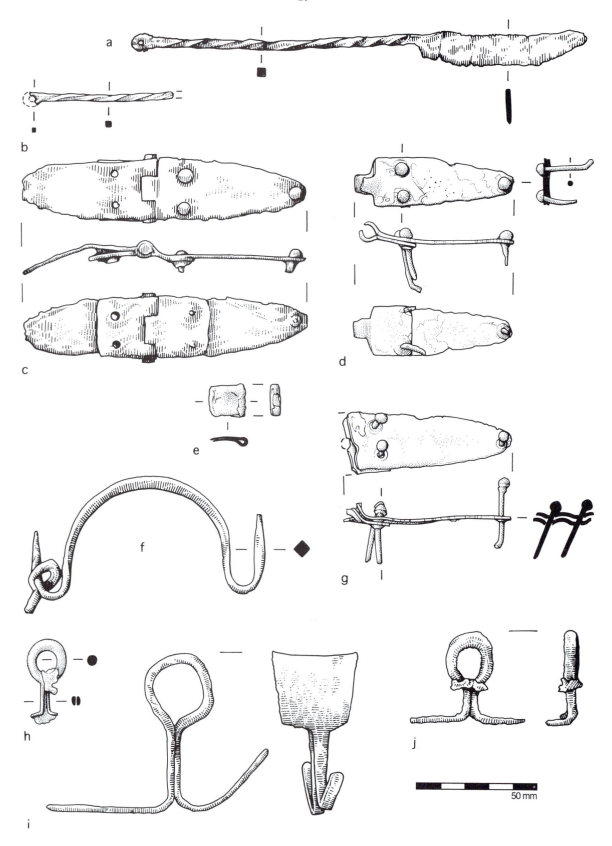

Fig. 70 *Copper alloy knives, hinges, handle and cotter pins from the Tomb of the Brick Arches.*

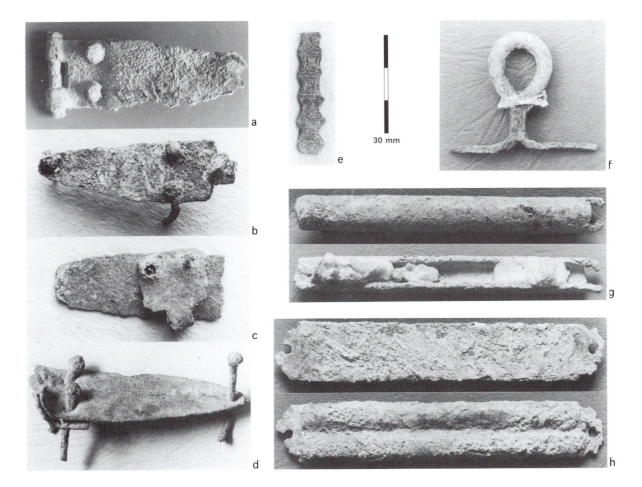

Fig. 71 *Copper alloy hinges, scalloped-edge strip, cotter-pin, semi-circular strip and grooved strip from the Tomb of the Brick Arches.*

Washers: Three of the iron 'flanged objects' (*q.v.,* p. 113, below) from Loculus J retain circular copper alloy washers partly obscured by the iron corrosion but apparently 19, 19 and 13 mm in diameter. A single example of different type (Fig. 69c) comes from Chamber B; it is square both overall (24 mm) and in perforation (10 mm). A slightly larger (28 mm) and unperforated item (Fig. 69d) came from Chamber B.

Knives: A complete specimen from Chamber B (Fig. 70a) is 187 mm in overall length, comprising a straight square-sectioned twisted handle, flattened and pierced at the extremity, and a flat tapering blade 12 mm wide and 3 mm in maximum thickness along the straight back; the cutting edge is gently curved. A second specimen (Fig. 70b), also from Chamber B, is a 59-mm length from the handle of a similar knife (cf. Munro-Hay 1989: fig. 15.71) retaining traces of the pierced extremity. Such thin knives could only have served delicate purposes.

Hinges: Two types are present. The first is represented by one complete (Fig. 70c) and seven broken (Figs 70d, g, 71a-d) specimens, all from Chamber B and possibly derived from a single object. It is a butterfly-type hinge with two near-identical plates 67 mm long and 20 mm wide at the hinge, looped to hold the pin (cf. Munro-Hay 1989: fig. 15.77-9). Each plate has three perforations, two parallel and chose to the hinge, passing through both the main and the looped parts of the plate, and one near the narrowing rounded end. The holes retain dome-headed nails with round-sectioned shanks. The seven broken specimens are all from single plates of similar hinges; in one case traces of wood are preserved adhering to the underside. A minimum of five hinges must be represented. The remaining example (Fig. 70e), from Loculus E, is probably a fragment from a smaller hinge of different type.

Handle: Chamber B yielded a semi-circular handle 98 mm long, formed of square-sectioned bar 4.0 by 4.5 mm (Fig. 70f; cf. Munro-Hay 1989: fig. 15.72). It is looped back at both ends; one such loop retains the cotter-pin with a pair of which the handle would have been fixed to its parent object.

91

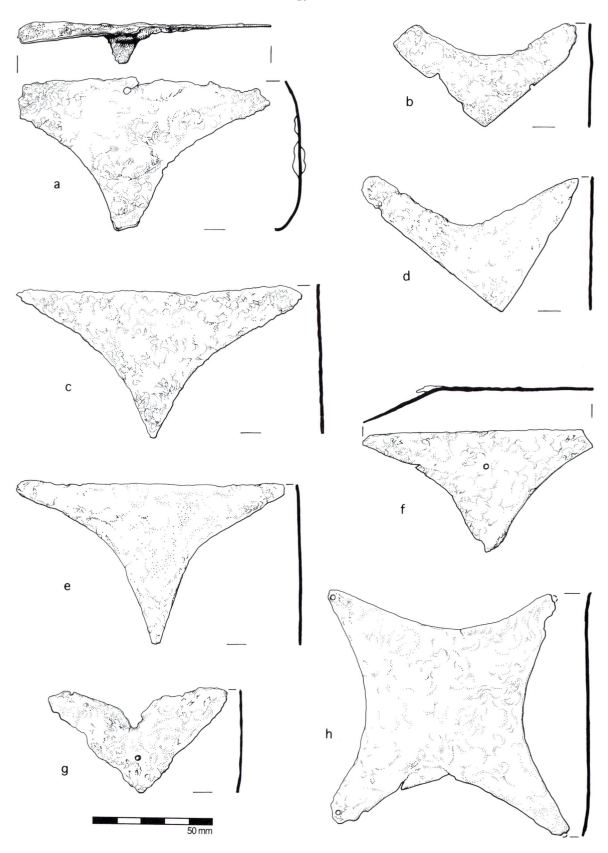

Fig. 72 *Copper alloy box-fittings from Loculus J, Tomb of the Brick Arches.*

Cotter-pins: There are six examples, all from Chamber B. One (Fig. 70i) is larger than the others, its loop formed of a plate 34 mm wide. The others are all similar (Figs 70h, j, 71f; cf. Munro-Hay 1989: fig.15.73-4) with the loop between 15 and 18 mm in external diameter and formed from round-sectioned rod. Another example of the smaller type is joined to the handle illustrated in Fig. 70f, also from Chamber B, showing one use to which such cotter-pins were put. A silver cotter-pin found embedded in a piece of elephant ivory is discussed above (p. 86).

Sheets and plates: Nine clearly related specimens (Fig. 72) came from the same level in three adjoining grid squares of Loculus J; the mirrors (*q.v.*) all come

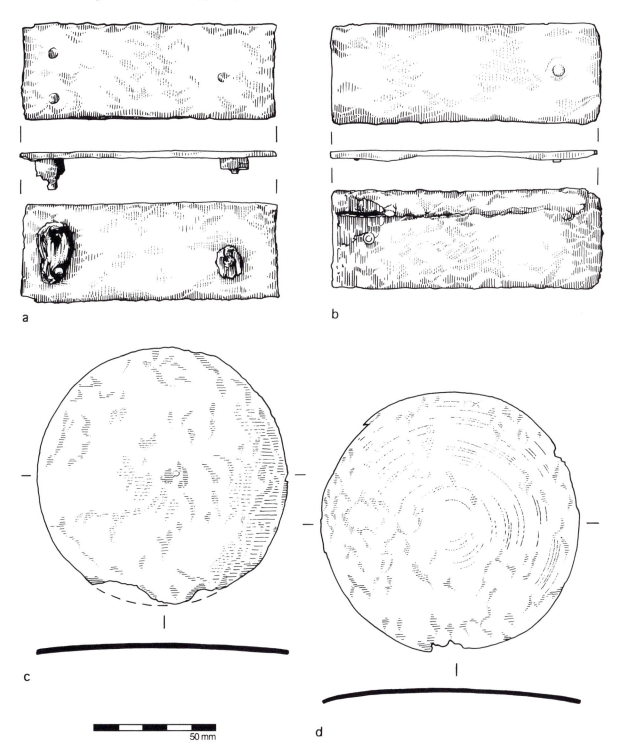

Fig. 73 *Copper alloy box fittings from Chamber B and mirrors from Loculus J, Tomb of the Brick Arches.*

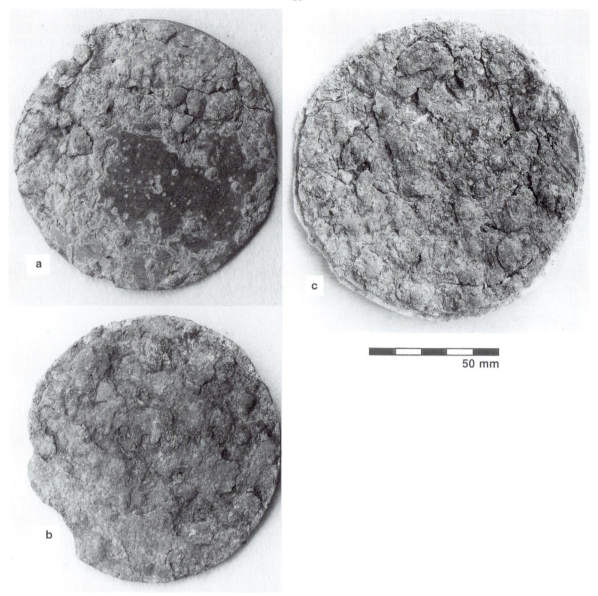

Fig. 74 *Copper alloy mirrors from the Tomb of the Brick Arches.*

from two of these contexts. All are made of thin copper alloy sheet. One (Fig. 72h) is star-shaped, or a 135-mm square with each side concave, each corner rounded and perforated. The other eight are triangular, sizes where apparent varying between 75 and 119 mm by between 48 and 78 mm. On four the two short sides are concave and the long one straight; on three it is the long side that is concave and the others straight. Three plus possibly another broken specimen are perforated near the centre. They may have been affixed to a receptacle which held the mirrors, although none retained traces of wood. From Chamber B came two thicker copper alloy plates (Fig. 73a, b) respectively 110 by 40 mm and 4 mm thick, and 100 by 38 by 3 mm (cf. Munro-Hay 1989: fig. 15.62), pierced for nails and with wood adhering. Eleven fragments of

thin copper alloy sheet were recovered from Chamber B and one from Loculus E. Of those from Chamber B, two are pierced and one retains poorly preserved traces of embossed decoration. A fragment of 5-mm thick curved copper alloy plate, apparently cast, was found in Loculus J.

Mirrors: There are eight examples, all from the same level in two adjacent grid-squares of Loculus J (Figs 73c, d, 74). The six non-fragmentary examples are all precise discs, remarkably standardised between 102 and 109 mm in diameter and concavo-convex in profile. A corrosion sample removed from one of them has been analysed by Ann Feuerbach and shown to have a tin-content suggestive of speculum or a high-tin bronze (Appendix IV). They are apparently cold-worked and polished like Roman mirrors, rather than

94

cast in the Chinese fashion. There is no sign of any design or elaboration on the polished slightly convex surface or on the reverse. Five of the nine triangular or star-shaped box fittings (see above) come from these same contexts, the others come from the same level in a third (contiguous) square.

Studs: Six specimens, all from Chamber B, are copper alloy studs identical to those at the centre of the turned ivory plaques, and are assumed to have come from such objects (cf. pp. 119-22, below).

Miscellaneous fragments: Seven pieces from Chamber B and one (hook-shaped) from Loculus G are too corroded or broken to permit description.

The hoard of scrap from Chamber A

As noted above on p. 39, a pit was located in the floor of Chamber A which had not been observed by the 1974 excavators. Although it was partly covered by the wall at the western side of Arch III separating Chamber B from Chamber A, it could not incontrovertibly be demonstrated that the pit predated construction of this wall. The pit was found to be filled with a dense mass of cuprous scrap metal weighing 37.93 kg (Fig. 75). The dense packing of the material suggests that it may have been held in some sort of bag, although no physical trace of such was observed. It was block-lifted (not without difficulty!) and removed from the tomb without damage to Arch III, then painstakingly dismantled in the Project's conservation laboratory by Noël Siver and her colleagues.

The block was found to comprise numerous fragments which could be reassembled as at least three large castings, presumably failed, plus 2029 other cuprous specimens as well as two complete and more

*Fig. 75 The 'block' of cuprous scrap from Chamber A, Tomb of the Brick Arches: **a** - as removed, 25-cm scale; **b** - in course of dismantling, scale in centimetres.*

100 mm

Fig. 76 *Tomb of the Brick Arches: the 'cover' as re-assembled.*

than 82 fragmentary coloured glass inlay-pieces. These objects are described below.

Although it was not feasible to record the positions of individual specimens within the block, a certain amount of layering was apparent. The upper part, as buried, was found to comprise plates with cut-out designs, bar fragments and nails. It was initially assumed that similar artefacts occurred throughout, but as dismantling proceeded this was found not to be the case. The lower part of the block, by contrast, contained fragments of castings which, on reassembly, were shown to have comprised most but apparently not all of the 'cover', 'trough' and rondel described below. The collection thus seems to have been built up by successively adding components of different types. Failed castings were probably intentionally broken so that the pieces would take up minimum space; and it was presumably for the same reason that the

pierced straps were so tightly folded. The collection as a whole may be interpreted as a hoard of scrap metal, presumably intended for reworking. The value of cuprous metal in Aksumite or post-Aksumite times is indicated by the extent to which, as argued below (pp. 108, 130-1), it had been selectively sought by robbers who entered the Tomb of the Brick Arches. Although neither they nor the 1974 excavators noted the hoard carefully hidden in the pit in the floor, the tomb does seem to have been an odd place for the concealment of such material in view of the difficulty inherent in its subsequent recovery. (The possibility that the hoard was hidden by the robbers may be discounted in view of the overlying deposits.)

'Cover': This was a massive cast object, 270 mm in diameter and 65 mm deep (Fig. 76), the metal averaging 7 mm in thickness. Ann Feuerbach's analysis (Appendix IV) indicates that it is made of brass.

The top or base is flat, with cast concentric flutes on the external surface extending around the near-vertical sides. There are five cast apertures in the flat surface: a rectangular one 33 by 15 mm in the centre and four approximately 18-mm square ones evenly spaced around it near the periphery, matched by four rectangular openings 39/40 mm high and 27/28 mm wide in the sides. The drawing (Fig. 77) attempts a reconstruction.

'Trough': Numerous fragments have been reassembled into two large objects, respectively 430 and 308 mm long which do not join: it is possible that two similar items are represented. Assuming that both come from the same item, it would have been a large rectangular trough-like receptacle with a flat base, upright back and two deeper sections possibly at each end. It is cast in metal which averages 8 mm thick. Drawings of the reassembled pieces are shown in Fig. 78, with tentative reconstructed views of the original object. If these views are correct, the object would have been more than 750 mm in overall length, with a 23-mm-

high ridge along the back, perforated as if for fixing to a wall; the deeper sections at each end measure some 75 mm square internally and are 42 mm deep. Two samples were analysed by Ann Feuerbach (Appendix IV) and both proved to be brass.

Rondel: This remarkable and massive failed casting was originally, as reconstructed, 380 mm in diameter (Figs 79, 80). Two samples have been analysed by Ann Feuerbach (Appendix IV), one of corroded metal and the other of clay which may derive from a casting core; both contained traces of zinc indicating that the rondel was made of brass. It has been tentatively reassembled from 80 fragments: even with the addition of 29 additional pieces which are thought to belong, by no means all of it is present. Its body is between 9.5 and 10.9 mm thick, although the relief decoration is 24.5 - 27.3 mm thick and the border, 7.2 mm wide, is 13.2 mm thick. It was cast with at least four square and one round holes near the edge, as shown in Fig. 80. Although the reconstruction cannot be regarded as definitive in all details, the centre clearly represents a

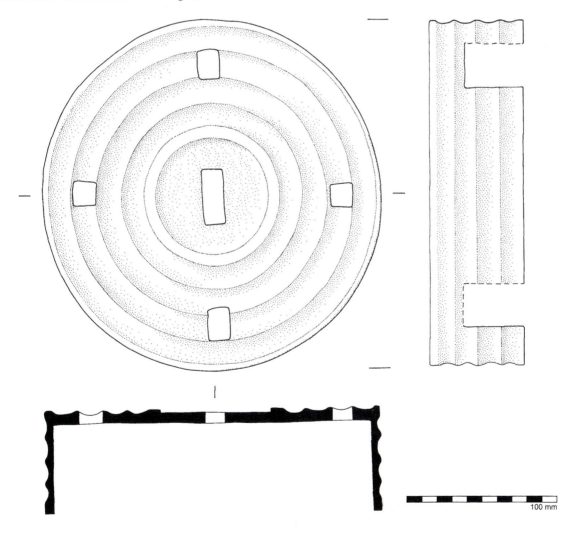

Fig. 77 Tomb of the Brick Arches: the 'cover' as reconstructed.

97

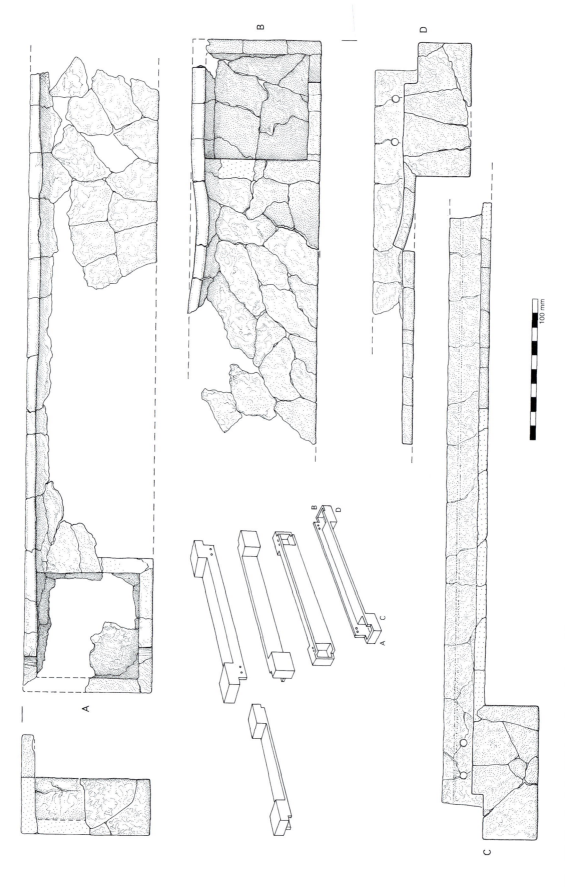

Fig. 78 *Tomb of the Brick Arches: the 'trough'.*

a

100 mm

b

50 mm

Fig. 79 *Tomb of the Brick Arches: the rondel: **a** - as re-assembled; **b** - detail of face.*

high-relief frontal human face with flowing hair and perhaps wearing a torque. Around this is an inscription in raised Ethiopic letters between 28 and 32 mm high; illustrations have been examined by Dr Roger Schneider, who considers that the form of the letters suggests a date in the second half of the third century AD, although he is unable to offer an interpretation or translation (Appendix IX). Although the function for which this object was intended cannot be ascertained with absolute confidence, it is considered that it was probably made to be set at the apex of a decorated stela. The far-reaching implications of this suggestion are considered below. The storeyed stelae all have on the side of their apex which originally faced south one or two recesses which may be circular (as on Stelae 4 and 6) or more elaborate in shape (as on Stelae 1-3 and 5). In each of these recesses are holes for pegs such as could have

held an inset; Stela 3 still retains looped metal pegs in these holes (p. 136 and Fig. 112a, below). The diameters of the circular recesses on Stela 4 are 330 and 345 mm; those on Stela 6 are significantly larger. The size of the rondel from the Tomb of the Brick Arches and the configuration of its holes are in accord with the view that it was intended to adorn the top of a stela, although it could be argued that such placement would have rendered the inscription extremely difficult to read.

Grille: Of unknown function, this is represented by 196 copper alloy fragments (Fig. 81a), weighing 1.93 kg and forming a series of interconnected octagonal rings some 47 to 50 mm in diameter, with a fluted moulded exterior. Each ring has four straight bars evenly spaced around the edge linking the ring to its neighbours in a latticework design (Fig. 82). A few

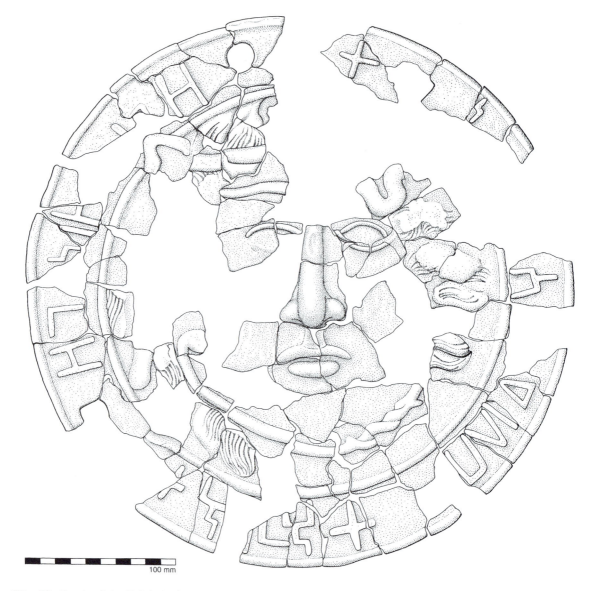

100 mm

Fig. 80 *Tomb of the Brick Arches: the rondel as reconstructed.*

30 mm

a

30 mm

b

*Fig. 81 Cuprous fragments from the 'block', Tomb of the Brick Arches: **a** - grille; **b** - plates with cut-out designs; **c** - bars and nails.*

30 mm

c

101

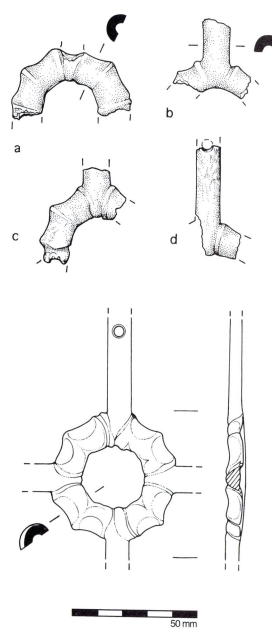

Fig. 82 *Tomb of the Brick Arches: grille fragments and reconstruction.*

four foliate shapes surrounding it, as shown diagrammatically in Fig. 84. At each end and/or side is a small circular hole, sometimes retaining a round-sectioned nail. A further 139 pieces are triangular or semi-circular in shape, often with nail-holes near the points, and each with three foliate cut-outs akin to those on the rectangular plates (Figs 84f, g). There can be little doubt that these plates originally housed coloured glass inlays, some examples of which were recovered in close association with the plates, and that they were affixed with nails to one or more wooden objects. They may have been detached from the wood and have lost much of their inlay long before they were folded and incorporated into the hoard of metal scrap.

Inlay: The glass inlay pieces are best described here since it is almost certain that they were originally inserted in the pierced metal plates. The two complete pieces are symmetrically foliate, pointed at both ends, 18 and 19.2 mm long by 6.7 and 7.3 mm wide, roughly chipped from flat translucent dark turquoise glass 1.3 and 1.4 mm thick (Fig. 84c, d). Two halves of similarly shaped pieces were recovered, one of the

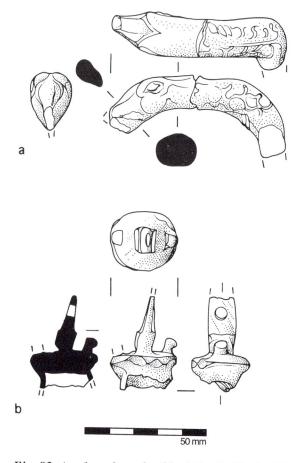

Fig. 83 *Artefacts from the 'block' in the Tomb of the Brick Arches: **a** - fragment of handle or bracelet; **b** - uncertain object.*

longer bars terminate in a broken edge retaining traces of a hole, possibly for attaching the grille to a wooden frame. The bars have half-round sections, grooved on the flat underside.

Plates with cut-out designs: The 248 specimens are remarkably standardised, weighing a total of 7.87 kg. All had been tightly folded so as to occupy the minimum space. One hundred and nine were originally rectangular, some 140 mm long, between 38 and 46 mm wide and 1.9 mm in average thickness (Figs 81b, 84a, b). Each was perforated with three wheel-like motifs comprising a central circle with

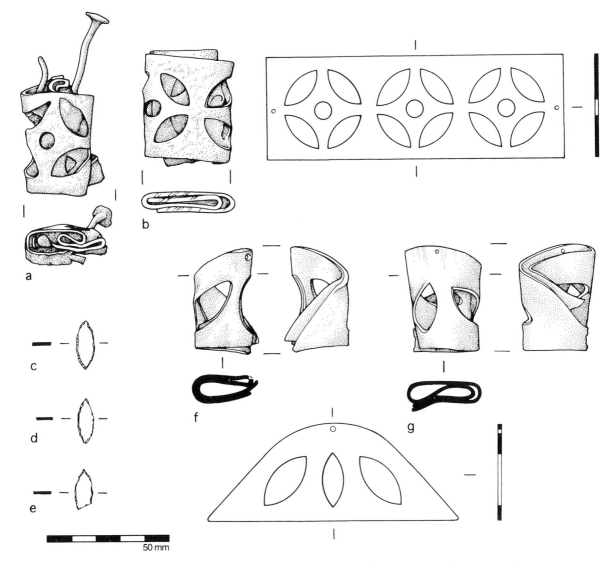

Fig. 84 *Tomb of the Brick Arches: plates with cut-out designs, glass inserts and reconstructions.*

same glass as the complete specimens, the other opaque white (Fig. 84e). In addition there were more than 80 smaller fragments of opaque white, translucent and opaque turquoise glass (see also p. 81, above). Far fewer pieces of inlay were recovered than would have been accommodated by the pierced plates, indicating that their occasional presence in a hoard of metal is fortuitous.

Bar fragments: All the 1051 specimens are broken, all but two from standardised bars of half-round section, often grooved on the flat underside, many pierced and some retaining copper alloy nails in the perforations. A representative selection is illustrated in Figs 81c and 84. The two exceptions (Figs 84a, e) have rectangular sections, with three and two perforations respectively. The total weight of these objects, including the 96 attached nails, is 10.53 kg.

Nails/rivets: There are 638, examples being shown in Fig. 85, including ten with eyelets; 96 are attached to bar fragments (*q.v.*). The remaining 532 weigh 1.00 kg and comprise 125 rivets, 132 nails with square-sectioned shanks and small flat heads some 4 mm in diameter, 274 nails with round-sectioned shanks and generally somewhat larger flat heads, and one shank-fragment. The ten examples with eyelets (*e.g.* Fig. 85c) have square-sectioned shanks tapering to the head which is bent into a loop at right angles to the axis of the shank. The rivets are between 6.2 and 14.8 mm long, of round-section copper alloy standardised at 3.6 mm diameter; the flat ends of most examples have been flattened by hammering.

Handle/bracelet fragment: The single specimen (Fig. 83a) is preserved to a length of 74 mm and is 14 mm thick. It is crudely moulded, perhaps in

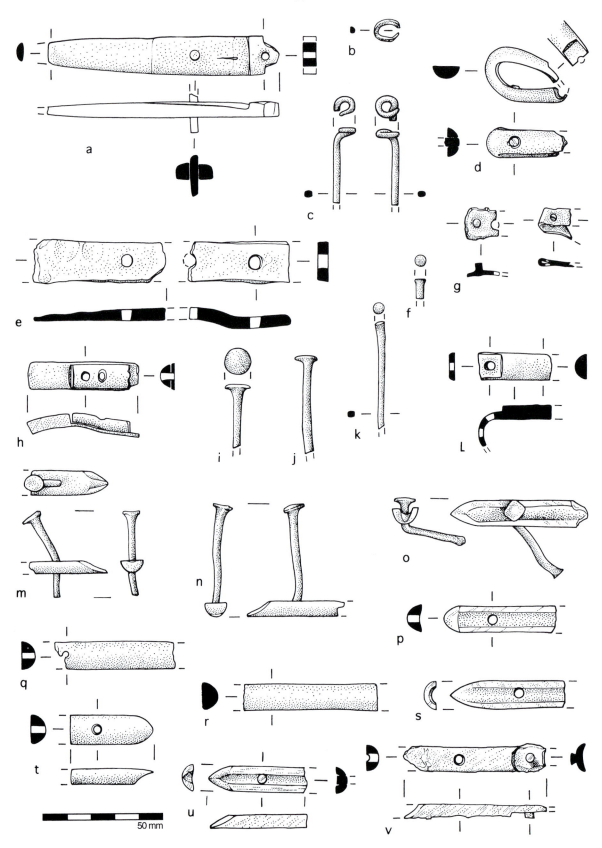

Fig. 85 *Tomb of the Brick Arches: bars and nails from the 'block'.*

representation of a snake's head; a faint body design may indicate scales. Tool marks indicate that it was intentionally broken.

Other fragments: An enigmatic, broken and distorted object forms, as preserved, a flat-topped cap with thin tubular sides (Fig. 83b). A rectangular-sectioned bar projects from the centre of the cap, with shorter ones on either side. There are 88 further miscellaneous fragments, weighing 530 g in total, of which 72 fragments are cast and 4 are pieces of copper alloy sheet.

Iron, copper alloy and glass paste

By far the most numerous single class of metal objects from the Tomb of the Brick Arches comprises fragments of composite plaques. The complete examples are all square, 113 by 113 mm in size, consisting of a sheet of copper alloy perforated to receive an elaborate design in coloured glass paste which was then mounted on an iron backing sheet of the same size (Fig. 88d). In a few cases it appears that the two metal sheets were fixed together by means of pins or rivets. Analysis of one fragment by Ann Feuerbach detected a zinc component in the copper alloy, indicating that it is in fact brass (Appendix IV).

In 1993-6[20] a total of 1096 objects was recognised as coming from these plaques; of these 1063 retained the iron component and 33 were exclusively of copper alloy. Significantly, in only three cases are both iron and copper alloy preserved on the same specimen, although many of the 33 copper alloy pieces retain traces of iron corrosion. No fewer than 1060 fragments are of iron only, of which 452 (43%) retain on their corroded surface traces of the design which had been inlaid in the copper alloy sheet to which they had formerly been fixed. Sixty-five specimens retain on the corroded iron sheet imprints or other traces of the wood to which the plaques had evidently been attached. Clearly, the fixing of the copper alloy and iron components was not completely secure, to judge from the fact that in nearly all cases they have become separated. That this separation often did not take place until the iron had begun to corrode is indicated by the fact that so many of the iron fragments retain traces of the design that was inlaid in the copper alloy (Fig. 88b).

Most of these plaques were found near the floor of the north side of Chamber B in what appeared

---

[20] Comparable figures for the 1974 excavations are not easy to calculate. It appears that one complete floral, one complete chequerboard and one near-complete chequerboard plaques were recovered, plus four copper alloy fragments with chequerboard designs and about 200 pieces of iron backing (Munro-Hay 1989: 215, 227-8, pl. 15.2, figs 15.64-5); all presumably came from Chamber B. The 1974 material, except where specifically stated, is not included in the discussion here presented.

Fig. 86 *Bimetallic plaques in situ in Passage G, Tomb of the Brick Arches.*

to be a mass of artefacts extracted from Loculi E and F during the Robbing 2 episode. One group of eight plaques (Fig. 86; cf. p. 49, above) was recorded in alignment, adjacent to one another, but proved on excavation to consist only of fragmentary iron retaining traces of wood in the corrosion.

Three designs are represented, here designated chequerboard (Fig. 87a), pinwheel (Fig. 87b) and floral (Fig. 87c). In the case of small or poorly preserved fragments it is sometimes difficult to distinguish between the last two designs. By remarkable good fortune, one complete example of each design was preserved, in addition to one chequerboard and one pinwheel example recovered in 1974. The designs are elaborate and highly standardised. The chequerboard design is made up of 5-mm square apertures, seven or eight being present in alternate rows both horizontally and vertically. These apertures had been filled with glass paste, now incompletely preserved, in which three colours may be recognised. The central four squares and the two in each corner were filled with red paste, as were the 28 forming a large outline diamond-shape (cf. Munro-Hay 1989: fig. 15.65). The remaining squares were filled with blue and yellow-green paste to form a symmetrical pattern (cf. Appendix IV). The pinwheel and floral designs employed the same colours and techniques and are similarly symmetrical, as shown in Figs 87b and 87c (see also Munro-Hay 1989: fig. 15.64).

Detailed examination in the field and by Ann Feuerbach permits some observations to be made concerning the manufacture of these plaques. The apertures in the brass plates intended to receive the coloured inlay must have been made before these plates were fixed to the iron. On some of the curvilinear designs scratched marking-out lines may be discerned (*e.g.* Fig. 88e), suggesting that the designs were individually plotted and cut, rather than cast. Use of this technique to produce the chequerboard design would have been difficult in view of the contiguity of the required apertures (Fig. 88c). Unless great care were exercised, small square sections of the brass plate would become detached; and Ann Feuerbach's work (Appendix IV) indicates that this may sometimes have happened, with the result that the design must have been built up with brass cubes before the coloured inlay was inserted.

It has unfortunately not proved possible to ascertain the precise nature of the coloured inlay

50 mm

Fig. 87 *Types of bimetallic plaques from the Tomb of the Brick Arches:* **a** *- chequerboard;* **b** *- pinwheel;* **c, d** *- floral, joined to a chequerboard fragment.*

Fig. 88 *Details of bimetallic plaques from the Tomb of the Brick Arches: **a** - traces of wood on the corroded back of an iron component; **b** - imprint of chequerboard design on the front of an iron component; **c** - detail of chequerboard design; **d** - section showing copper alloy and iron components; **e** - detail of pinwheel design.*

107

material. Whether it was inserted as a solid or paste, its bubbly texture suggests that it was subsequently heated. The pigments used seem to have given the different colours varying stability, as may be seem in the photographs (Figs 87a-c, 88c).

Only three plaques were preserved intact, two with the copper alloy and iron sheets still joined together, and one represented by the bronze sheet only. The predominantly iron fragments were often small, and their corroded condition meant that joins could rarely be made. Clearly the 1093 broken specimens represent the remains of a much smaller number of original plaques, but it is not possible to estimate their number. Consideration of the contiguity of find-spots suggests that not more than 299 plaques were represented, but the number could have been as small as 50.

Designs are represented on the extant specimens in the following proportions:

Chequerboard	25%
Floral	8%
Pinwheel	2%
Floral or pinwheel	5%
Indeterminate	4%
No trace preserved	55%.

The possibility that there was a significant proportion of undecorated plaques is rejected. None of the plaques from which the copper alloy component was preserved had been without decoration. It is felt that the 488 specimens which retain evidence for the inlay provide a reasonable indication of the proportions in which the designs were originally represented. The chequerboard pattern is significantly more common that the others, being represented on 63% of diagnostic specimens. The curvilinear floral and pinwheel designs cannot always be distinguished from one another, so less confidence should be placed on the fact that 19% of the decorated pieces fall in the former category and only 6% in the latter, 12% being indistinguishable between the two. It may, however, be accepted that roughly two-thirds of the plaques bore the chequerboard design and one-third one or other of the curvilinear designs.

In view of the reconstruction argued above, it is necessary to enquire why so few examples of the copper alloy components were preserved, particularly since conditions in the tomb were clearly more conducive to the preservation of copper alloy than of iron. The conclusion seems inescapable that robbers must have removed most of the copper alloy. As indicated above, separation of the two metal components seems not to have taken place until corrosion on the iron had begun (and this corrosion process would have assisted if not caused the separation). The robbing therefore may not have taken place until significantly after the plaques had been placed in the tomb. Although the copper alloy, being scarcer than the iron and more

readily re-worked into an unrecognisable and untraceable form, was clearly preferred, it seems unlikely that robbers would have sought to separate the two components while in the tomb if they were not already easily detached from one another.

It remains to consider the original function of the plaques. In some cases, perhaps all, they were mounted on wood (Fig. 88a). That they were mounted adjacent to one another is shown both by the discovery of eight plaques in alignment (Fig. 86) and also by the preservation of two plaques still joined together by a copper alloy strip (Figs 87c, d). This specimen comprises a complete pinwheel plaque and about one quarter of a chequerboard example, thus confirming that these two designs were used together. The centre-grooved strip is of a type represented by other examples in the tomb (*e.g.* Fig. 67l, above). It seems plausible to suggest that the plaques were used to adorn one or more wooden objects, perhaps boxes whose presence in the tomb is indicated by the presence of copper alloy hinges and other fittings. The 50 plaques suggested above as the minimum number represented would have covered a total area of approximately 0.65 sq. m, so there is no need to suggest the presence of more than one such box, which need not have exceeded 0.06 cu. m in size (*e.g.* 700 by 350 by 230 mm).

Iron and copper alloy

Strip with 'fasteners': An enigmatic object from Loculus H (Fig. 89a) consists of an elongated copper alloy strip to which are attached two identical 'Y'-shaped iron 'fasteners' (cf. that illustrated in Fig. 94d, below), 120 mm apart. At one end and midway between the 'fasteners', the copper alloy strip is pierced, the holes retaining remains of flat-headed copper alloy nails. Traces of wood are preserved on the underside.

Handle: Also from Chamber B is a 110-mm length of a tubular iron handle (Fig. 89b), 12 mm in diameter, with a rounded copper alloy knob 15 mm in diameter at the end. It is tempting to suggest, in view of its size, that this may have been the handle of a fly-whisk, sistrum or similar object.[21]

Projectile point: From Chamber B was recovered a projectile point (Fig. 89c; D.W.Phillipson 1995a: fig. 20) having a semicircular copper-alloy blade with curved outer edge continuing to a barb at either end, set into a round-sectioned iron haft forming a tang to which traces of wood still adhere. The blade, 2 mm thick, is 65 mm wide and the haft is 10 mm in diameter. A possible parallel from Hawelti is offered by de Contenson (1963: pls l, lii).

---

[21] The presence of fly-whisks in Aksum during the fourth century AD is clearly demonstrated on coinage portraits (Munro-Hay and Juel-Jensen 1995: *passim*).

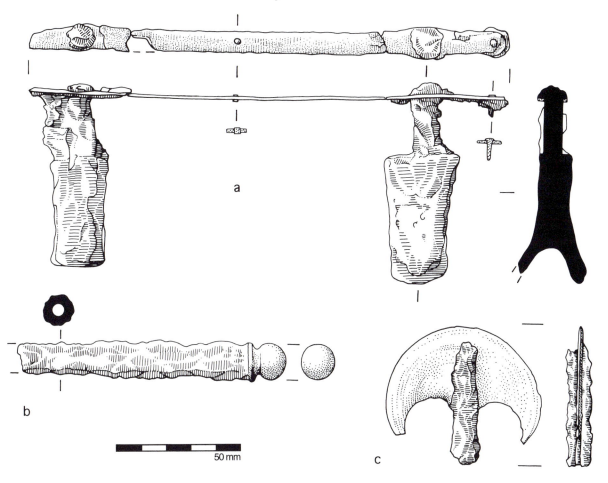

Fig. 89 *Bimetallic objects in iron and copper alloy from the Tomb of the Brick Arches.*

Iron

A total of 1205 iron objects or fragments was recovered in 1993-6, including the 1063 plaques and 4 others (described separately) in which iron had been used in conjunction with another metal, leaving only 138 objects made exclusively of iron. Iron was not generally well preserved, few artefacts being recovered intact; as a consequence precise dimensions and fine details could rarely be ascertained.

Knives: Twelve examples were sufficiently complete to be identified with confidence; in addition six objects are probably fragments from the blades of similar artefacts (Figs 90, 91). Seven comparable specimens were recorded in 1974 (Munro-Hay 1989: 225, fig.15.138). The principal feature is a blade with triangular cross-section and, for most of its length, parallel sides, one of which is straight and thick throughout, the other a thin cutting edge tapering at one end to a rounded point. At the other end of the blade is a solid tang, round or rectangular in cross-section, the former being more common. On several examples, notably that

illustrated in Fig. 90e, traces of wood were preserved in the corrosion on both sides of the blade, suggesting that the knife had been housed in some sort of wooden sheath. On examples sufficiently complete for measurement, blade-length ranges from 62 to 350 mm, width from 13 to 55 mm and maximum blade thickness from 2 to 8 mm. All except two of the knives and blade fragments come from Chamber B, there being one each from Loculus H and Loculus J. There are two exceptional knives: one of them (Figs 90h, 91a) has an integral solid iron handle, 15 by 8 mm in cross-section, in place of a tang. An exceptionally large knife, 272 mm in overall length, from Loculus J (Figs 90g, 91c) retains part of a poorly preserved ivory handle; it is also hooked at the point although corrosion (and the absence of x-ray facilities) make it uncertain whether this is an original intentional feature, as was undoubtedly the case with an example from the Mausoleum (p. 204, Fig. 180a, below).

Adze: No additional examples were recovered to accompany that found in 1974 (Munro-Hay 1989: 225,

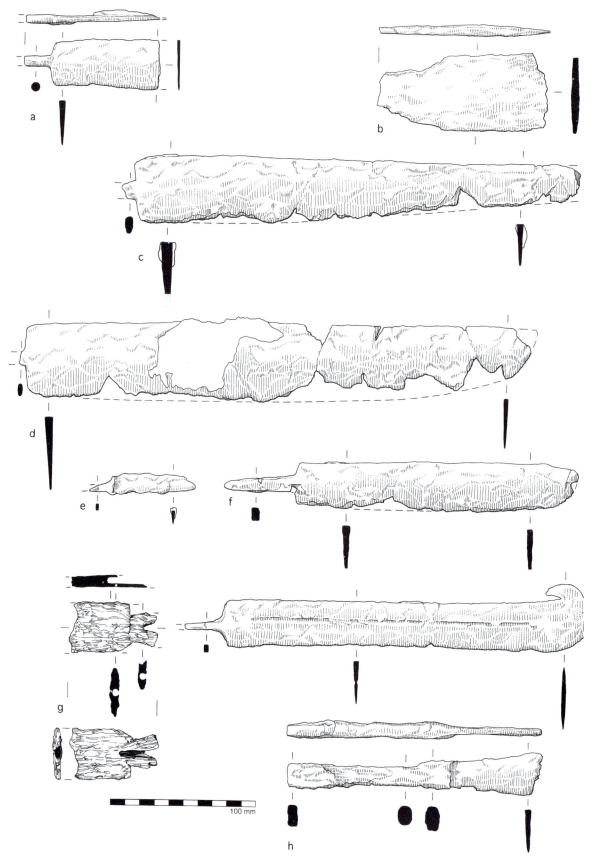

Fig. 90 *Iron knives from the Tomb of the Brick Arches.*

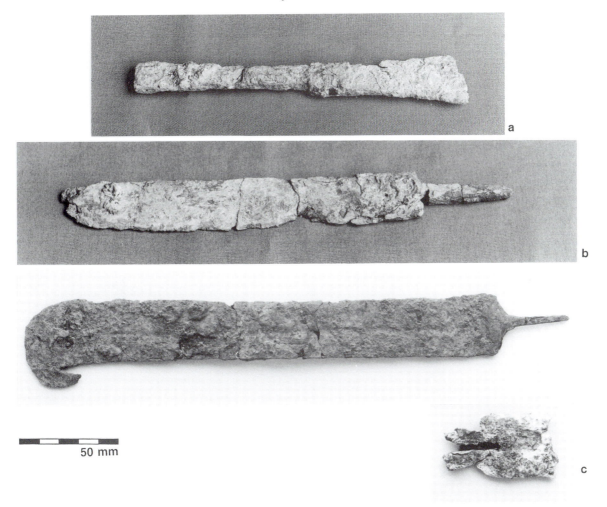

50 mm

Fig. 91 *Iron knives from the Tomb of the Brick Arches.*

fig. 15.142), with the possible exception of the object illustrated in Fig. 90b.

Hammers: The one or possibly two specimens recovered in 1974 (Munro-Hay 1989: 225, fig. 15.141) have no parallels from the excavations of 1993-6.

Spearheads, etc.: Thirty-one spearheads were recovered during the excavations of 1993-6: nineteen from Chamber B, two from Passage G and ten from Loculus H. All but one are of simple foliate shape with a tang, quite standardised also in size, the blade being 80 to more than 105 mm long and 24 to 56 mm wide (Figs 92j-q). With two possible exceptions, the blades have a longitudinal midrib on both sides, generally rounded in section but sometimes angular. In two cases (*e.g.* Fig. 92m) the midrib is exaggerated. Fourteen examples have a round-sectioned tang, on two it is squared. Traces of wood were found adhering to the tang in ten cases (eight of them in Loculus H), indicating that at least in this loculus the spears had been buried hafted. The exception is a very large example (Fig. 93) from Chamber B, 690 mm in overall length;

it has a pronounced midrib and very small tang. The thin blade is waisted *c.* 110 mm from the tip. It appears unserviceable as a weapon and may have served a symbolic or decorative function. Similar, but not identical 'lanceheads' were recovered from Tumulus III at El Hobagi near Meroe (Lenoble 1994; Lenoble *et al.* 1994), probably slightly later in date than the Tomb of the Brick Arches. At least eight further spearheads were recovered in 1974 (Munro-Hay 1989: 225, fig. 15.143-50), presumably all from Chamber B. They fall within the typological range of the smaller examples described above. The single arrowhead, from Loculus H, has a narrow foliate blade, 50 by 21 mm, 4.5 mm in maximum thickness with no midrib. Its tang is missing.

Latches: There are four new examples, two from Chamber B and two from Loculus J. The sole complete specimen, (Fig. 92i), is 128 mm long, rounded and perforated at one end, with a pronounced hook at the other. A second, lacking most of the hook, retains traces of iron rod in the perforation. The remaining

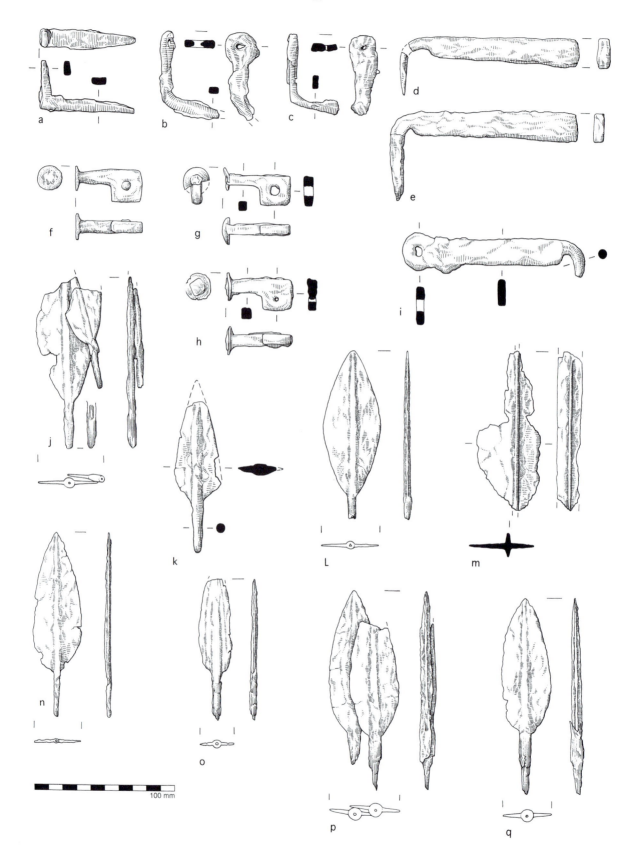

Fig. 92 *Iron cramps, latches, flanged objects and spearheads from the Tomb of the Brick Arches.*

examples (Figs 92d, e) lack the perforated end. The single specimen recorded in 1974 (Munro-Hay 1989: 255-7, fig. 15.152) was complete, 128 mm long, retaining part of an iron nail or rivet in the perforation.

Hinge-plate: In addition to two specimens recorded in 1974 (Munro-Hay 1989: fig. 15.151), a single example was recovered from Chamber B. It is represented by a piece of iron strip, 27 mm wide, looped at one end around an iron pin. Traces of wood are preserved on one side.

Flanged objects: Four enigmatic 'key'-shaped objects were recovered from Loculus J. No comparable items were recorded in 1974. They are highly standardised, 46 to 49 mm in length, comprising a shank with a perforated square projection to the side at one end (Figs 92f-h). On two the perforation is clear, on one it is obscured by corrosion, on one it retains a piece of solid iron rod. Three examples retain a copper alloy washer at the free end of the shank. Traces of wood adhere to one example.

Nails: Only four iron nails were recovered, all from Chamber B; none was recorded in 1974. Two have flat round heads 19 and 23 mm in diameter (*e.g.* Fig. 94b), traces of wood being preserved under the head of the smaller. One nail, 47 mm in surviving length, has a domed round head 16 mm in diameter (Fig. 94a). The fourth is a corroded fragment preserved in a perforation through a fragment of iron sheet. Clearly, copper alloy was the usual material for nails.

Angled spikes: In addition to five examples (designated 'clamps') found in 1974 (Munro-Hay 1989: 227, figs. 15.139, 140, 153), three specimens were recovered from Chamber B (Figs 92a-c). They consist of rectangular-sectioned spikes bent at right-angles near the centre. The new examples are all between 54 and 68 mm in maximum length. They are interpreted as having been used to fix something onto a wooden base or frame.

Eyelet spikes: Three iron spikes, all from Chamber B, each have an eyelet at the blunt end. No comparable specimens were recorded in 1974. Lengths are 69, 69 and 105 mm. On one example the metal rod had been bent to form a single loop; on the other two (*e.g.* Fig. 94c) the end had been hammered flat but it was not possible to ascertain whether the perforation had been made by bending the rod prior to hammering or whether it was drilled subsequently.

Plain spike: The sole example of a simple square-sectioned spike, from Loculus J, is 104 mm long. An eyelet has broken from the blunt end.

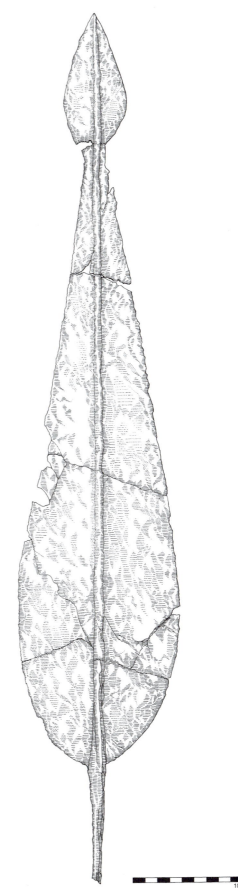

Fig. 93 (right) *Large iron spearhead from the Tomb of the Brick Arches.*

100 mm

113

Rods: There are 26 pieces of round- or rectangular-sectioned rod, two from Loculus J, one from Loculus H, one retaining traces of wood from Loculus E, one from Passage G and all the others from Chamber B. At least four similar specimens were recorded in 1974. In view of the rarity of iron nails in this tomb it seems likely that most are from the tangs of spearheads or knives, or from spikes, clamps *etc*. The specimen from Passage G (Fig. 94e) bulges in the centre to a maximum diameter of 18 mm and may be some sort of handle. Chamber B yielded a 67-mm length of round-sectioned rod, flattened in the centre and bifurcating at one end (Fig. 94d). It is broken at both ends and no interpretation can be offered, although there is a similarity with the iron components of the bimetallic object illustrated above in Fig. 89a. Another example from Chamber B (Fig. 94f) has an oval section and a

transverse ridge with traces of wood on one side: it may be from the tang or handle of an iron knife. Three others from Chamber B are perforated, retaining traces of copper alloy nails and, in two cases, wood to which they had presumably been affixed; the best example is shown in Fig. 94g, 112 mm long with two nails having large flat heads 18 mm in diameter (cf. Fig. 94h).

Strips: There are 13 fragments of iron strip or bar. One is grooved and retains traces of wood on the back, while six are pierced (Fig. 94i).

Fragments: Twelve fragments of iron from Chamber B and two from Loculus G are not further identifiable. Six pieces of iron sheet come from Chamber B, two from Loculus G and four from Loculus H; three of them are pierced, retaining copper alloy nails. In addition, one specimen from Loculus E and one from Chamber B are angled as if from the corners of boxes.

Iron and silver

A remarkable object from Chamber B (Figs 95, 96) is a rectangular iron sheet, apparently folded over and flattened to fit around a long diamond-sectioned object (not present), the two ends held together by an ornamental silver rivet. Incised or stamped on both external sides of the iron are rectilinear designs of Chinese aspect. Its present overall measurements are 73 by 38 mm, the head of the rivet is 17 mm in maximum diameter, and the iron sheet is *c*. 2.4 mm thick.

Many colleagues have examined this enigmatic object: although interesting technological information has emerged, none has been able to suggest an identification. Examination by Mrs Keren Butler using a scanning electron microscope has indicated that the purity of the iron is very high, but that of the silver only 55%. Dr J. A. Charles has noted the lamellar structure of the iron indicating that, contrary to its superficial appearance, the object was forged, not cast. X-ray photography by Ms Julie Dawson raises the possibility that the iron was originally in two pieces, which have corroded together at the object's thicker end. Close examination by Mrs Butler and others suggests that the designs are so uniform and regular that they were more probably stamped than incised, although there can be no certainty on this point.

The original suggestion that this object might have originated in China (D.W.Phillipson 1998: 67-8) was based both on the nature of the designs and on the suggestion that it might be made of cast iron. The latter argument is now disproved, but the former remains to be evaluated.[22] Authorities who have examined either the object itself or photographs

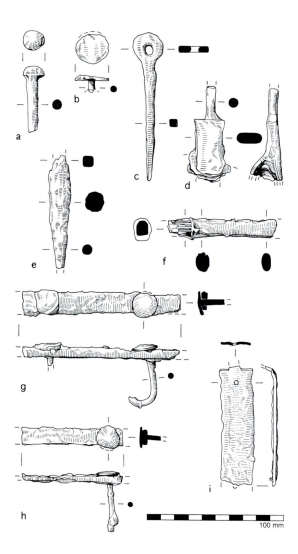

Fig. 94 *Iron nails, eyelet spike, strip, bars, rods and 'fitting' from the Tomb of the Brick Arches.*

---
[22] Thanks are due for the assistance and advice of Drs Raymond and Bridget Allchin, Dr Gina Barnes, Dr Dilip Chakrabarti, Dr J. A. Charles, Dr Ian Glover, Professor Charles Higham, Professor Michael Loewe, Professor David McMullen, Dr Jianjun Mei and Dr Jessica Rawson.

of it have commented on the superficial East Asian aspect of the designs, although none has been able to cite an exact parallel A central Chinese origin has been suggested as unlikely, although the possibility remains that the piece came from some other part of East Asia. The hypothesis that it is of local Aksumite manufacture needs also to be considered. Good evidence for the skill and ingenuity of Aksumite metalworkers is provided by this and earlier excavations.

Use of base silver and of rivets are separately attested at Aksum; and skills of working wrought iron were well developed. Stamping of designs in metal (although not in iron) was widely practised at the mint and elsewhere. The actual designs on this object cannot be paralleled at Aksum, but the force of such negative evidence is weak and the possibility remains that they were inspired by some import from East Asia not yet recovered from the archaeological record.

Fig. 95 *Iron and silver object from the Tomb of the Brick Arches.*

30 mm

115

30 mm

a

10 mm

b

Fig. 96 *X-ray and detail of iron and silver object, Tomb of the Brick Arches.*

Ivory
(D.W.P.)

A total of 423 pieces of ivory (after such reassembly as was possible) was recovered from the Tomb of the

Brick Arches during the 1993-6 excavations. All appear to be of elephant ivory. They were very unevenly distributed, 386 coming from Chamber B, 22 from Passage G, 12 from Loculus H, 2 from Loculus J and 1 from Chamber D. It is interesting that the 1974

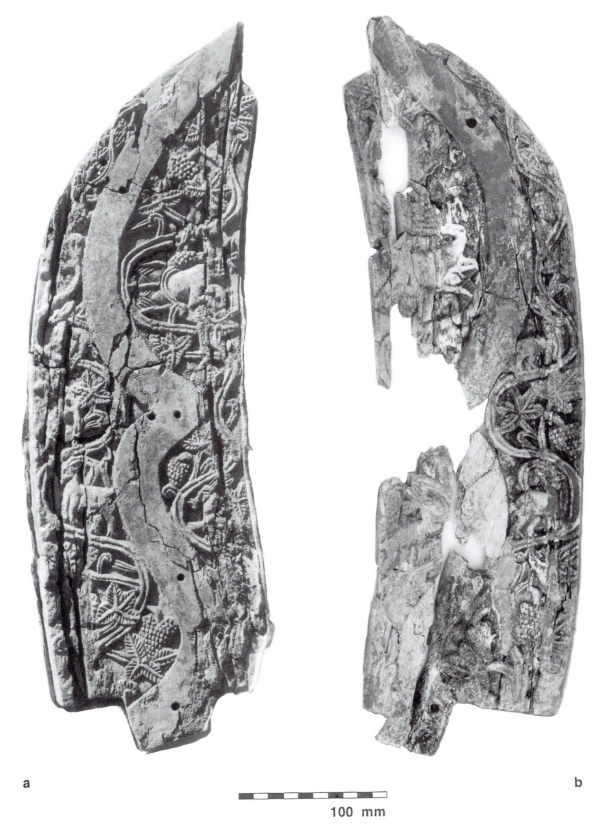

a

b

100 mm

Fig. 97 *Ivory throne components from the Tomb of the Brick Arches: panels. Drawings of these panels have been published elsewhere (D.W.Phillipson 1995a: fig. 22, 1998: fig. 32).*

excavators did not record any ivory: possibly it was not preserved in Chamber A which they excavated almost completely, but they also worked in Chamber B where ivory has been shown to be abundant. Perhaps, in the wetter conditions which then prevailed, ivory was not recognised.

Furniture components: Exactly 50 pieces appear to be derived from one or more elaborate items of ivory furniture. A detailed and fully illustrated

consideration of this material is being prepared for publication elsewhere, while the style and techniques of ivory-working are discussed below (pp. 461-70), so the account offered here is comparatively brief. The preferred interpretation of this material is that it represents a single chair or throne. There are two large elaborately carved panels, six posts / finials and 42 slats. A fragment of a third panel bears quite different decoration and may not belong to the same

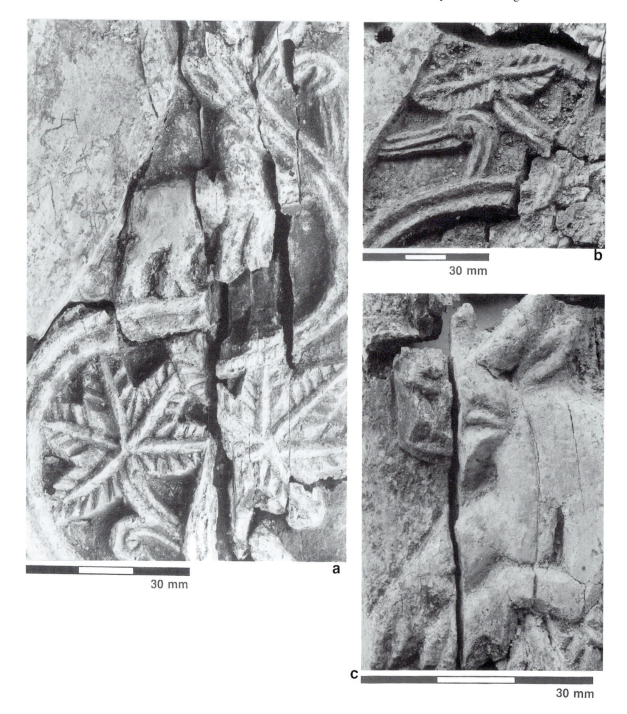

Fig. 98 *Ivory throne components from the Tomb of the Brick Arches: panel details.*

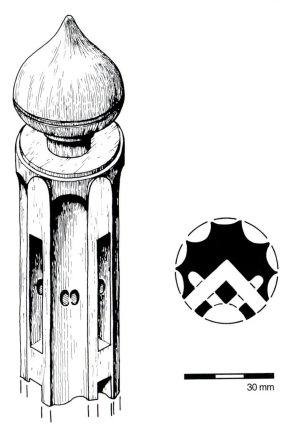

30 mm

Fig. 99 *Ivory throne components from the Tomb of the Brick Arches: reconstruction of finial.*

assemblage. With the exception of four of the slats (three from Passage G and one from Chamber D), all this material was recovered from Chamber B. The main panels each measure 490 by 160 mm and are virtually mirror images of one another, being 18 and 22 mm thick (Figs 97, 98). Each is carved on one side with an elaborate design of vines, birds and animals, the positioning of which indicates the original alignment of the panels. The leaves and bunches of grapes on the vines are carefully depicted, the animals are varied stylised quadrupeds and the long-beaked birds are probably ibises. Each panel has one edge very slightly concave and the other markedly but asymmetrically convex, producing a pointed top; they may have been mounted side-by-side with the nearly straight sides adjacent. Through each carved design runs a plain curvilinear band, between 24 and 35 mm wide, in which are drilled holes by means of which the panels were presumably mounted. Five of these holes, each 5.5 mm in diameter, are preserved in the better preserved of the two panels. The detailed configuration of posts and finials may only be seen on a single specimen (Figs 99, 100g), preserved to a total length of 130 mm and

comprising a 38-mm square post with eight fluted sides topped by an onion-shaped finial, apparently turned, measuring 38 by 35 mm resting on a straight neck 10 mm long. Two fine parallel horizontal lines are carved around the maximum diameter of the finial. A series of smoothly polished vertical grooves and deep mortises have been cut into the facets of the post, with holes for fixing pegs: their configuration is shown in the reconstructed drawing. In addition to this specimen there are three poorly preserved fragments which appear to come from analogous finials and four from posts, one of them from the top section retaining traces of the neck. The slats (Figs 100a-f, i-m), mostly fragmentary and poorly preserved, are generally rectangular in section and often retain carefully drilled pegholes *c*. 9 mm in diameter; no remains of pegs were, however, recovered. The maximum preserved length of the slats is 456 mm, with cross-sections up to 56 by 22 mm. Some retain informative traces of the methods by which they were produced, discussed separately below. The affinities of this material have been noted briefly by Jacke Phillips (1998). The ivory throne of Maximian in the Archepiscopal Museum at Ravenna (Rodley 1994 and references) is of particular relevance, as is the representation of an Aksumite throne on coins of Armah (Munro-Hay and Juel-Jensen 1995: type 152-3; Munro-Hay 1999). More detailed studies are in preparation.

Plaques: A large series of standardised square plaques, flat on one side, the other decorated with a lathe-turned design of concentric rings, is represented by no fewer than 108 specimens (Figs 101-3). A detailed account of the processes by which they were manufactured is presented below (pp. 467-9). These plaques, when sufficiently complete to be measured, were between 101 and 108 mm (average of 15 specimens: 103.3 mm) on the longer side, and between 92 and 98 mm (average of 13 specimens: 94.6 mm). Their thickness showed greater variation, between 4 and 11 mm (average of 69 specimens: 6.2 mm). Of the 108 examples, 80 retained a copper alloy stud in the centre of the design (Figs 102a-e, 103f). By contrast, four plaques had an integral turned ivory button in place of the stud (Figs 102h, 103g). In eighteen cases, no metal stud was preserved (Fig. 102f) but it seems likely that one had originally been present (six loose studs of identical type were also recovered and have been noted on p. 95, above: cf. Fig. 103d). The diameters of 70 studs were recorded, ranging only from 22 to 26 mm with an average of 24.1 mm. The studs' central shanks had been flattened at their distal ends so as to hold the studs in place; they were thus not used to fix the plaques themselves in whatever position they were intended to occupy. Only in four cases were there any signs of holes by means of which the plaques may have

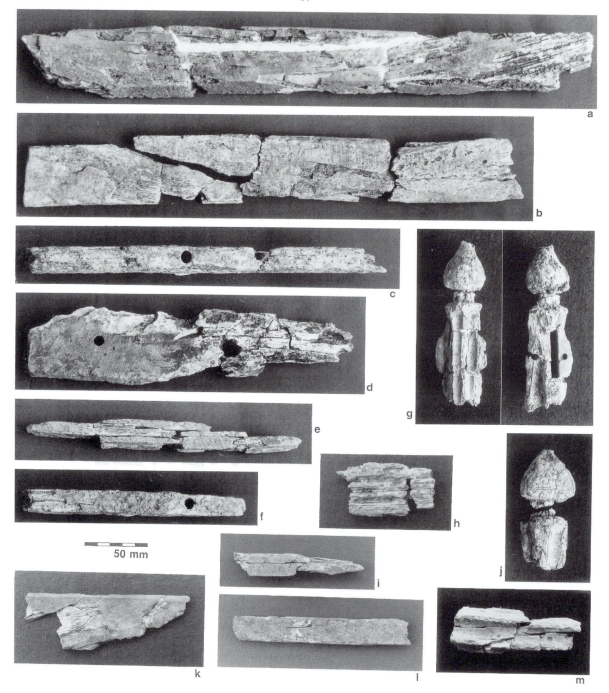

Fig. 100 *Ivory throne components from the Tomb of the Brick Arches: slats and finial.*

been affixed (Figs 103c, e); these holes were very close to the midpoint of an edge and no plaque preserved evidence for more than one such hole. The plaques may have been affixed by means of overlying strips which would have obscured their roughly worked edges. Most of the plaques come from a circumscribed area in Chamber B (Fig. 101; cf p. 39, above), but none appeared to be aligned in such a way

as to indicate their original inter-relationship. Their thinness and fragility strongly suggest that they were affixed to some more substantial substance, but its nature cannot be demonstrated.

Cylindrical boxes: Eleven fragments, all from Chamber B, are attributed to small ivory pyxides or their lids (Fig. 104). The most complete example, shown in Fig. 104a-d, is lathe-turned, well preserved

and almost complete. It is 76 mm in external diameter and has vertical sides, 61 mm high, decorated with five parallel horizontal raised bands each bearing a carved chevron design. The lip is flanged to receive a lid. Three other examples, represented by large fragments, were apparently 62, 70 and 86 mm in diameter, others perhaps smaller and at least one apparently oval in shape (Fig. 104e-g). Some were carved or turned from sections of ivory not from the centre of the tusk, which observation serves to explain the extent of their fragmentation. Turned discs were subsequently inserted as bases or used as lids (cf. p. 467, below). No other examples could be shown to have borne decoration such as that on the near-complete specimen.

Fig. 101 *Ivory plaques as block-lifted from Chamber B, Tomb of the Brick Arches.*

Fig. 102 *Ivory plaques from the Tomb of the Brick Arches: **a-g** - with central copper-alloy stud; **h** - with central ivory boss and notch in edge.*

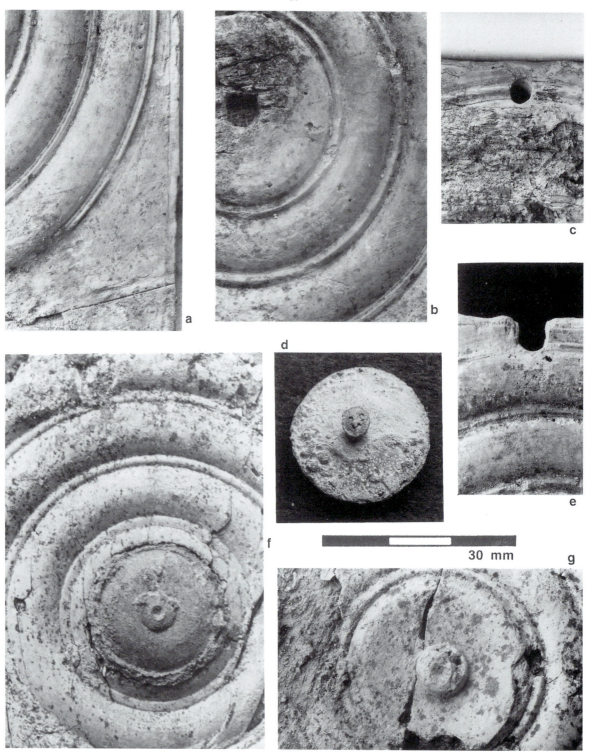

Fig. 103 *Details of ivory plaques from the Tomb of the Brick Arches.*

Fig. 104 *Turned cylindrical ivory boxes from the Tomb of the Brick Arches.*

Female figurine: This remarkable object from Passage G (Fig. 105; see also Fig. 404, below) represents a naked woman in *controposto* pose, the head, arms and lower legs (from just below the knees) being broken away and not recovered. As it survives, the figurine is 62 mm high and 24.5 mm wide across the shoulders. At the waist it is 9.3 mm thick, 4.7 mm at the neck. What appears to be a wide strap is shown from the front only, partly obscuring the left breast and supporting a pommelled dagger hanging diagonally between the breasts. This strap is not shown on the back, where long straight hair is somewhat roughly represented, extending down to the position of the shoulder blades. This object is stylistically strange, front and rear being reminiscent of Graeco-Roman representations (*e.g.* Whitehouse 1997: 29, 326), although the profile is markedly less voluptuous suggesting that the artist was better acquainted with relief-carving than with three-dimensional forms, or was copying another artwork that had not been fully understood. It is noteworthy that the hair of the figurine is not typically Ethiopian, contrasting both with that of recent populations and with that depicted on Aksumite

human-headed pottery jars (cf. pp. 68-72, above). As Dr B. Juel-Jensen has pointed out (*pers. comm.*), this is a manner which Ethiopian artists have for many centuries employed in order to show that the subject is a foreigner.

Handles: There are three examples, two of which are attached to metal objects which have been discussed above. That containing a silver cotter-pin is here illustrated (Fig. 106a; see p. 86, above); that attached to an iron knife has been described and illustrated above (Figs 90g, 91c). The third, from Chamber B (Fig. 106d) comprises two non-joining 48- and 42-mm straight lengths of ivory, 24 by 11 mm in ovoid cross-section, with flattened sides and carved scalloped decoration.

Rod: Also from Chamber B, this is straight, preserved to a length of 85 mm, with both ends broken (Fig. 106b). The round cross-section measures 8 by 7.5 mm.

Pierced rectangular piece: The specimen (Fig. 106c), from Chamber B, measures 86 by 54 mm and is 24 mm in maximum thickness. The holes are 12 and 7 mm in diameter. Although much of the original

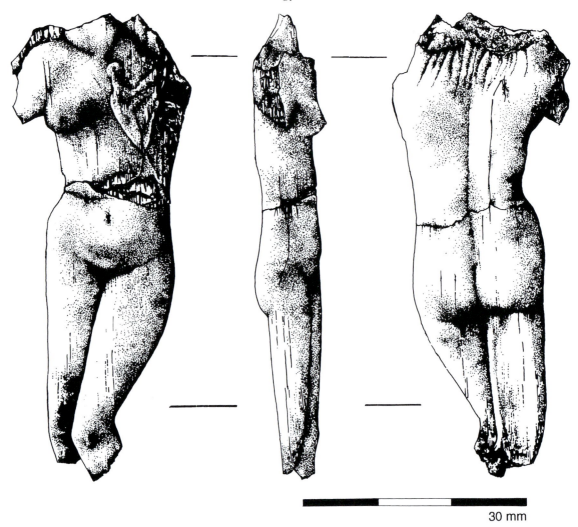

30 mm

Fig. 105 *Ivory figurine from the Tomb of the Brick Arches. For a photograph, see Fig. 404, below.*

surfaces has flaked away, enough survives to indicate that the original dimensions were not significantly greater than the present ones. The finish seems to have been significantly rougher than that of the slats. The smaller hole retains traces of drilling: both may have been drilled from both sides.

Lid: This dome-shaped specimen from Chamber B (Fig. 106e), surmounted by a roughly spherical knob, was found, much fragmented, inside a pottery bowl. Its rim was not recovered, so its original diameter cannot be ascertained; it survives with maximum dimensions of 80 by 83 mm, a height of 35 mm and a thickness of 5 mm. The knob is 7.1 mm in diameter. All pieces show signs of wear, to the extend that it is impossible to be certain whether the lid was lathe-turned.

Miscellaneous fragments: There are 246 pieces which could not be fitted onto other objects and of which the original form could not be ascertained. Of these, at least 55 show tool-marks, polishing or other signs of working. Some of these fragments may be hippopotamus ivory or bone.

Stone
(D.W.P.)

A single, heavily used lower grindstone was recovered from Chamber B; its position indicated that it may have been removed from Loculus E during the Robbing 2 episode. Made of variegated sandstone, it is heavily used, 320 mm long, 140 mm wide and weighs 3.3 kg (Fig. 107). It is noteworthy as one of very few artefacts from the Tomb of the Brick Arches which appears to have been used for some domestic purpose. Clearly, however, it was not recovered from what had been its original position within the tomb, and it is possible that it had been used within the loculus for some purpose to which its grinding function was irrelevant, *e.g.* for building stone or as a supporting prop.

124

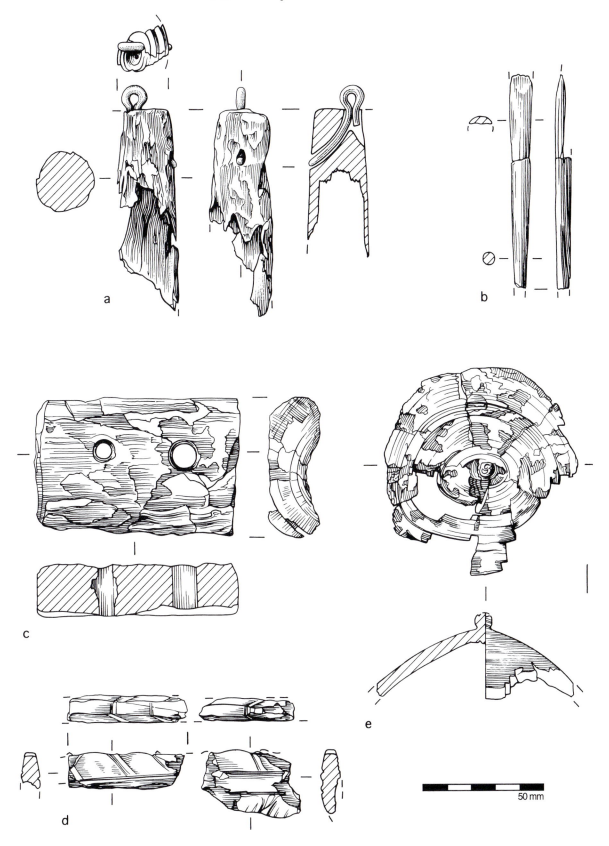

Fig. 106 *Miscellaneous ivory artefacts from the Tomb of the Brick Arches:* **a** *- handle with silver cotterpin;* **b** *- rod;* **c** *- pierced rectangular piece;* **d** *- handle;* **e** *- lid.*

Fig. 107 *Lower grindstone from the Tomb of the Brick Arches.*

100 mm

HUMAN SKELETAL REMAINS
(Helen Cook)

Over two hundred human bones or fragments were recovered during the 1993-6 excavations in the Tomb of the Brick Arches. In 1974 a human skull had been recorded near the foot of the adit (p. 37 above and Munro-Hay 1989: 234), while other bones from Chambers A and B were not firmly identified as human.[23] Despite the disturbance brought about by repeated robbing, limited reconstruction of individuals has been possible, at least three and probably four individuals being recognised. Age, sex and stature estimations were made using as many different calculations as possible, based on the various formulae presented by W. Bass (1995).

An elderly woman is represented by a partial skull recovered beside the bench in Loculus J(67)e. It displays bony nodules (moderate hypostosis frontalis) on the cerebral surface of the frontal bone (Fig. 108a). This is a common condition in post-menopausal individuals (Iscan and Kennedy 1989: 301). Left and right femora recovered from Chamber B may belong to the same individual, although precise measurements and stature calculations were not possible. Paired and articulating ulnae and radii found nearby permitted calculation that the individual represented had a height of *c.* 1.58 m. Female innominate bones and small, adult left and right humeri recovered from this area may also have been associated with this individual.

A complete male skull, seven articulating vertebrae and some possibly associated limb bones (see below) were recovered in different grid squares of Chamber B(8). The maxillary dental attrition suggests that this person was between 45 and 55 years old when

[23] The absence of animal bone from the 1993-6 excavations suggests that this material was human.

he died.[24] The maxilla displayed indications of periodontal disease and at least two teeth had been lost prior to death. This man suffered from vertebral osteoarthritis, possibly connected with a crush fracture that drew the vertebra out of alignment. The transverse foramen of the atlas vertebra is bent inwards, and there is eburnation on the dens of the axis vertebra (Fig. 108b). This pathology is consistent with the carrying of heavy loads on the head, either regularly over time or in a single traumatic episode. There are three right tibiae, any one of which might be associated with this cranium. The first was found in Passage G(9)d, in possible association with a left femur. Both these leg bones come from an adult approximately 1.80 m tall, probably male. Two further right tibiae, from Chamber B(8)n and Chamber D(47)b, come from individuals respectively *c.* 1.75 and 1.60 m tall, whose sex could not be determined. It was considered unlikely that the smallest femur, that from Chamber D, could have belonged to the elderly woman noted above. It was not possible to ascertain whether the skull recovered in 1974 could have belonged to one of these individuals.

Additional specimens, all from Chamber B(8), which could not be linked with any particular individual described above, show pathological features which are of interest. Five vertebrae have deep lesions on the superior body surfaces; at least two of them also have Schmorl's nodes (Fig. 108c), caused by pressure on the centrum and perhaps indicating intervertebral disk hernias (Aufderheide and Rodriguez-Martin 1998: 97). The final item of interest is a distal

[24] Most of the dental aging criteria used in this study are taken from the work of Brothwell (1981: 71-2) which, although based on British Neolithic and Medieval populations, have found wider application (Hillson 1986: 195). These criteria may require modification to take account of excessive tooth-wear due to eating stone-ground cereals.

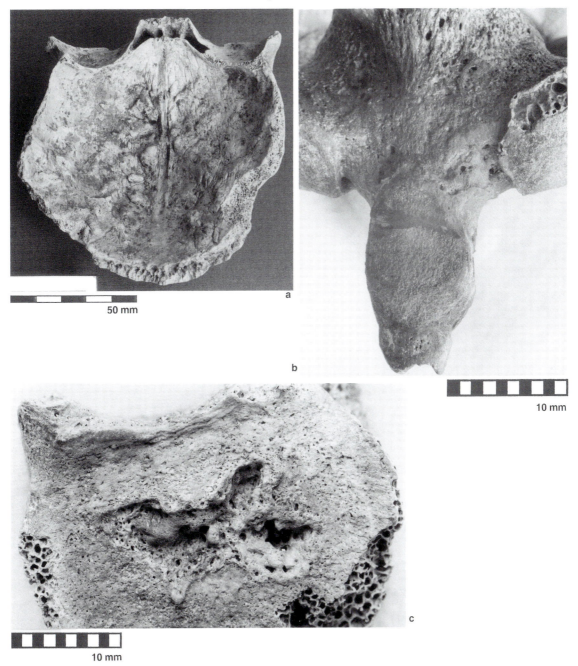

Fig. 108 *Human bones from the Tomb of the Brick Arches: **a** - female frontal, scale in centimetres;
b - axis vertebra; **c** - vertebra with deep body lesion and Schmorl's node.*

phalanx with a small hole cut through its shaft apparently after death; while it is possible that this bone was suspended on a cord, there is no wear around the hole where such a cord would have rubbed the bone.

ARCHAEOBOTANY
(Sheila Boardman)

The contents of almost one hundred intact or near-intact ceramic vessels from the Tomb of the Brick

Arches were investigated, together with ten samples of soil from around the block-lifted artefacts. Small fragments of ivory and other artefacts were recovered; and sparse plant remains were present in five vessels and three block-lifts. These comprise a few charred grains of cereals (barley, sorghum, emmer wheat) with isolated seeds of other cultivated/wild plants (cotton, linseed, grasses). One pottery vessel from a Robbing-2 context in Chamber B was found to contain a single desiccated grape pip, but this does not provide very convincing evidence for inclusion of plant tributes with the burials. The charred condition of most grains and their low numbers suggest that they may have been accidentally introduced into the deposits either at the time of the tomb's initial use or, less probably, during the Robbing-2 episode. A single sorghum grain associated with the cuprous hoard in Chamber A is likely to be be contemporary with the deposition of the hoard.

The limited number of wood samples examined by Rowena Gale included fragments identified as *Acokanthera*, *Ficus*, *Maytenus*, *Olea* and *Rhus*. It is uncertain which of these woods are derived from artefacts, perhaps including materials brought from afar, and which represent fuel or domestic residues of probable local origin.

OVERVIEW
(D.W.P.)

Configuration and use

The massive entrance to the tomb contrasts with its irregular, seemingly unplanned interior. Roof-collapse has undoubtedly contributed to the rough aspect of the rock-cut tomb, but its overall lay-out is markedly distinct, for example, from the ordered symmetry of the Mausoleum, despite the similarities emphasised by the use of brick arches to divide both tombs into sections. The impression of irregularity is partly erroneous: Chamber D has twinned mirror-image loculi on the right side of someone entering the tomb, each loculus being equipped with a stone-built bench. Loculi in the same position off Chamber B are apparently similar, perhaps also having benches. Chamber C has likewise two loculi, although they were laid out in a somewhat different manner. There is no indication that the tomb itself was constructed in stages or as other than a unity. The adit walls were, however, demonstrably subsequent to Arch I, although no significant interval is indicated.

It is clear that bodies and grave goods were originally placed in the loculi, not in chambers B, D nor passage G, where artefact-bearing deposits lying directly on the rock-cut floor are attributed to Robbing 1. Likewise, there is no evidence that artefacts were originally placed in Chamber A, other than in the pit in the floor. The question must be addressed whether the tomb was used once, the three or four interments for which arguments are offered below being placed there at essentially the same time, or whether it was re-used over a period. It is suggested above that the tomb was constructed as a unit, there being no evidence for sequential stages in its interior configuration. Certainly, it would seem impossible for the tomb to

have been extended once its use as a repository had begun. If this argument is accepted, the three principal chambers B, C and D where burial loculi were constructed, must have been prepared *ab initio*. The artefacts from the tomb show no evidence of having been manufactured over any length of time although the possibility that 'heirlooms' were included cannot be disregarded and, since so many artefact types are without parallel elsewhere, this argument must depend largely on the pottery. It cannot be ruled out that some modest time - years or even a decade or two - may separate the individual interments; but it seems safe to conclude that the tomb's contents are all essentially contemporaneous, with the probable exception of the rondel for which, as indicated below, typological considerations suggest an age some five to ten decades earlier than that suggested for the tomb as a whole. The significance of wear observed on the adit steps is discussed on p. 259 below.

Chronology

Evidence for the absolute age of the Tomb of the Brick Arches may be derived from three sources: radiocarbon determinations, seriation of artefacts with material from other Aksumite contexts, and comparative observations on the artefacts themselves. It is appropriate to consider these three sources separately, before comparing the conclusions to which they give rise.

A total of seven radiocarbon analyses has been conducted on materials from the Tomb of the Brick Arches. The calibrated results are summarised in Fig. 109 and full details of the analyses are provided in Appendix VI. In view of the indications noted above that only very little material was introduced into the tomb during successive robbing episodes, it is reasonable to assume that all the dated samples derive from material associated with the original disposition of burials, notwithstanding the fact that much of it had been repeatedly disturbed subsequently. The close agreement between the results of the seven analyses confirms this view; and they are here regarded as dating a single event. The three analyses from Passage G (OxA-8363-5) form a tight group with calibrated results at one standard deviation between AD 230 and 380. This is in accord with one of the samples (OxA-8340) from the block of scrap in Chamber A; although the other sample from this source (OxA-8341) gave a somewhat more recent result, there is overlap in the third and fourth centuries at two standard deviations. The single analysis obtained on a sample from the 1974 excavations (P-2314) is also in agreement with the others, although that obtained on burned bone from the floor of Chamber B (OxA-8984) is anomalously early. Paul Pettitt reports that the radiocarbon dates from the tomb, excluding OxA-8984, may be combined statistically to give a result of 1714 bp ± 17: when calibrated this indicates an overall range of AD 260 to 390 for the monument's construction and primary use, with the greater probability that the age falls late in this range, *i.e.* in the fourth century AD (see Fig. 109).

The specialised and idiosyncratic nature of the artefact assemblage from the tomb renders comparisons difficult. The most informative categories for this purpose are undoubtedly the pottery and the beads. Jacke Phillips and Michael Harlow have respectively noted the strong similarities with material from primary deposits in the Mausoleum, described below in Chapter 7. In the case of the pottery, there are indications that the Mausoleum assemblage could be slightly earlier than that from the Tomb of the Brick Arches (see pp. 194-6 and 456-7, below).

The artefacts themselves provide only limited chronological precision. The total absence of coins from the tomb may or may not be significant: gold and silver may have been removed by robbers, or the placement of coins in a tomb may not have been considered appropriate. The Aksumite coinage is generally believed to have begun *c*. AD 270 (Munro-Hay and Juel-Jensen 1995: 36-7) and coins from other sources are notoriously rare at Aksum. Dr Roger Schneider considers that the inscribed rondel from the Chamber-A hoard dates from the second half of the third century AD (Appendix IX). Richard Wilding (in Munro-

Hay 1989: 272) drew attention to the presence in the tomb of pottery vessels bearing applied disc-and-crescent symbols, paired in some cases with a cruciform appliqué: he suggested that the tomb dated from a transitional pagan-to-Christian period. No other symbols of recognisable religious significance were noted in the tomb. Although the formal adoption of Christianity at Aksum is believed to have taken place during the second quarter of the fourth century AD, there are indications of a Christian presence before that (Rufinus, cited by Munro-Hay 1997: 58).

Combining the lines of evidence summarised above, one is led to the conclusion that the construction of the Tomb of the Brick Arches and its use for interment dates to a comparatively brief period in the fourth century AD, perhaps in the third quarter of that century.

As argued above, very few artefacts if any seem to have been introduced to the tomb during the various robbing episodes; there is consequently no clear archaeological evidence for the date at which these episodes took place (but cf. p. 131, below).

Interments

Evidence has been cited above which suggests that Chamber D with its Loculi J and H may originally have housed a single interment with a wooden bier or coffin which was placed on the bench in Loculus J, Loculus H containing grave goods but no body, and

Laboratory number	Stratigraphy	Material	Uncalibrated age bp
OxA-8984	BB(15)	Charred bone	1925±50
OxA-8363	BG(15)	*Maytenus* charcoal	1725±35
OxA-8340	B/3\	*Ficus* charcoal	1705±45
OxA-8341	B/3\	*Acokanthera* charcoal	1655±40
OxA-8364	BG(9)d	*Ficus?* charcoal	1725±40
OxA-8365	BG(9)d	*Olea* charcoal	1750±35
P-2314	Chamber C	Charcoal not ident.	1680±80

If OxA-8984 is excluded as anomalously early, the remaining six age-determinations may be combined to provide an uncalibrated estimate of 1714±17 bp for the age of the Tomb of the Brick Arches.

Calibration of this combined result by means of the OxCal v. 3.5 programme provides the following values:

At 68.2% probability:
AD 260-280 (0.29)
AD 290-300 (0.02)
AD 320-390 (0.69)

At 95.4% probability:
AD 250-400 (1.00)

Fig. 109 *Radiocarbon dates from the Tomb of the Brick Arches.*

with Chamber D originally empty. The individual interred in Loculus J was an elderly woman approximately 1.58 m tall.

A second individual was interred in either Loculus E or F, probably the former. This was a middle-aged man, between 1.75 and 1.80 m tall, who had evidently been engaged at some stage of his life in carrying heavy loads.

The most economical interpretation of the other fragments which cannot be attributed to either individual noted above is that one further person had been buried in the tomb, of stature comparable with that of the man in Loculus E. Remains of this skeleton were mostly found scattered in Chamber B, while the 1974 discoveries of a skull near the foot of the adit and other fragments in Chamber A may also belong. It may be suggested, but cannot be proven, that the remains of this third person had originally been interred in Chamber C.

Evidence for a fourth individual is less conclusive. It rests primarily on the presence of the right femur of a comparatively small individual. Helen Cook considers that this femur, which was recovered in Chamber D, is unlikely to have belonged to the elderly woman of whom other remains were found in the same area.

The original disposition of the tomb contents is not easy to ascertain because of the extent of the subsequent robbing. Since material deposited in the course of Robbing 1 lay directly on the rock-cut floor of Chambers B and D and Passage G, it seems likely that grave goods were originally restricted to the loculi. There could thus have been a certain symmetry and order in the tomb's primary use, each pair of loculi housing an individual interment with the neighbouring loculus devoted to grave goods; the loculi were walled up and the main chambers left essentially empty. Despite the mixing brought about by repeated robbing and the concomitant removal of certain items, it is possible to recognise differences in the locations of some types of grave goods and to link these with the individuals with whom they were placed. The old lady in Loculus J was buried with a box of mirrors; hafted spears were placed in the adjacent Loculus H. The middle-aged man in Loculus E appears to have been accompanied by a much greater quantity and variety of grave goods, including the large ceremonial iron spearhead, objects covered respectively with ivory and bimetallic plaques and, probably, an ivory throne. Insufficient investigation has been undertaken in Chamber C to support conclusions about the interment there.

Grave goods
The archaeological materials recovered from the Tomb of the Brick Arches were noteworthy both for their

wealth and variety, but also for what was not present. Arguments have been presented above that items of gold and silver had for the most part been removed by robbers at an early stage. More striking is the absence of animal bone and almost all other food debris; a single grindstone was the only artefact which may have been specifically associated with the preparation of food. There were no flaked stone artefacts nor (with the possible exception of some of the knives) metal tools associated with agriculture or craft, such as were present in the GT II tomb which was excavated in 1974 in the Gudit Stelae Field (Munro-Hay 1989: 348). It must be concluded that the Tomb of the Brick Arches contained an artefact assemblage that was not only specifically funerary in character but which also reflected the status and activities of those who were interred there. There was no evidence that offerings of food were interred with the dead.

It seems likely that much of the pottery from the tomb was made specially to serve a funerary purpose. Very few vessels show signs of having been used. Much of it is elaborately decorated but poorly fired. The fugitive nature of the painted decoration suggests that these vessels were never intended to be used, but were produced as grave goods. Sizes are remarkably standardised, very large vessels being markedly absent although miniature forms are common. Some vessels represent types known only from funerary contexts. It may be doubted whether any of the vessels recovered from the tomb were actually intended to be used by the living. The total absence of imported pottery is also noteworthy. The question of the extent to which such a specialised assemblage should be regarded as characteristic of the Aksumite pottery that was in use at this particular time is addressed below (pp. 456-7 and 484).

Metal was present in substantial quantities. There were enough traces of gold and (largely debased) silver to indicate its former presence, although this may have been the prime focus of the robbers. The total absence of coins is noteworthy, since the tomb almost certainly dates from a period after the beginnings of Aksumite coinage: coins may not have been deemed appropriate grave goods, or coins formerly present may have been robbed. The differential preservation of components from the bimetallic plaques suggests that easily re-worked copper alloy may have been more attractive to the robbers than iron; nonetheless substantial numbers of copper alloy artefacts were recovered and may originally have been more plentiful than those of iron, although the quantity of iron removed from the tomb by robbers is not known. The assemblage of metal from the tomb indicates considerable expertise in casting, forging, cold-working, riveting, polishing, inlaying and plating. There were no metal objects recovered for which non-local manufacture is necessarily indicated.

The abundant ivory recovered from the tomb is of especial interest, very few objects of this material having been recovered from other Aksumite sites. There can be little doubt that the objects recovered were produced in Aksum, carving and turning being both attested, to high standards of artistry and technological competence. Ivory seems not to have been of interest to the robbers, perhaps both because of its commonness and because re-use or reworking were considered impracticable or inappropriate.

In the absence of imported pottery, and in view of the conclusion that the ivory and metal artefacts were locally made, the only items from the tomb for which a possible non-Aksumite origin needs to be considered are certain beads and glass vessels.

Lastly, it is necessary to consider - albeit inconclusively - the significance of the 38-kg mass of cuprous metal that had been buried in the pit in the floor of Chamber A. It appears to have been accumulated in layers, first broken pieces of three failed large and elaborate castings which have no parallels elsewhere; of none of the three items are all the pieces present. Above these was placed a mass of nails, rods and plates which formerly held glass inlay. Considerable effort was taken to fit the hoard into the smallest practicable space, by breaking the failed castings and tightly folding the plates. As already noted, the rondel may have been several decades old at the time the tomb was constructed; the same may be true of some or all of the hoard's other components. Very little non-cuprous material was included: no iron and only a few fragments from clay casting cores and the glass inlay. The usual archaeological interpretation of such a feature would be that it was a metal-worker's hoard of scrap, awaiting recycling. If this were the case, a tomb seems a strange place to deposit such a hoard in view of the difficulty or recovery. Placement under a wall and arch raises the possibility that the feature was in some way comparable with what is in other cultural contexts called a foundation deposit; this is a practice lacking other Aksumite attestation. No convincing explanation can be offered.

Robbing

The tomb appears to have been blocked after the final interment until the first robbing occurred. The floors of Chamber B, Passage G and Chamber D remained clear and free from inwash, debris from Robbing 1 being deposited directly on to the largely unworn floor. The rock from which this floor was cut is so soft that any significant use before it was covered with robbing debris would have resulted in clearly visible wear: no such wear was observed by the excavators.

The absence of intervening deposits might indicate that no great interval separated the date of the interments from that of the first robbing. In Robbing 1, artefacts including the big iron spear were extracted from Loculus E and strewn on the floor of Chamber B where they were subject to trampling and disturbance through subsequent episodes. The blocking of Loculus H was removed to the extent that was necessary to gain access; it may be assumed that some items of value were removed at this time, others being swept from the bench onto the floor, but the general impression is one of selectivity, perhaps haste. After Robbing 1 the first inwash of silt into the tomb took place. Robbing 2 was on a larger scale: much more material including the furniture components was extracted from loculi E and F into Chamber B, loculi H and J appear to have been ransacked. After a further interval, Robbing 3 and Robbing 4 may have concentrated their attentions in Loculi H and J (although this may be more apparent than real in view of the removal of the upper deposits from Chamber B in 1974), where walls were demolished and extensive pits dug in order to reach the already-ransacked artefact-bearing deposits beneath.

In contrast with the largely unworn rock-cut floor of the tomb itself, the treads of the steps in the adit show signs of significant use. All robbers entering and leaving the tomb must have done so by way of the adit. It seems unlikely that this was filled and re-excavated between each robbing episode, so it may have remained open, perhaps since the time of the original interments.

There is no clear evidence for the dates at which the various robbing episodes took place. It is argued below (pp. 481-2) that most ransacking of tombs in the Stelae Park took place in or after the seventh century, and this may have been the case also at the Tomb of the Brick Arches, indications of a substantial interval between deposition and robbing having been noted above. On the other hand, robbing at the Tomb of the Brick Arches, although repeated, was appreciably less thorough than at other tombs such as the Mausoleum (pp. 224-5) or the Tomb of the False Door (Munro-Hay 1989: 104-13).

Conclusion

The Tomb of the Brick Arches was used as the burial place of at least three individuals, including one elderly woman and one middle-aged man. No genetic testing having been undertaken, it is not possible to comment on their consanguinity. These individuals seem to have held broadly similar status: despite the evidence that he may have engaged in heavy labour, the male was accompanied by grave goods that were significantly more numerous and varied.

The date proposed for the tomb is broadly the same as that which is argued below for the principal storeyed stelae. Of the latter, Stela 1 and, probably, Stela 2, were markers of tombs with the magnificence of which the Tomb of the Brick Arches cannot compare. As argued below (p. 479), it is probable that the tombs marked by the storeyed stela were those of Aksumite kings. As noted below (pp. 480-1, cf. Fig. 416), the entrance to the Tomb of the Brick Arches lay just outside the boundary of the terrace which had already been demarcated as the area where the most elaborate burials took place. This tomb may have been used for the interment of individuals who, while clearly both prominent and wealthy, were not of the very highest rank.

No other Aksumite burial of comparable status has yet been found to retain so much of its original contents. Although the Tomb of the Brick Arches had been extensively robbed on at least four occasions, the depredations had been highly selective. Despite the wealth and variety of the tomb's contents, opportunities for comparison are thus severely restricted. The present Project has not investigated contemporary settlement sites and it is thus not easy to evaluate the extent to which the tomb's contents, particularly the pottery, are characteristic of the period, as opposed to a specialised funerary assemblage. In comparison with

later domestic assemblages, the absence of demonstrably imported artefacts (with the possible exception of some glass and beads) is striking. Unless such foreign items were for some cultural reason excluded from the burial assemblage or were particularly sought by the robbers, one may conclude that import of luxury goods into Aksum was mainly a development of later times. If that were the case, the local technological sophistication and expertise demonstrated by the tomb's contents, in metalwork, ivory carving and probably glass-working, not to mention the contemporary stone architecture displayed elsewhere, is all the more remarkable.

CONSERVATION
(D.W.P.)

In 1993 the collapsed western wall of the adit was reconstructed in Aksumite style and materials, to match the eastern wall. A watertight roof was erected over the adit, its height being kept to a minimum so that it does not intrude on the view of the area from outside the Stelae Park (Fig. 110).

At the end of each excavation season, with the approval of the Ethiopian authorities, the tomb was securely sealed by blocking the now-roofed adit at

Fig. 110 *Conservation measures at the Tomb of the Brick Arches: **a** - rebuilding the collapsed adit wall; **b** - roofing the adit; **c** - the adit roof completed.*

both ends. Arch I was closed with a double wall of concrete blocks and the entrance to the adit walled up and filled with earth. This served the double purpose of preventing unauthorised access and of preserving the unexcavated deposits within.

Despite its obvious interest, there are major difficulties to be resolved in making the Tomb of the Brick Arches accessible to visitors. There are potential dangers both to visitors and to the tomb itself. Regular access would quickly result in unacceptable wear to the soft rock of the tomb's floor. The roof is extremely friable and falls of decomposed rock are frequent: this process would accelerate if the tomb were kept open and allowed to dry out. The configuration of the tomb is such that reliable fume-less lighting is essential and that only a very small number of visitors could safely be accommodated at any one time; they would obviously need to be accompanied by an appropriate invigilator. Finally, the humidity and security of the unexcavated areas need to be maintained. In view of these difficulties, the authorities have taken the wise decision not to admit visitors to the tomb until such time as developments permit this to be done with safety.

Chapter 5

STELA 3
(D.W.P.)

Stela 3 is the only one of the great storeyed stelae of Aksum which still stands upright in its original position (Fig. 111). The investigations conducted by the 1993-7 Project were limited to visual inspection and evaluation of the monument's stability.

　　A detailed illustrated description of Stela 3 was published by the Deutsche Aksum-Expedition (Littmann *et al.* 1913, II: 20-2; D.W.Phillipson 1997: 26-32) and needs little augmentation. The present stepped configuration of its front and back baseplates, with the front one at a higher level, may or may not be original. Clearly, the underground features of the monument cannot be investigated by excavation without endangering its stability. Under conditions of

Fig. 111 Stela 3 from the southeast.

a

oblique sunlight which prevail in November/December for only 10 minutes each day, clear signs of divided tooling areas (Fig. 112b) are visible on the north face of the stela. Telescopic examination of the south side of the stela's apex revealed previously unrecorded details of the looped metal pegs which remain embedded in the stone, having presumably previously served to secure an inset (Fig. 112a). The possibility that such an inset may have resembled the cast brass rondel recovered from the Tomb of the Brick Arches is evaluated elsewhere (p. 100).

Stela 3 is not now perfectly vertical, but leaning to the north and to the east (Fig. 113). At first sight, the stela appears to lean at somewhat alarming angles; a view has sometimes been expressed that it is in danger of imminent collapse, and it has been suggested that consolidation work may be necessary in order to prevent this. In November and December 1993 detailed investigations were undertaken which sought to ascertain the precise extent of the stela's inclination, whether or not this was increasing, and whether there was danger of the stela falling. The methods adopted have been described elsewhere (D.W.Phillipson and Hobbs 1996), so only a summary of the conclusions is offered here.

A detailed survey was conducted by Douglas Hobbs, using a Wild T05 theodolite. This required a precise calculation of the stela's height, for which various figures had previously been published. It was decided that the most appropriate base from which to measure was the centre-point of the lower edge of the false door carved on the south face of the stela. Three independent sets of measurements were taken, giving results which differed by only 70 mm; this very close agreement suggests that the average figure of 20.57 m can be accepted for the height of Stela 3.

Theodolite measurements also indicate that the stela is inclined from the vertical by 1 degree 13 minutes northwards and by 2 degrees 6 minutes eastwards. These angles are significantly less than appears to the casual visitor, for the slope of the ground and displacement of the baseplate combine to provide an illusion of greater inclination. The ground on which the stela stands slopes down to the south at an average angle of some 5 degrees, which tends to magnify the monument's apparent northward tilt. Likewise, the front baseplate currently inclines downwards on its west side; it is approximately 3 degrees from the horizontal and this gives a visual impression that the stela is leaning more to the east than is actually the case. Elderly residents of Aksum confirm that the stela's inclination is not new, but that it has been noticed and commented upon over many years.

In 1906 the DAE took a photograph of Stela 3 from the east which shows very clearly its angle of northward inclination relative to Stela 21. This

b

Fig. 112 *Details of Stela 3: a - south side of apex, b - north face.*

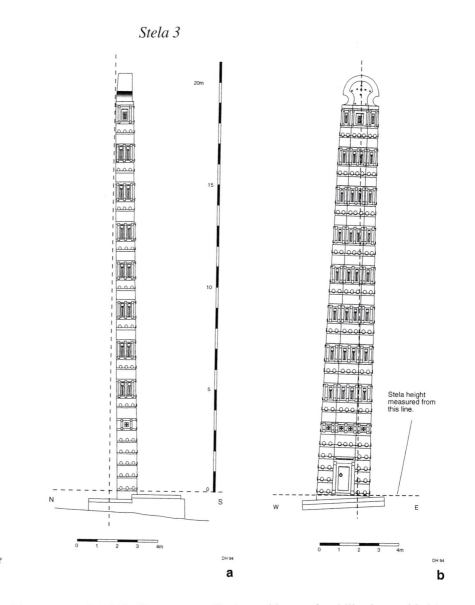

Fig. 113 *Present inclination of Stela 3: a - to the north, b - to the east.*

a

b

photograph, published by Littmann *et al.* (1913, II: fig. 40; see also D.W.Phillipson 1997: fig. 33), demonstrates that the two stelae diverged in 1906 at an angle of 4.5 degrees. Since Stelae 3 and 21 are widely separated, it is possible to ascertain very precisely the line on which the DAE photographer stood (D.W.Phillipson and Hobbs 1996: fig. 2). The exact position on the line from which the photograph was taken would make no difference to the apparent angle of divergence, only to the relative heights of the stelae as seen in the photograph. The 18-m distance between the two stelae also makes it highly unlikely that any movement of one would have affected the other. In 1992 a photograph was taken from a position on the fallen Stela 25 where it is intersected by the line on which the DAE photograph was taken. The 1906 and 1992 photographs (Fig. 114) show precisely the same angle of divergence between Stela 3 and Stela 21: 4.5 degrees. It may be concluded that there had been no perceptible change in the northward inclination of Stela 3 during the past 86 years.

Further evidence of stability is provided by the joints between Stela 3 and its front and back baseplates. These joints are cemented; and the various dates when the cement was inserted were ascertained from records and through local enquiry. The earliest known repair was in 1906, when the stone packing beneath the front baseplate was consolidated by the DAE; it was probably at about this time that the underpinning of the back baseplate was strengthened on the orders of Dejazmatch Gabra Selassie. An inscription - now poorly preserved - on the north face of the plinth records the latter event. Subsequently, in the early 1960s, further work was undertaken at the instigation of Ras Mengesha Seyoum: the steps to the south of the stela and the low castellated wall which surrounds it on the other three sides were all constructed at this time, while the joints between the stela itself and the front and back baseplates were carefully cemented. Examination of this work in 1993 showed no sign that any movement had taken place since the cement had been inserted; the joins are not strong enough for any movement on the part of the stela to have shifted the baseplates. Since the base of the stela is 2.7 m wide from east to west (cf. Fig. 113b), any increase in eastward lean would have been readily apparent.

It was concluded from these three independent lines of argument that there had been no perceptible increase in the inclination of Stela 3 since at least the 1960s, and probably for considerably longer. This gives rise to speculation whether in fact it was ever truly vertical. It has not been possible to locate documentary evidence older than that compiled by the DAE in 1906. The famous lithograph by Henry Salt (1809; reproduced in D.W.Phillipson 1998: fig. 9) is inconclusive in this respect, but the engraving by the same artist published by Viscount Valentia in 1809 appears to show an inclination similar to that seen today. We know that the ancient Aksumites experienced some difficulty with the erection of their larger stelae. Other than Stela 3 itself, all the nine stelae known to have exceeded 13.5 m in height have fallen. It is argued below (p. 223) that the largest of all was probably never successfully erected. It is plausible to suggest that Stela 3 has leant at the present angle ever since it was set up (see pp. 253-6, below, where this hypothesis is considered further).

The position of the stela's present centre of gravity was calculated, taking into account the stela's taper, but ignoring the length of stela which is below ground. The centre of gravity thus ascertained, projected vertically downwards, was found to lie comfortably within the base-area of the stela, which shows that the inclination is not such as to render the monument in imminent danger of falling. The fact that these calculations ignore the stabilising effect of the baseplates and of the stela foot being embedded in the ground provides a further, unquantifiable, safety-margin.

a   b

Fig. 114 *Stelae 3 and 21: **a** - in 1906 (after Littmann et al. 1913, II: fig. 40); **b** - in 1992.*

Chapter 6

THE STELA-2 SITE

*SUMMARY: The second-largest stela,
long fallen and broken, was removed to Rome in 1937.
Its original position has been located archaeologically
and exploratory excavation conducted in anticipation of its return from Italy.
Details of its massive substructure were revealed, together with evidence
that the stela had been intentionally toppled at some time in the past.*

INTRODUCTION
(D.W.P.)

The second-largest of the Aksum stelae was described with characteristic thoroughness by the Deutsche Aksum-Expedition (Littmann *et al.* 1913, II: 22-3; D.W.Phillipson 1997: 33-6), whose account and illustrations need not be repeated here. The stela was at that time lying on the ground, broken into five principal pieces. Like Stela 1, it was elaborately carved on all four sides. Only its undecorated front (southern) baseplate was preserved. The stela appeared to have had a total length of 24.6 m, of which 2.9 m had originally been set underground. Its cross-section at ground level measured 2.32 by 1.26 m and the original total weight of the monument may be calculated as having been approximately 170 tonnes. The position in which the fallen stela lay indicated that it had formerly stood on a virtually straight line between the bases of Stelae 1 and 3, somewhat closer to the latter than to the former. Stela 2 would have stood approximately 1.2 m higher than the adjacent and still-erect Stela 3, than which it was about 10 tonnes (6%) heavier.

In 1937, during the Italian occupation of Ethiopia, the five main pieces of Stela 2, together with the single extant baseplate, were taken to Rome on the personal orders of Mussolini (Monneret de Villard 1938). Elderly residents of Aksum still recall the original position of the supine stela, and the manner in which the Italian military secured its removal, Ethiopians being forcibly restricted from the area. In Rome, the monument was reassembled, missing pieces being reconstituted, and erected in the Piazza di Porta Capena. Some of the missing pieces were left behind in Aksum by the Italians. The fragment designated Stela 15 by the DAE and now preserved in the Cathedral precinct almost certainly falls into this category (D.W.Phillipson 1997: 49), as does a much smaller piece currently wedged under the front baseplate of Stela 3, in which position it may be discerned

in DAE photographs (D.W.Phillipson 1997: figs 34, 36). A worn fragment incorporated in the steps at the foot of the north wall of the Old Cathedral, noted by Ato Girma Elias (*pers. comm.*), may also be part of Stela 2. Other pieces were unearthed during the 1997 excavations, as recorded below (pp. 147, 149, 154-5).

During the half-century that has elapsed since the stela's removal, efforts have been made to secure its return. In 1997 it was announced that agreement on this matter had reached between the Ethiopian and Italian governments. At the time of writing (August 2000), however, the stela is still in Italy. Those involved in the negotiations and subsequent arrangements have undertaken detailed studies of the monument's transport to and re-erection in Italy: no attempt is made here to repeat or emulate those studies.

PRELIMINARY INVESTIGATIONS, 1993-4
(D.W.P.)

In 1993, before any conclusion had been reached concerning the return of Stela 2 to Ethiopia, the Project team made detailed studies of the plans that had been prepared by the DAE in 1906. This permitted the delineation of a 10 by 10 m square within which it was highly probable that the stela had originally stood (D.W.Phillipson 1994a: fig. 2). In 1994, under the supervision of Jenny Jones, a series of nine test trenches, designated S1-9, was laid out in this area. Six of the trenches were excavated, three of them being in due course joined to form a single L-shaped excavation, the total area opened being 30 sq. m (Fig. 20, above).

As work progressed, it became apparent that very extensive disturbance had taken place during the twentieth century. Like the surroundings of Stela 1, described below, the area had been covered with domestic buildings in 1906; these had been swept away in the course of landscaping during the 1960s. Removal of the stela in 1937 had also involved substantial disturbance. It was decided at the outset of the 1994 excavation that work would be limited to locating the original position of the stela, and that excavation would not be continued to a depth greater than was necessary to achieve this aim.

The topsoil over the areas investigated had apparently been deposited during the 1960s landscaping, and included lines of basalt blocks used at that time to produce miniature terraces and to delineate areas where hedges and shrubs were planted. Modern glass, china and metal were found, together with small amounts of redeposited Aksumite material. Below 0.15 m depth, increasing amounts of loosely packed stone rubble were encountered, of uneven size and density. Especially in the area of the L-shaped trench, this rubble was mixed with large quantities of broken twentieth-century bottle glass; there was also much animal bone and corroded metal of twentieth-century European type, including cans of the kind used for packaging food. There could be no doubt that this deposit dated from the time that Italian troops removed Stela 2, the rubble and artefacts being thrown into the resultant pit. A rough wall-like feature aligned slightly east of north in the western half of trench S5 appeared to represent the edge of this pit.

In the northern section of the L-shaped excavation was revealed an intact stela baseplate (Fig. 115), its overall dimensions being 2.02 by 1.54 m, and the indent to accommodate the stela-base 1.18 by 0.41 m. The position of this baseplate immediately below the topsoil, the fact that bottle glass was present beneath it, and the angle at which it lay extending into the Italian pit, all strongly suggested that it formed part of the backfill of the latter feature. From its size, there is no possibility that it had any original connection with Stela 2; rather it must have been installed at the foot of a stela comparable in size with Stela 12 which still stands, lacking baseplates, some 40 m to the north (cf. Fig. 20, above).

As removal of the pit-fill continued, a large stone slab was exposed at a depth between 2.2 and 2.4 m from the surface. Resting on it were broken pieces of a second slab. It was concluded that these stones probably formed the base and south side of the socket in which Stela 2 had originally been erected; since they were more fully exposed and more comprehensively investigated in 1997, they are not discussed further here. Traces of an ancient trench dug along the south side of the upper slab suggested that the stela had at some distant time been intentionally destabilised (D.W.Phillipson 1995a: 24-5). It was confirmed by this preliminary investigation that Stelae 3, 2 and

Fig. 115 Exploratory excavation of the Stela-2 site in 1994, showing displaced baseplate of a smaller stela and the slabs which formed the socket for Stela 2. Scale in 0.5-m divisions.

1 had been intended to stand in a virtually straight line, Stela 2 being 26 m from Stela 3 and 31.5 m from Stela 1.

The 1994 excavation did not seek to investigate the underlying layers. All artefacts from the 1994 excavation were originally processed and stored in the Museum at Aksum. In 1997 however, with the agreement of the Ethiopian authorities, uninventoried material from contexts which had suffered twentieth-century disturbance was discarded, retaining only a small number of representative examples for display purposes. Details of some of the artefacts recovered from the Stela-2 site in both 1994 and 1997 are presented on pp. 154-6, below.

At the end of the 1994 season, when the excavations were backfilled, the original position of the stela was marked on the surface of the ground by a simple cement plaque, inscribed in both English and Tigrinya, which generated considerable local interest. It was concluded that more detailed excavation of the site might prove exceptionally informative; and it was recommended to the Ethiopian authorities that thorough investigations should be conducted before any attempt was made to return the stela to its original place, should negotiations with Italy prove successful.

THE 1997 EXCAVATION
(Martin Watts)

The 1997 excavation was designed to investigate the original position of Stela 2 and any associated Aksumite or later features of archaeological significance in the immediate vicinity. It was undertaken at the request, and with the support, of CRCCH in anticipation of the return of the stela from Rome and its possible re-erection at Aksum. The immediate objective was to confirm the 1994 assessment of the stela's original location and to ascertain the nature of any surviving below-ground structures that may have been associated with it. It was anticipated that this information could then be used by the relevant authorities in reaching a decision as to whether it was desirable and practicable to re-erect Stela 2 on its original site.

The method and results of the excavation are summarised below, followed by a discussion of the results and their broader significance. A full context index with interpretative phasing is available in the Project Archive.

Methodology

The approximate position where the stela had stood, between Stelae 1 and 3, had been calculated from DAE records and confirmed by excavation in 1994, as described above. During the 1997 excavation, designated R, the principal L-shaped 1994 trench was cleared and enlarged, mainly to the south and east, attaining overall dimensions of 12.5 m from east to west and 9.0 m from north to south (Fig. 20, above). Deeper excavations were initially undertaken to the south and east of the 1994 trench, the two areas being separated by a baulk (Fig. 116a). Once natural deposits had been exposed in both areas, the baulk was removed, creating a single deeper excavation measuring 11.5 by 7 m. Excavation of deeply-cut features and intrusions then continued, reaching a maximum depth below modern ground level of 6.5 m in the northwest, 5.9 m in the southwest and 7.65 m in the northeast of the excavated area (Figs 116b, c).

All deposits were excavated manually using picks, shovels and trowels. Stratigraphic information was recorded on standardised single-context record sheets, with plans and sections drawn as appropriate at a scale of 1:20 (Figs 117, 118, 122). Site drawings were related to a grid based on permanent survey points within the Stelae Park, which had its point of origin to the southwest of the R excavation. All levels were related to the height of the permanent survey point close to the base of Stela 1, which was given an arbitrary value of 100 m, its true height being calculated as 2119.7 m above sea level.

All artefacts were cleaned as appropriate and summarily examined, chronological estimates being recorded where practicable. With the agreement of the Ethiopian authorities, all objects retrieved from deposits disturbed by the removal of the stela and later landscaping, excluding those entered into the inventory, were discarded after preliminary examination. All other artefacts are stored in the Aksum Museum compound; they have not been studied in detail.

Backfilling of the trench took place at the end of the excavation season in December 1997. At the request of the authorities the central and western areas of the trench, where the stela had formerly stood, were filled with stone rubble up to the level of the stela's basal slab. A dry stone wall was constructed to the east of this area, and the eastern third of the trench was completely backfilled. Since the 1997 excavation took place, further investigations have been initiated by CRCCH, including the removal of certain large stone features described below.

Results

The remains of two major Aksumite features were exposed in the excavation (Fig. 118). Lying centrally in the area of deeper excavation was a large subterranean structure, 6.0 m wide and extending beyond both the northern and southern edges of the excavation. Despite

Fig. 116 *The 1997
Stela-2 excavation:
a - an early stage, with
the baseplate discovered
in 1993 visible in the
right foreground: the
figure is standing in
trench 718, immediately
to the west of the stela
substructure; b - from
the southwest, showing
the slabs seen in 1993
(Fig. 115) fully exposed;
c - from the south,
showing the shaft.*

extensive later disturbance, it was clear that the stela had formerly stood directly over the northern end of this structure. Three components were recognised in the stela substructure and are described in detail below. The other major feature, a rock-cut shaft, was located to the east of the stela substructure. It extended beyond the northern edge of excavation and had also been disturbed by later activity. The shaft lay within a sunken area defined by the remains of two Aksumite walls on its south and south-west.

NATURAL DEPOSITS

Undisturbed subsoil was exposed on either side of the stela substructure, capped by a 0.4-m-thick layer of black clay at a depth of approximately 2.7 m below modern ground level. The earliest Aksumite surfaces directly overlay this black clay. To the west of the substructure the black clay sealed a substantial deposit of yellow clay at least 2.3 m thick, whereas to the east of the substructure it sealed multicoloured soft clayey bedrock. Where exposed in the side of the shaft, the interface between these two deposits was indistinct. Bedrock was also exposed at the eastern edge of the southern component of the stela substructure.

THE ROCK-CUT SHAFT

In the northeast corner of the excavated area (Figs 116c, 118) a shaft was encountered dug through the clayey bedrock to a depth of 7.65 m below the modern ground surface. Later robbing activity had truncated the entire top edge of the shaft (928), destroying all traces of its primary associations. However, it was clear that the shaft had been dug from the top of natural deposits, indicating that it was one of the earliest features investigated during this excavation.

At its top, the shaft measured at least 2.9 m from north to south, continuing beyond the northern limit of excavation, and just under 2.0 m from east to west at its southern end, narrowing to 1.5 m at the edge of the excavation. At a depth of 1.0 m, archaeological excavation of the shaft was stepped in by 1.0 m from the limit of excavation for reasons of safety. The shaft descended to a depth of 1.1 m with near-vertical edges. At this level a narrow ledge was located on the western side, narrowing the width of the shaft to 1.6 m. It was unclear whether this feature was part of the original shaft construction or resulted from later robbing activity, but a further 0.5 m of excavation revealed a second narrow ledge on the southern side of the shaft. Below this level the squared corners of the shaft gradually became more rounded. Although the eastern and southern edges continued downwards nearly vertically, the western edge was considerably undercut. The width of the shaft therefore gradually increased

with depth to form a 2.0-m-wide ovoid base, which sloped downwards from east to west at an angle of approximately 26 degrees. The deepest point was 5.45 m below the top of the bedrock. The sides of the shaft were generally smooth, with occasional unstable areas patched with stone. Its southeastern corner featured eight rock-cut niches (Fig. 119) between the base and ledge-level forming a crude series of irregular steps which would have provided access up the near-vertical face. There was no sign of a tunnel or other opening leading from the base of the western, southern or eastern side of the shaft; its northern side lay beyond the excavation area and was not exposed.

THE STELA SUBSTRUCTURE

Two huge stone slabs, (1014) and (1015), overlay and obscured the central component of the stela substructure. The slabs, exposed and recognised in 1994 (p. 140, above), had once formed part of the stela setting but had been displaced southwards when it fell (pp. 147-8, below). Details of the substructure were thus mainly exposed through the excavation of its construction trenches and of later robbing trenches to the south of these slabs. Further observations were made following the removal of natural deposits adjacent to the western edge of the substructure.

Remnants of a construction surface (1226) observed to the west of the substructure indicated, as with shaft (928), that it too had been built from the top of natural deposits. The remains of the substructure comprised at least three distinct types of construction, described here from south to north as the southern and central components and the stela podium itself.

The southern component

This comprised a compact rubble construction (1242) overlain by a layer of large boulders (1037) with more compact rubble above (1026, 1038, 1049). It extended beyond the southern limit of excavation. The western edge of the southern component had a neat uncoursed face, clearly built from a wide construction trench (730) to the west. Its base was located approximately 2.8 m below the top of the natural deposits.

The boulder layer was exposed across the entire width of the substructure, at an average depth of 1.4 m below the top of the natural subsoil. Although its upper surface was irregular (Fig. 120a), limited excavation of later robber trenches (718, 1040) showed that its lower surface was flat. Much of the primary construction over the boulder layer had been subject to later disturbance. The backfill of construction trench (730) comprised several layers of redeposited clay, which had also been disturbed by later robbing.

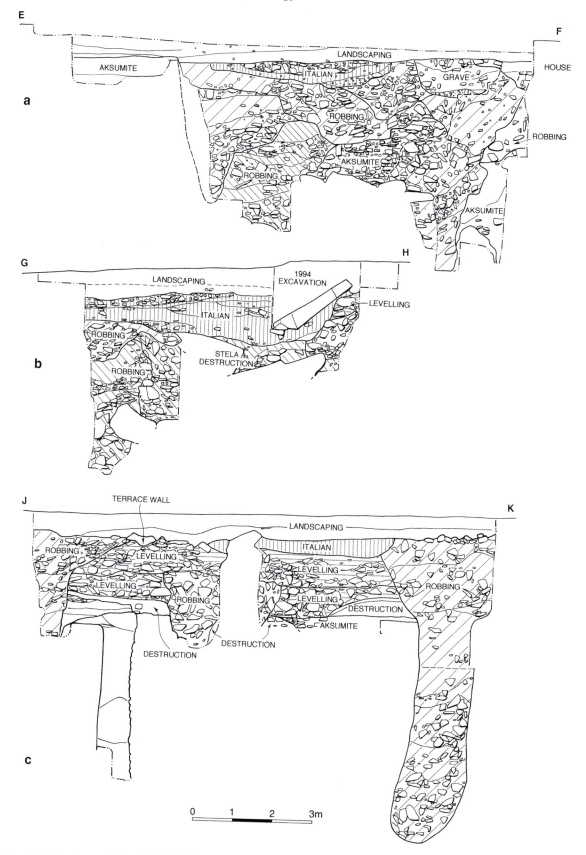

Fig. 117 *Sections of the 1997 Stela-2 excavation: **a** - south face; **b** - south-north section through the centre of the excavation; **c** - north face. The locations of these sections are marked on the plan at Fig. 122.*

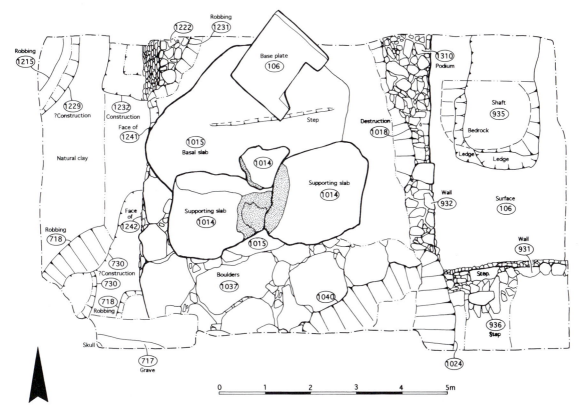

Fig. 118 *Plan of the 1997 Stela-2 excavation: Aksumite features.*

The central component

Due to the extent of later truncation, observations of the central component were only possible after the top of its western face had been freed from contiguous natural clay. The presence of this clay indicated that this part of the substructure had been built up from within. The upper 0.35 m of a rough stone component (1241) was observed, slightly set back from the southern component but abutting it and continuing the same alignment northwards. This was overlain by 0.4 m of soft grey clay (1245) containing several large stones that appeared to have been disturbed by later activity, being considerably less compact than the contemporary components to the south and north.

The stela podium

This northern component was by far the best preserved of the three, surviving to just above the top of the natural deposits on either side of the substructure and extending beyond the northern limit of excavation. Although slabs (1014) and (1015) had been displaced, it was clear that the northern component had formed a masonry podium on which the stela had originally stood. Like its southern counterpart, the western side of the podium was accompanied by a construction trench (1232), excavation of which exposed over 4.0 m of neatly-faced masonry without reaching its base.

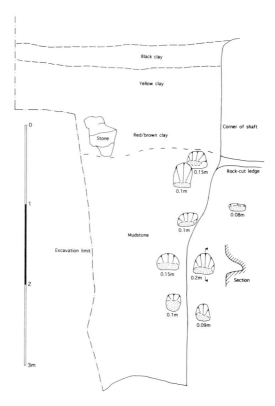

Fig. 119 *The east wall of the shaft exposed in the Stela-2 excavation.*

The western side of the podium had been built in at least four horizontal bands of rubble masonry (1222, 1238, 1239, 1240) of which the second (1239) abutted the central component and continued its alignment northwards (Fig. 120b). Although the western face had clearly been built from within construction trench (1232), the eastern side of the podium (1310) completely filled its construction trench (1319), and appeared to continue southwards to overlie the central component. Excavation to confirm this was prevented by the presence of overlying structures.

Close observation of the northern section revealed that the backfilling of construction trench (1232) with layers of redeposited clay (1233, 1236, 1237) had occurred in stages, as successive bands of masonry were completed. Once trench (1232) was completely backfilled, further layers were deposited (1221, 1224, 1247), spreading westwards over the natural black clay. To the east of the substructure, mortar surfaces (916, 1046, 1312) overlay the black clay.

OTHER AKSUMITE CONSTRUCTION

Although the stratigraphical relationship between the stela substructure and the shaft (928) was uncertain, the two terrace walls (931, 932) which defined the sunken area framing the shaft were clearly later than

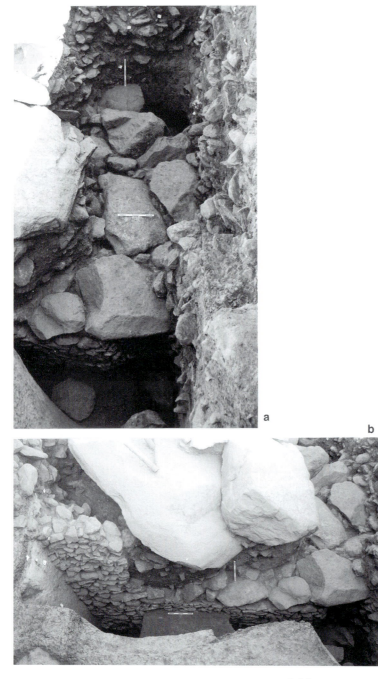

Fig. 120 *The Stela-2 substructure: **a** - boulder layer over the southern component; **b** - the western face. Scales: 0.5 m.*

146

the sub-structure. Wall (931), with a step at its western end, was built within a shallow trench (933) partly cutting surface (916). To the south of wall (931), the foundations of a second step (936) were exposed within a levelling layer of redeposited bedrock (912). Although the northern part of wall (932) was lost to later truncation, rubble (1045) associated with its surviving southern end sealed both surface (1046) and rubble (1038), part of the actual substructure.

Abutting the substructure to the west, a broad shallow trench (1227), of unknown function but cutting through layer (1247), was exposed. Further to the west, a second, deeper trench (1229) was observed in the northwestern corner of the excavation. The presence of a large robber trench (1215) within it suggests that trench (1229) may have been connected with an Aksumite structure lying immediately to the west of the excavation. The continuation beyond the western limit of excavation of construction trench (730), associated with the southern component of the stela substructure, may likewise indicate the presence of another Aksumite structure in this location.

The final episode of Aksumite activity appears to have been the infilling of shaft (928) and trenches (1227) and (1229), followed by further deposition which raised ground level on either side of the stela position. The infilling of trench (1229) with redeposited clay was followed by the deposition of clay and rubble layers which also infilled trench (1227). A compacted surface (1260) was then formed over these deposits, 0.6 m above the top of the natural.

Although shaft (928) had been extensively cleared by later robbing, at least one of its fills (925) appeared to be original. Within the sunken area, at least one deposit (909) survived from the original infill over the shaft.

EARLY ROBBING

With the exception of the southeastern corner, evidence of post-Aksumite disturbance was virtually continuous across the area excavated; differentiation between various phases of disturbance was hindered by the similarity of these various rubble deposits. However, at least one robbing episode clearly predated the destruction of the stela (see below). A large robber trench (1040), in the southeastern corner of the stela substructure, cut down through the Aksumite rubble (1038, 1049) and boulder layer (1037) of its southern component. Robber trench (1040), which extended beyond the southern limit of excavation, was filled with numerous rubble and clay layers prior to further disturbance of the Aksumite features.

DESTRUCTION OF THE STELA

Much of the disturbance to the stela substructure was caused by the excavation of a deep trench (1018), clearly intended to destabilise Stela 2. The upper part of this trench cut down through the Aksumite deposits on either side of the stela, reducing the height of the podium to just above the level of the natural subsoil (Fig. 121). To the south of the podium, trench (1018) dived sharply to a depth of 1.7 m, removing the upper part of the substructure's central component and truncating much of the rubble lying over the boulder layer of its southern component. At its southern extremity it also truncated the fill of robber trench (1040).

The remains of two syenite slabs (1014, 1015) lay within trench (1018). The lower of the two, slab (1015), measured *c.* 4.5 m in both length and width and was at least 0.5 m thick. It sloped downwards from north to south at an angle of 20 degrees. Its upper face had been dressed (cf. pp. 256-68, below) to form two flat surfaces separated by a north-facing shallow step 40 mm deep and extending for 2.7 m from east to west. The broken remains of the upper slab (1014) measured 4.2 m by 2.0 m, being *c.* 0.7 m in maximum thickness.

From their locations within trench (1018), it was clear that slab (1014) had originally supported the southern side of the stela, with slab (1015) acting as a basal foundation. The shallow step would appear to mark the original location of the southern edge of the stela on slab (1015). Originally, slab (1015) lay flat over the stela substructure, Stela 2 stood over the northern part of slab (1015) and slab (1014) was placed on edge over the centre of slab (1015), immediately adjacent to and supporting the southern side of the stela (Fig. 121). Once the stability of the stela had been undermined, slab (1015) tipped into trench (1018), and slab (1014) fell onto its side, crushed and broken beneath the weight of the falling stela. On the western side of trench (1018), a large stone (1228) appeared to have been pushed into adjacent deposits by the force of this event, a small part of it being broken beneath the weight of slab (1015).

Many splinters of slab (1014) were recovered from deposits filling the southern end of trench (1018). Several of these splinters, and one of the main slab fragments, bore quarrying wedge-marks. All of the lower fills of trench (1018) contained large quantities of stone rubble that probably fell into the trench during the destruction of the stela. Compact powdery deposits (1246, 1309) lying over the truncated remains of the stela podium probably represent demolition debris from the dismantling of masonry surrounding the stela base, of which no *in situ* remains were observed.

The deposition of further rubble layers filled trench (1018) to the top of the natural subsoil. Two fragments of the actual stela were recovered from these deposits (pp. 154-5, below). The uppermost fill

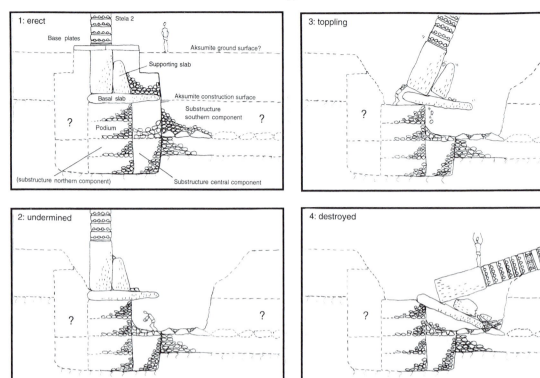

Fig. 121 *How Stela 2 was toppled.*

(1011), and a thin layer (1314) sealing demolition debris (1309), both appeared to be colluvial.

LEVELLING AND SECONDARY ROBBING

Further infilling around the remains of Stela 2 followed, with the deposition of carefully laid, compacted rubble (1044, 1217, 1218, 1316), filling trench (1018) by a further 1.4 m. A compacted surface (710) at this level suggested that a sunken area was created around the base of the fallen stela within trench (1018), some 1.5 m below the contemporary ground level. A small number of glass beads was recovered from surface (710). In the southeastern corner of the excavation, surface (908) may also have been formed at this time following some truncation of the Aksumite deposits.

A second robbing episode took place from the level of surface (710). A robber trench (1231 and 1318) was recorded to either side of the baseplate (106) that was left *in situ* within the backfill of trench (1013) (see p. 140, above and p. 150, below). Trench (1231/1318) was filled to the level of surface (710) before further infilling took place around the fallen stela.

Evidence of another robber trench was provided by its compacted clay fill (734) in the southwestern corner of the excavation. Later robbing (718) had removed all evidence of its primary associations, but the level of its fill (734) indicated that it was broadly contemporary with robber trench (1231/1318).

FURTHER LEVELLING AND EXTENSIVE ROBBING

Another deposit of carefully laid compacted rubble (708, 1042, 1311, 1315) further filled trench (1018) to *c.* 2 m above the top of the natural deposits or *c.* 0.9 m below the contemporaneous ground level. Although this was only recorded in the northern half of trench (1018), it may have been more widespread, but later robbing had removed any trace of it to the south. The compacted rubble was overlain by another layer of apparent colluvium (1317).

Extensive robbing then took place, with a further seven robber trenches in evidence across the excavated area. In the northeastern corner a deep robber trench (935) appeared to have emptied virtually all the primary fill from shaft (928): artefacts recovered from its numerous fills included ornate fragments of decorated glass and part of a crucible made of copper alloy.

Further robbing also followed over the southern end of the stela substructure. Two intersecting robber trenches (1051, 1024) truncated the fills of robber trench (1040). Further disturbance of the substructure's southern component occurred when another deep robber trench (718) was cut down through the Aksumite construction trench (730) in the southwestern corner of the excavation. Having reached the base of construction trench (730), it undercut boulder layer (1037) truncating the rubble face of construction (1242).

Disturbed human skeletal remains were noted in the section through the lower fills of robber trench (718), while its upper fill yielded another fragment of Stela 2. Yet another robber trench (737) was recorded in the southern section. All these robber trenches extended southwards beyond the area excavated.

A large robber trench (1215) in the extreme northwestern corner of the excavation had removed almost the entire primary fill of the Aksumite construction trench (1229). The upper fills of trenches (1215) and (718) appeared to be continuous, suggesting contemporaneity. In the northeastern corner of the excavation, further robbing of shaft (928) may have been attempted (robber trench 914), although this feature could have been caused by compaction and sinking of the fills of robber trench (935).

LATE BURIAL AND TERRACES

The features of more recent date noted in the 1997 excavations are shown in Fig. 122, with the exception of the only grave (717) that was encountered; this cut into the backfill of robber trench (718) in the southwestern corner of the excavation, approximately 1.3 m below modern ground level. It was left *in situ* by the expedient of re-aligning the southern limit of excavation 0.5 m to the north.

Two terrace walls (204, 205), broadly contemporary with the burial, had been constructed over the infilled robber trenches in the western half of the excavation. Wall (204), which extended beyond the northern limit of the excavation, had been truncated by later house construction; wall (205) had been truncated by both house construction and the trench dug in 1937 to remove the remains of Stela 2 (see below). Twentieth-century landscaping, probably in the 1960s, had truncated the tops of both walls.

THE ROUND HOUSE

At the western end of the excavation, the remains of a round stone-built house were exposed (Fig. 123). Subsequent landscaping had truncated this structure, but wall foundations survived within a construction trench (404) that cut through both earlier terrace walls and the top of grave (717). The foundations of the curved outer wall (203) survived around the edge of trench (404), which also contained a number of levelling deposits.

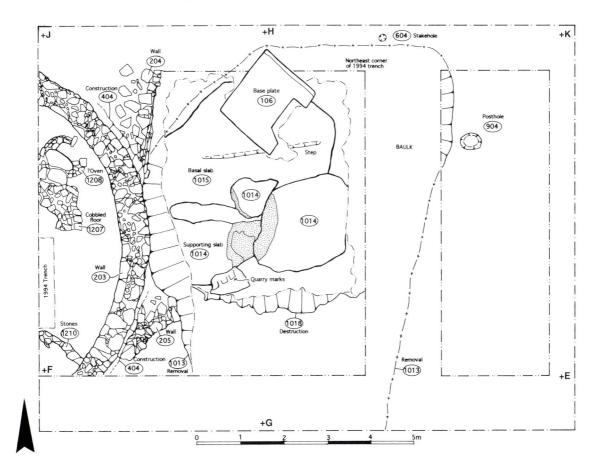

Fig. 122 *Plan of the 1997 Stela-2 excavation: Post-Aksumite features, showing locations of the sections presented in Fig. 117.*

Fig. 123 *The recent round house exposed in the western part of the 1997 Stela-2 excavation. Scale: 0.5 m.*

Some evidence survived for the internal arrangement of the house. The remains of a cobbled floor (1207) abutted the remains of a sunken oven-like structure (1208). At the southern end of the house an alignment of stones (1210) may represent an internal wall, perhaps associated with the entrance. Thin burnt layers overlay both the floor and the oven.

REMOVAL OF STELA 2

The trench excavated in 1937 for the removal of Stela 2 (1013) was readily distinguished by the large quantities of broken beer-bottle glass in its backfill (cf. pp. 155-6, below). This broad trench lay immediately to the east of the round-house remains and continued beyond the southern edge of the excavation. The northern end of trench (1013), which lay just within the limit of excavation, contained the stela baseplate (106) encountered in 1994 and described on p. 140, above; it had clearly been pushed into the open trench (1013) after the remains of Stela 2 had been removed. A posthole (904) and a stakehole (604) to the northeast of trench (1013) may represent a structure or structures used to lift the stela sections from the ground.

LANDSCAPING AND ARCHAEOLOGICAL ACTIVITY

The modern ground surface within the Stelae Park was created in the 1960s when the area was extensively landscaped (p. 30, above). The uppermost 0.5 m of deposits across the entire excavated area were derived from this activity, which also caused widespread truncation of features lying close to the surface. Two of the backfilled 1994 trenches were encountered: the L-shaped trench was entirely re-excavated, and the eastern edge of the southwestern trench S7 was exposed in the western edge of the 1997 excavation.

Dating

Of the 245 contexts recorded, 116 yielded assemblages of artefacts, predominantly pottery. Although it has not been studied in detail, all the pottery retrieved from the *in situ* remains of the substructure and from the original fill of the shaft may be attributed on typological grounds to the third and fourth centuries AD.

Deposits from all subsequent phases up to the episode of major robbing produced remarkably similar pottery assemblages with varying quantities and proportions of Classical Aksumite material and sherds of Late Aksumite date. The earliest deposit to contain exclusively post-Aksumite pottery was the backfill of robber trench (1024), although the subsequent robber trench (718) again yielded only Aksumite potsherds, presumably redeposited. Further finds of post-Aksumite pottery were made from robber trench (737), feature (914) and deposits associated with the round house. Deposits associated with twentieth-century events all yielded modern artefacts, notably fragments of Italian bottles, mixed with redeposited material of earlier origin.

Discussion

AKSUMITE

Despite the truncated nature of the remains it is evident that all the Aksumite constructions exposed during excavation had once formed a suite of interconnected features and that these probably belonged to an elaborate funerary complex. Although no actual burial chamber or tomb was located, there were strong indications that such structures may lie immediately beyond the limit of excavation to the northeast, south and west.

The principal feature exposed in the excavation was the substructure of Stela 2, overlain by the remains of the actual stela setting. When erect, Stela 2 marked the position of one or more subterranean, presumably funerary, features which were located just outside the excavation area.

Natural deposits

By chance, Stela 2 was erected over a geological discontinuity. Below a uniform layer of black clay, the natural subsoil differed on either side of the substructure. The substructure was built in a deep construction trench, chiselled out from bedrock to the east but dug in softer yellow clay to the west. This difference probably accounts for the presence of associated construction trenches to the west but not the east. It may also account for the different type of burial structures found on either side of the Stela-2 site within the Stelae Park, as argued further below (p. 480).

The shaft

In 1974, preliminary investigations were undertaken of a number of rock-cut shafts, each between 7 and 8 m deep, located to the north of Stela 3 and to the northeast of the Stela-2 site (Munro-Hay 1989: 69, 78-83, 91-4, 155-6, fig. 6.24). At the base of each shaft was at least one tunnel leading to a complex of rock-cut burial chambers or catacombs. Sketches made at the time indicate that one branch of these catacombs extended towards the location of the Stela 2 excavation. The catacombs have been incompletely investigated but are known to contain artefacts, apparently disturbed by robbers, suggesting a funerary purpose (D.W.Phillipson 1997: 187).

Shaft (928), from which fragments of prestige artefacts such as decorated glass, a metal crucible and high-status pottery were recovered, was undoubtedly another of these features. The absence of a tunnel leading from any of the three sides that were exposed strongly implies the presence of one at its northern side, in all likelihood leading to a rock-cut chamber lying to the east of the Stela-2 position just beyond the northern edge of the 1997 excavation. It is

possible that such a chamber was entered in 1974 at the end of the southwestern branch of catacombs (Shaft Tomb C), although the presence of a shaft in that location was not recorded during the brief survey then conducted.

Stela 2

Although no *in situ* traces remained of Stela 2 itself, it has been possible to deduce its original position in relation to the remains of the substructure. It is clear that slab (1015) had acted as a basal foundation for the stela, with slab (1014) having originally supported the stela on the south and the shallow step having delineated the southern edge of its base. It was also clear that both these slabs had been displaced southwards from their original position over the podium.

In their original position, when the erect stela and the supporting slab (1014) both rested on the basal slab (1015), the latter would have projected a further 1.75 m to the south of slab (1014). This distance approximates to the width of the central component of the stela substructure (Fig. 118, above). Furthermore, there was no evidence of the earliest Aksumite surface (1046), which was probably contemporary with the construction of the substructure and the erection of the stela, overlying either the central component or the podium. It is thus possible to propose with some certainty the original configuration of the overall structure: both the stela and the supporting slab originally lay directly on the podium, with the southern limits of both the basal slab and the central component coinciding with the northern limit of the surviving Aksumite construction-surface.

The central component thus appears to have been directly associated with the stela position. Its precise purpose is unclear, but it may have been associated with the successful erection of the stela rather than providing structural support once it was upright.

Although the northern end of the podium was not exposed, a reasonable estimate of its full extent may be made. From DAE records (D.W.Phillipson 1997: 33-6) it is evident that Stela 2, with a thickness of 1.26 m, would not have projected beyond the northern limit of the basal slab. In the absence of evidence for a northern supporting slab, it may be postulated that the northern limit of the podium coincided with that of the basal slab. There may have been further construction similar to the central component to the north of the podium; certainly the rear baseplate of the stela would have projected beyond the postulated northern limit of the podium, and was probably supported by further substructure masonry, as shown in Fig. 121, above.

The proposed reconstruction of the stela arrangement shows the southern component of the stela substructure to have served no obvious structural function, yet it was built within the same construction trench apparently before the stela was erected. Although no evidence of a burial chamber was uncovered, it is possible that this component represents the northern extremity of an Aksumite tomb marked by Stela 2. All the robber trenches truncating the southern component of the stela substructure continued beyond the southern edge of excavation, and robber trench (718), which appeared to burrow beneath the boulder layer, contained human skeletal remains. Furthermore, the construction of the burial chamber prior to erection of its associated stela appears to be paralleled in the case of Stela 1, which probably fell during erection, the Mausoleum being already effectively complete (cf. pp. 221-5, below).

It thus appears likely that a tomb lay beyond the southern edge of the 1997 excavation, the boulder layer perhaps representing either its northern edge, or packing material in a deep construction trench common to both the stela substructure and the tomb itself.

Other Aksumite constructions

No stratigraphy survived to indicate the sequential relationship between the stela substructure and the shaft (928). However, the walls framing the shaft and the Aksumite construction trench at the western limit of excavation both clearly post-dated the substructure. The walls defined a sunken area which was reached using stone-built steps in its southern wall; the steps may have remained in use for some time before the area was infilled.

The purpose of the western construction trench is unclear. Located within the yellow clay, it is probably not another shaft and may represent the eastern limit of tombs associated with Stela 1. Although the Mausoleum has been largely excavated (Chapter 7, below) the extent of its easterly counterpart, the East Tomb, remains unknown. If the East Tomb were symmetrical with the Mausoleum, its eastern end would lie just to the west of the Stela-2 excavations.

Aksumite ground level

Later robbing and extensive 1960s landscaping appear to have removed all evidence of the original Aksumite ground surface within the area of excavation. Although the surviving Stela 2 baseplate is undecorated, it is clear that baseplates generally were exposed to view. While it is possible that they were originally set on raised pedestals, akin to the modern configuration of Stela 3, it seems much more likely that the Aksumite ground surface was somewhat higher than its modern counterpart and that the baseplates lay at or just above ground level. Furthermore, the level of the present ground surface, a result of the 1960s landscaping,

approximates to that shown in the 1906 DAE photographs (*e.g.* D.W.Phillipson 1997: fig. 31). The eroded nature of the 1906 ground surface may also indicate the former presence of ground level *c*. 0.5 m higher than the present one.

Aksumite surfaces recorded during the excavation were probably temporary, used only during the various construction phases. However, the remains of terrace walls to the east of the substructure suggest that surface (916/1312) may have had longer use, perhaps at the base of an adit leading down to the shaft. It was partly re-exposed during destruction of the stela, coinciding with the truncation level of the stela podium. Another Aksumite construction surface (1260), near the western edge of the excavation, appears to have been re-exposed prior to post-Aksumite levelling and may have been within a similar adit leading to a structure immediately west of the excavation. This structure may have been the East Tomb associated with Stela 1, discussed on pp. 219-21, below.

Chronology

Although the shaft is stratigraphically isolated, the sequence of construction for the other Aksumite features seems clear. The southern component preceded the stela podium, which was followed by the sunken area around the shaft and by further construction to the west. On current evidence from the 1997 and previous investigations (Munro-Hay 1989), the chronological relationship between the catacombs and the three giant stelae remains unclear. However, if construction trench (1229) is indeed related to the East Tomb, the erection of Stela 2 must have preceded construction of the subterranean funerary monuments associated with Stela 1 (cf. p. 478, below).

POST-AKSUMITE
Robbing, levelling and destruction

The earliest robber trench recorded (1040) truncated the eastern half of the exposed southern component of the stela substructure, and represents the beginning of a period during which Stela 2 was destroyed and the tombs of the Aksumite élite were repeatedly broken into and robbed. This period may have begun after the waning of Aksumite power from the seventh century AD, and appears to have lasted for several centuries.

The toppling of Stela 2 was clearly a deliberate act involving extensive truncation of the stela substructure, and occurred after the first robber trench had been infilled. When the stela fell, it and its associated slabs must have slipped southwards by at least 1.0 m before tipping into the destruction trench. This movement is reflected by the location of stone (1228), which was pushed laterally into the soft clay edge of the destruction trench before the basal slab tipped and broke it. It is unclear why the southern edge of this destruction trench appears undercut, but this may have resulted from the impact of flying splinters from slab (1014) when the stela was toppled.

At least two attempts were made to remodel the site following the destruction of the stela, suggesting periods of relative calm in post-Aksumite times. The first of these appears to have focused on infilling the destruction trench up to the level of the basal slab of the fallen stela, where surface (710) was established. Some truncation of deposits may also have occurred to the east with the formation of surface (908) which lay at approximately the same height as surface (710).

Further robbing occurred to the north of the fallen stela before the next levelling episode was undertaken. The location of this robber trench over the stela podium is curious, and suggests that the robbers were unsure of the location of the associated Aksumite tombs. Secondary infilling of the destruction trench seems also to have involved the robber trench to the north of the stela base. Accumulations of hillwash over these infill deposits suggest that it was some time before further robbing took place.

Later robbing disturbance was extensive, providing evidence of the likely location of Aksumite burial structures outside the area of excavation (see above). The shaft was located and virtually emptied, as was the Aksumite construction trench to the west of the substructure. However, the majority of these late robber trenches concentrated on the substructure's southern component, where at least three episodes were attested. Each of these robber trenches appeared to have been deliberately infilled, suggesting that, at least by some sectors of the community, the area was still regarded with respect.

Chronology

The post-Aksumite sequence indicates that the various episodes of levelling and robbing occurred over a considerable time. However, although datable pottery assemblages were recovered from many post-Aksumite deposits, there are several reasons why it is not possible to assign an absolute chronology to these events.

Firstly, as many of these deposits comprised similar soil and rubble, differentiation between them during excavation was exceedingly difficult; discrete robber trenches could often only be identified in section. This inevitably led during excavation to some contamination of earlier deposits with later pottery. Secondly, a post-Aksumite pottery chronology has not yet been established (p. 458, below), and many of the deposits produced remarkably similar assemblages, with late material mixed with redeposited Aksumite pottery.

RECENT

Burial and round house

Re-use of the site for burial was demonstrated by grave (717), which cut through the fills of robber trenches in the southwestern corner of the excavation. The nature and alignment of the burial strongly suggest that it was Christian. It may have been associated with the burial ground excavated in the 1950s some 30 m to the southwest in the vicinity of Nefas Mawcha, which probably dated between the mid-seventeenth and early nineteenth centuries AD (de Contenson 1959). The absence of further graves in the 1997 excavation area suggests that it lay in the extreme northeastern corner of the burial area which may have been delineated in this direction by the fallen Stela 2.

When the DAE visited Aksum in 1906, the remains of Stela 2 were enclosed within a walled compound, with two traditional round stone-built houses located to the east of the stela (D.W.Phillipson 1997: fig. 12). The truncated remains of one of these houses were partly exposed in the western half of the excavation, overlying the late burial noted above. The house was probably built in the mid- to late nineteenth century, and appears to have been still standing when the stela was removed in 1937, as the trench dug by the Italians at that time respected its outer wall.

Commentary

The 1997 excavation revealed remains of a large and complex structure comprising at least three distinct types of construction, overlain by the remains of two huge stone slabs which originally held Stela 2 erect. It is likely that the two northern substructure components were directly associated with the original position of Stela 2, just within the northern limit of the excavation. Aksumite ground level appears then to have been about 0.5 m higher than it is today.

There was clear evidence that Stela 2 had been deliberately toppled in post-Aksumite times. This provides a striking parallel for the widespread tradition, first recorded by Salt (in Valentia 1809, III: 98), that the stelae were cast down by Queen Gudit late in the tenth century (cf. Trimingham 1952: 52-3).

No direct evidence of any associated tombs was exposed. However, the presence of a rock-cut shaft to the east of the substructure implies the presence of an underground burial chamber immediately to the northeast of the excavation area. The top of this shaft lay some 3 m below the Aksumite ground level, at the base of a stone-built adit with stepped access on its southern side. The southern substructure component, with no obvious structural function relating to Stela 2, may be the northern edge of another burial chamber

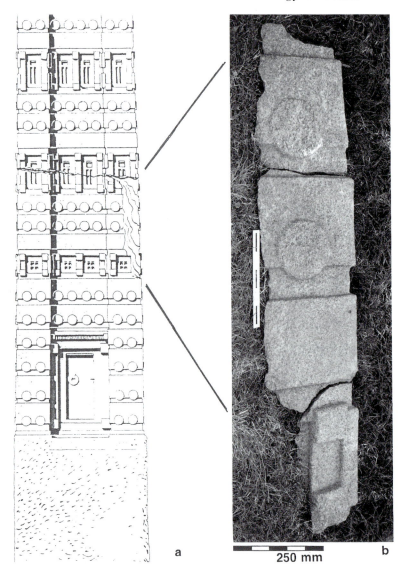

a

250 mm

b

Fig. 124 *Stela 2:*
a - drawing by D.
Krencker in 1906
showing the splinter then
missing (after Littmann
et al. 1913, II: pl. vii);
b - the splinter
recovered in three
pieces during the 1997
excavations.

built within the same construction trench as the stela substructure. A later Aksumite construction trench to the west of the substructure may represent the eastern extent of a tomb associated with Stela 1.

Further work is required if the objectives of the excavation are to be fully realised. Extension of the excavation to the north might expose more of the stela podium and *in situ* evidence of the precise original setting of the stela. Excavation of the northern part of the shaft is likely to confirm the presence and precise location of any associated rock-cut burial chambers. Extension to the south would enable the southern substructure component to be more fully investigated, and may confirm the presence of a burial structure. Extension to the west would similarly confirm the nature of any burial chamber in that direction, and may determine the eastern limit of the tomb known to exist to the east of Stela 1.

ARTEFACTS FROM THE 1994 AND 1997 EXCAVATIONS
(D.W.P. and Martin Watts)

Artefacts from these excavations have not been examined in detail, the 1994 work having been exploratory and largely restricted to disturbed areas, and that in 1997 conducted under severe time-constraints. This section therefore merely draws attention to a few items of particular interest.

Stela fragments
The 1997 excavation revealed three fragments of carved syenite which originally formed part of Stela 2 (Fig. 124b). The contexts from which they came are noted above (pp. 147, 149). The three pieces fit together to form a single large splinter, *c.* 1.7 m long, which had

formed the northwestern corner of the stela as it originally stood, extending from the lowest to the next lowest line of windows, as shown in Fig. 124a. The scar formed by the detachment of this splinter is clearly shown in the DAE drawing (D.W.Phillipson 1997: fig. 41; cf. Fig. 124a). Evidence from these long-buried and relatively unweathered fragments for the stone-working techniques that were employed is discussed on pp. 262-7, below.

Intaglio

In 1994, the uppermost undisturbed levels yielded an intaglio depicting two clasped hands (Fig. 125a). It is carved from a variegated orange, white and purple stone, probably chert. Photographs have been examined by Dr Martin Henig (Institute of Archaeology, University of Oxford). The clasped hands motif was commonly used on Roman rings of the first three centuries AD which are generally interpreted as marriage rings (*e.g.* Henig and Whiting 1987: nos. 314-5; Henig 1990: nos. 50-1; Zwierlein-Diehl 1991: nos. 2036-45). In the eastern Mediterranean, as at Alexandria, the use of such rings seems to have continued longer than it did in the west (Buckton 1994: 47). This is, however, not the only occurrence of the motif in Roman art: it was also used during the first three centuries AD as a reverse type on the imperial coinage, usually symbolising military or political concord rather than matrimony. Dr Henig notes that the Aksum specimen shows two features for which he is unable to suggest any parallels. First, it appears not to have been a ring bezel, but to have been pierced vertically, perhaps for suspension, either directly by means of a cord or to receive a metal plug to which a loop

10 mm

10 mm

10 mm

30 mm

Fig. 125 *Artefacts from the Stela-2 excavation:* **a** *- intaglio with clasped hands;* **b** *- inlaid glass fragment;* **c** *- Venetian gold coin;* **d** *- Italian beer bottles.*

may have been attached. Secondly, all known Roman examples show the forearms truncated, whereas on the Aksum specimen they run off the edge of the stone. These observations, together with the fact that the type of stone appears to differ from those usually employed for such purposes in the circum-Mediterranean world, lead Dr Henig to suggest (*in litt.* August 1998) that 'although there may be influence from the Roman marriage type, the stone is an individual creation by a local gem-cutter'.

Coins

The five Aksumite coins recovered, all from disturbed contexts, are noted in Appendix V.

A context which had been disturbed by recent landscaping yielded a Venetian gold ducat (Fig. 125c), struck under Ludovico Manin (1789-97), the last doge.[25] The coin has twin perforations, made by piercing from the obverse rather than by drilling. This implies that, at least latterly, it was used as adornment rather than circulated as currency.

Glass

Two fragments of fine glass with inlaid cobalt blue squares (Fig. 125b) are almost certainly derived from the same object. One of them came from a disturbed context in 1994, the other being recovered in 1997 from the fill of the Aksumite shaft.

The most recent levels yielded large quantities of broken bottle glass, mostly derived from beer-bottles bearing embossed designs and inscriptions indicating production in Trieste during the 1930s. Representative pieces, clearly left by the Italian soldiers who removed Stela 2 in 1937, are shown in Fig. 125d.

ARCHAEOBOTANY

(Sheila Boardman)

Three bulk soil samples were collected from the hearth and floor of the round house. The charred seeds and fruits include oat, finger millet, teff, barley, bread wheat, emmer, noog and cress. A single fruit of

[25] The coin has been examined by Professor Wolfgang Hahn, and photographs of it by Professor Philip Grierson. The coin is a regular issue, not one of the common imitations (Ives and Grierson 1954). Professor Hahn has kindly drawn to our attention references (summarised by Pankhurst 1990) for the presence of such coins in Tigray and adjacent regions during the early nineteenth century.

Ethiopian buckthorn (*Rhamnus prinoides*), or *gesho* was identified: the leaves of this evergreen shrub are today widely collected and used in the preparation of beer.

OVERVIEW

(D.W.P. and Martin Watts)

Detailed examination of the Stela 2 site did not form part of the 1993 Research Strategy. Once the original location of the stela had been located by trial excavation in 1994, intense local and national interest was aroused. Following progress in negotiations with Italy for the monument's repatriation, the Project was asked in 1997 to conduct a more intensive investigation.

It was not possible during the limited time at the Project's disposal to excavate the stela location totally. Enough was done, however, to indicate the nature of the substructure, its approximate date, the manner in which the stela had been supported and its likely association with one or more monumental tombs. Fragments of the stela itself were located, and clear evidence was obtained that the monument had at some distant time been intentionally destabilised.

The Project had been asked by the Ethiopian authorities to pay particular attention to ascertaining whether it would be desirable or practicable to re-erect the stela in its original position. It rapidly became clear that such a development would inevitably involve destruction of associated archaeological materials of considerable interest and importance. A further factor requiring investigation is the proximity of the underground tomb-chambers or 'catacombs' recorded in 1974 (Munro-Hay 1989: 78-100 and fig. 6.24). It is known that these extend very close to the Stela-2 site, but their precise location has not been ascertained. It is very probable that the shaft discovered in 1997 only 3 m northeast of the stela position leads into this subterranean complex, which incorporates major voids. The danger of subsidence, which could endanger the stability of Stela 3, needs to be fully evaluated.

The Ethiopian authorities have been advised that, while the 1997 excavations should be regarded as preliminary, they have provided a clear picture of the dangers inherent in attempting to re-erect the stela in its original position, together with guidelines for future investigation. It is understood that further work was undertaken on the site at the instigation of CRCCH during 1998 and 1999.

Chapter 7

THE COMPLEX OF MONUMENTS ASSOCIATED WITH STELA 1

SUMMARY: The largest of the Aksumite stelae,
probably never successfully erected,
was intended to mark two elaborate monumental tombs,
only one of which appears to have been completed and put to its intended use.
The archaeological evidence is difficult to interpret,
but it seems that the complex was originally built in the fourth century AD,
abandoned when the stela fell, and subsequently extensively robbed.

The present configuration of the Stela-1 complex
(D.W.P.)

The monumental complex which includes the largest of the Aksumite stelae is located close to the western end of the present Stelae Park (Fig. 20, above). Today, the readily visible features other than the fallen Stela 1 itself, which is described below, are the terrace wall (now reconstructed) over which the stela broke when it fell and the lowered area immediately to the west of the stela in which are several carved or dressed stones including a slab with a rectangular aperture resembling a doorway. This lowered area is reached by means of modern steps and a passageway which leads under the stela, permitting a view of the false door carved on

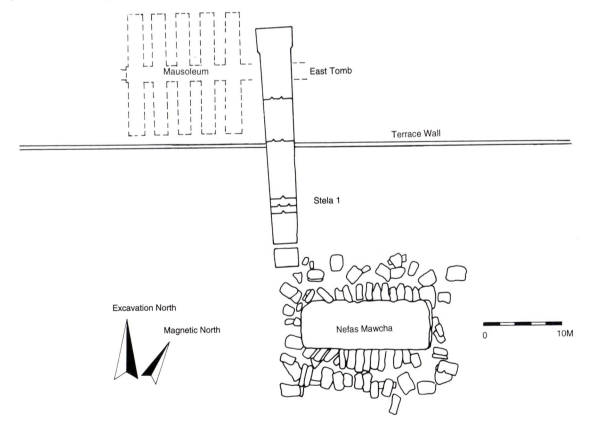

Fig. 126 *Plan of the Stela-1 area including Nefas Mawcha.*

Fig. 127 *Stela 1 and Nefas Mawcha:* ***a*** *- from the south;* ***b*** *- from the east.*

what is now its lower face. The southern end of the fallen stela (formerly its apex) lies adjacent to the megalithic structure known as Nefas Mawcha. The inter-relationship of these features may be seen in the plan (Fig. 126) and the photographs (Fig. 127).

Much of this modern configuration is misleading, having been developed in recent times particularly when the modern Stelae Park was laid out during the 1960s. Photographs and plans prepared by the 1906 Deutsche Aksum-Expedition (Littmann *et al.* 1913; D.W.Phillipson 1997: 13, 37-43) show the former position of walls and houses surrounding and in some cases overlying the stela. The DAE appears to have undertaken some clearance below the stela in the area of the present passageway, the actual configuration of which dates, however, to the 1960s. In 1906 the badly ruined terrace wall was much obscured; it was exposed during excavations in 1956 (Leclant 1959) and subsequently reconstructed in Aksumite style following the original alignment. The lowered area to the west of the fallen Stela 1 (Fig. 128) is apparently part of the 1960s landscaping operation, inspired by construction of the stepped passageway under the stela and by the discovery of carved stonework during levelling and the removal of recent houses. The slab with the rectangular aperture, noted above, was found recumbent close to its original position (Fig. 154 and pp. 177-8, below). Its present vertical setting has no archaeological justification and is almost certainly misleading. The original associations of the other carved stones currently set in this area are not known; at least one of them was probably brought to the Stelae Park from elsewhere in modern times, and the positions of several others have been adjusted since 1974. The steps leading down beside the terrace wall to the area immediately west of Nefas Mawcha were also constructed in the 1960s. The stone revetments surrounding the lowered area likewise date from that time, except for the rectangular extension on the west side which was constructed in 1993 to protect a shaft leading to the underlying Mausoleum.

Nefas Mawcha itself has not been a focus of study under the Project here described, other than for details of the stone-dressing and construction techniques that were employed by its makers (see Chapter 9, below). Its architectural form has been discussed elsewhere (Munro-Hay 1989: 116-20; Lewcock in Munro-Hay 1989: 165-7; D.W.Phillipson 1997: 68-71, 189-90). This monument covers an area some 23 by 16 m overall, comprising a rectangular central chamber, presumably funerary in purpose, surrounded on three sides by a passage. The central chamber was covered with a single huge capstone, weighing about 360 tonnes, which rested on top of the passage roof slabs. The capstone is very carefully dressed on the underside but

Fig. 128 *The lowered area west of Stela 1, seen during the excavation from atop the fallen stela. The three stone-lined trenches in the foreground lead to the Mausoleum shafts; trench M6 (with ladder) is visible in the background.*

still uneven and apparently unfinished on the top and edges. This suggests that some of the working was done *in situ*. Its unfinished state could be due either to a decision to cover the structure with earth rather than finely finish areas which would be hidden, or to the interruption of work on Nefas Mawcha when it was hit and ruined by the falling Stela 1. In any event, it is clear that Nefas Mawcha was in place but not completed before Stela 1 collapsed, and that no attempt was made to repair it subsequently.

The area surrounding Nefas Mawcha was excavated under the auspices of the Ethiopian Institute of Archaeology in four annual field seasons 1954-7, successively directed by J. Doresse, P. Pironin, J. Leclant and H. de Contenson (Leclant 1959; de Contenson 1959). A considerable length of the ruined terrace wall (designated M1) was exposed: its condition may be seen in the photographs published by Leclant (1959: pls v, viia). During this work, the southernmost

Fig. 129 *Stela 1 from the southwest, showing fractures.*

surviving fragments of Stela 1, smashed in antiquity through impact with the northwestern corner of Nefas Mawcha, were investigated. It appeared that some of these fragments were overlain by deposits containing coins of the late-fourth-century king Ouazebas (de Contenson 1959: 29-32). If this observation is correct, it might imply that the fall of Stela 1 (and the destruction of Nefas Mawcha) had already taken place by that time, as proposed by de Contenson. The date and circumstances of Stela 1's collapse are considered in

greater detail below. Subsequently, the area between Nefas Mawcha and the terrace wall, east of Stela 1, was used as a cemetery (Leclant 1959). Recent use of the Stelae Park area is discussed in Appendix XII.

The 1973-4 excavations revealed important additional information (Munro-Hay 1989: 74-6, 100-2, 104). The presence of two major tombs was established, providing invaluable guidance for the work of 1993-5 described below. Excavation was also conducted next to the foot of Stela 1, revealing the existence

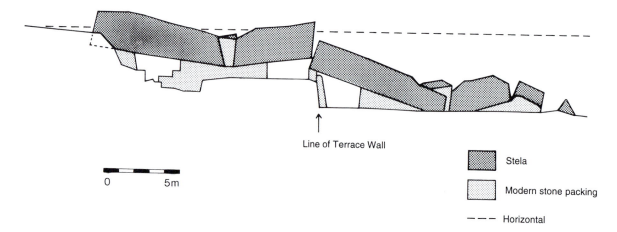

Line of Terrace Wall

0   5m

■ Stela

▨ Modern stone packing

– – – Horizontal

Fig. 130 *Section along Stela 1.*

of a wall extending from east to west approximately 1.5 m north of the stela foot; there was rubble packing against the northern face of this wall which was interpreted as having formed the northern end of a sunken court giving access to the Mausoleum and East Tomb. This wall was traced to a depth of 6.8 m below the modern surface, but its base was not encountered. Evidence for the original configuration of the area is discussed on pp. 220-3, below.

The present position in which the stela fragments lie permits certain conclusions to be drawn concerning the configuration of the area at the time of its fall. The terrace wall must have been already in place, for the fracture between the second and third main stela pieces (counting from its northern end, originally intended as the base) coincides with the line of the wall. The dip at the break between the first and second pieces shows that the ground at this point was either lower than the top of the terrace wall or not fully consolidated. The lowered court between the entrances to the Mausoleum and East Tomb (see Fig. 202, below) must have been largely or completely filled before the stela fell. The area to the south of the terrace wall and north of the west end of Nefas Mawcha could not have been much higher than it is at present. The photographs (Figs 127b, 129, 132) and section (Fig. 130) which are reproduced here serve to make these points and inter-relationships clear.

Stela 1
(D.W.P.)

Stela 1 is probably the largest single block of stone which people have ever attempted to put into an upright position. Although its apex was shattered through impact with Nefas Mawcha and cannot now be reconstructed with certainty, comparison with the intact apices of other stelae suggests that the monument was originally intended to stand at least 29.8 m high which, with the addition of 2.8 m intended to be set in the ground, gives a total length of about 32.6 m. Wildly different estimates of its weight have been published (Munro-Hay 1991: 136). In fact, if the above length-estimate is accepted, direct measurements and calculation of the specific gravity of the syenite permit a mass of 517 tonnes to be proposed with reasonable certainty.

It is clear, as may be seen from the roughly trimmed area shown in Fig. 131 that only 2.8 m of the stela, 8.5% of its total length, was intended to be set in the ground. The loose stony rubble in which the stela was to be erected would have provided much less support than a rock-cut socket. Indeed, it will be argued below that Stela 1 was never successfully erected, but that it fell and broke whilst the attempt was being made to set it up (cf. pp. 222, 252-4).

The most detailed record and reconstruction of Stela 1 remain those prepared by D. Krencker for the Deutsche Aksum-Expedition (Littmann *et al.* 1913, II: 24-7; D.W.Phillipson 1997: 37-43, fig. 52). It may be noted, however, that Krencker's drawings tend to minimise the irregularities in the carving such as

Fig. 131 *The base of Stela 1, seen from the east. Scale: 0.5 m.*

Fig. 132 *The view southward along the top of the fallen Stela 1, towards Nefas Mawcha.*

those which may be discerned in Fig. 132. The more fanciful reconstructions published by the DAE (*e.g.* Littmann *et al.* 1913, II: pl. x) include features for which there is no extant evidence. These include the row of dentils over the southern false door, and the shape and crescent-and-disc decoration of the apex; baseplates likewise, although essential to hold the stela vertical had this position ever been attained, do not survive.

Stela 1 is carved on all four faces in representation of a 13-storey building. Although broken by its fall, virtually all the pieces remain except for the very

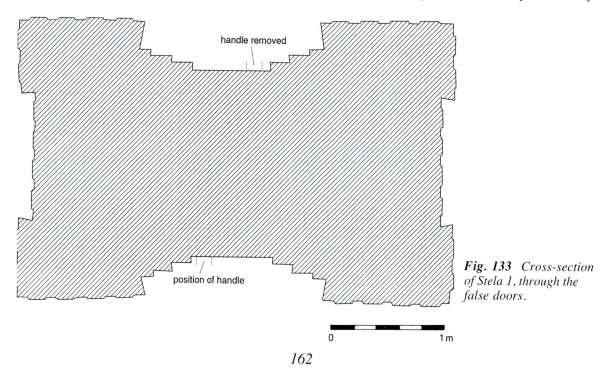

Fig. 133 *Cross-section of Stela 1, through the false doors.*

top which was presumably shattered by its impact with Nefas Mawcha. The rows of bosses, conventionally known as monkey heads, represent the ends of wooden beams. The indentations on each side of the stela are deliberately undercut (Fig. 133), a sophistication which causes the strong Aksum sunlight to throw double shadows and which enhances the apparent relief of the carved surfaces. The representations of windows on some upper storeys contain elaborate tracery of a type for which almost identical parallels may be found in later Ethiopian ecclesiastical architecture (*e.g.* Matthews and Mordini 1959: fig. 11; D.W.Phillipson 1998: fig. 54). At the foot of the stela, both front and back, are false doors; that on the former south - now lower - surface retains its finely carved handle (Fig. 134). Despite the apparent overall regularity of the design, close examination reveals numerous minor inconsistencies in its execution: the cross-section for example is slightly skewed, and many of the windows are imperfectly aligned. This suggests that layout was essentially by eye, rather than by measurement. (Carving, stone dressing and methods of stela erection are further discussed in Chapter 9, below.)

Stela 1 was carved with false doors on its northern and southern faces. That on the southern side would have faced the associated tombs and the direction from which it may be assumed that the monument was intended primarily to be viewed. Following the stela's fall this southern face became the underside and the carving on it was obscured from view. Excavation by the DAE early this century revealed the southern false door and its finely carved handle (Fig. 134). In contrast, as noted by Littmann *et al.* (1913, II: 26), the handle from the upper - originally northern - false door had been carefully chipped away (Fig. 135). The patination of the scar shows that this must have been done in ancient times, and serves to explain why this feature has not been more widely remarked. This upper false door would, of course, have been the one that was still visible after the stela's collapse. After that disaster the requirement to symbolise a method of entry may no longer have been deemed appropriate and the means of attaining it therefore removed.

There is increasing evidence (p. 220, below) to support the view that the stela was never successfully set upright, but that it fell and broke whilst in process of erection. The long-term significance of this catastrophic event is discussed elsewhere (D.W.Phillipson 1994a, 1997: 95-111; see also pp. 477-80, below). This, the largest of all the Aksumite stelae, was originally intended to serve as a marker for two monumental underground tombs. It represents the apogée of a very long and widespread tradition (D.W.Phillipson 1997: 95). Arguments are presented below that the

Fig. 134 *The lower (formerly southern) false door of Stela 1: **a** - general view; **b** - handle.*

complex was constructed in the fourth century AD. It appears increasingly likely that the fall of Stela 1, broadly coinciding with the adoption of Christianity at Aksum, led to the abandonment of the use of large, elaborately carved monumental stelae as markers of élite graves.

100 mm

Fig. 135 *The upper (formerly northern) false door of Stela 1, and (**b**) the scar where its handle has been removed.*

The Mausoleum

STRUCTURE
(Michael Harlow and D.W.P.)

It was known from the 1974 excavations that major tombs survived on either side of Stela 1 (Fig. 136). That on the west side, designated the Mausoleum by Chittick (1974), was fully investigated in 1993-5 under the supervision of Michael Harlow, who had acted in the same capacity during excavations in the Stelae Park two decades earlier.

In 1974, trench ST XIII was excavated along the northern end of Stela 1 to the north of the modern

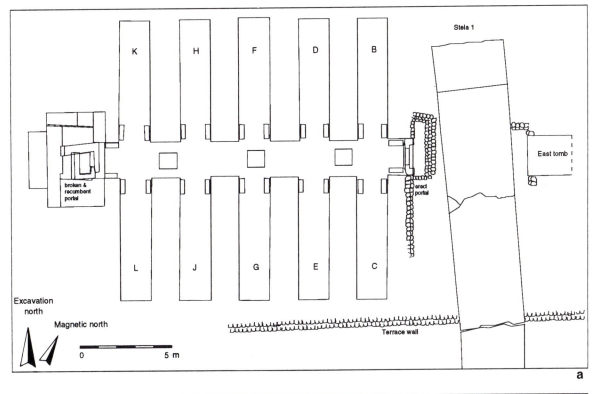

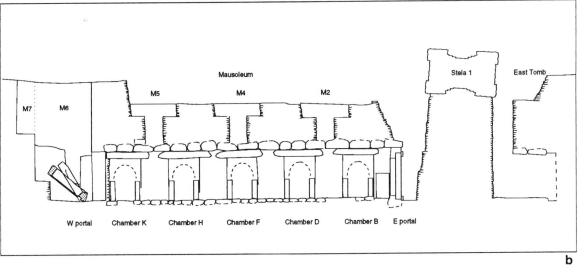

Fig. 136 *Plan and section of the Mausoleum and East Tomb.*

Fig. 137 The eastern portal of the Mausoleum. Scale: 0.5 m.

east-west retaining wall which had been constructed during landscaping of the main Stelae Park in the 1960s. Trench ST XXIV, in which the Mausoleum's eastern entry-portal was exposed, was excavated immediately to the south of the wall adjoining the north-west corner of the stela base. The portal was found to be blocked with accumulated deposit, but what was later recognised as the eastern vertical roof-shaft of the Mausoleum was revealed in the centre of the trench. This allowed relatively easy access to the narrow space between the underside of the roofing blocks and the top of the accumulated deposit within. The upper surface of the roof slabs over the northwestern corner of

the Mausoleum (sidechamber K) were also exposed in trench ST XXVII. It was thus possible to obtain rough measurements of the interior of the structure and to prepare a plan (Munro-Hay 1989: 75-7, 100-02, 104). When the Mausoleum was re-entered in 1993, there was no sign that any disturbance had taken place during the intervening nineteen years.

The east portal

Excavation in 1993 re-exposed the tomb's monumental eastern portal, carved from a single slab of nepheline syenite (Figs 137, 138) at least 2.55 m tall by 1.93 m wide. The portal is carefully dressed on its

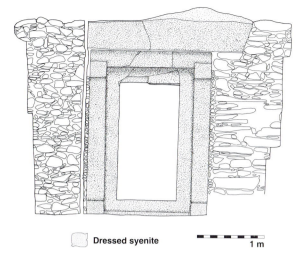

Dressed syenite

1 m

Fig. 138 *Photogrammetry of the Mausoleum's eastern portal.*

Fig. 139 *A view westwards along the central passage of the Mausoleum.*

a

b

c

Fig. 140 *Inner faces of the Mausoleum entrances:
a, b - the inner face of the eastern portal,
showing the upright syenite slabs which
formerly supported a brick arch; **c** - the
western arch as exposed, before excavation
of the deposits with which it was blocked.
Scales: 0.5 m.*

chamber D west side

Sidechamber D north end

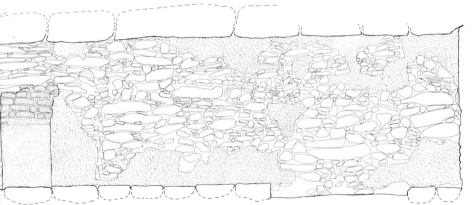

Sidechamber E east side

Sidechamber E south end

er

1   2m

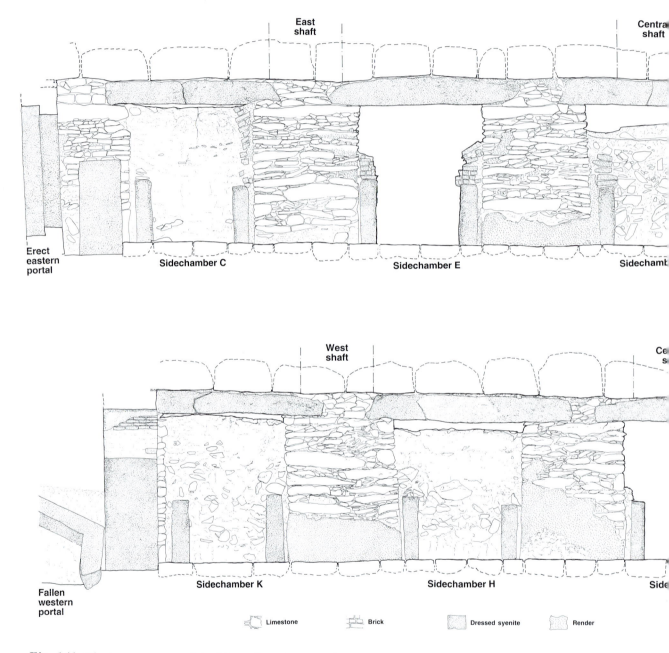

Fig. 141 *Photogrammetry of the Mausoleum's central passage.*

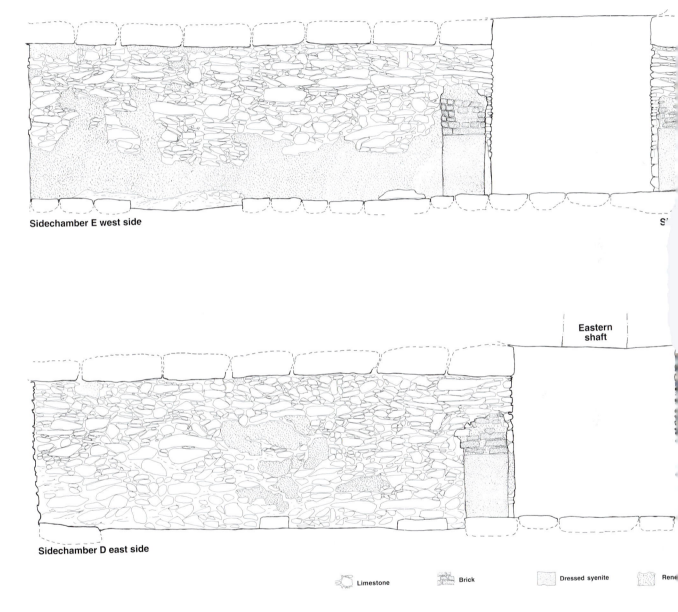

Sidechamber E west side

Eastern shaft

Sidechamber D east side

Limestone   Brick   Dressed syenite   Ren

Fig. 142 *Photogrammetry of Mausoleum sidechambers D and E.*

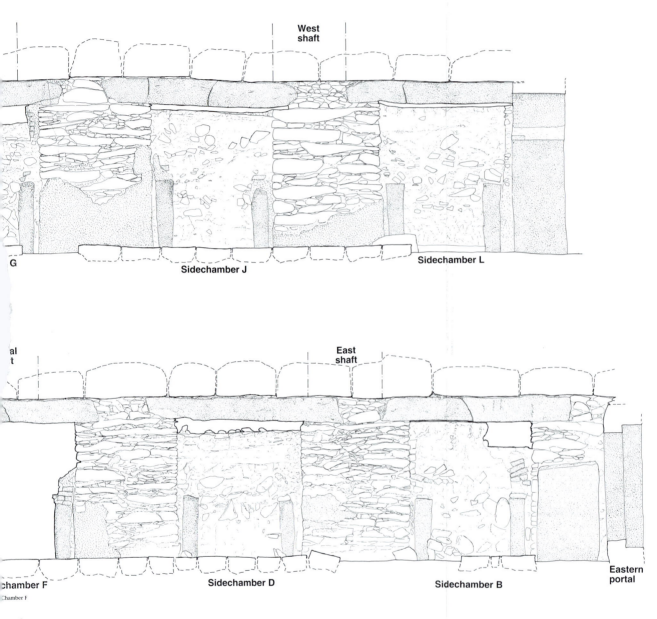

West
shaft

G   Sidechamber J   Sidechamber L

East
shaft

al
t

chamber F   Sidechamber D   Sidechamber B   Eastern
portal

Chamber F

0
1   2m

Fig. 143 *Inside the Mausoleum after excavation:* **a** *- an oblique view in the central passage, from the southeast, showing the sidechambers opening to the north;* **b** *- the view from the northern end of sidechamber D, looking across the central passage into sidechamber E. Scales: 0.5 m.*

outer surface in the same form as the false doors carved on Stela 1 except that the aperture is open and, being 1.79 m high and 0.94 m wide, larger than those represented on the stela. The inner (west) surface of the portal is only roughly trimmed, having originally been virtually obscured by a brick arch which, it will be argued below, formerly abutted it. Wedging of small packing stones on either side of the portal, clearly seen in Figs 137 and 138, indicates that the east wall of the Mausoleum was built first, leaving an aperture some 2.1 m wide into which the portal-slab was inserted. The virtually identical western portal is described below (pp. 174-5).

The central passage
The portal leads into a passage, 16.7 m long and 1.9 m wide, its walls built of undressed and poorly sorted stones set in mud mortar, and its roof spanned by a series of seventeen massive dressed transverse slabs of nepheline syenite between 0.7 and 1.2 m wide. The passage (Figs 139, 141, 143a) has a ceiling height of 2.3 m, and its floor is 5.9 m below the modern ground surface. At its western end, it leads to a brick arch set upon large blocks of dressed syenite (Fig. 140c). The arch has an interior width of 1.53 m and rises 0.69 m above its supporting slabs, giving a total height of 2.04 m above the floor. It is likely that a similar arch was originally located immediately inside the eastern portal; the brickwork has not survived *in situ*, but the stone slabs from which it sprang have suffered only minor displacement (Figs 140a, b).

The sidechambers
On each side of the central passage are five sidechambers, ten in all, each between 6.3 and 6.6 m long and between 1.7 and 1.9 m wide (Figs 142, 143). The sidechambers were designated B to L (omitting I), starting from the northeast and proceeding westwards on alternate sides of the passage, as shown in Fig. 136, above. They vary between 1.85 and 1.95 m in height, their ceilings aligning with large syenite lintels at their entrances on which rest the ends of the transverse ceiling slabs spanning the central passage. These lintels, set into the passage walls, average some 2.9 m long and 0.42 m thick; all were cracked in antiquity except those over the entrances to sidechambers D and E. Four of the sidechambers (D, E, F and K) were totally excavated, as was part of J. Excavation of sidechambers D and E revealed a complete north-south section of the Mausoleum (Figs 142, 143b).

The entrance to each sidechamber is flanked by a pair of rectangular syenite blocks which range from 0.80 to 0.86 m high above the paving, 0.70 to 0.74 m wide and 0.20 to 0.24 m thick. Most of these blocks retain at least some remnants of the brick

arches that originally rested on them, notably those of sidechamber E and the eastern side of G (D.W.Phillipson 1994: fig. 21). The bricks were set in lime mortar, unlike the adjacent stonework, which was mud-bonded (Figs 144a, b). Although apparently shaped with the use of mould boards, the bricks show little standardisation in size: three complete examples are rectangular, measuring 79 by 128 by 173 mm, 63 by 125 by 134 mm and 55 by 147 by 255 mm. The arches appear to have been 1.0 to 1.1 m in interior width at their bases and about 0.7 to 0.8 m high above their supporting slabs, relatively low and flat but otherwise having a horseshoe shape resembling Arch I in the Tomb of the Brick Arches (see p. 31, above), with protruding brick capitals on each side. They were clearly built primarily for decorative effect rather than for structural reasons as all had load-bearing lintels above them. Several of the bricks were given the required angle to their neighbours by the insertion of potsherds in the mortar: some of these sherds derived from a single vessel (see p. 194, below).

A piece of *Acacia abyssinica* charcoal (identified by Rowena Gale) embedded in the mortar used in construction of the brick arch at the entrance to sidechamber F has been subjected to radiocarbon analysis, giving an age of 1745 bp ± 30 (OxA-8366).

In general, the sidechamber ceiling slabs are than those of the central passage, averaging over 1.0 m; some, as in sidechamber K, are more finely dressed and up to 2.8 m wide. Initial exploration of the Mausoleum in 1974 indicated also that sidechamber B, not investigated by the present Project, was roofed by a single slab (Munro-Hay 1989: 100 and fig. 6.37). Sidechambers C and L, in analogous corner positions, have not been investigated so it remains unknown whether their roofs share this characteristic.

Sidechamber K (Figs 144c, 146) was found to display further interesting features not represented elsewhere. On the floor lay two large dressed syenite slabs, 1.65 and 1.30 m long and clearly displaced; their original function or significance could not be ascertained. These features, like the finely finished roof noted above, suggest that sidechamber K may have had particular significance at the time of the Mausoleum's construction and original use. As noted below (pp. 186, 190-1), a tunnel was subsequently dug through the 1.3-m-thick western wall into this chamber, causing displacement of the roof-slabs.

Paving
The whole of the interior floor of the Mausoleum was originally paved with roughly dressed sandstone slabs. These vary considerably in size and shape (Fig. 147; see also Figs 143a, b) but are typically sub-rectangular, averaging some 0.5 by 0.3 m in plan and between

*Fig. 144 Mausoleum sidechambers: **a** - the entrance to sidechamber D; **b** - the entrance to sidechamber F, with sidechamber G in the background; **c** - sidechamber K from the southeast, showing props inserted to support the roof where the wall had been removed by digging a tunnel through the outer wall. Scales: 0.5 m.*

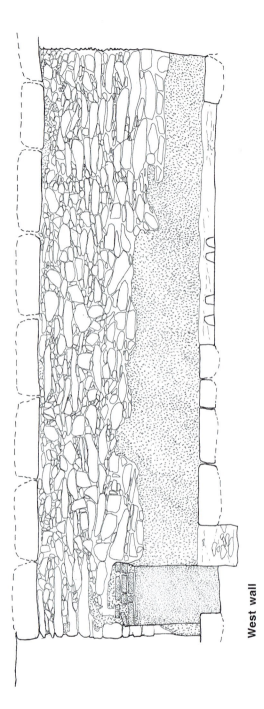

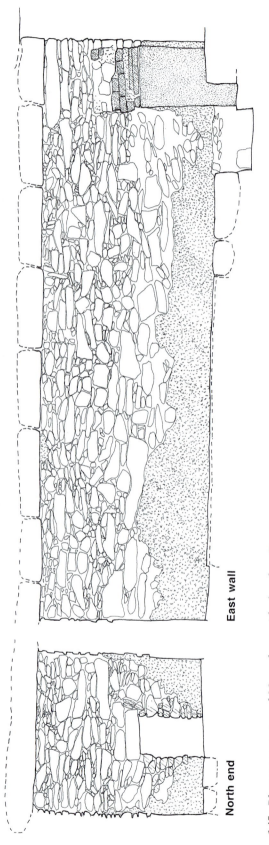

West wall

East wall

North end

Fig. 145 Photogrammetry of Mausoleum sidechamber F.

West wall

East wall

North end

Brick

Dressed syenite

Render

Fig. 146 Photogrammetry of Mausoleum sidechamber K.

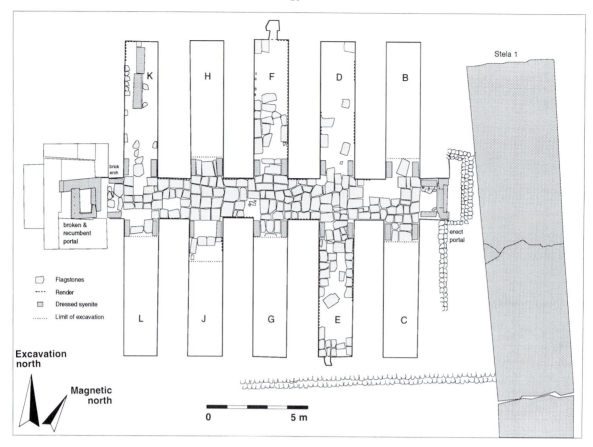

Fig. 147 *Plan of paving surviving in the Mausoleum.*

0.08 and 0.12 m thick. They were laid after the walls were built but before the render (see below) was applied. The paving slabs had been prised up, presumably by robbers, in six places in the central passage, virtually throughout sidechambers D and K, and in the southern and northern halves respectively of sidechambers E and F. During the excavations, 58 of the stones thus removed were found scattered about the floor of the Mausoleum.

Excavations below paving level in sidechambers E and F indicated that their side walls were built directly onto a thin layer of mortar and small stones above the natural yellow clay (Fig. 148). A lack of substantial foundations was also revealed below the east portal.

The west portal

Removal of the earth blocking the western arch (Fig. 149) revealed that the syenite roof-slabs did not continue further to the west. It was therefore necessary to excavate down from the modern surface in order to investigate the western side of the arch. This excavation, designated trench M6 and described in detail below, eventually reached a depth of over 5.5 m and revealed a

second monolithic portal nearly identical to that preserved at the Mausoleum's eastern end, but broken and lying at an angle, as shown in Fig. 150. Like its eastern counterpart, this portal is of syenite, fully dressed only on the outside and has, so far as may be ascertained in its present position, the same size and form, although one of the beam-end representations is imperfectly squared, perhaps unfinished. The two entrances to the tomb thus appear to have been identical.

Fig. 148 *Excavation below the Mausoleum floor in sidechamber F. Scale: 0.25 m.*

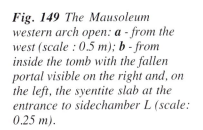

Fig. 149 *The Mausoleum western arch open: **a** - from the west (scale : 0.5 m); **b** - from inside the tomb with the fallen portal visible on the right and, on the left, the syentite slab at the entrance to sidechamber L (scale: 0.25 m).*

The monolithic portals at either end of the structure were each flanked on the inside by two large rectangular dressed blocks of nepheline syenite. The southern block by the east portal measured 1.40 m high above the paving, 0.73 m wide and 0.22 m thick, being comparatively roughly dressed for the 0.50 m which lay below the original paving level. The other blocks at both portals have almost exactly the same dimensions above the paving level. The blocks at the west end still support a shallow brick arch. No remains of such an arch survive in place at the eastern portal although some 5 kg of brick were found below it within the central passage, and it is clear that a shallow arch originally spanned this entrance too.

Fig. 150 *The western entrance to the Mausoleum:* **a** *- the fallen portal and the west side of the arch in trench M6, seen from above;* **b** *- looking west through the western arch to the fallen portal from inside the Mausoleum. Scale: 0.5 m.*

Render

The internal walls of the Mausoleum had originally been thickly plastered with a coarse, gritty render (Figs 145, 151). The render had also been applied to the cracks between the roof slabs, and to all exposed brickwork of the western arch and the arches at the entrances to the sidechambers. Sidechamber J is the only part of the Mausoleum where the render, which seems originally to have covered all the interior walls of undressed stone, is preserved to its full height. This render contains small gravel chips and gives the surface an appearance very similar to that of the dressed syenite. It may thus have given the whole structure the appearance of having been constructed out of solid syenite. No trace of paint or other decoration could be found on the surface of the render. Samples of the render have been examined by Dr Graham Morgan whose report (reproduced below as Appendix X) indicates that they are a type of lime mortar.

A large quantity of fallen render was found in the deposits on the floor of the Mausoleum, particularly in sidechamber F where it had apparently slumped off the walls and in places become mixed with small pieces of glass. (Since glass fragments were not observed in the render elsewhere, it may be concluded that they were not an intentional component.) The manner in which the fallen render hardened around the glass fragments suggests that the thickness of its application and the damp atmosphere prevailing in the Mausoleum had prevented it from setting on the walls.

Inscription

The walls and roof of the excavated portions of the Mausoleum were found to be without any surviving mark or inscription with the sole exception of an isolated glyph measuring about 100 by 70 mm roughly incised into the next to southernmost roof slab in sidechamber E (Fig. 152). Dr Roger Schneider (Appendix IX) reports that this is the Aksumite form of *'alef*, a glottal stop. He is unable to suggest a meaning for the glyph but considers that its morphology does not postdate the fourth-century reign of king Ezana.

Shafts

In the roof of the main passage are three square apertures surmounted by stone-lined vertical shafts that originally led to the ground surface. Each was carefully cut at the junction between two massive syenite

a

b

c

d

*Fig. 151 Render: **a** - extending from floor to ceiling in sidechamber J; **b** - on the roof of sidechamber E, filling gaps between the syenite slabs; **c** - on the walls of sidechamber E at floor level; **d** - at the entrance to sidechamber G. Scales: 0.25 m in **b**, others 0.5 m.*

roof-slabs (Fig. 142a, above). The shafts are each approximately 0.92 m square, separated by about 3.7 m from each other and 3.0 m from the two ends of the passage. Above the ceiling slabs, the eastern shaft retains its original stone walling (Fig. 153a) which is similar in construction to the Mausoleum walls but retains no trace of render. The walling of the central and western shafts has largely disappeared. The western shaft is of particular interest: the western of the two roof slabs through which it was cut had cracked, evidently before construction was completed, and been reinforced with a second syenite slab laid over it (Fig. 153b).

A rectangular syenite slab with a carefully cut central aperture 0.92 m wide (Fig. 154) was set upright in the 1960s immediately to the south of the central shaft where it was reported by eye-witnesses

Fig. 152 The inscribed letter on the roof of sidechamber E. Scale in centimetres.

Fig. 153 *The Mausoleum roof shafts seen from below: **a** - the eastern shaft, with original walling; **b** - the western shaft showing reinforcement.*

to have been found during landscaping operations. It is clear that the aperture was originally square (0.92 by 0.89 m) but had been extended at some unknown time in antiquity to form a rectangle (1.68 by 0.89 m); the reason for this extension is not known.[26] The present position of the slab may be seen in Fig. 128, above. It seems likely that it originally formed the top of the shaft, perhaps sealed by the two large and heavy rocks with flat under-surfaces which now lie near it, having been moved from positions adjacent to the eastern

shaft during the 1974 excavations. They may originally have sealed that shaft; similar slabs adjacent to the western shaft were encountered in trench M5 (Fig. 160b, below). Such a method of closing the Mausoleum shafts would have been analogous to that which was used to seal the steps leading to the ambulatory at the Tomb of the False Door (Munro-Hay 1989: pl. 6.32).

Overall dimensions

The external dimensions of the Mausoleum are easily measured along the main east-west axis, being 18.3 m, but the width from north to south is harder to determine as the outer edge of the north wall was only exposed by the clearance of a tunnel in sidechamber F

---

[26] The extension was never finely finished and a further extension was marked out but not cut. The full size of the intended aperture, *c.* 1.8 by 0.9 m, is approximately the same as that of the Mausoleum portals, raising the possibility that work might at some time have begun on making a replacement for the broken western portal.

Fig. 154 *The slab from the central shaft, erected vertically, seen from the southeast. Scale: 0.5 m.*

which extended through this wall to a length of 0.6 m. The outer edge of the south wall is represented by the line of the main terrace wall, as was revealed in trench M8, described below (p. 188). This suggests that the overall width of the structure is some 17 m.

EXCAVATIONS WITHIN THE MAUSOLEUM
(Michael Harlow and Jacke Phillips)

The Mausoleum's total floor area is approximately 143 sq. m and, when it was first entered, archaeological deposits extended to within 0.1 - 0.35 m of the roof. It thus contained *c*. 270 cu. m of deposit, of which about 65% has been excavated. The excavation was conducted by trowel with the aid of electric light supplied from a portable generator, all the deposits being removed in buckets hauled up through one of the three vertical shafts noted above or passed through the eastern portal. Material requiring particularly close examination was sieved in daylight through 5-mm mesh. The greater part of the Mausoleum's contents

clearly represents secondary deposition and includes much Late Aksumite and post-Aksumite material, with abundant faunal and human skeletal remains. The lowest levels associated with the flagged floor, however, although greatly disturbed in many places, contained a distinctive artefact assemblage which is described below. The excavations revealed no evidence for primary burials.

Excavated areas inside the Mausoleum were designated as follows. The central passage (MA) was divided into 1-m strips (MA10 to MA25 from east to west); MA21 to MA25 were excavated in two halves dividing the passage lengthwise in order to reveal the profile of the deposits along that axis while retaining the same cross-passage 1-m strip numbering. The ten sidechambers were, as noted above, designated MB to ML (omitting MI), starting from the northeast and proceeding westwards on alternate sides of the central passage. Each excavated sidechamber was then divided into 1-m strips given unique numbers starting from the strips adjoining the central passage, as summarised in Fig. 155.

Deposits in the central passage (Fig. 156a) had accumulated in a variety of ways and at different periods, but were greatly disturbed in many places as a result of tomb robbing, deliberate filling and possible disposal of unarticulated human and animal (especially dog) bones. Five or six contexts were distinguished in each of the sixteen strips and provide evidence for several phases of deposition. The contexts were numbered in separate series for each strip, from (1) at the top to (5) or (6) at the bottom.

The central passage was found to be partially filled by large irregular stones, which extended only to the entrances of the sidechambers. Notable were many roughly dressed ellipsoid stones, the largest of which, over 1.2 m in length, was found in the first 1.0-m strip in sidechamber B (MB130). The function of these stones is unclear, but some could have been used to form part of blockings for the sidechambers, although no evidence for such blocking was found *in situ*.

Beyond the first 1-m-wide strip, the stratigraphy in the sidechambers only partially paralleled that in the central passage, especially in the lowest levels (Figs. 156b, 157). That these chambers had been extensively robbed in antiquity was indicated by the disturbed nature of the deposits and by the high proportion of the paving stones that had been removed or uprooted.

Five phases can be distinguished in the fill of the central passage and sidechambers, above the paving and basal yellow clay. These are designated by Roman numerals (Fig. 158), to distinguish them from the Arabic numerals employed for the exterior phasing described below. The points of linkage outlined below

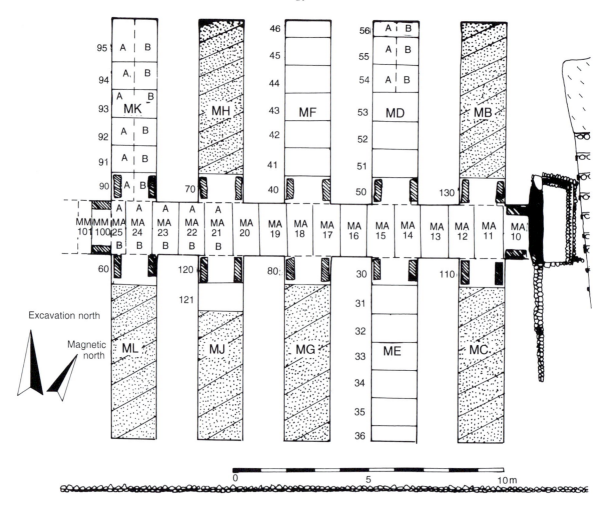

Fig. 155 *Plan of the Mausoleum showing excavation divisions. Stippling indicates areas which were not excavated.*

do not permit precise correlation of the stratigraphic sequences recorded inside and outside the Mausoleum. It is, however, possible to present the sequences in parallel and tentatively to suggest approximate dates for certain stages. The results of this exercise are summarised below in Fig. 167.

Phase I

In the central passage the earliest phase is represented by very thin deposits just below, between and immediately above the paving slabs. In the holes from which paving stones had been removed, a basal yellow clay layer was exposed. Extending from MA11 along the central passage but petering out around MA21 was a thin layer of distinctive fine red silt overlying the paving stones. These red and yellow layers, attributed to phase I, generally excavated as contexts (5) and (6), comprised disturbed but artefact-rich deposits filling holes in the paving and extending up to some 0.5 m

above it in some places, often between uprooted paving stones. The abrupt end of these deposits at both main entrances to the Mausoleum suggests that the portals may have been closed whilst the red layer accumulated, although they may have been at least partly unblocked during the subsequent robbing.

Banks and patches of the distinctive yellow clay from below the paving level extended up to half the total depth of deposits in sidechambers D and F; in sidechamber D this material was mixed with displaced paving stones, indicating that robbing had involved large-scale digging to and through the paving. Although the red layer immediately overlying the paving in the central passage generally extended only 1.0 m or so into the sidechambers, contexts at or immediately above the paving level further back were similarly rich in artefacts.

Fragments of charcoal from a phase-I deposit at the rear of sidechamber E, ME34(5) have yielded a

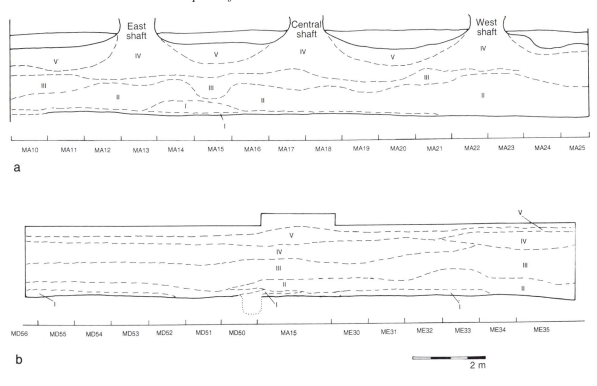

Fig. 156 *Sections of deposits within the Mausoleum:* **a** *- along the central passage;* **b** *- through sidechambers D and E.*

radiocarbon date of 1645 bp ± 35 (OxA-8367). The charcoal was identified as *Ficus* sp. by Rowena Gale. The significance of the radiocarbon dates from the Mausoleum is assessed on p. 223, below.

Much of the primary deposit seems to have been deliberately, even systematically, removed from most of the sidechambers. Clear differences were nonetheless apparent between the types of artefact present in various areas. Thus, in sidechamber D, contexts MD52(5) and MD53(5) contained most of the metal and shell objects, sidechamber E produced numerous fragments of coloured glass inlay, while in strips 43-45 of sidechamber F contexts (4) and (5) yielded very small shattered fragments of colourless and cobalt blue glass often mixed with the render slumped from the side walls. Only the northernmost 2.0 m of sidechamber J was excavated, but context (5) there contained several copper alloy nails, an iron spearhead, glass beads, and over 10 kg of pottery including three fragments from human-headed jars; no joining fragments were noted and it is possible that this collection represents material removed from other sidechambers. The artefacts contained in these deposits may be regarded as contemporary with the construction of the Mausoleum and with its primary use. Many places were observed where the phase-I deposits had suffered post-depositional disturbance, as where floor slabs had been

prised up and, in some cases, removed. As a result the phase-I artefact assemblages incorporated occasional items of demonstrably later date.

Following phase I, the whole of the Mausoleum interior had been largely but not completely cleared in antiquity before becoming filled with rubble and clay mixed with bone and pottery. In this report, particular attention has been attached to distinguishing between materials which date from the monument's construction and primary use, and those which represent subsequent activity. It has been assumed that the distinctive material recovered from between the floor-paving stones, immediately on that paving, and in related contexts directly above with similar material should be considered primary (*i.e.* belonging to phase I), together with that used as chinking between the bricks of the arches. Overall, this distinction between primary and later contexts appears to be valid, since most of the artefacts in the former comprise an assemblage markedly different from that contained in the overlying fill. The extent of disturbance and mixture is emphasised by the presence of a few sherds from stratigraphically higher contexts which appear to belong to, or actually join, floor-level material. In a subsequent section of this chapter, the artefacts which are attributed to primary and later deposits are described separately.

Fig. 157 *Deposits at entrances to Mausoleum sidechambers: **a** - B; **b** - J. Scales: 0.5 m.*

Phase II

The second phase in the central passage was marked by a dark brown clay containing accumulations of large and medium undressed stones rarely exceeding 0.5 m in maximum dimension. These appeared to have been deposited through all of the three shafts in the roof, rising to about 1 m above paving level below the eastern and western shafts, but lower under the central one. Similar stones at the same level at the east and west ends of the passage may have been introduced through the portals. As noted above, some of these stones may also originally have been used to block the sidechamber entrances, but no clear evidence of such blocking remained *in situ*. The sidechamber contexts above the phase-I layer incorporated much water-laid material, contained fewer artefacts and had been heavily disturbed. The quantity of brick and mortar fragments recovered at this level near the sidechamber entrances suggests that the brick arches may have collapsed at this time, or have been demolished to facilitate access to the sidechambers.

Deposits attributed to phase II began just above the floor and were mixed with phase-I material in some areas; they were probably laid shortly after the tomb had been thoroughly robbed. Comparison with material from D site (pp. 312-34, below) suggests that the phase-II pottery dates around the sixth or seventh century. A coin of Armah, recovered near floor level in the central passage close to the entrance of sidechamber J may have been introduced at this time (cf. pp. 200, 223).

Phase III

Above the phase-II accumulations in the central passage, but possibly laid only shortly afterwards, were deposits of dark brown silty clay containing smaller (0.2 m) stones together with concentrations of bone (over 4 kg per cubic metre), particularly in contexts (3) below the central and western shafts but also in MA11(3). The occurrence of pottery in these deposits was markedly less dense.

Towards the top of context (3) in the sidechambers were found deposits of disarticulated animal and human bone together with much fallen render. Such deposits occurred in ME31-5, MF41-2 and the east side of MF45-6, similarly on the east side of MD51 and the northeast corner of MD56, as well as in MK94A(5) and MK94B(4). They suggest a period

	Area	Phase I	Phase II	Phase III	Phase IV	Phase V
MA	Central passage	(7), (6), (5)	(4)	(3), lower(2)	–	upper(2), (1)
MB	Sidechamber B	(5)	(4)	(3)	–	(2), (1)
MC	Sidechamber C	(5)	(4)	(3)	–	(2), (1)
MD	Sidechamber D	(5), (4a)	(4)	(3)	–	(2), (1)
ME	Sidechamber E	(6), (5), ME31(4), ME36(2), ME36(1)	(4), ME31(3)	(3), ME31(2), ME30upper(4)-lower(2)	–	(2), (1)
MF	Sidechamber F	(6), (5), MF47(2), MF47(1)	(4), MF44(3)	(3), MF44(2)	MF40(2) MF40(1)	(2), (1)
MG	Sidechamber G	(6), (5)	(4)	(3)	(2)	(1)
MH	Sidechamber H	(6), (5)	(4)	(3)	–	(2), (1)
MJ	Sidechamber J	(5)	lower(4)	upper(4)	–	(2), (1)
MK	Sidechamber K	lower(5)	upper(5), MK90(4)	(4), MK90(3) MK90(2)	–	(3), (2), (1)
ML	Sidechamber L	(6), lower(5)	upper(5)	(4), (3)	–	(2), (1)

Fig. 158 *Excavated contexts within the Mausoleum attributed to phases.*

when access to the Mausoleum was relatively easy and when it may have been used as a refuge for dying animals or for the disposal of unwanted bones or carcasses. No evidence of formal burial was noted, except that in some cases, as in MA10 under the east portal, dog skulls were found aligned beside each other but separated from other mixed bones. Two human skulls (pp. 216-7, below) were found beside each other in MF41(3), carefully placed immediately north of the eastern syenite slab at the entrance to the sidechamber as if they had been moved during clearance.

Although rich in disarticulated human and animal bone, this phase produced little pottery. Its distribution, concentrated in the immediate vicinity of the eastern and central shafts, showed little correlation with that of the bone, and much of it may be better placed in phase IV. Occasional joins between sherds found in deposits attributed to phases III and IV emphasise the difficulty of isolating these phases stratigraphically. The pottery, described below, is predominantly post-Aksumite, some apparently recent.

Phase IV

Substantial deposits are attributed to the fourth phase, mainly below the eastern and central shafts, forming cones of material which had been introduced through the shafts, eventually blocking them. The western shaft may also have been open for part of the time. These cones contained fewer and smaller stones, but had high densities of pottery and bone. Sherds scattered on either side of the shaft were found to join. This phase was barely represented in the sidechambers, and then only in the first 1.0 m strips as part of the cones below the eastern and central shafts, as in MD56(1)-(2), ME31(2), MG80(2), and MH70(2). Material from MK90(2) may be connected with the tunnel dug from outside the Mausoleum into sidechamber K, discussed below (pp. 186, 190-1).

These contexts were densely packed with pottery, clearly deposited through the shafts to break and spread out in a conical formation; in some cases substantially whole vessels could be reconstructed. Use of the shafts to dump refuse was probably related to the initial stages of industrial activity revealed in trenches M5 and M6 and described below.

Phase V

The final phase was represented by water-borne deposits of red and dark brown or black silty clay which, particularly between the vertical shafts and to the rear of the sidechambers, showed clear varves marking successive periods of flooding. Bone and pottery were sparse, generally less than 50 g of bone and 1 kg of pottery per cubic metre. Seepage at this time may have caused shifting in the underlying deposits.

EXTERNAL EXCAVATIONS
(Michael Harlow and Jacke Phillips)

Excavation outside the Mausoleum, but associated with it, was undertaken in front of the east portal,

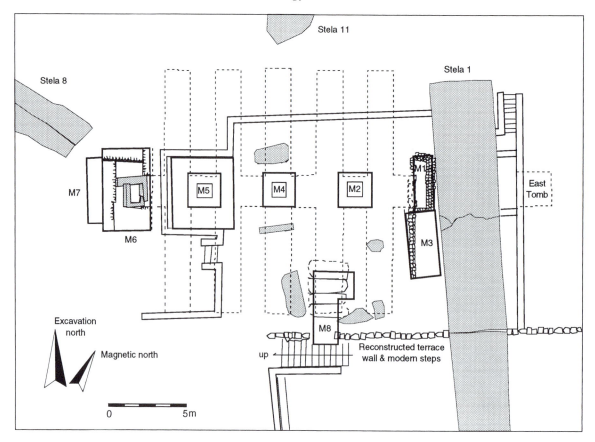

Fig. 159 *Plan of trenches external to the Mausoleum.*

where the trenches excavated in 1974 were cleared and extended; at the west end to reveal the fallen west portal; around each of the three vertical roof-shafts; and through a section of the main terrace wall in order to examine its relationship with the south side of the Mausoleum. These trenches, all excavated from the 1993 ground surface, were laid out in the manner shown in Fig. 159.

Trench M1 (5.3 by 2.55 m), adjacent to the east portal, cut through backfill from the 1974 excavation.

Trench M2 (2.6 by 2.6 m) was over the eastern shaft, likewise excavated in 1974.

Trench M3 (4.0 by 2.5 m) lay immediately to the south of M1 alongside Stela 1. It was not excavated below levels which could be attributed to the 1960s landscaping or the 1974 excavations.

Trench M4 (2.6 by 2.6 m) was over the central shaft (Fig. 160a). As noted above, most of the Mausoleum now lies below a terrace levelled and paved during the 1960s landscaping of the area to the east of Stela 1.

The upper contexts in M4, like those described below in M8, represented material disturbed during the levelling. M4(5) and M4(6) were of similar type and may have been the place where the rectangular slab shown in Fig. 154 once lay. Nothing remained *in situ* of the shaft's original walls above the ceiling slabs of the Mausoleum passage, although context (4) contained rubble which may have come from this wall or its surrounding packing.

Trench M5 (5.0 by 4.0 m) took the area around the western shaft down to the level of the terrace formed by the 1960s landscaping.[27] It was subdivided from north to south into sections M5A, M5B and M5C. Under the surface topsoil were found remains of stone walls, floors and fireplace areas which may represent structures recorded by the DAE in 1906; some traces of these were also discerned to the west in the upper contexts of M6 and M7. The earlier deposits below were only investigated in the immediate vicinity of the western shaft. M5(10) and (11) contained scattered rocks from the shaft's walls and packing, with two

[27] Trenches M5, M6 and M7 were the only ones dug from a level which had not been significantly lowered during the 1960s landscaping.

184

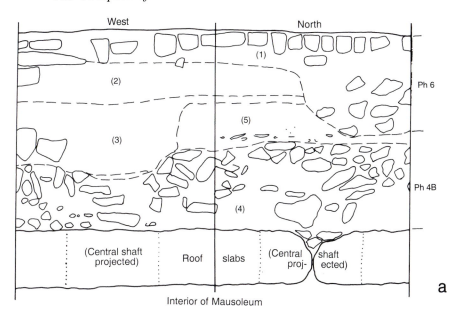

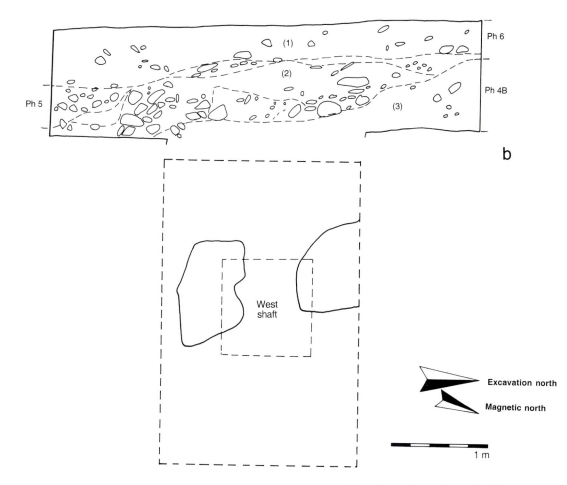

Fig. 160 *Mausoleum external trenches: **a** - trench M4: west and north sections of trench M4; **b** - west section and plan of trench M5.*

Fig. 161 *Trench M6 from the southwest, showing the tunnel dug through the Mausoleum wall into sidechamber K. The figure stands in the Mausoleum's western arch.*

large slabs of dressed syenite which may originally have sealed the shaft (Fig. 160b). M5(13) comprised the fill of the shaft and may be correlated with phase-IV deposits inside the Mausoleum.

Trench M6 (5.0 by 3.0 m), beyond the Mausoleum to the west and overlying the west portal, was subdivided from north to south into sections M6A, M6B, and M6C. The upper contexts (1) to (4) represent domestic occupation which continued at least as late as 1906; walls and surfaces, M6(3) and (4), demonstrably contemporary with those in M5, extended to *c*. 1 m below the ground surface. Below, for almost a further 2 m, a succession of ashy deposits was excavated as contexts (5) to (9) with brown/grey clayey silts and concentrations of ash, bone and pottery around fireplace areas. These deposits indicate occupation or specialist activity rather than a rubbish tip or deliberate fill, at least in M6C and M6B. Below context (10) at *c*. 3.5 m below the surface, the nature of the deposits changed markedly, becoming very loosely packed with concentrations of massive broken stones. Part of contexts (9) and (10) in M6A and M6B may represent the fill of a tunnel which, unfortunately, could not be fully distinguished during excavation except where it penetrated the walls of the Mausoleum. The date of

this tunnel is discussed on p. 191, below. Contexts (13) to (15) in M6A and M6B, starting from some 0.5 m above the Mausoleum paving level and extending down to a rough stone paving slightly lower than that inside, contained brick and mortar derived from the tomb structure: they therefore post-date the primary use of the Mausoleum. M6C(10), a hard red deposit around vestigial remains of an east-west wall abutting the north-south wall, may also belong to this phase.

This trench revealed a complex of walls, all of undressed stone set in mud, which lay outside the Mausoleum's western entrance. The original outer wall of the Mausoleum was exposed, extending northwards from the brick arch. Some 0.9 m north of the arch an east-west wall abutted onto it at approximately 90 degrees. This wall was preserved to a total height of 3.3 m. Its junction with the outer wall of the Mausoleum had been disfigured by the digging of a tunnel (Fig. 161) which, as noted above, passed obliquely through the 1.3-m-thick masonry into sidechamber K. A wall at right-angles to the outer wall of the Mausoleum 0.9 m north of the western portal, and approximately parallel to but 2.4 m west of it, formed the edges of what seems to have been a small courtyard (Fig. 162). There were traces of a north-south wall close to the western limit of the excavation; its upper

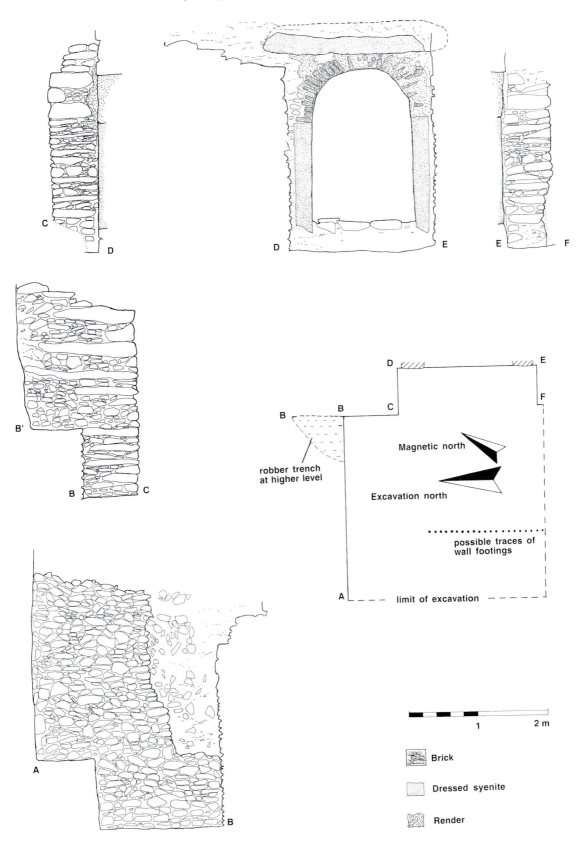

Fig. 162 *Plan and photogrammetry of walls exposed in trench M6 outside the west end of the Mausoleum.*

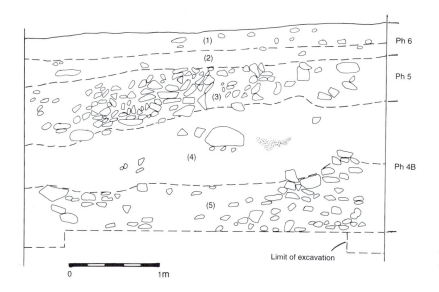

Fig. 163 Mausoleum trench M7: west section.

courses were parallel to, and 1.7 m west of, the Mausoleum wall. These external walls preserved no trace of render. Their generally unweathered state confirms the stratigraphic evidence, noted below, that they were buried soon after they had been built. The excavation was extended southwards as far as was considered safe, but no sign was found of a southern east-west wall: if such was indeed present it must have been further from the Mausoleum's western arch than was its northern counterpart. Such asymmetry is considered unlikely. This western entrance to the Mausoleum may originally have been reached by a re-entrant from the main Aksumite terrace, although it was not possible to check this by excavating the intervening area.

Trench M7 (4.0 by 1.0 m) was a western step-extension of M6, excavated to a depth of 2.1 m below the modern surface. Contexts (2) and (3) represented the remains of buildings and living areas analogous to those in trench M6, but these deposits were considerably thicker to the south than in the north (Fig. 163). Below this was a westward continuation of the ash deposits seen in M6A/B(5), with iron slag and vitrified material. There was no sign of any structure in which ironworking might have been conducted.

Trench M8 (1.5 by 4.0 m) cut into the south terrace wall and the adjacent rubble overlying the Mausoleum. M8A (1.5 by 1.5 m) and M8B (1.5 by 0.5 m) were respectively easterly and southerly extensions of M8. This excavation, designed to examine the relationship between the southeast wall of the Mausoleum and the ancient terrace wall which bounded the stelae area on the south side, confirmed that the ancient wall lay directly below the modern terrace wall. It constituted the outer (southeast) face of the 1.8-m thick Mausoleum wall, from which it could not be distinguished. Since the south wall of sidechamber E appears to be integral with its east and west walls, the terrace wall was probably constructed at the same time as the Mausoleum. Trench M8B uncovered the south face of the original Aksumite wall foundation set on undisturbed orange clay, and also a ledge of the type characteristic of Aksumite architecture. The 1.0- to 1.4 m-thick layer of rubble covering the roof-slabs of the Mausoleum had been disturbed at its southern margin, perhaps when the terrace wall was reconstructed in the 1960s or prior to that by natural erosion, but even at this level no sign could be found of a northern face to the terrace wall which must therefore have comprised an outer facing for the rubble. At the base of the trench, below the rubble, were revealed the undressed upper surfaces of the three southernmost roof slabs over sidechamber E. Contexts (1)-(3) in M8 and M8A overlay the rubble packing (4), and they probably represent later ground-surfaces. At the south end, modern reconstruction of the Aksumite terrace wall extended to about 1.6 m below the present surface (Figs 164, 165).

The deposits excavated within these trenches can be attributed to seven main phases. The contexts assigned to each phase are summarised in Fig. 166, while Fig. 167 offers a correlation between the phases recognised inside and outside the Mausoleum.

Phase 1

The earliest phase is represented by features contemporary with or integral to the construction and primary

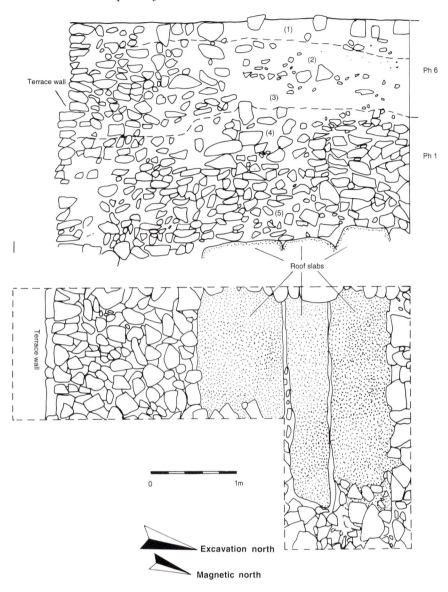

Fig. 164 *Mausoleum trench M8: west section and plan.*

use of the Mausoleum. Although several architectural elements of this phase were exposed, no contemporary artefact-bearing deposits were encountered in the external trenches. Features uncovered include the walls of the eastern shaft in trench M2 and the capping stones and original rubble packing in trenches M5 and 8/8A, the original terrace wall in trench M8B, as well as the slab floor surface, east-west wall and oblique north-south wall in the west courtyard of the Mausoleum in trench M6A. The east-west courtyard wall abuts the Mausoleum's exterior west wall, and the oblique north-south wall abuts the east-west wall, and so were constructed sequentially but probably within a short period as they are based at the same level as the Mausoleum itself. Other original architectural elements,

such as the broken west portal in trench M6B and the walls of the central and western shafts in trenches M4 and M5, as well as the capping stones removed from the eastern and central shafts and now exposed on the surface, were later displaced and not found *in situ*.

Phases 2A and 2B

Deposits of these subphases, mainly mixed and disturbed, occur in the lower levels of trench M6B and the adjacent part of M6A south of the east-west wall. The west entrance to the Mausoleum seems to have been open during phase 2A, since the lower half of the west courtyard fill represented a continuation of MM100(4): it was excavated as the lower portions of M6A(12) and M6B(14), together with M6A(13) and

a   b

Fig. 165 *Trench M8: the upper side of the Mausoleum roof-slabs with stone packing over them: **a** - with terrace wall in foreground; **b** - detail. Scales: 0.5 m.*

M6B(15), extending for about 0.5 m above the paving level. Subsequently, during phase 2B, the entrance was blocked and the courtyard filled by deposits that were excavated as M6B(13) and the the upper half of (14) with M6A(11) and upper (12). Below the Mausoleum's west arch, the blocking is represented by the lower part of MM100(3). The upper part of the blocking may have been removed subsequently and replaced in phase 4A or early 4B. Dating evidence is provided by material found within this deposit: brick and mortar fragments derived from the Mausoleum walls and arches indicate a period after the sidechamber arches had begun to collapse, while other artefacts suggest a date broadly contemporary with the Late Aksumite occupation of D site (Chapter 10, below).

Phase 3

Further accumulation in the west courtyard area is represented by a continuous layer of weathered undressed stones up to 0.4 m in maximum dimension: M6B(10-

12) and MM101(1), probably tipped from the north and completely obscuring the western arch. Unlike the phase-2 fill, this did not include brick and mortar fragments. A less stony layer, M6B(9), may represent the subsequent accumulation over an unknown period of time of overburden that completely obscured the exterior courtyard walls and the lintel over the western arch. Artefacts were generally worn and fragmentary, but far more numerous than in the phase-2 deposits. Joining fragments of two ceramic vessels link deposition levels M6B(9), (10) and (12). A coin of Hataz from M6B(10), level with the top of the brick arch, if not intrusive, provides a *terminus post quem* for this phase. All that may be concluded is that accumulation of these deposits may have begun around the seventh century and continued for a long time.

Phase 4A

A tunnel had been dug through the phase-3 layers beside the east-west wall marking the south face of the

Trench	1	2A	2B	3	4A	4B	5	6
						Phase		
M4	+					(5), (4)		(3), (2), (1)
M5	+					(13), (12), (11), (10), (5)	(9), (8), (7), (6)	(4), (3), (2), (1)
M5A						(10), lower(5)	(6), upper(5), (3)	(4), (2), (1)
M5B						lower(3)	(4), upper(3), (2)	(1)
M5C						(10)	(4), (3), (2)?	(2)?, (1)
M6A	+	(13), (12), (11)		(10)*, (9)*	(10)*, (9)*	(8), (7), (6)	(5), (4), (3)	(2), (1)
M6B (1994)		(15), (14), pt(13)		pt(13), (12), (11), (10)*, (9)*	(10)*, (9)*	(8), (7), (6), (5)	(4), (3)	(2), (1)
M6B (1995)		(15), (14), (13)		(12), (11), (10), (9)		(8), (7), (6), (5)	(4), (3)	(2), (1)
M6C				(10)		(9), (8), (7), (6), (5), (4)	(3)	(2), (1)
M7						(8), (7), (6), (5), (4)	(3)	(2), (1)
M8	(6), pt(5), pt(4)							pt(5), (4), (3), (2), (1)
M8A	(5)							(4), (3), (2), (1)
M8B	(2)							(1)

Fig. 166 *Excavated contexts in the Mausoleum external trenches, attributed to phases. Phases marked + are represented by structural features only, not excavated contexts.*

western courtyard. Unfortunately, the tunnel fill was not immediately recognised during excavation of M6A(9) and (10), and no distinction could be made between the surrounding phase-3 deposits and the later tunnel fill. The tunnel then turned to break through the west wall of the Mausoleum into sidechamber K; this must have involved considerable effort and suggests that its diggers were unaware that the west entrance lay only 2.0 m to the south. They may have been following the face of the east-west wall, the top of which would have been exposed at that time near the top of M6B(9). The age of the tunnel may only be estimated by reference to artefacts contained in its fill or by seeking correlation with the stratigraphy of deposits inside the Mausoleum. Neither method is straightforward. The tunnel deposits could not be isolated stratigraphically except where it passed through the Mausoleum wall, and material from M6A(9)-(10)

probably also contained sherds from phases 3 and 4B. Equivalent layers (9)-(10) in the northeast corner of M6B also probably included parts of the tunnel fill. Fragments of a handled pot (Fig. 188c), recovered in a circumscribed area at the northeast corner of M6B(10), may come from the phase-4A tunnel fill, being apparently of more recent type than other pottery from this level. If this attribution and stratigraphic provenance are both correct, the vessel could provide a *terminus post quem* for the tunnel fill. The chronology of 'recent' activity in the Stelae Park area remains uncertain (cf. p. 223 below and Appendix XII), but the date of the phase-4A tunnel could possibly be as late as the seventeenth century.

Phase 4B

Trenches M6 and M7 revealed numerous isolated ashy concentrations of varying size and depth above the

191

Estimated century (AD)		Interior		Exterior
4	I	original construction and primary deposits	1	walls in western court, terrace wall, wall outside easturn portal, rubble in M8
4–6			2	lowest deposits in western court (M6B). 2A before first blocking; 2B after blocking
c. 6	II	large and medium stones in clay to c. 0.5 m above paving	3	second blocking of portal and subsequent fill of western court
c. 17	III	smaller stones in clay, with bone accumulations	4A	robber tunnel and fill
			4B	later ashy deposits, eventually filling shafts
c. 18	IV	cones under eastern and central shafts	.	
	V	water-laid silts between shafts and in sidechambers	.	
19			5	buildings
20			6	landscaping

Fig. 167 *Correlation of phases inside and outside the Mausoleum*

level of the lintel at the west entrance to the Mausoleum. Some 2 m in overall thickness and separated by layers of clayey soils, these deposits appear unrelated to the Mausoleum. They are clearly later than the tunnel and earlier than the construction of the phase-5 building. The earliest layer, spread over most of M6B and M6C filling a depression directly above the courtyard, was excavated as M6B(8) directly overlying phase-3 layer M6B(9), and as M6C(6). Subsequent concentrations, including M6A(6)-(8), M6B(5)-(7) and M6C(4)-(7), were smaller and distinctly separate. It was late in this phase, probably around the third quarter of the nineteenth century, that fragments of porcelain cups and of mass-produced, presumably imported, glass first appeared. Iron slag and other vitrified fragments suggest industrial activity, probably ironworking of some kind conducted in open hearths. No associated buildings were revealed.

This level was barely penetrated by the M5 excavation, although iron slag recovered in layers M5(11)-(13) suggests that industrial activity extended into this area. The western Mausoleum shaft does not appear to have been used at this time as a dump in the same way as the other two shafts. Scattered rubble in M5(10) and (11) suggest that its walls may have been demolished during this phase.

In M4(4), a similar scatter of rocks represents the remains of the walls of the central shaft, at the same stratigraphic level. Quantities of charred seeds were also recovered and are discussed below (pp. 217-8). Context M4(5) covers this wall debris, being

similar to M5(10). Both shafts may have been destroyed at a similar date, following the phase-IV deposition within the Mausoleum. The absence of slag suggests that the ironworking activity area did not extend this far to the east. The fact that porcelain coffee-cups are represented in the later phase-4B deposits but not in the Mausoleum fill or the rubble sealing the shafts suggests that the Mausoleum had been sealed and the central and western shafts destroyed before the end of phase 4B and its associated ironworking.

The thickness of these layers suggests that phase 4B lasted for a considerable time. The associated pottery indicates that the ironworking was probably relatively recent, perhaps lasting until the phase-5 buildings were erected late in the nineteenth century.

Phase 5

The major feature of this phase was a substantial rectilinear building exposed in trenches M5 and M6 with some remnants in M7 (Fig. 168). Its south wall (running east-west) and at least two internal north-south walls were exposed, together with a poorly preserved east-west wall immediately downslope that apparently provided an east-west passageway. This last wall may have collapsed during the life of the building further upslope, since it is not shown in the DAE sketch plan (Littmann *et al.* 1913, II: fig. 8; D.W.Phillipson 1997: fig. 12). An ash concentration and part of a large storage jar suggest domestic use. Another ash concentration in the southwest corner of trench M5C may represent an earlier feature.

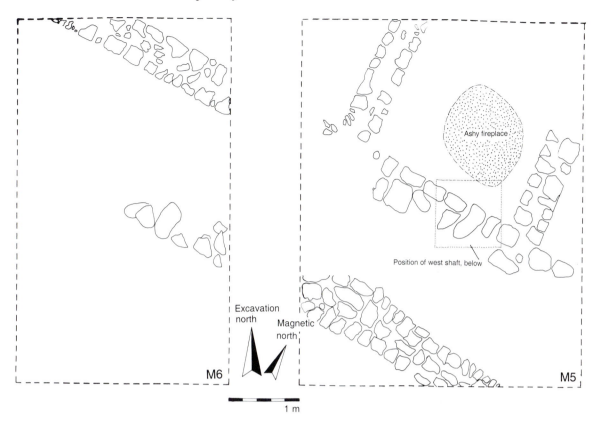

Fig. 168 *Plan of phase-5 house walls in Mausoleum trenches M5 and M6.*

The building was of rubble construction analogous to that used at the present day, perhaps employing mud-mortar but without foundation trenches or regular facing stones. It may have been located within a substantial compound, as the adjoining premises reportedly belonged to the Governor of Tigray in 1906 (Littmann *et al.* 1913, II: 24; D.W.Phillipson 1997: 37). Its angular plan contrasts with the more usual circular form of domestic structures at that time. No recollection of its function seems to survive, nor was this determined in excavation. It was probably erected late in the nineteenth century.

The building was present in 1906 but had been demolished before 1954 (Doresse 1956: 44-5). Its east end was removed by the phase-6 landscaping, with the result that no trace of it was noted in trench M4, although it is likely that the building originally extended over the site of the central shaft.

Phase 6

As noted above, much of the central stelae area was cleared in the mid-1960s and landscaped to create the open space now known as the Stelae Park. The area immediately west of Stela 1 was terraced at a level about 1 m lower than the surrounding surface, with several monumental stones exposed. The landscaping layer was revealed in all excavated trenches, and included a few features such as the ash concentration in M5/5A(4) and others exposed in the west section of trench M5A and south section of trench M6C, stratigraphically above the preserved tops of the phase-5 walls. In trenches M8 and M8A phase-6 deposits immediately overlay elements attributed to phase 1.

ARTEFACTS FROM PRIMARY CONTEXTS

In the following sections, discussion of the artefacts recovered from the Mausoleum and adjacent trenches is separated into two parts. Material from the primary (phase I) contexts within the Mausoleum, where most of the non-ceramic artefacts were concentrated, is presented first. Later material is then described and distinguished, where appropriate, by phase. An account of the most recent occupation of the Stelae Park area is provided in Appendix XII.

Pottery
(Jacke Phillips)

The pottery recovered from phase-I contexts in the Mausoleum forms a largely uniform group distinct from that contained in the overlying deposits. The latter do, however, contain a few sherds which appear to belong with, or even actually join, those found in the primary contexts. This is hardly surprising since the plunderers must have dug through the primary deposits in order to reach the paving stones, many of which they removed and overturned. Much of the original floor material is thus disturbed and mixed. Pottery recovered from floor contexts but considered on typological grounds to be of later date is not specifically discussed in this section.

Very little pottery was demonstrably *in situ*, with the notable exception of a basin (Figs 169a, 171b), whose sometimes widely separated but joining fragments were used as chinking for the brick arches of sidechambers B, C, D and F; no attempt was made to remove those sherds which were still in position between the bricks, and the vessel has been reconstructed from sherds found amongst the fallen bricks and mortar. Other sherds heavily encrusted with mortar were recovered at floor level and elsewhere, and had probably also been used for this purpose or for containing the mortar itself; for example a bowl (Fig. 169d) had much mortar adhering to its interior and to the top of its undulating rim.

Pottery from these contexts amounted to 52 kg, but its fragmentary condition precludes detailed description. In comparison with material from the Tomb of the Brick Arches, some similarities and differences are nonetheless apparent. The terminology established for the latter material (Appendix II) is employed here.

Although beaker sherds are readily recognisable, few were recovered from the Mausoleum. All bowl types are represented, although there are proportionately greater numbers of smooth-surface types, many with a groove below the rim. The only rim embellishments are discontinuous scalloping, a solid extended ridge and a coil handle; no applied bird figures were present. A small number of bowls have incised decoration. Rims are incised diagonally or, more rarely, vertically, or undulated by finger-pinching (Fig. 169e) at the edge. The few basins chiefly have a deeply incised herringbone pattern on the interior (Figs 169a, 171b). No animal model fragments were recovered, and only three coarse 'footrests' from large 'footwashers'. Some possible rebated pots may be recognised by the use of horizontal incised decoration on what may have been their necks. An underfired bowl with a wide ledge-rim and grooved rim top (Fig. 169f) may be

compared with the deliberately reduced black bowls from the Tomb of the Brick Arches (p. 60, above) and may likewise imitate a Roman form. Numerous jar sherds were recovered although few can be reconstructed; both horizontal lug handles and pierced flat strap handles are recorded, so presumably several types of jar are represented although none was noted with pre-firing suspension holes or with applied crosses or crescent-and-disc motifs. Human-headed jars are represented by two faces (one shown in Figs 169c, 171a) and a hair fragment, all from different vessels. Other sherds are interpreted as representing a brazier and a ladle. At least five pedestal vessels, mostly bowls (Fig. 169b), were recovered. Two sherds apparently re-used as lamps may have belonged to the plunderers, being found in sidechambers E and J where extensive robber activity is indicated.

Classical Aksumite incised decoration (presented here in terms of the classification devised for material in the Tomb of the Brick Arches, see Appendix II) was frequent, usually on jar shoulders or undiagnostic body sherds. Recognisable vessel forms included a beaker [3], bowls [1]-[3], and jars [2]-[4], [A]-[D], [F]-[G], [a] and [b]. Only one bowl sherd has moulded [3] relief decoration, and one otherwise plain jar shoulder fragment has a large incised diamond below its ledge-handle. Decoration on the body of a jar combining infilled diamonds, corrugation and dashes (Fig. 170a) is not paralleled in the Tomb of the Brick Arches, although its incomplete horizontal shoulder pattern [F] probably is. There seems to be a larger proportion of decoration [4] on the jars and [1] in general than in the Tomb of the Brick Arches. Paint was rarely preserved, being found only on one human-headed jar and possibly the other (Fig. 169c), with highlighting on some of the pedestal bowls (Fig. 169b) and the exterior of one basin.

A number of ceramic features present in the Mausoleum primary deposits were not found in the Tomb of the Brick Arches, including rim-top applied decoration and a rim-edge ledge-handle on basins, a lug handle on a ledge-rim jar, a prominent horizontal ridge on a jar neck, a tripod vessel, and a unique jar with grooved imitation of horizontal corrugation and a strap handle from the rim (Fig. 170d). The human-headed jars also exhibit features not found in the Tomb of the Brick Arches, having red-slipped faces and carefully incised hair of different patterns. It is difficult to assess whether the few miniature vessels recorded are early features or intrusive. In contrast with the Tomb of the Brick Arches, horizontal lug handles are larger and more frequently found on vessels other than bowls (Fig. 170c). On typological grounds, it appears that the Mausoleum primary material is not fully contemporary with that recovered in the Tomb of the Brick

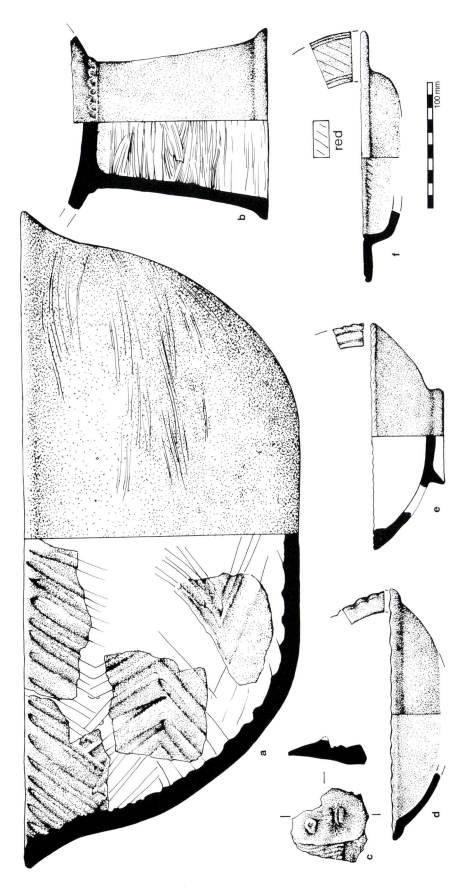

red

100 mm

Fig. 169 *Pottery bowls, basin, jar and pedestal from phase-1 contexts within the Mausoleum.*

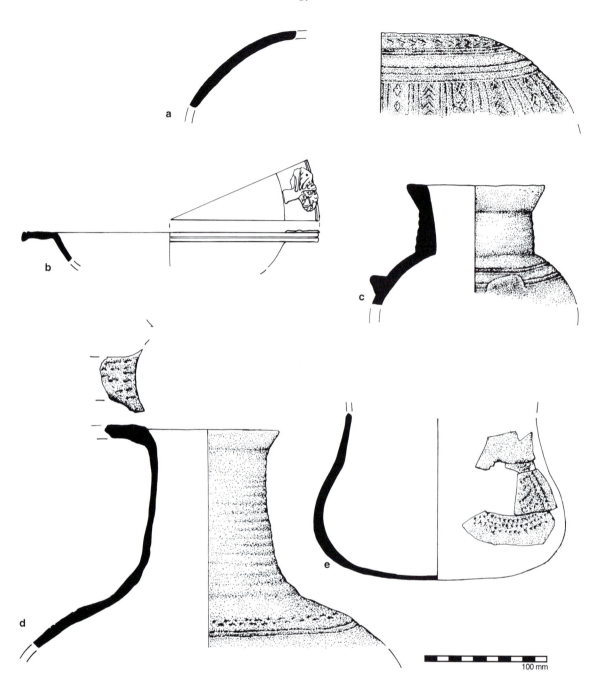

Fig. 170 *Pottery jar, pots and African Red Slip bowl from phase-I contexts within the Mausoleum.*

Arches; it is suggested that the Mausoleum assemblage may be the earlier of the two, perhaps by half a century or so (cf. pp. 456-7, below).

Fragments of a pot in a grey fabric with elaborate punctated decoration (Fig. 170e) might be an import, although no source-area can be suggested. As noted above, a number of fragments are, on typological grounds, considered intrusive to the primary contexts in which they were recovered, including possibly

the two bowls re-used as lamps, one of which bears an elaborate post-firing incised cross. Notable amongst the recognisably intrusive sherds are two ribbed fifth- or sixth-century AD amphora fragments, although an African Red Slip ware bowl with applied tree motif (Figs 170b, 171c) could be contemporary. Others are of types not found in the East Tomb (p. 220) or the Tomb of the Brick Arches, but paralleled in later contexts elsewhere at Aksum.

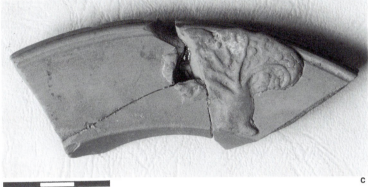

Fig. 171 *Pottery from phase I within the Mausoleum: **a** - face-jar fragment; **b** - sherds used as chinking (cf. Fig. 169a); **c** - sherd of African Red Slip ware.*

Glass and beads
(Michael Harlow)

GLASS

A total of 528 glass fragments (excluding beads) was recorded from Mausoleum phase-I contexts. Of these, 130 were pieces of inlay, and almost all the remainder were so comminuted as to be undiagnostic of the type of object from which they came. Glass beads are discussed separately.

The principal colours represented are summarised in Fig. 172. The following Munsell colour-

Fig. 172 *Summary of Mausoleum phase-I glass.*

Area	cobalt blue	pale/medium blue	blue/colourless cased	colourless	yellow-tinged colourless	green-tinged colourless	brown	turquoise	green/yellow	other	Total
MA	-	-	-	1	-	-	-	-	-	-	1
MD	105	1	-	4	30	9	1	-	-	4	154
ME	57	54	-	6	6	4	1	2	1	4	135
MF	69	4	23	2	117	3	-	-	1	10	229
MG	1	6	-	-	-	-	-	-	-	1	8
MJ	-	-	-	-	-	-	-	1	-	-	1
Totals	232	65	23	13	153	16	2	3	2	19	528

10 mm

a

b

10 mm

Fig. 173 *Glass from phase I within the Mausoleum.*

numbers were recorded: medium cobalt blue 5PB 4/9, pale blue 2.5PB 7/6, medium blue 2.5PB 5/8, dark blue l0B 3/5, pale turquoise 2.5BG 7/2, dark turquoise 6BG 4/5, yellowish green 5GY 6/4, and burgundy red 9RP 5/8.[28]

A large proportion of the colourless, yellow-tinged and cobalt blue fragments were in very small angular pieces often found together in clear phase-I contexts on or around the paving of the Mausoleum (Fig. 173a); some of them were mixed or embedded in mortar from the walls, as in sidechambers D and F. Some were fragments of cased glass, usually blue on colourless, their shape and size being similar to fragments of cased glass from other sites at Aksum, much prone to disintegration (pp. 80-1, above; Munro-Hay 1989: 201). One fragment of totally colourless glass, highly fractured internally but still holding together, was retrieved from a phase-I context in sidechamber D together with many small angular fragments of cased,

colourless and cobalt blue glass. These have the appearance of deriving from a base, being thick with a smooth flat interior surface and the beginning of a fairly steep curved side to the vessel. The same context yielded a short thick rod of bubbly black glass which may have been used for bead making or some other glass-working activity. Another fragment from a phase-I context, a purplish pink ring from the paving level inside sidechamber H (Fig. 173b), could represent either the rim of a flask or a thick disc bead with a very large central perforation, damage to the edge of which prevents certainty. Finally, a piece of 4-mm-thick translucent dark olive green glass came from a primary context in sidechamber F, associated with tiny fragments of cased blue and clear glass. It is very like modern bottle glass but could be ancient.

All 130 inlay pieces (Fig. 174) came from phase-I contexts, mainly from contexts (5) and (6) in ME30-4, with five from MG 80(5) and (6) and one from MD52(5). They comprise pieces of flat glass between 0.9 mm and 2 mm thick which had been

---

[28] These Munsell references should be treated with caution, having been obtained in the field and being dependent on the eyesight of the author only.

30 mm

10 mm

Fig. 174 *Glass inlay from phase-I contexts within the Mausoleum.*

roughly cold-clipped into geometrical shapes: mainly small squares (78), ranging from 6.5 mm to 10 mm along each side, and discs (32) between 6.7 mm and 10.5 mm in diameter, with rare teardrop, diamond, semi-circular, and irregular (possibly broken) pieces. Single instances of 'dagger', 'trumpet', crescent, triangle and 'olive leaf' forms were also found. The commonest colours were dark or cobalt blue (59), medium or pale blue (41) with rare examples in burgundy red, pale green, dark turquoise and colourless or colourless with a greenish or yellowish tinge. Close parallels in turquoise, deep blue and colourless glass have been found in the Tomb of the Brick Arches and under Nefas Mawcha (pp. 81, 102, above; Munro-Hay 1989: 208, figs 14.208-14). They may have been used as an inlay in a material such as wood or copper alloy which has either disappeared or been removed, although it is possible that they were used as decorative elements

on textiles, in the way that shaped mirrors are still used on some Indian fabrics.

BEADS

The table at Fig. 175 lists the 24 beads recovered from primary contexts in the Mausoleum. All are of glass.

It is noteworthy that more than two thirds of the glass beads from primary contexts are of the standard biconical hexagonally faceted type (Fig. 176), large numbers of which also occurred in the Tomb of the Brick Arches. Morrison notes that this particular form of bead (her type IIb) is common at Aksum in the Stelae Park area, the Gudit Stelae Field and at Enda Sem'on (Munro-Hay 1989: 169); she cites parallels from Gheyta and Firkwa, dating from the fifth or sixth century, as well as from Meroe. The area of maximum circumference where the two faceted cones meet sometimes presents a smooth curve (cf. Munro-Hay

Form	Area	Colour	Number
I a	J	turquoise T	1
II b	A	white O	1
II b	E	green T	1
II b	G	green T	1
II b	H	turquoise O	1
II b	J	turquoise O	1
II b	J	cobalt blue T	7
II b	J	blue T	1
II b	J	turquoise T	1
II b	J	yellow-brown T	2
II b	K	turquoise O	1
IV b	J	cobalt blue O	1
VI	G	green O	1
VI	G	red O	1
XIX a	J	turquoise T	1
?	J	turquoise T	1
disc	H	purple T	1
			24

Fig. 175 *Summary of Mausoleum phase-I beads.*
(O = opaque, T = translucent).

1989: figs 11.3-10), but equally often a band of rectangular or diamond shaped facets. As with the very similar beads from the Tomb of the Brick Arches (pp. 83-5, above), it seems that the facets were produced by grinding. The colours of these beads are predominantly translucent cobalt or pale blue, pale green or turquoise or opaque dark turquoise.

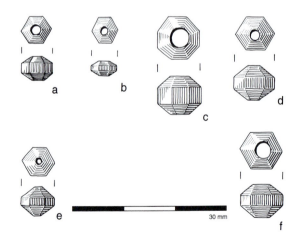

Fig. 176 *Beads from phase I within the*
Mausoleum.

Seven other glass beads from phase-I contexts represent a range of types and colours (Fig. 175), including two drawn beads from MG80(5), identical to those found in large numbers in the immediately overlying deposits: it is argued below (p. 213) that the two examples from phase-I contexts could be intrusive.

Metal
(D.W.P.)

Coin
The only coin (M/155\) from the interior of the Mausoleum was of type 153 [Armah AE 1], attributed to the seventh or eighth century, found at floor level in the central passage, in a context attributed to phase I, adjacent to the western support of the arch giving entry to sidechamber J. The implications of this occurrence are considered on p. 223, below.

Gold
A total of 96 fragments of gold was recovered from phase-I deposits within the Mausoleum, excluding those where gilding was attached to objects of other materials. All are tiny, 87 being wrinkled fragments of gold foil (Fig. 177b) which must have become detached from other artefacts such as are described below. Two pieces of foil, one found adhering to mortar, were examined by Ann Feuerbach (Appendix IV) who notes that they contain traces of silver, but no copper. Another may possibly be an intact square inlay (Figs 177a, 178a); while nine fragments of twisted gold thread (Fig. 177d) attest either the former presence of cloth of gold or the use of gold thread for embroidery. The spatial distribution of this material is informative: of the foil, only one piece came from the central passage, 30 pieces from MD, 54 from ME (which also yielded all the gold thread), and three from MG. This distribution may reflect not only the original distribution of gold or gilded objects, but also the ease and thoroughness of robbing.

Silver
Eleven silver items were recovered from primary contexts within the Mausoleum. Three tiny fragments of silver sheet were found together in ME; one, on analysis, proved to be debased with copper. The other items are all debased silver nails or shanks (Figs 178b-d, f, h, i), six from ME and two from MD. The nail heads, preserved on five examples, were all round and flat, suggesting decorative use. One example of this type contained copper with traces of gold and tin; another was debased with bronze only. The shanks were squared, showing signs of hammering in some cases.

10 mm

Fig. 177   Gold and gilded artefacts from phase-I contexts within the Mausoleum.

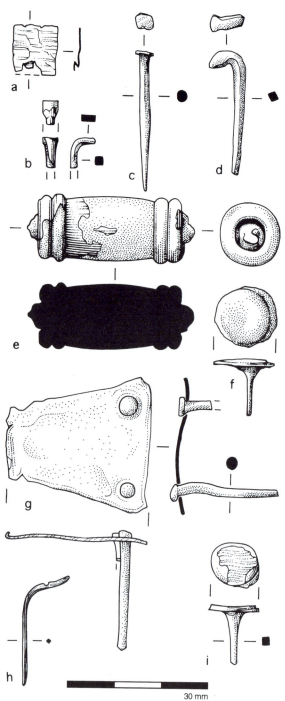

cylinder with double collars at each flat end, 13 mm in maximum diameter. It is likely that this was produced by casting. The gilding, now incompletely preserved, probably once covered the entire object. What appears to be a longitudinal perforation, 6 mm in diameter, is blocked with copper alloy which may be the remains of a tang. Ann Feuerbach considers that mercury gilding was employed; below the gold is a layer of cuprite (cf. Appendix IV).

There were 25 fragments of thin gilded copper or copper alloy sheet; all appeared flat but were so small (only one piece exceeded 14 mm in maximum dimension) that large-diameter curvature would not have been apparent. Gilding was in each case restricted to one side. Two specimens have been analysed (Appendix IV): one had traces of silver in the gold foil but no tin or zinc in the copper; the other comprised virtually pure gold over copper which contained a trace

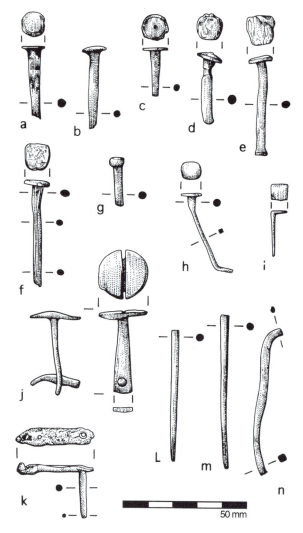

Fig. 178 *Mausoleum phase-I artefacts of gold (**a**), gilded copper alloy (**e**), silver (**b-d, f, h, i**) and silvered copper alloy (**g**).*

Gilded copper alloy

There were 37 specimens from primary contexts within the Mausoleum (eighteen from MD, eighteen from ME and one from MJ).

The most informative item is a handle (Figs 177f, 178e) from MD comprising a 30-mm-long

Fig. 179 *Copper alloy artefacts from phase-I contexts within the Mausoleum.*

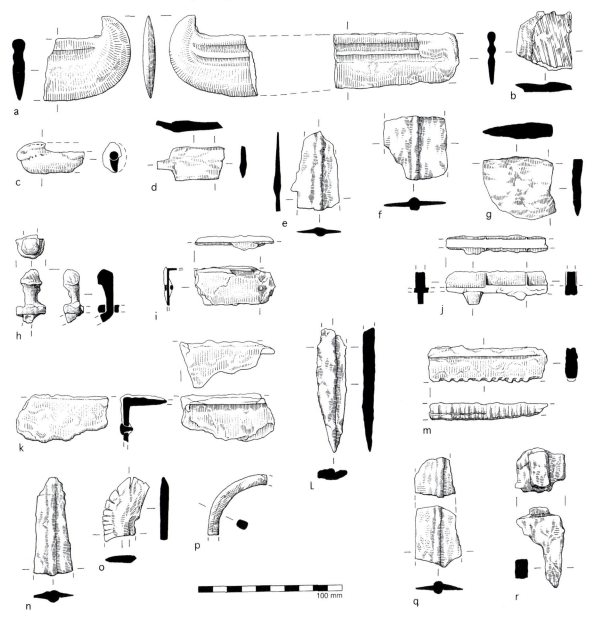

Fig. 180 *Iron artefacts from phase-I contexts within the Mausoleum.*

of zinc. On two specimens (*e.g.* Fig. 177e) the gilding could be seen to have been restricted to a narrow stripe across the surface of the copper alloy.

There were four nails, six shanks and one miscellaneous fragment. One nail was found to comprise a pure copper base with gold containing traces of silver and copper; a shank had a trace of silver in the gold, the copper again lacking both tin and zinc.

Gilded iron
Four pieces of gilded iron were excavated from primary contexts in MD. They comprise two fragments of knives, one bar and one strip. All are too poorly preserved to merit description.

Silvered copper alloy
Only three pieces were recovered from primary contexts, all in ME, and comprise one fragment of sheet retaining rivets or nails (Fig. 178g), and two broken shanks.

Copper alloy
Forty-six copper alloy objects came from primary contexts within the Mausoleum. They comprise twenty-one nails (Figs. 179a-j), eighteen shanks (Figs 179l-n), one strip, one bar with rivet (Fig. 179k), one rod, one sheet fragment, one piece or wire and two miscellaneous fragments. One shank was analysed and found to contain traces of both silver and gold.

Copper alloy and iron

One object from a primary context in sidechamber D, perhaps a knife, appears to have been bimetallic, incorporating iron and copper alloy components. It was unfortunately too broken and corroded to permit further description. A shank from a primary context in ME proved on analysis to contain both copper and iron.

Iron

Ninety iron objects (excluding bimetallic specimens) were recovered from phase-I contexts: one in MB, seventy-one in MD, eight in ME and ten in MJ.

With 34 examples, spearheads (Figs 180e, f, n, q) were the type most commonly represented. All are fragmentary and appear to represent simple foliate blades with a central midrib, analogous to the more complete specimens from the Tomb of the Brick Arches. The object illustrated at Fig. 180l may represent a thicker type of spearhead without a midrib or, alternatively, part of the blade of a dagger.

There are fourteen knives (Figs 180a, c, d, g). A large blade represented by two well preserved pieces (Fig. 180a) was originally at least 200 mm long, with a hooked point and double longitudinal grooves on both sides. The specimen illustrated in Fig. 180c appears to represent the tang of a knife embedded in the remains of a bone handle.

Ten poorly preserved objects (Figs 180i-k, m), all from sidechamber D, are provisionally interpreted as fragments from the casing of a rectangular box. One piece retains a nail by which it was presumably fixed to a wooden frame.

A large iron ring (Fig. 180p), represented by a single fragment, was originally some 60 to 70 mm in internal diameter and may have been a bracelet or anklet. Other iron objects, too fragmentary or poorly preserved to merit detailed description, include four pieces of shanks, a tang (Fig. 180r), seven bars, five blades (*e.g.* Fig. 180b, o), a knob (Fig. 180h), nine pieces of plate or sheet, two discs and five miscellaneous fragments.

Shell
(D.W.P.)

Primary contexts in MD yielded pieces of nineteen shell plaques (Fig. 181). They are for the most part poorly preserved and the original surfaces have often flaked away. They appear to have been originally chipped to roughly rectangular shapes, 49 to 66 by 40 to 55 mm; the maximum thickness preserved is 7.9 mm, but most specimens are much reduced by flaking of the surfaces. Twelve of the plaques retain traces of red paint and ten (including eight painted examples) have incised decoration: motifs include circles, spirals and a swastika-like design. One plaque, retaining no decoration, is perforated.

The only other shell objects found within the Mausoleum are two large, worn, scoops from low levels in the central passage and sidechamber E: it is possible that they were used for applying render to the walls. It has not proved possible to ascertain the species of shell from which these objects were made.

10 mm

Fig. 181 Shell plaques from phase-I contexts within the Mausoleum.

Lithics
(Laurel Phillipson)

Only four chipped stone artefacts were recorded from phase-I contexts on the floor of the Mausoleum. Noteworthy is a steep, possibly burnt, chert scraper (Fig. 182a), not of the same pattern as the numerous highly standardised convex chert scrapers collected from surface sites to the west of Aksum. It is partly covered with mortar apparently identical to that with which the

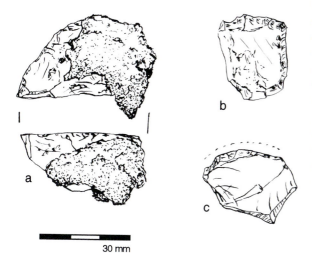

Fig. 182 *Lithics from phase-I contexts within the Mausoleum.*

interior walls had been plastered, and may be assumed to be contemporaneous with or to predate construction of the Mausoleum. Also recovered from primary contexts were a chert shallow flake scraper similarly affected by fire (Fig. 182b), another, unburnt shallow scraper on a chalcedony flake (Fig. 182c) and a chert chip 48 mm in maximum dimension. The only other stone artefact, from sidechamber F, is a wedge-shaped slab, 224 mm long, showing possible signs of utilisation at one end.

ARTEFACTS FROM LATER CONTEXTS

Pottery and other clay objects
(Jacke Phillips)

POTTERY FROM INTERNAL CONTEXTS
Phase II
Characteristic features of the phase-II ceramics include multi-line incised designs sometimes with cross-hatching, jars with bulging neck profile, shallow bowl forms, ledge-rim bowls with incised grooves which may imitate Roman types, semi-globular bowls, jars having a collar groove, and both horizontal and vertical strap loop handles, some having incised lines along the length. Many of these features also appear in phases 2 and 3 outside the Mausoleum (pp. 208-9, below), as well as in the Late Aksumite levels at D site (pp. 312-34). A few sherds of Pre-Aksumite types were also present.

Phase III
Features already encountered in phase II continued into phases III and IV which were, as noted above, sometimes difficult to separate stratigraphically. New features include punctate embellishment at junctions of multi-line incised decoration, large body bosses, highly burnished dishes, thumb-impressed pulled lug handles on rims of shallow bowls, tall cylinder-neck jars, thick loop-handled lids, and both double-pierced thick horizontal lug handles and large roughly punctated holes through vertical strap handles on jars and pots. An porcelain bowl of East Asian origin, represented by a single rim fragment (Fig. 183a), is of a

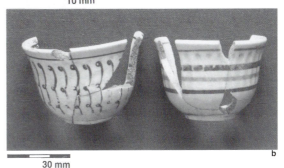

Fig. 183 *Glazed pottery from Mausoleum post-Aksumite and recent contexts: **a** - imported porcelain; **b** - coffee cup.*

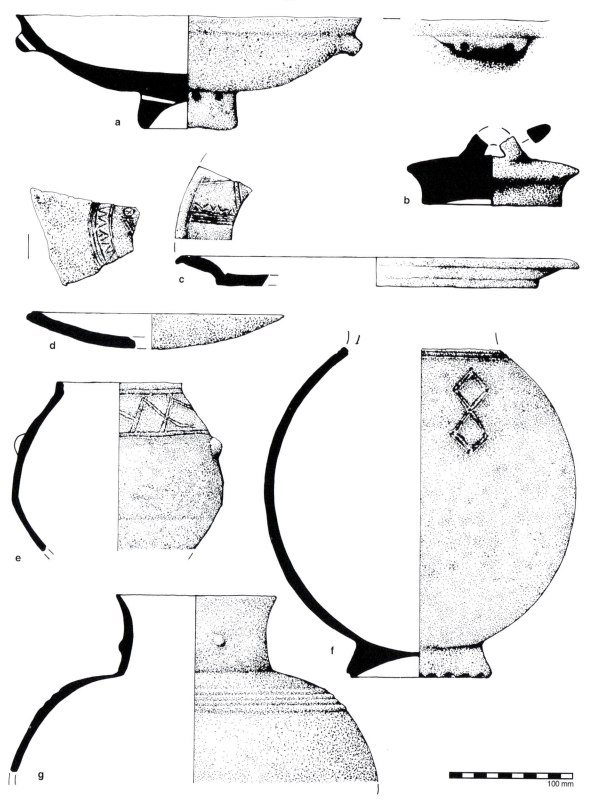

Fig. 184 *Pottery bowls, jar and lid from later contexts within the Mausoleum.*

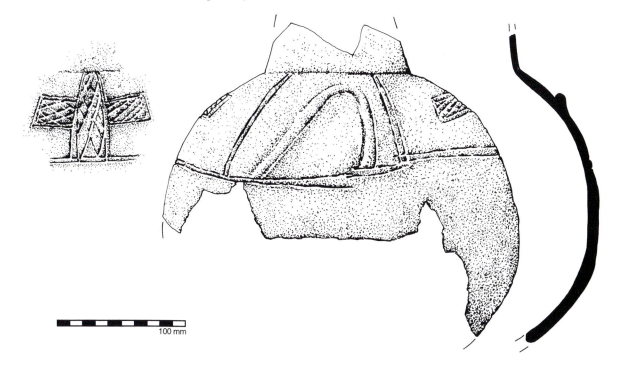

Fig. 185 *Post-Aksumite jar from within the Mausoleum.*

type which does not pre-date the eighteenth century (Ms J. Harrison-Hall, British Museum, *pers. comm.*), being wholly distinct from the coffee cups common from phase 4B onwards. None of these features is re-presented at D site, and they may be regarded as post-Aksumite, although some older sherds were recovered, including a Late Aksumite semi-globular bowl with a post-firing incised cross.

Phase IV

Contexts of this phase are limited to those immediately below the eastern and central shafts, although it is possible that the western shaft may also have been open for part of the time. The deposits were densely packed with pottery which had been thrown into the shaft to break and splay out in cones inside the Mausoleum. Numerous joining sherds confirm this interpretation; and in some cases substantially whole vessels could be reconstructed. This use of the shafts for rubbish disposal probably correlates with the beginning of phase-4B activity noted in trenches M5 to M7. If the sherd of porcelain noted above is correctly dated and attributed to phase III, these deposits cannot be earlier than the eighteenth century.

Features described in phase III continue in phase IV, but the fragments are generally more substantial and profiles more complete. Most vessels are either a badly fired grey with numerous reduction marks or black burnished wares, although some finely gritty yellowish vessels also appear. Shallow bowls having rounded (Fig. 184d), flat (Fig. 184c) or ring-bases (Fig. 184a) and a normally burnished surface are common, many with long horizontal lug handles pierced twice presumably for suspension. At least one has vertical handles. Large cylinder-neck jars with globular bodies have incised and applied designs on the shoulders (Figs 184f, 185). The yellowish vessels tend to be more finely made but less heavily decorated, with only some fluting and bosses (Fig. 184g). An inset lid has a loop handle (Fig. 184b). A unique jar (Fig. 186) with splayed pedestal base and double-strap handle employs vertical combed bands partly obscured by finger-rubbing, alternating with applied vertical ridges. Pots (Figs 184e, 187b) are differentiated by their wide mouth and short collar neck, sometimes with a vertical strap handle.

Phase V

Other than the pot illustrated in Fig. 187a, very little pottery was recovered from deposits which represent the final silting of the Mausoleum.

POTTERY FROM EXTERNAL CONTEXTS

In the following section, illustration is restricted to types not figured above. Much of the pottery from the external trenches is probably of fairly recent date but the chronology of this material is poorly understood.

Phase 1

The external trenches revealed no artefacts that were demonstrably contemporary with the construction and original use of the Mausoleum.

Phase 2

Very little pottery was recovered from these deposits, most of it being worn and highly fragmented but otherwise resembling that from the phase-I deposits

within the Mausoleum, whence it probably derived along with mortar and brick fragments during early clearance of the tomb. A few fragments akin to Late Aksumite pottery from D site were also present, including sherds of imported African Red Slip ware bowls (Fig. 188a), a ledge-rim with two grooves in imitation of ARS types, and rims of semi-spherical and shallow bowls.

Phase 3

Similarly mixed material was recovered, again generally worn and fragmentary but in far greater quantity.

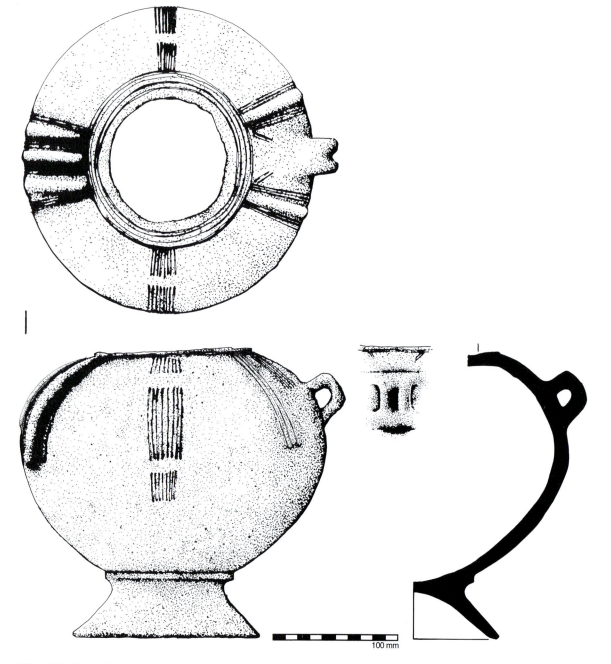

Fig. 186 *Post-Aksumite jar from the Mausoleum trenches.*

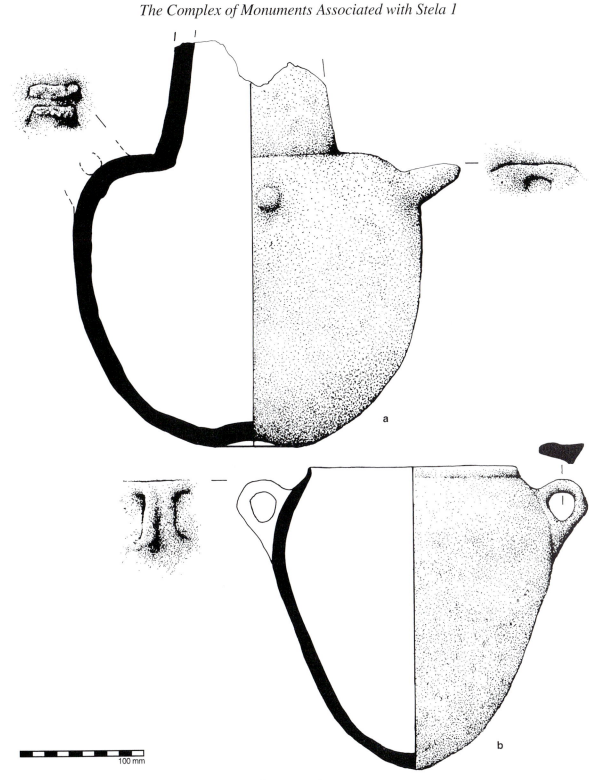

100 mm

Fig. 187 *Post-Aksumite pots from the Mausoleum trenches.*

Some large joining sherds in M6B(9) and (12) (*e.g.* Fig. 188e) suggest rapid deposition. Fewer sherds were encountered which appear to be derived from the primary deposit and these were more worn; the later material again includes forms and decoration comparable with the Late Aksumite pottery from D site, together with some which is probably of post-Aksumite or recent date. The high proportion of black burnished wares suggests that this phase post-dates the abandonment of D site.

Phase 4A

This phase represents the tunnel in M6, deposits associated with which were not distinguished during excavation from those of phases 3 and 4B. The worn and fragmentary pottery that was recovered indicates a mixture of early and late material. A nearly complete coarse grey handled pot (Fig. 188c) from the northeast corner of M6B(10), may come from the tunnel fill.

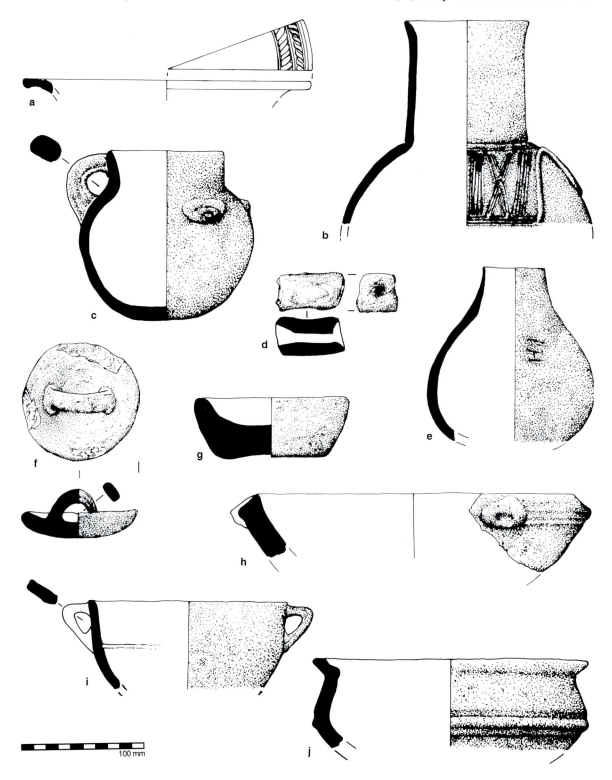

Fig. 188 *Pottery bowls, jars, pot and lid from the Mausoleum trenches.*

Although its age remains uncertain, pottery of this type could be as recent as the seventeenth or eighteenth centuries.

Phase 4B

The pottery again represents a mixture of several periods, with a marked increase in the poorly made grey wares indicative of recent ceramics. Although the western shaft does not appear to have been used as a dump as were the other two shafts, the iron slag recovered in these contexts suggests that the area immediately above was used for some industrial purpose. The fragmentary pottery includes numerous examples typical of recent wares: jars with tall cylindrical necks (Fig. 188b) or short collars and vertical strap handle, incised multi-line shoulder patterns with punctated junctions and butterfly and applied arch designs, pattern-burnished cups or goblets, deep open bowls with angular handles (Fig. 188i), shallow bowls including highly burnished examples with a carinated profile and pierced horizontal ledge-handle. A crude lid (Fig. 188f) is of the convex type with strap loop handle. Small porcelain coffee cups appear in the upper layers of this phase. A shallow thick-walled flat-bottomed bowl (Fig. 188g), thickly encrusted with blackened oily residue, may have been used as a lamp or for some industrial purpose, as may a small elongated spout fragment (Fig. 188d), square in section, similarly soot-encrusted on the interior and one open end, and marked by fire on either side.

Phase 5

The house occupation level likewise produced large quantities of pottery, including some joining fragments. Recent forms and decoration predominate, generally with a burnished black or unslipped grey surface, most with flash marks indicative of uncontrolled firing. Most common are thick-walled shallow bowls (Fig. 188h), as well as jars, pots and carinated bowls. A tall neck of a jar of type paralleled in a late nineteenth-century context at K site (Fig. 346, below) was found *in situ* in a room corner, its body deliberately removed. Small porcelain coffee cups (Fig. 183b) were scattered, their joining fragments linking phases 5 and 6 in trenches M5 and M6; some may have been imported but at least two bear the stamps of an Asmara factory. Pattern-burnished goblets or cups are common, one with a rough post-firing Ethiopic inscription *birr* (= silver, money).

Phases 6-7

The highly disturbed nature of these deposits denies any stratigraphical value to their contents, which include demonstrably recent pottery (*e.g.* Fig. 188j) as well as material derived from earlier horizons.

OTHER CLAY OBJECTS

Five clay objects, other than pottery vessels, were recovered within the Mausoleum, all from secondary contexts. From phase III came two small cones; one (Fig. 189b) is perforated, 15 mm thick and 24 mm in diameter. The other (Fig. 189a), unpierced but decorated with randomly incised vertical lines, is only 10 mm thick but 34 mm in diameter and may be a boss broken from a vessel surface. From phases III and IV

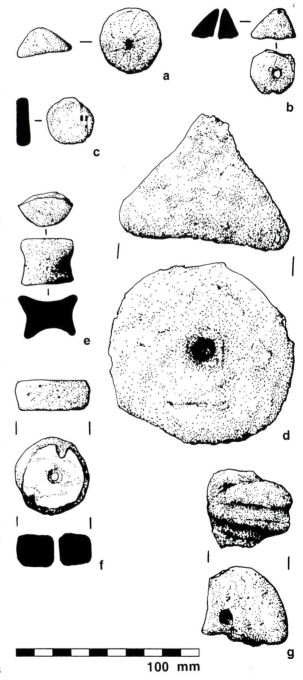

Fig. 189 *Mausoleum clay objects.*

100 mm

come two large cones with battered points. One is 87 mm in diameter and 53 mm tall, the other (Fig. 189d) is 94 mm in diameter and 68 mm tall; they are best interpreted as bungs. The last object is a sherd (Fig. 189c) abraded to make a 26-mm unperforated disc.

Of the clay objects recovered in the area surrounding the Mausoleum, most were sherds abraded as discs, sometimes pierced, although large cones and other objects were also present. They are concentrated at the phase-5 level and above; most presumably date to the last century or so.

Two cones were recovered in phase-6 contexts, both larger and flatter than those found elsewhere and displaying a strongly convex profile. Their contexts provide no clue to possible date; those of similar profile at D site are much smaller and cannot be cited as parallels. Dimensions are 41 and 72 mm in diameter, 18 and 26 mm in height, the smaller example having a hole diameter of 8 mm (the other could not be measured).

The earliest discs come from phases 3 and 4, made from potsherds which retain the Classical Aksumite decoration of the original vessel. The more numerous later specimens are in varied fabrics and include one made from a sherd of imported porcelain bearing a transfer design. All are roughly abraded, ranging from 14.7 to 16.2 mm in thickness and from 41 to 47 mm in diameter. One has an abortive drill mark near the centre on either side. Pierced discs (*e.g.* Fig. 189f) are less numerous and more carefully produced; again the majority come from phases 4 to 6 although two are from phase 2.

What may be the head of a bird-vessel is illustrated in Fig. 189g. Its phase-3 context, outside the west portal of the Mausoleum, suggests that it may have been derived from the tomb.

Phase 6 yielded an unusual clay object (Fig. 189e), possibly an ear stud despite its size: 29 mm in diameter by 24 mm thick.

Glass and beads
(Michael Harlow)

GLASS

When demonstrably modern material from the upper levels of the external trenches is excluded, the glass from post-primary deposits is far smaller in quantity and variety than that attributed to phase I, being restricted to 21 fragments only (Fig. 190).

Two undiagnostic body fragments of medium blue translucent glass came from phase-II contexts within the Mausoleum. Phase III yielded, beneath the western brick arch of the Mausoleum, two pieces of

Phase	medium blue	colourless	green-tinged colourless	brown	turquoise	green/yellow	Total
II	1	-	-	-	-	-	1
III	-	-	-	-	1	2	3
IV	1	-	-	-	-	1	2
4	-	4	3	-	-	-	7
5	-	2	-	-	1	1	4
6	-	1	-	3	-	-	4

Fig. 190 Tabulation of glass from later Mausoleum contexts.

translucent olive green glass (4GY 6/5): a ring-base fragment originally some 100 to 130 mm in diameter (Fig. 191a) and what seems to be a fragment from a neck or shoulder some 25 mm in diameter. If the two pieces are from the same vessel this would seem to have been a ring-based flask or jug. Two other undiagnostic body fragments from phase-II contexts are of medium blue translucent glass. Also from phase III within the Mausoleum was an everted rim fragment from a dark turquoise (6BG 4/5) vessel about 200 mm in diameter. From phase IV came a body fragment of yellowish green (5GY 8/4) from a mould-blown vessel with a raised honeycomb pattern on the exterior surface, and a rim fragment of unusual opaque medium blue glass (2.5PB 5/8).

Outside the Mausoleum in trench M7, a phase-4B fireplace area predating the nineteenth-century houses yielded a fragment from a shallow bowl or cup in translucent colourless glass with a turquoise tinge: it retains a rolled-edge rim with a horizontal groove immediately below. Phase-4 deposits in trench M6 contained four colourless fragments from a bottle or flask, and two turquoise body fragments.

Glass from phase-5 contexts redeposited during recent landscaping included fragments which probably derive from earlier deposits. One (Fig. 191b) is a pale turquoise (2.5BG 7/3) body fragment with a U-shape applied trail, clearly from a goblet of type B (Munro-Hay 1989: 189-90, figs 14.2-5). The other, of translucent colourless glass 1.3 mm thick with a shallow S-profile and one rolled edge, may come from a bowl rim or the foot of a goblet.

A small fragment of mould-blown colourless glass from unstratified backfill has decoration in the

10 mm   a

10 mm   b

Fig. 191 *Glass from later Mausoleum contexts.*

form of a waisted protruding knob very similar to that illustrated by Munro-Hay (1989: fig. 14.169). It represents a distinctive and well known form of decoration from the fourth-century Roman world (Price and Cottam 1998: 32, fig. 5.2, pl. 4.4).

A total of 2234 fragments of apparently modern glass came from the upper contexts of the trenches outside the Mausoleum, particularly M5, M6, M7, and M8. It was translucent and colourless, light green, dark green, reddish brown, or light blue. Two were demonstrably Italian.

BEADS

Post-primary contexts in the Mausoleum trenches yielded 255 glass beads, two of stone and two of clay

(Fig. 193). Of these, 228 came from inside the Mausoleum (166 from phase II, 60 from phase III and 2 from phase V). Twenty-seven beads came from the external trenches (seven from phase 4, five from phase 5 and fifteen from phase 6).

In contrast to the primary contexts only two biconical hexagonally faceted beads came from these contexts, in phase V, one being unusually of translucent yellow glass, the other of translucent cobalt blue (Fig. 192a).

Drawn beads dominate numerically. The largest group came from the first 1-m strip of sidechamber G, where 224 drawn beads were recovered - 58 from phase III, and 166 from phase II (Fig. 194a). The majority (208) were opaque dark red short and standard cylindrical beads but there were also a few green, dark blue and turquoise examples. It is noteworthy that two similar specimens were recovered from immediately underlying deposits attributed to phase I (cf. p. 200, above). Two common types of drawn bead are illustrated (Figs 192b, c) to record their presence in phase 6. The first is short and almost discoid, the second standard and almost barrel-shaped.

Six ring beads (type XII of Munro-Hay 1989: 172) came from phase 6 in the M5 and M6 trenches. Four are in translucent cobalt blue glass (Fig. 192d) and two, more barrel-shaped, are opaque white. Beads of this type are currently used at Aksum to decorate

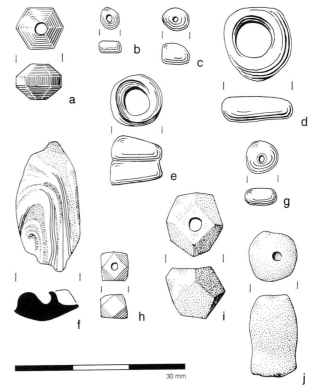

30 mm

Fig. 192 *Beads from later Mausoleum contexts.*

	cobalt blue O	cobalt blue T	blue O	blue T	green O	green T	turquoise O	turquoise T	red O	yellow T	white O	other glass	stone	clay	Total
Interior															
Phase I	1	7	-	2	1	2	3	4	1	2	1	-	-	-	24
Phase II	-	-	9	-	1	-	2	-	154	-	-	-	1	-	167
Phase III	-	-	1	-	1	1	2	-	55	-	-	-	-	-	60
Phase V	-	1	-	-	1	-	-	-	-	-	-	-	-	-	2
Exterior															
Phase 4B	-	2	-	-	1	1	-	-	1	-	-	2	-	2	9
Phase 5	-	3	-	-	-	1	-	-	-	-	-	1	-	-	5
Phase 6	-	4	1	1	-	3	-	2	-	1	2	1	1	-	16

Fig. 193 *Summary of beads from later Mausoleum contexts. (O = opaque, T = translucent).*

10 mm

a

10 mm

b

Fig. 194 *Beads from later Masusoleum contexts.*

leather baby-carriers, and the excavated examples are probably of fairly recent date. A variant is a double-ring bead from M5(3) (Fig. 192e; cf. Munro-Hay 1989: fig. 11.44).

Four unusual glass beads are worth noting:
- a fragment of a large ellipsoid bead in translucent green and opaque red and white glass, from phase 4 (Fig. 192f);
- a large opaque black oblate with green, cream and pink marvered spots, from phase 5 (Fig. 194b; cf. Dubin 1987: 328-41, no. 367 on chart);[29]
- an oblate with a white opaque core surrounded by red translucent glass, from phase 6 (Fig. 192g); and
- a cube with chamfered corners in translucent dark green glass, from phase 6 (Fig. 192h, cf. type XIII of Munro-Hay 1989: 172).

[29] Dubin (*loc. cit.*) describes the bead as of 'wound glass with marvered crumb decoration' and attributes it to the 'Roman Empire', AD 300-50.

The two stone beads comprise an off-white rectangular marble cube with chamfered corners from phase II in sidechamber E (Fig. 192i), and a barrel bead in reddish brown marble with tiny black inclusions from phase 6.

The two clay beads were both long cylinders and came from phase 4 (Fig. 192j).

Metal
(D.W.P.)

Four Aksumite coins (cf. Appendix V) were recovered during investigation of the Mausoleum area. One, possibly from phase I, has been noted above (p. 200). Two came from unstratified contexts outside the tomb: M/166\ and M/198\, respectively type 131/2 [Ioel AE 1] and type 76 [Anonymous AE 2]. M/404\ was recovered at a depth of 4.04 m in trench M6B(10), outside the western portal, associated with other Late Aksumite artefacts: type 137 [Hataz AR 1].

Only a single piece of gold foil came from post-primary deposits within the Mausoleum. It was recovered in sidechamber D in a context attributed to phase II; the possibility that it derived from the phase-I deposit cannot be precluded.

The fill of the phase-4A tunnel leading through the Mausoleum's exterior wall into sidechamber K yielded a copper alloy nail (Fig. 195b), the round head of which is elaborated with a design of three concentric rings picked out in silver. Again, it is possible that this was derived from the Mausoleum's primary deposit.

Metal from post-primary contexts was otherwise remarkably rare. There are seven objects of copper alloy, of which the only ones worthy of note are a needle (Fig. 195a) from phase 4B in M5 and two small rings of rod or wire from phase-3 deposits in M6A. Within the Mausoleum, ten iron objects came from secondary contexts: two in the central passage, seven in sidechamber D and one in sidechamber G. They comprise one strip, one shank, one box fragment and seven pieces of bar. Outside, a small iron knife with a curved blade (Fig. 196a) came from an apparently undisturbed context of phase 4B in M4, with a second example (Fig. 196b) retaining a long looped-ended tang from a deposit much disturbed during landscaping. The other metal objects are demonstrably modern, associated with the destruction of the nineteenth-century houses and subsequent landscaping.

Shell
(D.W.P.)

Seven cowrie shells, all but one perforated and bearing traces of red paint, were recovered. They came exclusively from horizons post-dating the secondary fill of the Mausoleum, five being associated with the house construction in trenches M5 and M6, and two with the 1960s landscaping.

Stone
(D.W.P.)

A broken stone cylinder (perhaps part of a small pestle), 126 mm long by 46 mm in diameter, and a piece of slate came from phase-II contexts in the central passage. The former may be compared with a complete example from D site (Fig. 305, below),

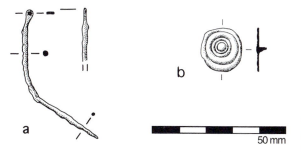

Fig. 195 *Copper alloy artefacts from later Mausoleum contexts.*

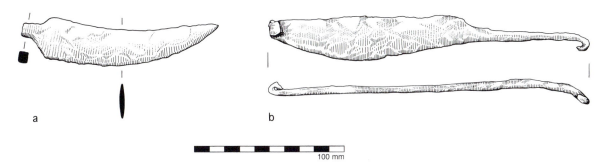

Fig. 196 *Iron knives from later Mausoleum contexts.*

Fig. 197 *Stone artefacts from later Mausoleum contexts: **a** - slate disc; **b** - inscribed burnisher.*

One obsidian chip with a maximum dimension of 19 mm, from a topsoil landscaping level, had a heavily utilised edge and heavy polish, presumably from being finger-held, on both faces. It was not possible from such a small fragment to reconstruct the original shape of the artefact, but the wear patterns are not inconsistent with its having been used as a small knife or cutting tool. Three other chips and flake fragments, two in obsidian and one in chalcedony, were recovered from these disturbed horizons. None of these lithics need be regarded as having been used at the late date implied by the post-primary levels in which they were found; all are likely to have been redeposited from earlier contexts.

Fig. 198 *Likanos flake from a Mausoleum phase-V context.*

while the latter may have been some sort of plaque. Later horizons of phases 4B to 6 in trenches M5 and M6 yielded four lower grindstones, three rubbing stones, one pestle, one door-socket or mortar and three slate discs (*e.g*. Fig. 197a). Also from phase 4B in M6B was a rectangular green stone (probably hornfels) burnisher, 45 mm long and 27 by 25 mm in section, rubbed smooth on one face and finger-worn all over through repeated use (Fig. 197b). The smoothed face is lightly scratched with the three Ethiopic characters *salaha* (= to rub or grind), clearly executed after the main period of use for that purpose.

Lithics
(Laurel Phillipson)

A phase-V level of fill in sidechamber E yielded a Likanos flake (see pp. 360-1) in obsidian; this (Fig. 198) is the only example of this class of artefact found away from D site. Also recovered from post-primary contexts were two joining mudstone flakes, and a few chips and flakes, one in chert/chalcedony and the others in obsidian.

HUMAN SKELETAL MATERIAL
(Helen Cook)

Just over 160 human bones and teeth were recovered from the Mausoleum. None was from the primary deposit, and the mixed nature of the later fill meant that the age of the skeletal material which it contained could not be estimated with any precision. Furthermore, the repeated robbing and disturbance to which the tomb had been subjected meant that few individual bones could be associated with others; it was therefore

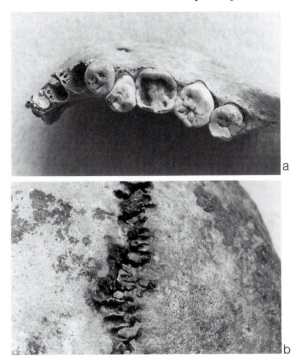

Fig. 199 *Human remains from the Mausoleum: a - mandible showing extra cusp in the second molar; b - bilateral pitting of a parietal bone.*

enamel hypoplasia. This indicates a period of life-threatening stress during the time of tooth-formation. The two main causes of enamel hypoplasia are inadequate nutrition and childhood sickness (Langsjoen in Auferheide and Rodriguez-Martin 1998: 405-7). Its high incidence in the sample may suggest a generalised origin. Dental caries occur in 20% of the sample, mainly around the crown. There were a few abscesses, both healed and unhealed, which must have been very painful if not immediately life-threatening. In a few cases tooth wear was uneven, possibly due to using teeth as tools or to over-compensation for prior tooth loss (W.Bass 1995: 300-1).

One final point of interest from the dentition is an extra cusp or enamel pearl on the occlusal surface of an *in situ* left second molar (Fig. 199a). Extra cusps may have genetic significance in tracing populations if the sample size is sufficient (W.Bass 1995: 292-6), but the single example recovered from the Mausoleum may be a solitary mutation.

Non-dental pathologies were comparatively rare in the Mausoleum skeletal material. Grooving on one patella indicates arthritis, possibly rheumatoid but probably osteo-arthritis (Brothwell 1981: 143-51). Two femurs in the sample show slight anterior bowing, the cause of which is often dietary, such as mild vitamin D deficiency during childhood or, which is more probable at Aksum, lathyrism caused by incorrect preparation of grass pea *Lathyrus sativus* (Yusuf and Lambein 1995). The final pathology can be seen in the pitted eye sockets (cribia orbitalia) of two specimens, and possibly in the lesions on the cranial vault of another (Fig. 199b). These pathologies are commonly associated with haematological disorders such as iron-deficiency anaemia which can result from diet, chronic disease or parasitic infection, extreme blood-loss through injury or childbirth. (All three affected bones from the Mausoleum came from young adult females.) However, similar osteo-effects are produced by genetic anaemias such as the sickle-cell anaemia which is common in parts of Africa today, providing the sufferer with protection from malaria, and may have been prevalent in the past.

necessary to address the sample in terms of separate bones rather than of individual people. The majority of the bone fragments recovered were identifiable as to element, while a few provided information as to the age, sex and physiology of the people represented.

One fifth of the bones could be sexed according to the criteria of W. Bass (1995); almost twice as many male as female bones were recorded. All age groups are represented: of 41 elements, representing at least 9 individuals, for which age estimates could be made, 22% were from children under the age of 10 years, 39% were from adolescents aged 10 to 17 years at death, 14% came from young adults between 17 and 25 years old and 24% were 25 to 45 years old. The apparently high frequency of adolescent elements may result more from sample size than from mortality patterns or burial practice.

The sample contained 70 teeth displaying a range of pathologies. Over a third showed signs of periodontitis, where inflammation of the gums has been transmitted to the bone, resulting in reabsorption of the alveolar bone and exposure of the tooth roots Dental calculus is a primary cause of periodontal infection (Brothwell 1981: 159), and there is a correspondingly high incidence of calculus in the Mausoleum sample. A quarter of the dental sample displayed

ARCHAEOBOTANY
(Sheila Boardman)

Two samples from the Mausoleum yielded charred plant remains. Both come from deposits attributed to phase 4B, possibly dating as late as the seventeenth or eighteenth centuries. In M7(6) a sample was taken from one of a series of ashy deposits, probably associated with iron working activity outside, and unrelated to, the Mausoleum. This produced a concentration of seeds/grains of possible teff (*Eragrostis* sp.), grasses and other wild plants. The sampling of similar, adjacent deposits did not produce evidence for extensive domestic activity in the area at this time. A sample from M4(4) derives from the apparently deliberate use of domestic rubbish to fill the central shaft during phase 4B (p. 192, above). More than 1 litre of solid charred and fused cereal grains were collected from this deposit. The remarkably uniform remains were predominantly *Sorghum bicolor* grains, with isolated grains and chaff fragments (glume bases) of emmer (*Triticum dicoccon*) and seeds of noog (*Guizotia abyssinica*). This material probably derives from a single incident.

ARCHAEOZOOLOGY
(Chester R. Cain)

Detailed study, following the methods explained in Appendix VIII, was restricted to those deposits which, it has been argued above, probably represent primary

fill dating immediately after the monument's construction. Most of the excavated deposits were dry-screened through 5-mm mesh. A non-archaeozoologist discarded all bone deemed non-identifiable, leaving 191 fragments of which 119 (62%) were identified above the taxonomic level of Mammal.

The following species were represented: *Bos*/Bovid size-class III, Bovid size-class II (cf. caprine), *Equus, Canis* sp. (cf. *C. familiaris*), indeterminate small carnivore (cf. *Felidae* or *Mustelidae*), and *Rodentia*. The surface preservation varied widely, which may suggest that the material did not derive from a single deposition event. The elements did not seem evenly distributed through the structure, but this was not studied systematically. Little human modification was noted on the specimens. One fragment exhibited burning, one possessed probable cut marks, and one may have been gnawed by a carnivore. In view of the shallowness and disturbed nature of these deposits and the large amount of bone in the overlying layers, it is likely that some of the bone recovered in this lowest layer was derived from above.

The East Tomb

STRUCTURE AND EXCAVATION
(D.W.P.)

Exactly opposite the Mausoleum portal, on the east side of the fallen Stela 1, is the entrance to the East Tomb (Figs 201a, b), located in 1974 (Munro-Hay 1989: 75, 77) and further examined in 1993 under the supervision of Gavin Rees. This tomb lacks a monumental portal, but the two entrances are otherwise remarkably similar in style, dimensions, construction and position. However, the east-west Aksumite wall seen on the west side of the fallen Stela 1 immediately south of the Mausoleum's eastern portal, was not present in an analogous position relative to the East Tomb, although such a wall was encountered 0.5 m to the north of the entrance. The entrance is formed by a massive nepheline syenite lintel at least 3.1 m long, now cracked in the centre, supported at each end by a wall which also continued over the lintel, leaving an aperture 2.02 m wide and at least 2.05 m high (Fig. 200). The upper surface of the lintel was 2.4 m below the modern ground level. The lintel must have been in place before the east-west wall, noted above, was built; the significance of this observation is considered on pp. 222-3, below.

It was only practicable to excavate the East Tomb to a distance of 2.4 m from the entrance: the

main lintel and the first roof slab were both broken, the second roof slab appeared to be missing or seriously displaced, and the south wall had slumped (Fig. 201c). It was concluded that the tomb could only be

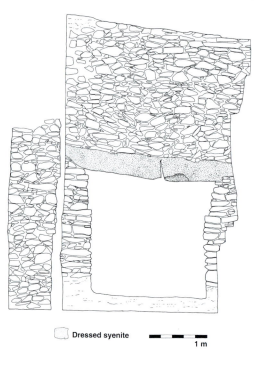

☐ Dressed syenite ▬▬ ▬▬
1 m

Fig. 200 *Photogrammetry of East Tomb entrance.*

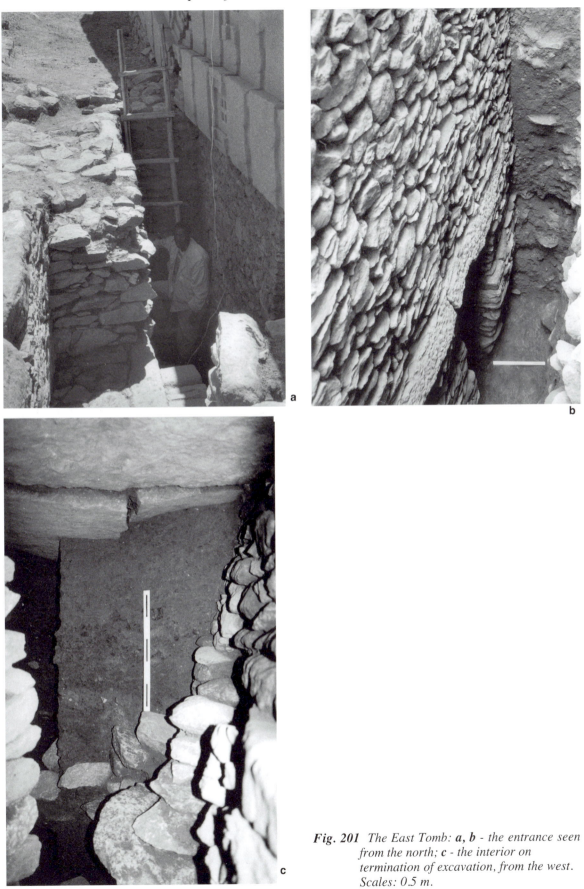

Fig. 201 *The East Tomb: **a, b** - the entrance seen from the north; **c** - the interior on termination of excavation, from the west. Scales: 0.5 m.*

excavated with safety by working down from the modern surface; this was not attempted. The ancient floor lies at a depth of 6.4 m below the modern ground surface and the extent of the East Tomb remains totally unknown. The overall symmetry of the Stela 1 complex suggests the possibility that the East Tomb was, at least in its original design, a mirror-image of the Mausoleum. If this were the case, it would have extended close to the site of Stela 2 (where possible traces of it were, in fact, observed, cf. pp. 147, 152, above), thus explaining why the distance between Stelae 1 and 2 is greater than that between Stelae 2 and 3. It may be noted that excavation inside the East Tomb did not penetrate so far as the point where, assuming symmetry with the Mausoleum, the first sidechambers or roof shaft would have been encountered. At the easternmost limit of excavation there appeared to be a step in the clay floor, perhaps leading to a lower level.

ARTEFACTS
(Jacke Phillips and D.W.P.)

Excavation outside the entrance of the East Tomb was limited to the removal of backfill from the 1974 investigation. The only discovery of note was an Aksumite coin (E/5\), probably of fifth-century date: type 76 [Anonymous AE 2].

The tomb contents appear to be significantly less disturbed than those in the Mausoleum. The 3.2 kg of pottery comprises the following recognisable vessel forms: unembellished smooth-surface vessels including a beaker, plain-rim bowls both with rounded bottom and with footed base, ledge-rim bowls with punctate rim top and with scalloped rim embellishment, a pedestal vessel, a jar with flat strap handle and one with a grooved ledge-rim and horizontal loop handles, and a third jar with a horizontal flat loop handle on the shoulder. Vessels with Classical Aksumite decoration are more limited in range, including two bowls with plain rim, five basins with deep interior zig-zag incision, and two jars with flat strap handles. One base of a footed vessel has a moulded medallion on the interior bottom, and another has an underfoot relief design. A large straight flat-strap handle attached to the exterior of a large closed vessel has no parallel in the Tomb of the Brick Arches. An imported smooth-surfaced amphora body-sherd and a filter-neck fragment were also recovered. None of this pottery retains traces of paint. Although no joining sherds were noted, the general uniformity of the ceramic assemblage strongly suggests that the integrity of the deposit was not compromised by later intrusions. Glass fragments, seven tiny fragments of gold foil, an iron tang and a copper alloy nail were also recovered from these deposits. Overall, the artefacts are very similar to those from phase-I Mausoleum contexts.

Overview
(D.W.P.)

Configuration and use

The original plan for Stela 1, Mausoleum and East Tomb may now be viewed as a unitary design. The stela was intended to mark and to stand between two monumental tombs set behind the front terrace wall of the stelae area (Fig. 202; see also Fig. 416, below).

The Mausoleum was built within an excavated cutting before being covered with stone rubble. The absence of butt joints in its structure strongly suggests that the Mausoleum was built as a single planned entity. Its area must first have been cleared down to a level in the clean natural clay subsoil some 0.25 m below the eventual floor. The walls were built directly on this clay, with no foundation trenches. The main terrace wall also appears to have been built at this time to a total thickness of 1.8 m, integral with the south wall of the Mausoleum's southern sidechambers. When the walls were complete and the roof slabs in position, the whole structure was covered with a thick layer of field stones, 0.3 to 0.4 m in

maximum size. This packing, which survives in places to a thickness of 1.6 m, continued around the walls of the vertical shafts over the central passage, and was faced by the higher courses of the main terrace wall. This work must have been completed before erection of the stela was attempted, although the stela may have been brought to the north of its intended footing at an earlier stage in the proceedings.

Entrances to the Mausoleum and the East Tomb were set in opposite sides of a sunken courtyard, some 17 m long by 8 m wide. Although the East Tomb has been very incompletely investigated, the intended overall symmetry of the complex is apparent: the entrances to the two tombs being virtually identical. Although precise comparisons are difficult, the three entrances investigated - at both ends of the Mausoleum and the west end of the East Tomb - all appear to have been between 1.95 and 2.05 m wide by 2.1 to 2.3 m high. The East Tomb may have been intended represent a mirror image of the Mausoleum.

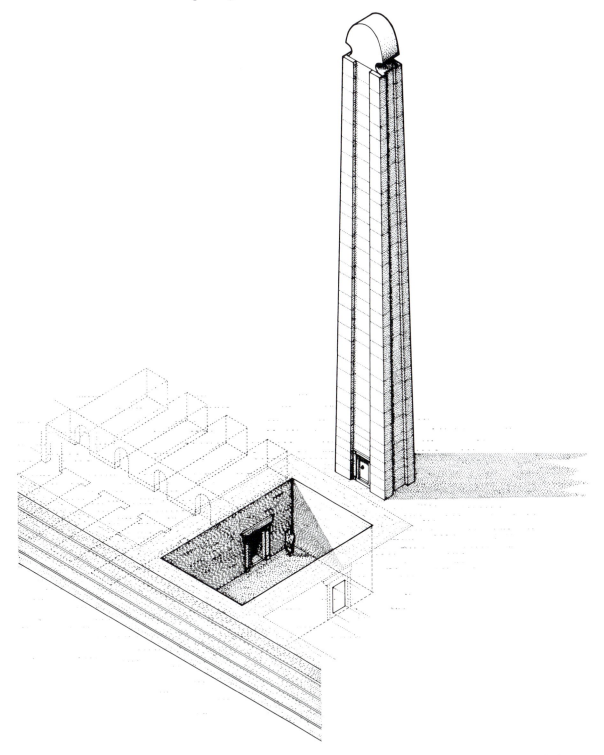

Fig. 202 *Reconstructed bird's eye view of the intended Stela-1 complex. The pit must have been filled before erection of the stela was attempted.*

Some doubt must remain whether the East Tomb was ever completed: it appears to lack a stone flagged floor analogous to that in the Mausoleum, and no evidence was observed that its walls had ever been coated with render. Furthermore, if the East Tomb entrance was originally designed to receive a portal, it seems more likely that this was never inserted than that it was subsequently removed. Remarkably few artefacts were recovered from the apparently undisturbed deposits inside the tomb, and they were not restricted

221

to the floor levels. The fill may have been inserted deliberately within a limited period of time soon after the complex's construction and broadly contemporary with the initial use of the Mausoleum. This would support the hypothesis that the East Tomb was never put to its originally intended purpose but was abandoned before completion, perhaps due to instability and cracked ceiling slabs sequential to the fall of Stela 1. Much further work is needed before the East Tomb can be fully understood.

A hypothesis that the stela was intended to stand in the floor of the courtyard seems unlikely for two reasons. The present position of the stela foot close to the ancient (and modern) ground surface cannot be explained if the erection process involved its setting at a level some 6.5 m lower. Since, as shown above (pp. 157-61), the falling stela broke over the terrace wall, with an intervening fracture over the courtyard, it seems impossible for the stela foot to have flipped up so far, or at its present angle. Secondly, the suggested method of stela erection (pp. 251-4), involving use of a ramp located to the north of its intended position so as to utilise the natural slope of the ground, would have required that the 500-tonne stela be dropped about 9.3 m if its socket were located in the floor of the sunken courtyard. It seems far more likely that the stela was intended to stand a short distance back from the northern edge of the court and that the court itself had been at least partly filled in before erection of the stela commenced. The cross walls noted above, including that immediately north of the entrance to the East Tomb, would have been inserted at that time, presumably in an attempt either to consolidate the infill or to restrict the part of the court which was filled so as to retain access to the tombs.

It is likely that vibration caused by the fall of the stela caused considerable damage to the associated tombs. It is tempting to attribute to this event the fact that, as noted above, the lintels to Mausoleum side-chambers B, C, F, G, H, J, K and L were cracked. The collapse and fracture of the Mausoleum's western portal must have taken place at a time when the courtyard at the western end of the structure was still open, *i.e.* not later than phase 2A, and probably also dates from the fall of the stela. At the East Tomb damage was more substantial: the lintel over the entrance was cracked, walls had slumped and the roof slabs were significantly displaced.

If a connection is accepted between the fall of the stela and the structural damage to the Mausoleum and East Tomb, it is possible to speculate further. Evidence has been cited above for the presence in the Mausoleum of rich objects, probably funerary in association, which were not entirely removed by subsequent robbing. Similar material may also have been

placed in the East Tomb. It seems unlikely that these valuables would have been laid out after the collapse of the stela. It follows that one or more interments, or at least the disposition of their grave-goods, had taken place before the unsuccessful attempt was made to erect the stela. If, as suggested above and supported by the absence of wear on the eastern portal, the court between the two tombs had been filled before the attempted erection, the western portal would have provided an important means of access to the Mausoleum. (Perhaps there was a similar entrance to the East Tomb at its eastern end.) The fact that no attempt seems to have been made to repair the Mausoleum's western portal after its collapse may offer an indication that the whole complex was abandoned as a funerary monument after the collapse of the stela (but cf. footnote 26 on p. 178, above).

Unless Nefas Mawcha had, for some reason not now apparent, been previously abandoned in an unfinished state, it too must have been still under construction at the time Stela 1 collapsed (see pp. 157-61 and Chapter 15). The apex of the falling stela hit the northwestern corner of Nefas Mawcha, depressing that end of the capstone and causing extensive displacement of the walls and roof-slabs of the passage which surrounded its central chamber (Lewcock in Munro-Hay 1989: 165-7).

There is increasing evidence to support the view, originally proposed by van Beek (1967), that Stela 1 was never successfully set upright, but that it fell and broke whilst in process of erection. The case for this may be summarised as follows:

- The stela, three times greater in mass than any other at Aksum, must have been intended for erection in loose rocky soil or at a level at least 9.3 m below the end of the ramp on which it was positioned.
- Only 2.8 m (8.5% of its total length) was intended to be set in its socket: far too little to achieve stability.
- There is some stratigraphic evidence from earlier excavations, noted on p. 160, above, that the stela had fallen by the late fourth century.
- It is clear that the placement of baseplates was the final stage in the placement of a stela. No trace of baseplates survives at Stela 1, nor is there any indication that they were ever installed.
- The fall and fracture of the Mausoleum's western portal was probably caused by vibration when the stela fell and must have occurred before significant deposits had accumulated in the western court; sealing of the tomb, had the stela been successfully erected, would probably have involved the filling of this court.

The detailed configuration of the two courts is not clear. No excavation has been conducted to ascertain whether the main terrace wall continued across the southern end of the western court. The traces of cross-walls in the eastern court are hard to interpret, excavation having been severely restricted by the presence of the fallen stela.

Chronology of primary use

The date at which the Stela-1 complex was constructed is not easy to estimate precisely. Two radiocarbon age-determinations are available on samples that were selected so as to minimise chances of contamination: OxA-8366 on a piece of charcoal embedded in structural mortar and OxA-8367 from phase-I deposit near the rear of sidechamber E (see Appendix VI). The results, when calibrated at two standard deviations, overlap for the period AD 260 to 390. Of the two results, the former is to be preferred as demonstrably associated with the construction of the Mausoleum: at one standard deviation the calibrated result falls in the period AD 240 to 335. The possibility that the sample represents wood that was old at the time of the complex's construction cannot be ruled out. The radiocarbon evidence does not allow us to offer any more precise estimate than mid-third to late fourth century to be proposed for the date at which the complex was constructed. Apart from the coin of Armah, which must be considered as having been introduced through the activity of robbers, there is nothing in the assemblage of artefacts associated with phase I to contradict this estimate. Chapter 15 will present arguments based on architectural and pottery seriation in an attempt to refine this chronology, concluding that a date around the middle of the fourth century is most probable.

Robbing and subsequent use

After phase I, the stratigraphy in and around the Mausoleum is confused and difficult to interpret. It is clear that the structure was thoroughly robbed in and/or after Late Aksumite times, and that thereafter it was repeatedly entered and used for a variety of purposes, including the disposal of rubbish. By contrast, there is no evidence from the limited excavation so far conducted that the East Tomb was entered or re-used at this time. The most recent datable artefact found inside the Mausoleum is a sherd of oriental porcelain for which an age not prior to the eighteenth century has been proposed. If this specimen has been correctly recorded and identified, it follows that the interior of the Mausoleum must have been accessible at least as late as the eighteenth century. Such access may have been gained either through one or more of the roof shafts, or through a tunnel which, it has been argued above, was dug at about this time through the western external wall of the Mausoleum into sidechamber K. Such access makes less remarkable the knowledge of the Mausoleum implied by a passage in the *Liber Axumae* (Conti-Rossini 1910: Munro-Hay (1989: 116). From around the beginning of the early nineteenth century, if not before, the Mausoleum appears to have been sealed, its shafts covered with domestic occupation which evidently continued until the landscaping programme of the 1960s. Recent use of the Stelae Park area is further discussed below by Jacke Phillips in Appendix XII.

Conservation
(D.W.P. and Michael Harlow)

On conclusion of the excavations, those Mausoleum sidechambers not excavated (*i.e.* B, C, G, H, J and L) were walled up with cement blocks set in mud mortar, both for security and in an attempt to maintain the humidity of the deposits (Fig. 203a). The surviving render was consolidated by applying a solution of slaked lime, following Michael Mallinson's advice. The robbed walls at the western end were consolidated with stone rubble and mud mortar. A reinforced metal roof was then installed over trench M6 at a depth of 2.1 m below the modern surface (Figs 203b, d), permitting the area of the western court to be reached through the Mausoleum while remaining protected from the elements. Following reconstruction of the central and western vertical shafts, all three shafts were walled for protection and the whole structure was carefully sealed, with the original ground-surface reinstated. The upper part of the east-west Aksumite wall immediately south of the eastern portal was reconstructed, and a new north-south wall built in Aksumite style on the line of the fallen stela's western edge, to provide safe access to the portal. Similar measures were undertaken on the other side of the fallen stela and the entrances to the Mausoleum and East Tomb were both securely roofed (Fig. 203c), care being taken to ensure adequate drainage and to avoid both visual disfigurement and obstruction to visitors' access to the passage beneath the fallen stela. Suggestions and recommendations were presented to the Ethiopian authorities concerning the long-term conservation and presentation of the Mausoleum, and the means by which visitors may in due course be permitted to gain access.

Fig. 203 *Conservation measures undertaken at the Stela-1 complex: **a** - Mausoleum sidechamber walled up to preserve unexcavated deposits, 0.5-m scale; **b** - walling in trench M6 consolidated; **c** - roof over the East Tomb entrance (cf. Fig. 201a); **d** - roof over trench M6, permitting access to its archaeological features from inside the Mausoleum.*

Chapter 8

THE GUDIT STELAE FIELD

(Ayele Tarekegn and D.W.P.)

The Gudit Stelae Field lies to the west of Aksum, immediately south of the road to Shire and opposite the Dungur ruins (Fig. 204). It was known to the Deutsche Aksum-Expedition as the Western Stelae Field (D.W.Phillipson 1997: 62-5). Although it seems likely that certain works, probably involving the re-erection of fallen stelae, were undertaken without record during the Italian occupation, the first archaeological excavations known to have been carried out there were those of Dr Neville Chittick in 1974 (Munro-Hay 1989: 142-9). Further work was undertaken as part of the 1993-7 campaign under the supervision of Ayele Tarekegn, who has incorporated an account of his work in a doctoral dissertation prepared at the University of Cambridge (Ayele 1997; see also Ayele 1996). Since the dissertation is completed and publication by Dr Ayele is in preparation, only a summary account is presented here.

The name by which the stelae field is currently known is derived from that of the queen Gudit, who is said to have sacked Aksum in the late tenth century AD (Trimingham 1952: 52-3; Sergew 1972: 225-32; Belaynesh *et al.* 1975). It was already known by this designation at the time of the German visit in 1906 (Littmann *et al.* 1913, II: pl. xxvii).

The site covers an area of about 40 ha, sloping slightly downwards to the south, with maximum measurements of 460 m from east to west and 300 m from north to south. Its northern edge has been obliterated by the main road from Aksum to Shire, but elsewhere it is clearly demarcated by an ancient terrace, the line of which has recently been emphasised by the erection of a protective fence. The plan published by Littmann *et al.* 1913, II: 34 and reproduced with minor modification by Munro-Hay 1989: 142 is very incomplete. Survey in 1995-6 (Fig. 205) revealed the

Fig. 204 *View in the Gudit Stelae Field.*

225

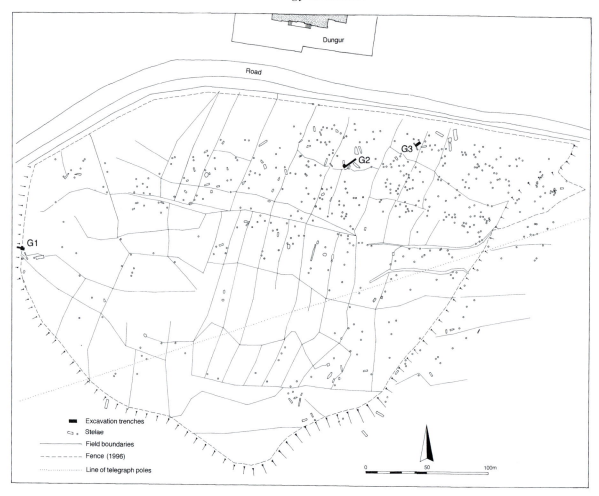

Fig. 205 *Detailed map of the Gudit Stelae Field.*

presence of 594 large stones, most of which were probably stelae. They include a few large dressed examples with rounded tops, but most are rough and undressed. Only about two dozen stelae remain upright. The whole area is currently under traditional cultivation but there are indications that this may be a twentieth-century development. In the course of cultivation several fallen stelae have been intentionally buried; others may have been broken or removed.

Chittick's excavation revealed the presence of an earth-dug tomb, designated GT II, containing abundant pottery, fine glassware and numerous iron tools, probably dating from the second or third centuries AD (Munro-Hay 1989: 142-9, 347-8). Despite its plentiful contents, it clearly belonged to a less elevated place in the socio-economic hierarchy than the broadly contemporary burials in the main Stelae Field. Research in 1994-6 was designed to evaluate the hypothesis that the Gudit Stelae Field represented the burial ground of the middle and/or lower strata of Aksumite society.

In 1994 a trench of 32 sq. m was opened across the terrace which demarcates the western edge of

the site; its location is shown as G1 on Fig. 205. This revealed a 4-m length of a well preserved retaining wall with, abutting its inner face, a stone platform some 4 by 2.5 m, approached by a flight of four stone steps (Fig. 206a). The wall, of rough stone construction, survived to a height of 1.3 m and preserved a single rebate 0.75 m above its foot. Although it cannot be demonstrated that this configuration of the terrace continued around other parts of the site's perimeter, it does suggest that the confines of the Gudit Stelae Field were at some stage clearly set out with the expenditure of considerable effort. The wall and platform both rested directly on a layer of black cotton soil which had formed over natural yellow clay; they thus represent an early phase of human activity at the site. There was evidence that the higher parts of these structures, now destroyed, may have incorporated brickwork. The excavation did not permit an estimate to be made of the absolute age of these features.

In 1995 excavations were conducted in an area of 20 sq. m, designated G2 (Fig. 206b), in the northeastern quadrant of the site adjacent to the small undressed stelae 193, 194, 195 and 196. The archaeo-logical deposits were found to attain a depth in excess of 4 m. The foundations of two stelae were revealed. No. 193 was found to extend to a depth of only 0.26 m below the modern ground surface: it may have been re-erected comparatively recently and may not be in its original location. No. 196, on the other hand, reached a depth of 1.16 m, resting on a large stone slab sup-ported by substantial packing. A fragmentary human burial was located in a deep pit which had been dug from a level 1.5 m below the modern surface. Further down in the same pit, at a depth of 4.0 m was a sec-ond human skull associated with glass and pottery fragments, glass beads and an iron knife. Elsewhere in the trench poorly preserved skeletal material was inter-preted as representing five additional burials in simple

stone-filled pits, the grave goods being limited to small amounts of pottery, glass beads and, in one case, two copper alloy rings. Three of these burials were close together in intersecting pits.

Work at G2 was continued to completion in 1996, when excavations were also conducted in an area of 14 sq. m at G3, some 65 m to the east-northeast, adjacent to stelae nos 121, 122 and 124 (Fig. 206c). These are irregularly shaped but comparatively large stelae, no. 121 still standing 3.5 m high, while the fallen no. 124 was 3.6 m long and 2.9 m in max-imum width. The area was shown to have been ex-tensively disturbed in recent times to a depth of 1.4 m. Below this, two grave pits were located, the stone fill-ing of which formed low mounds above the pits. The human skeletal material was fragmentary and poorly

Fig. 206 *The Gudit Stelae Field:* **a** *- steps exposed by excavation in trench G1;* **b** *- trench G2;* **c** *- trench G3;* **d** *- re-used stela baseplate at Dungur. Scales: 0.5 m.*

preserved, being associated with potsherds, glass beads and heavily corroded iron, as well as animal bones attributed to a bovid and to sheep/goat. In one pit was preserved the broken foot of a stela that had evidently been erected above the burial. Charcoal from successive horizons containing human burials but predating the principal grave-pits noted above has been dated: the lower to 1825 bp ± 40 (OxA-8358) and the higher to 1780 bp ±40 (OxA-8342).

Soil samples from both G2 and G3 were wet-sieved by Sheila Boardman, but were found to contain no identifiable archaeobotanical remains.

Despite the very small scale of the investigations so far undertaken, and the extensive disturbance to which the site has been subjected, it is possible to offer some tentative conclusions. It appears that at least some of the stelae had been erected to mark graves, but no built or rock-cut tombs have been found analogous to those in other burial grounds at Aksum. The Gudit Stelae Field may be interpreted as a place for the interment of less prominent or wealthy members of Aksumite society. One tomb excavated by Chittick, apparently comprising a single pit or chamber, contained an extensive series of grave goods including pottery, ironwork and a fine set of six matching glass goblets, probably of eastern Mediterranean inspiration or manufacture and of early third-century date (Morrison in Munro-Hay 1989: 188-91). Other graves, comprising simple pits, had far fewer accompaniments and were filled with stones before being marked by stelae.

The interments at the Gudit Stelae Field may have taken place at a somewhat earlier date than most of those in the main Stelae Park area. Radiocarbon analyses (Appendix VI) from trench G2 yielded calibrated dates which overlap in the late second and third centuries AD, broadly contemporary with the age of the GT II tomb suggested both by the typology of its glassware and, in general terms, by the radiocarbon date (P-2315: 1720 bp ± 220) obtained in 1974 (Munro-Hay 1989: 26). The cemetery may have remained in use for a long time: religious belief and practice, status and date are all unknown variables. The fact that a stela baseplate (Fig. 206d) was re-used in constructing the adjacent Dungur edifice of probable sixth-century date may suggest that the Gudit Stelae Field had fallen out of use by that time, although it is equally possible that the baseplate could have been brought from elsewhere. It may be concluded that the Gudit Stelae Field was in use for non-élite burials during at least the period from the mid-second to the mid-fourth centuries, and possibly for much of the first five centuries AD. The area was subsequently used for craft or industrial purposes, as indicated by the proliferation of the stone scrapers (see pp. 437-43) of the type to which the site has given its name.

Chapter 9

QUARRIES, STONE WORKING AND STELA ERECTION

The Aksumite quarries at Gobedra Hill and Adi Tsehafi
(Jillian B. Phillips and Jennifer P. Ford)

Stone was employed extensively in Aksumite times both for stelae and in building construction. The material most commonly used was the intrusive igneous granitic rock known as nepheline syenite, a coarse-grained felspathic rock consisting essentially of the minerals feldspar, augite, hornblende and nepheline (cf. Morton 1978). Extraction of building stone on this scale required a major quarrying industry. Wylde (1901:146) believed that the quarry supplying the stelae was situated close to Mai Shum. The Deutsche Aksum-Expedition also drew attention to traces of quarrying in this area and further north, east of the route leading to the Tombs of Kaleb and Gabra Maskal (Littmann *et al.* 1913, II: 62). Such evidence for ancient quarrying as still survives in this area is, however, on a small scale. Traces formerly visible on Mai Qoho have now been almost completely obliterated. More recently, attention has been drawn to similar evidence on Beta Giyorgis (Fattovich *et al.* 2000). This section describes five quarry sites on Gobedra Hill and one at Adi Tsehafi (Fig. 207).

Gobedra Hill is a rocky ridge situated approximately 5 km to the west of Aksum and rising to a height of 200 m above the bottom of the valley which separates it from Beta Giyorgis. Prior to the 1960s its rocky slopes were virtually bare; but reforestation with *Eucalyptus* and the regeneration of native shrubs during recent decades have had a marked effect, and vegetation now obscures many boulders and rocky outcrops interspersed, in the ancient quarrying areas, with worked blocks mainly of large to enormous size (for definitions, see Fig. 208). Terracing, using many small and medium boulders and anciently worked blocks, has recently been carried out all over the hillside, resulting in further modification to the landscape. Furthermore, medium and small blocks and boulders have probably been removed over many centuries by local people whose houses, animal shelters and field boundaries, as elsewhere in Tigray, are constructed of stone, some of which appears to have been worked, although stone-dressing is not now practised except on

an industrial scale. More intensive extraction of building stone and road-construction material has been established since 1991 at the southern foot of Gobedra Hill and threatens to destroy traces of ancient quarrying in that area.

The presence of ancient quarries on Gobedra Hill has been known since at least the 1950s, but they have never been systematically recorded. Previously published notices include those of Anfray (1972a, 1990), while Kobishchanov (1979) referred to them as workshops. Following preliminary visits by members of the Project in 1993-5 (J.S.Phillips 1996), and a reconnaissance by Rebecca Bridgman in 1996, a more intensive investigation was undertaken in 1997 by Jillian Phillips and Jennifer Ford, with Tom Pollard as surveyor and Laurel Phillipson assisting with photography. With advice and guidance from local residents, a physical examination of the area was undertaken in search of tangible evidence for ancient stone extraction. A total of five quarry-areas (designated Quarries I to V) was located at Gobedra; although ancient quarrying appears to have been concentrated in these five areas, wedge-holes and other evidence suggest that stone was also removed in a more opportunistic manner from suitable outcrops on most parts of the hill.

Each quarry was surveyed using an EDM theodolite, with the exception of Quarry V and Adi Tsehafi which were hand-measured. Each quarry was inspected for evidence of extraction methods, rough-outs, working marks and habitation; detailed recording of wedge-holes was undertaken. Magnetic susceptibility measurements[30] (Williams-Thorpe and Thorpe 1993) were recorded at a variety of locations, and further readings were undertaken at selected monuments

---

[30] Magnetic susceptibility is a non-destructive method of measuring the extent to which magnetism may be induced in igneous rocks such as granite and syenite which contain ferromagnetic minerals. For accurate readings the surface to be measured should be flat, unweathered and at least 0.10 m in diameter. The manufacturers of the equipment recommend corrections to be applied to readings obtained from uneven or weathered surfaces.

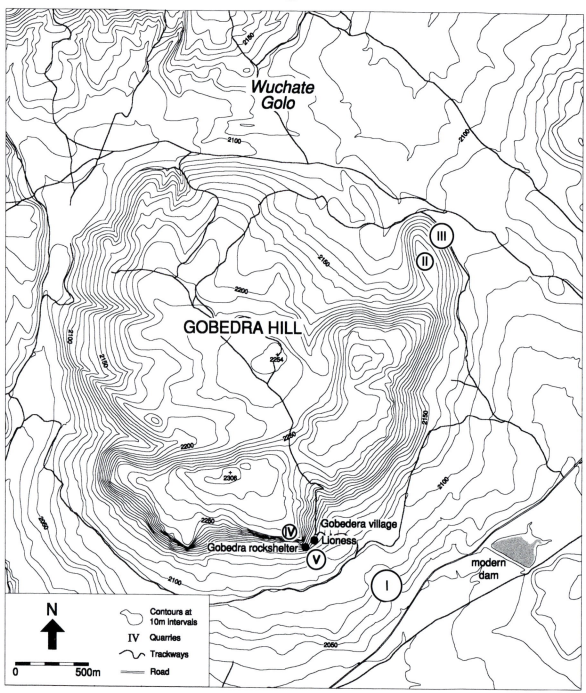

Fig. 207 *Map of Gobedra Hill, showing location of quarries. For the location of the Adi Tsehafi quarry, see Fig. 2, above.*

in Aksum with a view to ascertaining the possible sources of the stone employed: the combined results are presented below in Appendix XI.

Although each of the five areas showing evidence for the removal of blocks was recorded as a quarry, only Quarries II and III show features generally attributed to quarrying areas as conventionally defined. These are: a quarry face or faces from which stone was purposefully removed, a quarry floor where the

extracted stone was initially accumulated, a working area to which the stone was moved for subsequent working, a slipway for the transportation of the worked blocks, and an area where there is an accumulation of waste stone. Under these criteria, Quarries I, IV and V are more correctly defined as stone-extraction areas. In all five areas it was difficult to assess the amount of stone that had been removed, as the original contours of the hillside could not be reconstructed.

BLOCKS

small — pieces of extracted stone less than 0.125 cu m

medium — pieces of extracted stone varying in size from 0.125 to 1.0 cu m

large — pieces of extracted stone varying in size from 1 to larger than 4 cu m

enormous — pieces of extracted stone 4 cu m

BOULDERS   similar to blocks but lacking signs of separation by human agency

CHANNELLING   a deep cut, sometimes made by joining a linear set of wedge-holes, used to separate a block from a quarry face. Larger channels, termed trenches, could be deep enough to accommodate a quarryman

FLAKES   the term is used here to signify the waste product from fine working of stone blocks

OFFCUTS   small pieces of stone, the waste product from extracting blocks

PICK MARKS / PUNCHING   man-made linear furrows on the surface of a stone, made by a pick on a quarry face or by a punch in subsequent stone-dressing

SLIPWAY   man-made steeply down-sloping road used for the purposeful moving of stone

WEDGE-HOLES   sockets cut out to accommodate wedges for splitting the stone

WASTE SLIDE   area of hillside where stone-working waste material is discarded

Fig. 208 Definitions of terms used in descriptions of quarries.

The close proximity of Aksum, Wuchate Golo (de Contenson 1961) and numerous ancient homesteads could be the reason why none of the quarrying areas shows signs of contemporary occupation; only in one small area in Quarry I was any pottery found. As the quarries were easily accessible, they may have been used on a casual basis as need arose, rather than for regular removal of stone over a prolonged period or periods.

Although only two stone-working tools (p. 240, below) were recovered, marks left on the quarry-faces and on the extracted blocks themselves provide evidence of the techniques that were employed. The main method involved channelling, use of wedges and punches. Small indentations at the base of some of the wedge-holes indicate that they were made by means of sharp metal tools. Marks on the quarry faces, on some of the blocks, and on certain monuments show that metal picks may have been employed for rough dressing (*e.g.* Figs 213b, 219f; see also pp. 254-66, below). Although no metal tools were found at the quarry sites, excavations elsewhere provide abundant evidence for Aksumite use of iron and other metals (*e.g.* D.W.Phillipson 1998: 56, 77-8).

Gobedra Quarry I

Quarry I is the most accessible of the Gobedra quarries: it is situated at the south end of Gobedra Hill immediately north of the Shire road. Stone extraction is carried out in the area today, adjacent to the road. The ancient working area (Fig. 209) is represented by a wide scatter of waste blocks and natural boulders bearing wedge-holes. These are concentrated in an area situated between two dry stream-beds to the west of the modern workings. The area suffers erosion during heavy rains, and some of the blocks now visible in the stream-beds may have been displaced, so their present

distribution is not necessarily an indication of the ancient working-area or storage-point. It is thus difficult to assess how much ancient working has taken place in the area. A total of 106 worked blocks was recorded, ranging from medium to large with a few enormous examples. There is no evidence for a formal slipway, which may not have been needed in view of the quarry's hill-foot position.

The majority of the tooling in this working area comprises wedge-marks where the boulders or outcrops have been broken into smaller pieces (Fig. 210f). Blocks 101 and 133 also have channels. Block 101 (Fig. 210a) shows evidence of wedging and channelling in preparation for the removal of a rectangular stone measuring some 11.0 by 2.5 m. On the eastern side, wedge-holes show where stone was being removed to shape the outcrop into a rectangular block (Fig. 210d). The channel on the western side runs from the southern end towards the northern tip (Figs 210b, c). The rest of the block has been roughly dressed with punched tooling. It is conceivable that Blocks 102, 103 and 104, all of which bear wedge-holes and lie adjacent to Block 101, are waste from this working. Block 111 exhibits two rows of wedge-holes beneath which are large areas of punched tooling at an oblique angle. Many of the boulders in this quarry have had their tops removed to produce flat upper surfaces; such flat-topped boulders may then have been worked into smaller dressed blocks. In many instances the surface has been removed in one piece, the waste section lying next to the mother block, both pieces having been for some reason abandoned.

There are few offcuts or chippings to show that stone was dressed before removal from this quarry. One dressed rectangular block found lying down the bank of the eastern stream-bed, Block 188 (Fig. 210e), has a line of fine pecking all around its perimeter,

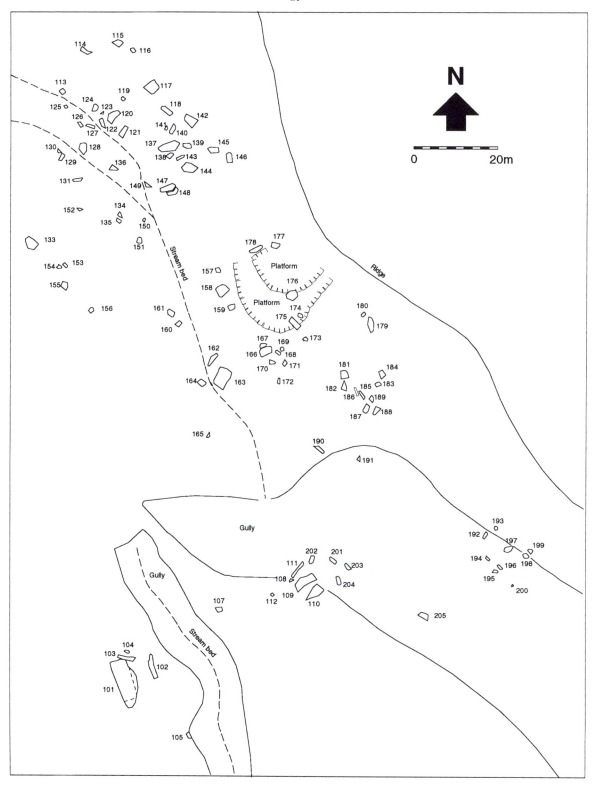

Fig. 209 *Plan of Gobedra Quarry I.*

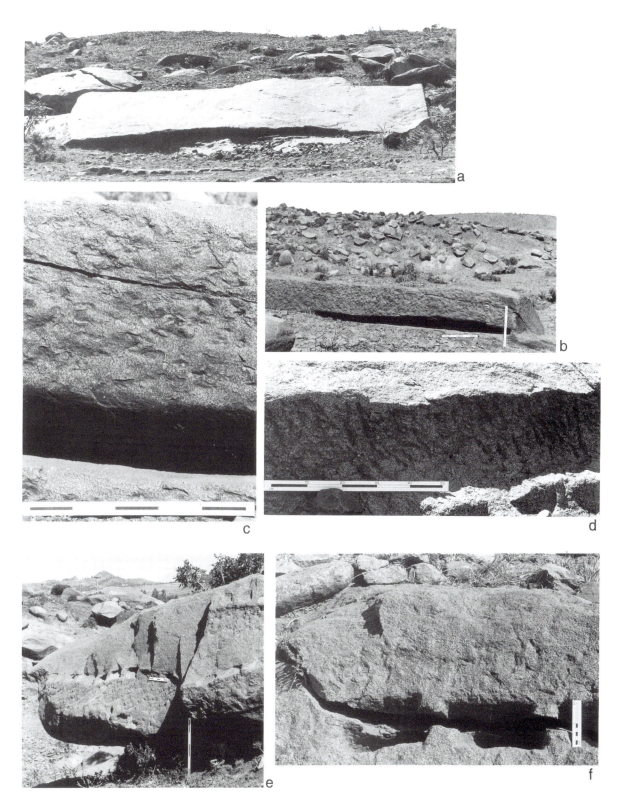

Fig. 210 *Gobedra Quarry I: **a** - general view of Blocks 101, 102 and 103 from the east; **b** - Block 101, west side; **c** - Block 101, west side detail; **d** - Block 101, south end; **e** - Block 188; **f** - Block 132.*

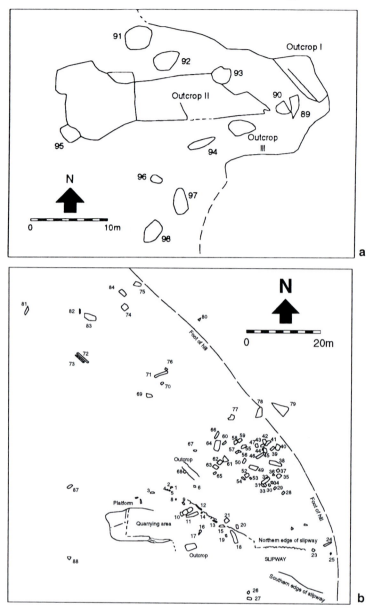

Fig. 211 Plans:
a - Gobedra Quarry II;
b - Gobedra Quarry III.

perhaps indicating the intended size of the block for use as a lintel or ceiling-slab.

No quarry-floor is visible in this area, the whole of which has been subject to erosion. The workings, comprising groups of blocks with wedge-holes, are widely spaced across the hillside. Some fragments of Aksumite pottery and a concentration of lithic flakes were observed on a centrally located le-velled and cleared area, but there is no reason to be-lieve that this was necessarily contemporary with the quarry.

There is no tangible evidence for a working platform. As many of the worked blocks are situated on high ground above the stream beds, those in the stream beds may represent waste. Around Block 101 there may have been a working area for the extraction

of blocks; indeed, such an area may have been estab-lished in any part of the quarry as need arose. Blocks 109, 110, 111 are in their working positions above the stream beds on level ground which may have been used as a working platform. Block 188 was found in the stream bed, its angled position on the slope sug-gesting that it is not in its original working position, having been shifted through erosion and/or deliberately discarded as waste. Blocks 201 to 205 had been stabi-lised in position by means of small boulders. No con-centrations of waste blocks or chippings were noted in the quarry such as might indicate that stone had been shaped there after its extraction, although it is recog-nised that erosion or subsequent removal of stone from areas close to the road may have contributed to this picture.

Fig. 212 *Gobedra Quarry II: **a** - general view to west; **b, c** - Outcrop II; **d** - south face of Outcrop III; **e** - view to northwest over Wuchate Golo, with possible slipway in foreground; **f** - Blocks 89, 90.*

Gobedra Quarry II

Quarry II (Figs 211a, 212a) is located on the plateau of Gobedra Hill, above and to the south of Quarry III. It overlooks the Aksumite site of Wuchate Golo (de Contenson 1961), with which it may have been connected. It is a small compact horseshoe-shaped quarry which extends back into the hillside. The face is horizontal and stone has been taken from the outcrops on the edge of the hill over an area *c.* 30 by 10 m.

Evidence of extraction methods in this quarry is restricted to wedge-holes and channels. Outcrop I has a channel extending from its western to its eastern side, worked in the standard way using parallel pecked lines to define the wedging area. Outcrop II (Fig. 212b) has pecked parallel lines running north to south with complete and partial wedge-holes between them (Fig. 212c). A further set of very large wedge-holes over 0.6 m in length has been made on the eastern side of the outcrop in preparation for removal of a block. Outcrop III (Fig. 212d), partly obscured by recent soil-deposition, is worked with successive rows of wedge-holes approximately 0.12 m apart. It appears that the quarry workers were trying to level the surface of the outcrop before extracting a block.

The quarry-floor is comparatively level, with the western side, used as a working area, containing four blocks set in a line from southwest to northeast. Three of these blocks are propped into working positions. Between Block 92 and Block 93 is a pile of waste offcut blocks and large chippings, indicating a working area. Block 89/90, now partly covered with soil, has been split by means of wedges (Fig. 212f).

There are two disposal-areas within the quarry. In the northwestern corner, nearest to Wuchate Golo, is a large rectangular stone bearing a series of wedge-holes. Further down the hillside, in a vegetation-free area, are some medium-sized unworked blocks. The small amount of waste in the quarry lies to the southeast and comprises a few large blocks, some of which bear wedge-holes. The numerous modern terraces in the vicinity may account for the absence of waste. The only evidence for what may have been a steep slipway is in a much overgrown area on the west-northwestern side of the spur, facing and leading towards Wuchate Golo (Fig. 212e).

It appears from the size of the blocks and the distances between wedge-holes that the stone in this quarry was being extracted in sizes suitable for paving slabs and building blocks.

Gobedra Quarry III

Quarry III is situated on the northeast face of Gobedra Hill facing Beta Giyorgis and overlooking the valley some 40 m below (Fig. 211b). The main working area is between 15 and 20 m high, with three sections

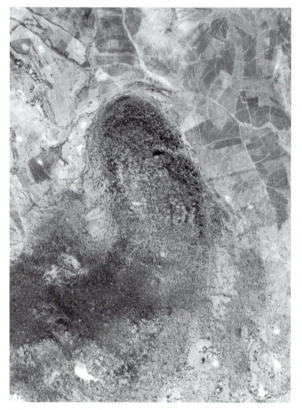

Fig. 213 *Gobedra Quarry III and slipway, from the air.*

facing north, west and east, the total width being between 15 and 20 m (Fig. 215a). The north-facing section has punch-marks and three rows of wedge-holes. One set, made with a stepped punch, is situated low down on the northern end of the face. The second set, at the same level, is about 6 m to the south and comprises two horizontal areas dressed with punch marks in a series of steps, each approximately 0.40 m high (Fig. 215b). The third set is high on the face, about 4 m above ground level.

There is a large gently sloping quarry-floor, now covered with trees, scrub and modern terracing. The undergrowth is thickest below the western face

100 mm

Fig. 214 *Basalt pounder from Gobedra Quarry III*

Fig. 215 *Gobedra Quarry III:* **a** *- south face of main quarry;* **b** *- northern pecked area at foot of quarry face;* **c** *- Block 10;* **d** *- Block A on valley floor* **e** *- circular hole in Block 20;* **f** *- split block 72/73.*

Fig. 216 *Slipway at Gobedra Quarry III: **a** - general view of the hillside; **b** - general view of the slipway;*
***c** - the lower and middle sections of the slipway.*

Fig. 217 *Gobedra Quarry IV: **a, b** - Block 249; **c-f** - Block 251.*

where it is impossible to ascertain whether ancient workings are present, although no working debris is visible.

The majority of the blocks in this quarry are in size-categories large or enormous. A few medium and small blocks remain, but others may have been removed by local residents. Three blocks have 90-mm-deep circular or oval pecked holes (Fig. 215e). Block 63 also has a single pecked line extending along the length of the block just above a circular hole. This type of working has not been observed elsewhere at Aksum. Two blocks, 28 and 87, show how the wedge-holes were marked out. Parallel lines of tiny punched holes were initially prepared; between these lines at regular intervals further lines were pecked at right-angles to mark positions for the wedges. Block 72/3 has been split vertically (Fig. 215f) although neither section was subsequently removed.

Near the base of the hill beneath this area is a large group of worked blocks. The majority of the 88 blocks recognised at Quarry III are in this general area, indicating a regular point of disposal (Fig. 215d). Many of the wedge-holes on these blocks are on their undersides, concealed from initial view, indicating that the blocks had been tumbled down from above.

To the east of the quarry-face is a working area containing worked Blocks 10 and 11 which each bear pecked areas and wedge-holes. Block 10 has two channels dividing the rectangular block into three rough squares, possibly intended for paving, baseplates or ceiling-slabs (Fig. 215c). Below and to the north of Block 10 is a small revetted working area extending eastwards towards the slipway.

The slipway faces east and connects with the level route to Aksum along the foot of Beta Giyorgis (Fig. 213; see also pp. 247-51, below). It runs for approximately 50 m down the hillside from the east side of the quarry floor, at an angle between 35 and 40 degrees (Fig. 216a). Its lower sections (Fig. 216b) consist of a cleared grassy slope, and there is an area of chippings and small offcut blocks just above midway (Fig. 216c). It is revetted on the north side by a series of rocky outcrops and artificially placed boulders, its southern edge being defined by the slope of the hill. The few worked blocks present on the slipway are situated on the northern edge adjacent to the revetments.

Surface finds at Quarries II and III represent the only objects from Gobedra which may plausibly be interpreted as tools used in stone-extraction. Both are cylindrical basalt pounders, that from Quarry III measuring 77 by 76 mm in cross-section and 195 mm long (Fig. 214). One end tapers to a rough conical point and bears evidence for heavy use; the other end is broken. A 40-mm-thick slab of sandstone, 152 by 136 mm, showing signs of having been used to sharpen

metal tools, was another surface find at Quarry III but not necessarily contemporary or associated with stone-extraction.

Gobedra Quarry IV

Quarry IV is situated on the flat summit of Gobedra Hill at its south end, overlooking the Shire road and directly above Quarry V. It is reached by a path which passes Gobedera village and the lioness carving (D.W.Phillipson 1997: 160-2).

This small area comprises three utilised outcrops. The main area lies above and to the west of Quarry V, consisting of two outcrops designated Blocks 249 and 250, on the very edge of the plateau. Both contain wedge-holes which are close to the edge of the outcrops. Those on Block 249 (Figs 217a, b) are situated towards the southern end near a natural fissure and the edge of the plateau, with a sheer drop to Quarry V below. They comprise two almost parallel lines running from east to west along the top of the rock with a third set extending from north to south down the western side of the outcrop. These wedges would have facilitated the removal of an enormous block. Block 250 contains one row of wedge-holes aligned from north to south.

The outcrop numbered as Block 251, the only block worked in this particular area, is situated to the east and north of outcrops 249 and 250. It was being worked into a block measuring 14.1 by 2.0 m with a worked depth of 0.7 m to soil level on the western side, and bears 31 wedge marks in groups along its sides (Figs 217c-f).

The worked blocks are scattered over a large area and there is no evidence of a specific working area. Extraction methods are represented by wedge-holes and punch-marks. Wedge-holes can be seen on all five of the worked blocks; punch-marks are found on Block 251. Two triangular free-standing blocks, 247 and 248, adjacent to each other with 41 and 7 wedge-holes respectively, are propped into their working positions; but no flakes, chippings or offcut blocks are present.

To the east of Blocks 247 and 248 is an area where a few blocks are situated on the very edge of the plateau, immediately above Quarry V. It is possible that blocks could have been pushed over the edge here, but any that were so treated would almost certainly have shattered on impact many metres below. Transport of stone quarried from this hill-top area must have been problematic.

Gobedra Quarry V

The quarry is situated to the northwest of Quarry I and slightly higher up the lower slope of Gobedra Hill. It comprises four extraction areas set amongst fields and

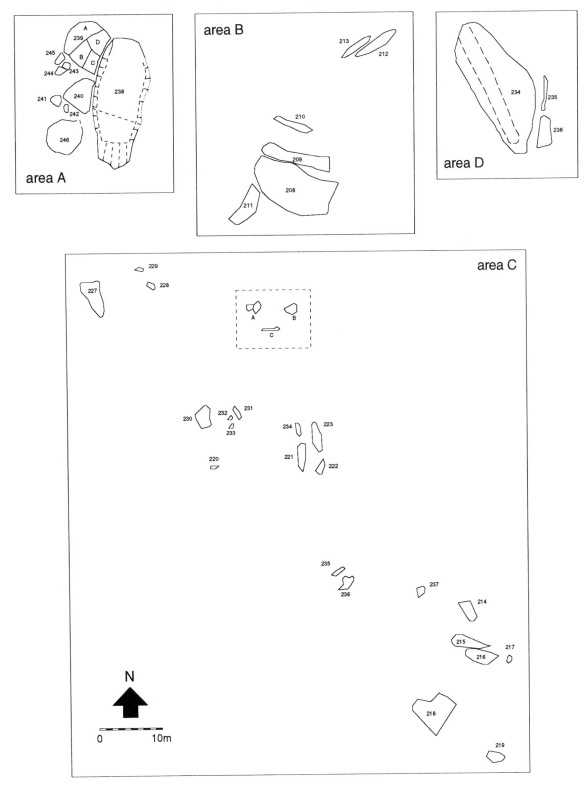

Fig. 218 *Plans of Gobedra Quarry V.*

homesteads on the tablelands directly beneath the rocky outcrop of the hill (Figs 218, 219e). There is no single face in this area as each of the four stone extraction areas A, B, C, and D utilises large outcrops.

Area A comprises a large outcrop of stone measuring approximately 20 by 30 m. Block 238 (Figs 219a, b) is a large rectangular stone, 8 by 20 m. There is a hollowed area through the centre with

Fig. 219 *Gobedra Quarry V: **a** - Block 238; **b** - Block 238, detail of channelling; **c** - Block 246 from west, showing rounded top; **d** - Block 246, detail; **e** - Blocks 208 and 209, showing location at the foot of Gobedra Hill; **f** - Block 208, detail.*

wedging and channelling to the north of the outcrop. Upper and lower grindstones found here, of basalt and syenite respectively, were associated with potsherds of post-Aksumite type and need not be connected with use of the quarry. Block 239, in the outcrop to the west of Block 238, is naturally divided into four areas, each of which contains a series of wedge-holes. A broken stone, Block 246, to the southwest of Block 238, is coarsely dressed on all visible surfaces and has a deliberately rounded end similar to that on certain Aksumite stelae (Figs 219c, d).

Area B lies to the east of Area A, just above the plateau where the land starts to rise towards the main rocky outcrop of Gobedra Hill. In this area are five stela-shaped blocks. The largest, numbered 208 (Figs 219e, f), is roughly rectangular and has a channel running along its length. It has a stepped base and irregular wide linear punch marks worked in an attempt to separate a smaller block. Block 209, propped against Block 208, is dressed and one end is rounded. Block 210 is rectangular with wedge-holes along its longest (northern) side. Blocks 212 and 213 are rectangular with wedge-holes, situated to the northeast of Blocks 208-10. Block 211 is a rough outcrop with three wedge-holes.

Area C, southeast of Area D, extends across the hillside above Area A. The blocks, numbered 213-23 and 226-37, all contain wedge-holes varying in number from one on Block 237 to eleven on Block 227. On Block 234 in this area were found the only physical traces of metal noted at any of the Gobedra quarries: a few small fragments of uncertain age, scattered in one small area, may have been the result of tool-sharpening or repair.

Area D is situated to the northwest of Area A on raised ground directly beneath the main rocky outcrop of Gobedra Hill. It comprises an enormous block, 224, which has a rectangular shape pecked out on the upper surface. There are 52 wedge-holes along its western side: the greatest number of wedge-holes found on any single block in the quarries surveyed. Block 225, adjacent to Block 224 from which it had at one time been removed, bears five wedge-holes.

Quarry at Adi Tsehafi

The settlement known as Adi Tsehafi is situated *c*. 5 km to the northwest of Aksum on the eastern side of Melatta Hill. Its rock-cut tanks, probably of Aksumite age, have long been known (D.W.Phillipson 1997: 162-5, 1998: 59-60) and the place features prominently in historical tradition. The quarrying and stone-extraction areas are mainly positioned in the bed and on the banks of the Mai Goda tributary of the Mareb river (Fig. 220a) close to the school *c*. 1.5 km east of the principal settlement. A unique feature of this quarry, in comparison with those at Gobedra, is the presence of pecked Ethiopic inscriptions and zoomorphic petroglyphs which are not necessarily of Aksumite age (see pp. 423-4, below). In the rainy season the stream rises several metres and it may then have been used in some form of transportation. At the point where the track from Aksum to Adi Tsehafi crosses the Mai Goda is a shallow ford reached by a broad artificial slope or slipway on the right (southeast) bank. This does not appear to be of recent construction and its gentle inclination may have been designed to facilitate hauling stone up from the river crossing on its way to Aksum.

The face in this quarry is mainly horizontal and has been worked in a stepped fashion, though some stone has been extracted vertically from blocks making up the stream bank (Fig. 220e). The horizontal face measures approximately 16 by 30 m, forming a flat plateau to the west of the main stream gully. Other limited working has taken place on the banks downstream to the northeast, northwest and southeast, over a total distance of approximately 1 km. The quarry floor comprises a flat area to the west of the horizontal face. Blocks C and D are situated at the northwesterly point of the working floor and both contain rows of wedge-holes (Figs 221b, c).

Wedges and points have been used throughout the quarry. The form of pecking that was employed here is different from that used on Gobedra Hill, the points being much larger in order to make holes 40 mm in diameter. This pecking was executed in a linear form, widely spaced. The same tools were used in the cracks between the blocks to prise them apart. Another working method found here is the insertion of small pieces of stone between blocks to maintain a gap when the block was being forced apart. Block E, measuring 2.7 by 1.3 and 0.3 m thick, shows the distinctive linear pecked or punched marks associated with this quarry (Fig. 220c); along its northern edge small ovals of stone have been chipped away by the use of metal points so as to prise the stone from the rock face.

Block G, a rectangular shaped, 0.3-m-thick slab measuring 7.8 by 1.0 m, lies in the stream to the south of the main quarry. It is partially submerged in the river gravel, with only a small portion visible above water level at the time of the survey (Fig. 220d). On the hill to the southeast of the main extraction area, Block M, on top of the bank, is a stela-shaped stone abandoned whilst being worked into a rectangular shape. The upper surface has two pairs of parallel pecked lines 6.0 m long and 0.98 m apart (Fig. 220b), one of which served to align a series of wedge-holes. The process of cutting these holes is well illustrated elsewhere (Figs 221a, d).

Fig. 220 *Adi Tsehafi quarry: **a** - general view; **b** - Block M; **c** - quarrying in stream bed; **d** - Block G in stream; **e** - quarrying in stream bank.*

Fig. 221 *Adi Tsehafi quarry: **a** - row of four wedges showing stages of production; **b** - Block C; **c** - Block D; **d** - Block A, showing squared wedge-marks.*

SUMMARY AND DISCUSSION

It is difficult to establish a chronology for the Gobedra and Adi Tsehafi quarries in relative or absolute terms. No dating evidence was recovered that was indubitably associated with their operation. Use of finely dressed monoliths and masonry at Aksum is best dated between the third and seventh centuries AD and this would be a reasonable but unproven estimate for the date of the quarries.[31] The working practices at the Aksum quarries show little evidence of change during the period of operation and are concordant with those attested in Egypt and around the eastern Mediterranean at the general time-depth here proposed.

Comparanda must, of necessity, be drawn from a considerable distance. Ancient African quarrying other than in Egypt was almost invariably casual. Previous studies of ancient Egyptian quarries have concentrated almost exclusively on those of pharaonic age (Klemm and Klemm 1981; Arnold 1991), which employed techniques markedly distinct from those attested at Aksum. It is unfortunate that virtually nothing is known about quarrying techniques employed in southern Arabia during the early centuries AD. Techniques that developed in the Mediterranean region around the mid-first millennium BC provide the best parallels and were introduced to Egypt in Roman, if not Ptolemaic, times. Wedges, probably not used in Egypt during earlier periods (Roder 1965; Nylander 1968), then became widespread (Ward-Perkins 1971). We know that iron tools were being used in Greek quarries around the early sixth century BC and that both wooden and metal wedges were employed (Waelkens *et al.* 1988).

The use of wedges in the removal of a block of stone requires great skill (Benfield 1990: 89-96). Firstly the suitability and size of the stone has to be assessed. An experienced quarryman can do this from the sounds obtained by striking the stone with a hammer, although hidden joints and seams may flaw the extraction process. A natural joint in the rock can be enlarged to lever the block from the quarry-face. Wedges can also be used, involving cutting a row of holes along an appropriate seam. According to Benfield (1990: 94) the wedge-holes should be shaped in such a way that the wedge may be inserted without actually touching the base. Once wedges have been inserted they must then be hit, initially to tighten them and subsequently in rotation. The quarryman knows by feeling the vibrations when the stone will split.

Kozelj (1988), describing the varying techniques used for the extraction of marble from ancient Greek quarries, believes that techniques were dependent on the function of the resulting blocks. Simple methods, such as using a form of crowbar in the bedding planes and natural cracks, were used to prise off blocks which could then be split and used without further work. Blocks produced by this method, from quarries close by, were used for the covering of the Neolithic tombs at Castri, Thasos. At Adi Tsehafi we see a similar method of inserting stones in cracks of the bedding planes in order to prise off blocks of stone.

In antiquity, much of the more prestigious stone appears to have been quarried either on a casual basis for the erection of local monuments, or extracted in a systematic and structured manner for commercial use. The Roman-period quarries at Mons Claudianus and Mons Porphyrites in eastern Egypt fall into the latter category (J.B.Phillips and Wright 1996; J.B. Phillips and Ford 1997; Peacock and Maxfield 1997). The coarse-grained granodiorite quarries at Mons Claudianus cover an area of approximately 1.5 sq. km. The 130 small extraction areas/quarries average 20 m across and were supported by a fort, animal lines and a network of slipways, working platforms and huts. The stone was quarried and worked on site; and the resulting columns were transported across to the Nile and then to Rome. Stone removal was by use of wedges.

Mons Porphyrites, consisting of three main extraction-areas, each with a series of quarries, produced Imperial Porphyry, initially for the sole use of the Roman emperor and then on a more commercial basis. This complex of quarries, supported by villages and slipways, was expanded to support the increasing requirements for porphyry (J.B.Phillips and Wright 1996; J.B.Phillips and Ford 1997; J.B.Phillips 1998). An extremely structured approach was adopted at these quarries with the extracted blocks of porphyry, in some instances, being stacked and numbered. Iron tools were used, evidenced by the small quenching basins found at individual quarries and centrally located smithies.

Kobishchanov (1979) described the Gobedra stone-extraction areas as workshops; and this appears to be a justified term. In the areas here defined as Quarry I, Quarry IV and Quarry V, stone appears to have been removed in an opportunistic method repeatedly using areas that had traditionally provided stone of a suitable quality and size. This view is strengthened by the evidence of several isolated outcrops throughout the foothills showing evidence of stone extraction in the form of wedge marks. The survey shows that small clusters of rock were habitually worked confirming that, once a suitable quality of rock had been found, it was regularly extracted from that location.

The quarries on Gobedra Hill appear to have employed fairly uniform methods of extracting the stone. Wedge-marks, channels and point-marks were

---

[31] There is, however, evidence that dressed stone was employed in central Tigray during earlier times, although not at Aksum itself.

discovered in all the quarries inspected. Working practices, on the other hand, appear to have been systematic only at Quarries II and III which have working areas and slipways; more random extraction took place in the other three quarries, where there is no evidence that the stone was dressed on the quarry site.

Stone extraction at Quarry III appears to have been a well structured process. Working area, slipway and waste area provide the appearance of a formalised way of removing the stone. Considering the size of both the quarry and the waste blocks it seems that the stone extracted from here was used for lintels, ceiling- and paving slabs and building blocks possibly at Dungur and other élite buildings in Aksum. There is no evidence that the large stelae came from this quarry, although some of the smaller ones such as those in the Gudit Stelae Field may have come from here.

The dimensions and methods of extraction in Quarry II indicate that the extracted stone was also being used for paving, ceiling slabs, lintels, and building stone. As the majority of the stone appears to have been taken down the northwestern side of the spur it is logical to assume, pending further investigation, that it was used at the Aksumite site of Wuchate Golo (cf. de Contenson 1961).

Some of the blocks from Quarry I could possibly have been used to form smaller stelae, although the wedge-marks on many of them indicate that the stone was being worked into smaller pieces such as building blocks. One block displays fine pecking on its upper surface which corresponds to the size of a door-lintel.

The scant extent of workings at Quarry IV, inaccessibly located on the summit of Gobedra Hill, implies that this quarry was abandoned soon after it was started. The removal of stone without damage would have presented logistical difficulty.

The large outcrops in Quarry V produced blocks 20 m long and could have been a source for larger stelae, rough-outs for which are clearly visible, although no evidence was found for the production of blocks analogous to the very largest monoliths.

A random selection of wedge-holes was measured in each of the quarries, the results being recorded in the Project Archive. Although they vary in size within and between the quarries, overall they are fairly consistent within the size-range 150 to 220 by 50 to 90 mm and between 80 and 150 mm deep.

Comparison of magnetic susceptibility readings permits tentative conclusions to be drawn concerning the likelihood that stone for certain monuments was obtained from particular Gobedra quarries. (Unfortunately, it has not been possible to obtain readings from the quarry at Adi Tsehafi.) The principal conclusions so far available, tabulated in Appendix XI, must be regarded with caution. It is not possible at this stage of research to attribute a monument to a particular stone-source. Many monuments clearly come from quarries other than those for which magnetic susceptibility readings are currently available. Several stone-sources were evidently in use at the same time for the same construction project. Much more detailed research will be necessary before Aksumite stone quarrying is properly understood.

Transport and stela erection
(D.W.P. and Laurel Phillipson)

TRANSPORT

It is clear from the evidence both at the quarries and, as will be shown below, on the monuments themselves that blocks were only roughly shaped at the point of extraction and that much of the finer dressing was carried out at the building- or erection-site. It follows that most blocks were transported to their final destinations in an unfinished state. Although, as shown above and in Appendix XI, only tentative conclusions may yet be drawn concerning the places where the stone for Aksum's monuments was extracted, the possible quarries are all located at some significant distance from the places where the monuments were erected. For example, a straight line from Gobedra Quarry III to Stela 1 measures 3.35 km, while one from Gobedra Quarry 1 to Ta'akha Maryam is 3.45 km. In each case the shortest practicable route, avoiding steep gradients etc., would be in the order of 4.0 km. It is pertinent to

consider both the routes and the motive power that may have been employed to shift stones which, in the case of Stela 1, weighed more than 500 tonnes.

The routes followed must, at least for the larger stones, have been broad, unencumbered by vegetation or boulders, and relatively level. A view of the terrain between Gobedra and central Aksum suggests the possibility that a route meeting these requirements may have existed along the southern flank of Beta Giyorgis (Figs 222-4). In 1997 this hypothesis was strengthened by close examination on the ground and by detailed mapping. Cultivation and intensive soil-erosion during the past one and a half millennia have combined with twentieth-century terracing, stone removal, dam building and road construction to modify the ancient configuration of the terrain, but the general lie of the land as revealed by the contoured map, and the distribution of minor Aksumite remains, suggest

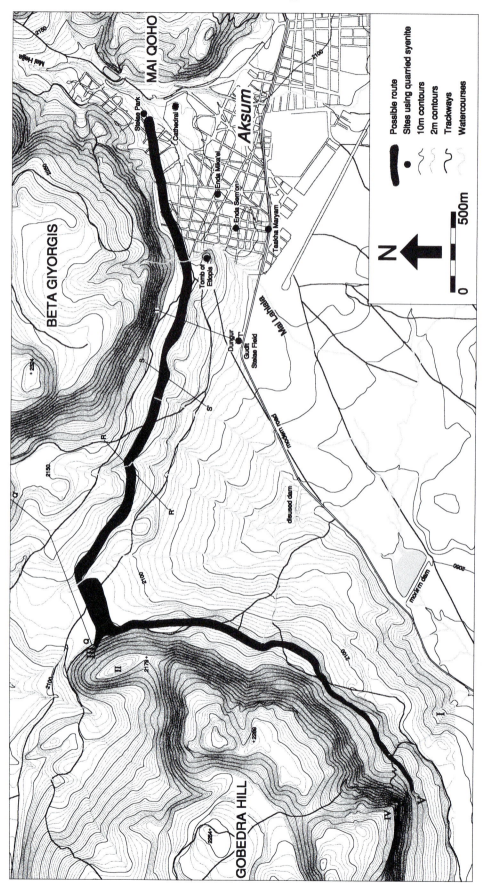

Fig. 222 *Contour map of the area between Gobedra and Aksum, showing the probable route by which quarried stone was transported. Depending on the amount or erosion that has taken place since Aksumite times, the route across the valley between Gobedra and Beta Giyorgis may have been to the south of that shown here.*

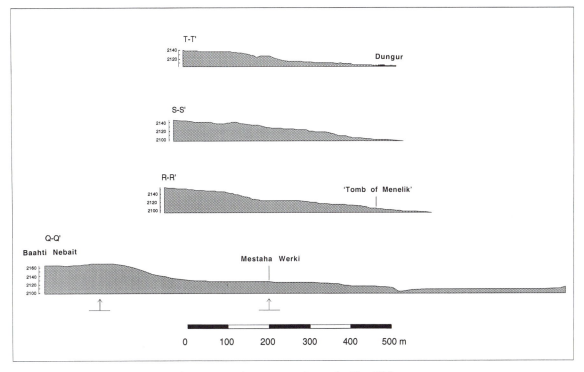

Fig. 223 *Cross-sections across the proposed route, as shown in Fig. 222.*

that such a route may have passed from the foot of the Quarry III slipway in a direction somewhat north of east across the flat head of the valley at 2110 m altitude to the southwestern flank of Beta Giyorgis. Depending on the extent of post-Aksumite soil erosion in this area, it is possible that a second route could have led more directly to this point from Quarries I and V. It could then have followed the foot of Beta Giyorgis in a remarkably straight east-southeasterly line, gaining only 20 m in altitude over a distance of 2.1 km, to a crossing of the Mai Lahlaha stream immediately north of the Tomb of Etiopis (Figs 222-4). Since the head of the valley has clearly been lowered by erosion since Aksumite times, the ascent would have been even less than the 0.9% here calculated. The apparent crossing-point of the Mai Lahlaha has been much disfigured by erosion and recent road building, as well as by the Aksumite building recorded by the Deutsche Aksum-Expedition as Ruin D (D.W.Phillipson 1997: 122). From this point, the route could have continued on an alignment slightly to the north of due east across the slope now occupied by the built-up area of Maleke Aksum, losing some 8 m over 0.95 km (0.85%) to the area where the major stelae were erected at an altitude of 2119 m. The linear distance of such a route is almost exactly 4.0 km. Much of the route has been modified by erosion, exposing boulders which would previously have been hidden. Areas may still be discerned on the southwestern flank of Beta Giyorgis where terrace walls of

probably ancient origin provide levelling across declivities in the route.

No primary archaeological evidence is available to suggest the manner in which the quarried stone was transported. Egyptian records provide examples of ways in which loads comparable with those at Aksum could be moved long distances by means of a comparatively simple technology (Arnold 1991). Indeed, the Aksumites had two technological advantages over their earlier Egyptian counterparts: iron tools and a relatively abundant supply of wood. Leather thongs, ropes and harnesses would also have been abundantly available from the vast numbers of cattle herded by the Aksumites. Timber would have been employed in many ways: to encase the stone blocks; for a cradle, sledge or wheeled conveyance; and perhaps for rollers and/or paving the trackway. Such use of timber would have minimised fraying and breakage of the leather and other ropes needed for haulage, and have reduced friction, as discussed below.

Motive power is likewise uncertain. Egyptian evidence demonstrates that a large well organised labour force can move stones similar in size to the Aksumite ones. The extent to which cattle were used at Aksum as draft-animals remains unknown; they and donkeys may have been used to transport timber and other materials, in a manner not always practicable in Egypt. Using data presented by Cotterell and Kamminga (1990: 193-233), it is possible to suggest that dragging stelae such as nos 2 and 1, weighing 160 and

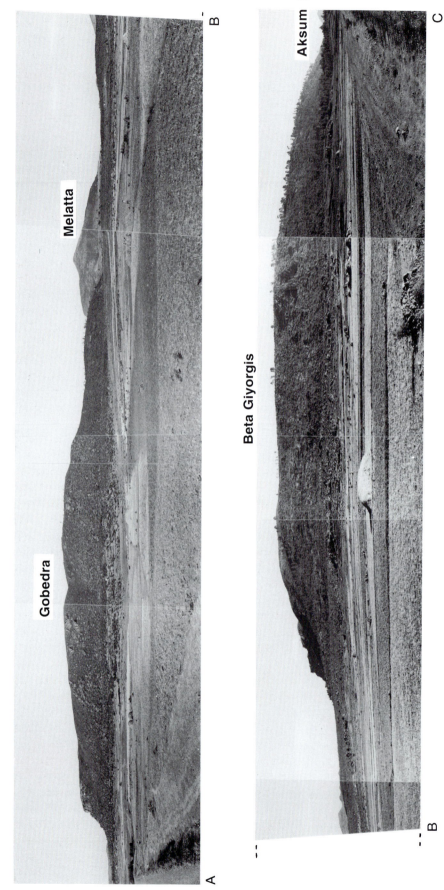

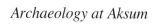

Fig. 224 *Photo-panorama of probable stela-route, taken from the Shire road at a point some 700 m west of Dungur. Gobedra Hill is on the right (upper section), Beta Giyorgis to the right (lower section) and the outskirts of Aksum town are on the extreme right.*

500 tonnes, along a relatively level but unpaved route would require respectively some 1800 and 5600 men (cf. also Burford 1960, Lewis 1985). These figures could be reduced to about one third (*i.e.* minima of 600 and 1900 men) if rollers or lubricants were used. These numbers are so large as to be almost inconceivable, leading to the question whether some sort of wheeled conveyance may not have been employed. The description of king Kaleb in a chariot, recorded by John Malalas (Sergew 1972: 138; D.W.Phillipson 1998: 52), suggests that the ancient Aksumites were familiar with wheels; and there is evidence that huge carts were used in Roman Egypt (whence many aspects of Aksumite quarrying technology appear to have been derived) to transport monolithic columns weighing up to 200 tonnes (Peña 1989; Peacock 1997). Such carts could have been pulled by animals, numbers of 1.3 cattle or 2.5 donkeys per tonne being required (Peña 1989; Cotterell and Kamminga 1990).[32] There are pervasive traditions at Aksum today that elephants were used to transport the stelae (cf. Fig. 225): although primary archaeological evidence is lacking, this is by no means impossible. The common belief that only Indian and not African elephants can be domesticated is demonstrably untrue (Sikes 1971: 296-7); indeed, African war-elephants were imported to Egypt by the Ptolemies (Scullard 1974; Burstein 1989; Sidebotham 1995). In the sixth century AD, Nonnosus recorded seeing large protected herds of elephants in the Aksum vicinity, and king Kaleb's chariot, noted above, was described as pulled by elephants (D.W.Phillipson 1998: 25, 52).

STELA ERECTION

Previous sections of this chapter have presented descriptions of some of the quarries where certain Aksumite stelae may have been extracted, and of the route and manner whereby they may have been transported into Aksum. It remains to consider the erection of the stelae. General observations are presented first, followed by a more detailed consideration of how the largest example, Stela 1, may have been erected.

Some stelae at least (most notably no. 8) appear to have been transported in an unfinished state. This is particularly clear in the case of no. 8; several (*e.g.* nos 17, 19 and 110) were erected without complete removal of the wedge-marks derived from their initial quarrying (D.W.Phillipson 1994a: fig. 5). Stela 5 was apparently broken, perhaps in transit, after carving of its decoration had begun, and redesigned in a different format (D.W.Phillipson 1997: 16-21). The two largest stelae are unusual in being carved in a similar manner on all four faces. The others are either plainly dressed on the back or have much simpler

[32] Ancient references (including Aksumite inscriptions) to draft animals rarely specify their species.

carving there. It is almost certain that the carving was done before the stelae were erected. This must have been the case if, as argued on p. 222 above, Stela 1 (which is fully carved on all four sides) fell and broke whilst attempts were being made to erect it. Carving and stone-dressing are further considered in a later section of this chapter.

The largest decorated stelae were all characteristically set on gently sloping ground. In those cases where one face has no or comparatively simple decoration, that face was on the uphill side. This supports the topographic indication that the decorated stelae were primarily intended to be seen from the southern, downslope, direction of what was, and still is, the main urban centre. It seems likely that the stelae were set upright from the north, utilising the slope of the ground: the area immediately upslope from each of the major storeyed stelae is apparently unencumbered by earlier features, and there would thus have been room for the construction of a ramp large enough to accommodate the length of the stela concerned (Figs 20, 21, above; Munro-Hay 1989: figs 4.1-7).

Two stelae are particularly informative in the present context. Stela 3 is the only one of the elaborately carved multi-storeyed stelae which remains intact and erect. It offers a good impression of the original configuration of such a monument, although it is possible that the stepped arrangement of its front and back baseplates may not be original. Clearly its underground features cannot be investigated by excavation without endangering its stability. This difficulty is to some extent remedied by one of the smaller storeyed stelae, no. 4, located near the churchyard of Enda Yesus. It has fallen and, although no excavations have been undertaken in the vicinity, the original arrangement of its component parts is readily apparent (D.W.Phillipson 1994a: fig. 9). Vertical stone slabs were set below the ground surface to line a pit into which the stub of the stela was set. The two baseplates were then installed, each being recessed to fit closely around the stela at ground level. The front baseplates of Stelae 3 and 4, like several others, were elaborately carved with designs incorporating hollows which could have served for the receipt of offerings.

The 1997 excavations on the site of Stela 2, described above on pp. 141-56, provide further indications of the below-ground setting of a major stela. Here, on a huge foundation, was set a horizontal stone slab on which the stela was to stand. On this slab rested vertical stones which demarcated the socket.

It is now possible to suggest how the larger stelae may have been erected. A socket was prepared in the position where it was intended the stela should stand. A ramp was constructed extending northwards from this position, its top being horizontal or only

Fig. 225 *Transport and erection of stelae, by Berhane Meskel Ftsah, Aksum, 1996.*

very gently inclined, and its length proportionate to that of the stela. The stela, its carving and dressing completed, must then have been brought to the site and laid on the ramp, as shown in Fig. 226. The next stage would have involved moving the stela horizontally southwards so that its foot extended beyond the end of the ramp, over the previously prepared socket. When, in the course of this process, the stela's centre of gravity approached the end of the ramp, the stela would be tilted so that its base entered the socket. It would then be necessary to adjust the stela into a position as nearly vertical as possible.

It seems likely that timber was extensively employed as levers and supports. A stela must have been gradually manoeuvred into position, then tipped into the socket that had been prepared for it. Following adjustment into a vertical position, the space between the stela-stub and the socket-lining was tightly packed with stones to hold the stela in position. Evidence for such packing has been observed in several places (*e.g.* Munro-Hay 1989: 77). Installation of baseplates was the final stage, enhancing the stability of the whole assembly.

One of the most difficult and dangerous parts of the operation would have been the final adjustment of the stela into its socket. It has been suggested above (p. 222) that Stela 1, with a mass three times that of any stela previously erected at Aksum, toppled southwards in this process and was smashed. It may also be that the misalignment of Stela 3 dates from the time of its original erection (cf. p. 138, above; D.W.Phillipson and Hobbs 1996).

OBSERVATIONS ON THE ATTEMPTED ERECTION OF STELA 1

Chapter 7 provides an account of the present state of this monument, and of excavations conducted in its vicinity. With an estimated length of *c.* 32.6 m and a weight of 517 tonnes, this was by far the largest of the Aksumite stelae. It seems most probable that the broken portions of Stela 1 have not been moved since the time of its catastrophic fall and that its base remains very near the position at which it was intended that the stela should stand. Furthermore, the contour defined by the lower face of the stela as it now lies may be taken as indicative of the then existing ground level if allowance is made for ground compaction resulting from the force of impact. Discounting the effect of consolidation in the area between the entrances to the Mausoleum and East Tomb, the positions in which the northernmost portions of Stela 1 now lie define a ground slope of about 6 degrees (cf. Figs 21, 130, above). Taking the top of the pre-existing terrace wall over which the stela fell and broke as indicative of the surface height at that point, a probable transect of the terrace as it then was can be reconstructed.[33] The nature of this terrace wall is confirmed by the fact that a free-standing or insecurely supported wall in the area between the Mausoleum and the East Tomb would not have resisted the impact of the falling stela.

[33] Additional indications of the approximate ancient ground level are provided by the baseplates of Stela 3 and by the surface of Stela 2's basal slab plus the 2.9-m length of its below-ground foot (cf. p. 152, above). On average, it appears that the ground level at the time the stelae were erected was *c.* 0.5 m above the present surface.

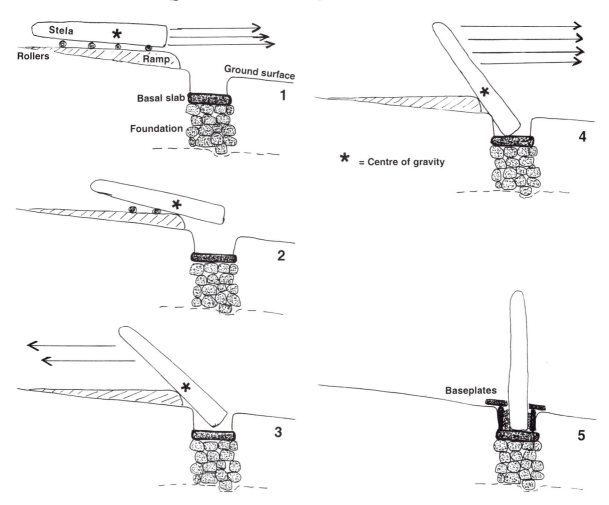

Fig. 226 *Possible method of stela-erection.*

As argued above, it is probable that the attempt to erect Stela 1 involved the use of a ramp extending approximately northwards, or uphill, from the place of its intended erection. Such a location would take advantage of the natural slope of the ground to permit a rise at the southern end, or lip, while ensuring that the upper surface of the ramp remained horizontal or almost so.

Three phases would have been involved in the 'launching' of the stela from its face-up horizontal position on the ramp to its intended vertical position. First a very large force would be required to overcome stationary inertia and set the mass into motion. Second would be a smaller force necessary to overcome friction and to keep the stela in motion along the length of the ramp. Third, and most crucial, would be the need to check and control the stela's descent as it slid base-first from the end of the ramp. Shaping the lip of the ramp to provide either a gentle curve or a reverse slope could have assisted in guiding the stela into position (Chevrier 1970: 34).

As the stela descended from the ramp, three directional forces would have been acting upon it, each of which would have required control in order to permit a safe landing. These were a continuation of the horizontal momentum from its projection along the ramp, the downward force of gravity, and a torque or rotational force about the stela's centre of gravity resulting from gravity acting on the leading or basal portion of the stela while its upper end remained supported by the ramp. Failure to control the horizontal momentum would have resulted in the stela landing face-up with its base to the south; failure to control the pull of gravity would have resulted in the stela landing heavily and shattering on impact with the ground. Only a failure adequately to control the stela's angular momentum could have resulted in the monument's landing in the position in which it is now found: face-down and with its base to the north, a reversal of 180 degrees or slightly more from the position which it must have occupied while it lay on the ramp.

The desired and intended position for a large stela upon descent from its ramp was most likely that it should have a slight backwards tilt, leaning against the lip of the ramp, from which it could be pulled and pushed into a vertical position. Too great a backwards tilt would make the job of righting it very difficult; too vertical an initial position would increase the risk of overshooting the mark and seeing the stela collapse in a forward direction. The stela's length, slippage and a component of horizontal momentum as it left the ramp would cause the foot of the stela to touch ground a some distance beyond the ramp's base. Without knowing the speed at which the stela moved nor the height of the ramp, this distance cannot be calculated. Likewise, we do not know the angle at which the stela was intended to lean before its final righting.

The process of stela erection would have been complicated by the fact that the top of the stela would not lose its rotational momentum as soon as its base touched ground, but would have continued to move forward with the centre about which it rotated transferred from the stela's centre of gravity to its base. If this angular momentum were absorbed and halted before the stela reached near verticality all would be well, the stela coming to rest in a position from which it could be pulled upright. If, however, rotation carried the stela beyond the point of verticality, the pull of gravity added to the residual momentum would make collapse inevitable. A small misestimation in the ramp's necessary height would have been sufficient to cause the destruction which did in fact take place. That this possibility was anticipated and allowed for is evident from the configuration of Stela 1 with a small basal portion and a centre of gravity almost 15 m above its lower end, which is very close to its linear midpoint. (Since the travelling speed of a point on a rotating object is proportional to its distance from the centre about which it turns, the lower the centre of gravity, the faster the top of the stela would have travelled as it descended from the ramp.)

The position of the stela as it first landed would have been affected primarily by the total height from the lip of the ramp to the surface on which it rested and by the location of the stela's centre of gravity. The higher the ramp, the steeper the angle at which the stela could be expected to come to rest, but the greater its impact with the ground and the more crucial to control its vertical descent to prevent shattering as it landed. More difficult to retard than the stela's vertical descent would have been its rotational torque. To do so would require that the upper end of the stela be vertically as well as horizontally restrained as it descended. Failure to do so would result in the monument's toppling irretrievably past the vertical position before its base was securely grounded. On the other hand, if the upper end of the stela were held down too firmly while the descent began, the strain on such a long, slender piece of stone would be likely to break it along any possible line of weakness.

While the lack of a massive stela base would be a major advantage, probably a necessity, if there was to be any hope of success in setting it upright, a heavy base would have been needed for stability once the monument had been erected. The construction described above (pp. 251-2) of a stela foot set into a stone-lined and stone-packed pit would have served this function provided that it was capped with baseplates sufficiently massive to prevent any elements of the construction from shifting. It may be expected that baseplates would have been prepared in readiness for installation as soon as Stela 1 was erected: such baseplates are not now, however, in evidence.

The more one contemplates it, the more the process of stela erection seems to have been fraught with difficulties. However, the use of an elementary system of pulleys might have made the task easier. Even a very simple construction of fixed or hinged tripods and single pulleys located to the south of the stela's intended position, perhaps in the cleared space between the terrace wall and Nefas Mawcha, would have permitted it to have been pulled upright from a less vertical position after descending from a lower ramp than would have been possible without the use of such auxiliary tools. We know that the timbers and ropes necessary to construct such a system were available at Aksum, and we may surmise that people who were able to quarry and transport these massive stones had a high level of practical mechanical knowledge. However, as there is no evidence for or against their use in ancient Aksum we cannot make any assumptions on this point. What we do know is that both Stela 2 and Stela 3 were successfully erected, Stela 2 only having collapsed several centuries later as a result of intentional undermining. Stela 1 was not successfully erected and great must have been the consternation and probably injuries and deaths as the hundreds or thousands of people involved in the attempt witnessed its destruction.

Stone dressing

(Laurel Phillipson)

It has long been recognised that several of the Aksumite stelae are, as well as being among the largest monoliths ever erected anywhere, very finely worked; the logical question of how this was accomplished appears, however, not previously to have been addressed. From a careful inspection of the surfaces of the major monuments and dressed stones, it is possible to retrieve information about the processes and tools employed in their shaping. Particularly revealing in this study are several dressed stones which had remained buried, and thus unexposed to the vicissitudes of wear and weather, for most of the time since their original shaping. These include especially the blocks of the Tomb of the False Door (Munro-Hay 1989: 104-10), several stones which comprised the foundation structure beneath Stela 2, three contiguous fragments of Stela 2 which became detached and remained buried from the time when it was toppled in antiquity until their recovery in 1997 (pp. 154-5, above), and the stonework of the Mausoleum, discovered in 1973 and excavated in 1993-5 (pp. 165-79, above).

An important component of the decorative aspects of the stelae is the colour of the syenite of which they are composed. This is a white to pale grey stone with numerous close packed angular inclusions between 1 and 3 mm across. When freshly exposed these inclusions are a striking blue colour, being in the Munsell range 2.5Pb: 4/2, 3/0, 3/2, 3/4, and 2/2, and 7.5B: 4/0, 4/2, 3/0, and 3/2. Sunlight shining on the fresh stone surfaces, as it would have on the south-facing stelae and other monuments when newly erected, makes a brilliant spectacle. Eventually the surfaces weather to a pleasant but less impressive medium grey. We continue to be awed by the size and quality of carving on the Aksumite monuments; the ancient Aksumites would also have admired their colour and glitter. Syenite is reputed to be less hard and easier to carve than granite, with which it has sometimes been confused. Hammerstones of basalt or granite are preferred today for redressing sandstone and syenite

grindstones, and it is noteworthy that a cylindrical basalt pounder was found at Gobedra Quarry III (p. 240 and Fig. 214, above). Samples of freshly broken syenite can only be lightly scratched with a penknife, indicating a Moh's hardness of about 5 or somewhat above. Iron tools used to work this stone would require to be sturdy and well forged, perhaps with a rather high carbon content, and would nonetheless require frequent resharpening and replacement. Experiment has demonstrated that the stone is somewhat softer when freshly quarried, but hardens with prolonged exposure to the air.

All the exposed monuments in the main Stelae Park were examined for evidence of dressing techniques. In addition to photographs and rubbings of dressed surfaces, plasticine casts and direct measurements were made of individual tooling marks, and latex casts were made of some larger areas. Few previous studies of this type having been conducted (*e.g.* Bessac 1988), this investigation began with basic principles. While the length and depth of individual tooling marks give an indication of the relative sizes of tools used to dress the stones and of the force employed in doing so, owing to subsequent weathering and to the fracture properties of the stone they do not give a measurement of actual tool-size. Similarly, casts of individual tooling marks are more indicative of the shapes of the tip or edge of the tools employed than of their sizes.

It is noticeable that the exposed stelae near the eastern end of the Stelae Park are more worn than those in the western portion. Stela 27, for example, seems to have been dressed in a manner similar to Stela 19, but on the former the stone has been so eroded by exposure to the elements that tool marks on its surfaces have been very largely effaced. While it may

Fig. 227 Modern mason's tools.

be tempting to conclude that the degree of weathering might indicate the relative ages of the stelae, this argument would be difficult to support as the individual blocks of syenite from which the monuments were carved vary somewhat in their density, porosity and fracture properties. Stela 21 in particular exhibits a different fracture pattern from the others. Likewise, the individual monuments differ in their particular histories. Although the detached, recently recovered portions of Stela 2 retain even their finest tooling marks despite apparently having been exposed to the atmosphere for several centuries before the monument was toppled, Stelae 1 and 3 at similar heights above their bases have been so worn as to retain almost no evidence of individual tooling marks.

Initial stages of shaping and dressing the stone blocks which were to become the stelae and other monuments took place in the quarries as part of the extraction process. There is no definitive evidence as to where the final stages of stone-dressing were carried out, but it seems likely that this was often at or near the places of erection of each monument. The close and sometimes complex fit of architectural blocks to one another, as at the Tombs of Kaleb and Gabra Maskal (pp. 427-31, below; D.W.Phillipson 1997: 73-88, 1998: 107-9) or the Tomb of the False Door (Munro-Hay 1989: 104-12), could most easily be obtained by the adjustment and finishing of individual components on site as the construction work progressed. Also, delaying the final dressing of the larger blocks until after they had been transported from their place of quarrying would have reduced the risk of accidental damage in transit, while transport in a semi-finished state would have lessened the weight and bulk of stone to be transported. That such was the case in some instances is attested by the unfinished Stela 8 (D.W.Phillipson 1994a: 192, fig. 4), which is well dressed on one face, less well dressed on another, and unfinished at either end. The ends of a stela would have been the portions most vulnerable to damage while being lowered from its quarry site and transported to its intended place of erection. That not all stelae were transported in such an unfinished state is, however, indicated by several partially extracted specimens in the Gobedra quarries and elsewhere which carefully rounded or otherwise shaped tops.

Although hammerstones and stone polishers were probably used, most of the stone-dressing tools must have been of high-quality iron or steel, as is indicated by the sharpness of individual tooling marks. The tool for which there is most evidence is a blunt metal punch, or possibly a pick, with a tapered profile and an approximately square cross-section near the tip, probably very similar to that used by traditional stone masons at the present day (Fig. 227). Various sizes of

Fig. 228 *Internal impressions of stone-dressing marks: a - profiles of individual punches, Nefas Mawcha; b - profiles and plans of individual punch-marks, wedge holes on slab (1014) associated with the base of Stela 2; c - Plans of running punch-marks, Stela 19. Tracings of stone-dressing marks: d - individual punch-marks and chisel-marks on the lintel of the Tomb of the False Door; e - chisel- and multi-tined hammer- / punch-marks, T-shaped block at the Tomb of the False Door; f - stone-dressing marks on the upper part of the detached portion of Stela 2; g - multi-tined hammer- / punch-marks on the lower part of the detached portion of Stela 2; h - lengths of running punch- and possible chisel-marks, Stela 19; i - chisel- or running punch-marks, Stela 21.*

256

this tool were used, presumably in conjunction with an iron-headed hammer, depending on the amount of material to be removed from the stone's surface and the final appearance that was desired. For some purposes, such as carving out the deep holes into which quarrying wedges were inserted, sculpting some fine details, and sometimes for reducing ridges between other punch-marks, the punch was struck at right-angles to the stone surface. Most frequently it was applied at an inclination to the stone's surface and struck three, four or five times, producing a short running line with an uneven bottom reflective of the several hammer-blows. The quality of the finished surface will have depended upon the size of the punch used, the force with which and angle at which it was struck, and the length and spacing of the individual tooling lines. Occasional tooling marks with a flat bottom of even depth and indications of a corner at one or both ends - rather like a square bracket,] - indicate that a flat chisel was sometimes used instead of or in addition to a punch. Other marks indicate the occasional use of a stout, multi-toothed chisel or punch and several more delicate tools for the final finishing of dressed surfaces: a small, round punch, a light-weight hammer with a row of four or five square teeth, and rounded hammers of stone or metal which were used to obliterate other tooling marks without adding distinctive new scars (Fig. 228).

Most often, the use of larger punches was followed by those of progressively smaller sizes, the smaller marks tending to overlie the larger and to be at approximately right-angles to them. Where vertical single punch-marks were used to reduce the high spots between areas of chased tooling, the same size of punch appears to have been used for both operations. Most of the stelae and architectural blocks were left with their hidden surfaces roughly chased or punch-dressed and their exposed surfaces finely dressed, the texture of the dressing marks providing an important decorative element. Most of the stelae have had the finer details of their finishing obliterated by gradual weathering, but on a few monuments there is clear evidence of the deliberate erasure of dressing marks, whether by overall hammering or, perhaps, by the use of a stone abrader.

The several stages of stone dressing which have been recognised (use of larger and smaller punches, hammering and polishing) were apparently sequential and applied to all flat surfaces, the sizes of the tools, skill of the artisans, and point in the sequence at which work was stopped largely determining the fineness of the finish obtained. Sculpted decoration always comprises flat surfaces in moderate or low relief; there is no trace of carving in the round. Lines of close-set,

individual circular punch marks were used to delineate decorative areas, as may be seen on the front of Stela 3 and the lintel at the Tomb of the False Door. No use was made of a drill or similar tool for detailed work.

Nefas Mawcha

Despite having been exposed to the elements for a long period, the stonework of this monument (D.W. Phillipson 1997: 68-71, 189 and references; also pp. 157-61, above) retains many indications of its primary shaping and final dressing. The upper surface of the great capstone has been dressed with running punch-marks in fairly regular, approximately parallel rows oriented in areas which would correspond to a stone-mason's reach from a kneeling or crouched position. These tooling marks are in three size-ranges: 75 to 105 mm, 43 to 58 mm, and 20 to 26 mm long. Some of the smallest tooling marks appear to have been made with a straight-edged chisel rather than a punch. In places, the rows of tooling marks can be seen to overlap at approximately right-angles, the smaller marks overlying the larger (Figs 229b, c). Only the larger punches were used in the area closest to the remaining undressed bulge on the capstone. On the bulge itself are several rectangular marks which must have been made by a particularly massive chisel or wedge struck vertically to the surface with considerable force. Three or four other marks were apparently made by a stout toothed or notched chisel struck diagonally. The edges and lower surface of the capstone are more carefully dressed.

A variety of running punch-, single punch- and chisel-marks occur on the smaller roof-slabs and other blocks (Figs 229d-f). The roof-slab at the north-western corner was first roughly dressed, then finished with a blunt square-ended punch applied vertically to produce marks 7 to 12 mm square and up to 9 mm deep (Fig. 228a). A stone lying on the ground at the western end of Nefas Mawcha and presumably once part of it has a tooled line across its exposed face. Below that line the major tooling marks were largely effaced by the strokes of a blunt punch or hammer which has left shallow, faintly delineated scars 5 to 8 mm in diameter. Above the line, the stone is only roughly dressed. The outer blocks and roof-slabs of this monument have mainly running punch- and square, single punch-marks; some have also been hammer-dressed. In general, the lower faces of the roof-slabs are more carefully dressed than the upper faces and their edges and corners are particularly carefully finished. Adjoining faces of the blocks, which would have been completely hidden from view, were also well dressed to enable them to fit closely against one another.

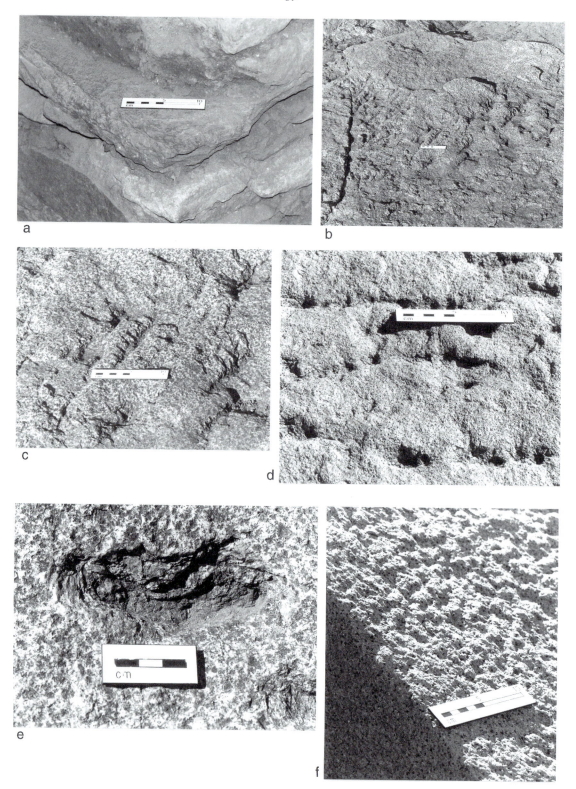

Fig. 229 *Stone-dressing, Tomb of the Brick Arches and Nefas Mawcha:* ***a*** *- support for Arch 1 at the Tomb of the Brick Arches, topped by trimmed undressed slates;* ***b, c****- medium and large chisel--marks on the Nefas Mawcha capstone, some clawed or toothed, showing overlapping areas of parallel rows;* ***d*** *- roof-slab at the northwest corner of Nefas Mawcha, dressed with a 4-toothed punch c. 80 mm long;* ***e*** *- detail of the Nefas Mawcha capstone;* ***f*** *- finely dressed (hammered) face of a Nefas Mawcha roof-slab.*

The Tomb of the Brick Arches

It is a conspicuous feature of this monument (pp. 31-57, above) that almost no dressed stone was used in its construction (Fig. 229a). The pilasters supporting the brick arches are topped by naturally flat, roughly trimmed slates; the roofing slabs of the adit are roughly trimmed with their major surfaces undressed; and only undressed stones and mud mortar were used in the adit and partition walls. Some stones of the stair-treads were dressed, but only to the extent necessary to provide moderately level surfaces, individual tooling marks being irregularly spaced and 30 to 37 mm long. In view of the very finely dressed stonework exhibited in Pre-Aksumite and later structures, the absence of well dressed stone in the Tomb of the Brick Arches is a notable feature, particularly in contrast with the relatively advanced architectural features of the brick arches themselves.

While the stair-treads have not been worn into concavities, they clearly exhibit more wear than can be attributed to the passage of archaeologists and visitors during several seasons of excavation. It would seem most likely that the tomb was open and repeatedly visited at some stage in its history as, indeed, is confirmed by the archaeological evidence for repeated robbing noted above (pp. 36-7, 131-2).

The Tomb of the False Door

This is the most finely finished of the monuments in the Stelae Park (Munro-Hay 1989: 104-13; D.W.Phillipson 1997: 192-3). On their exposed faces all stones, including the slab on which the false door is carved, have been hammered to obliterate most tooling marks (Fig. 230a). Contiguous faces of these well squared blocks were also finely finished, particularly near their edges, to allow for their close fit. Internal faces of the same blocks were undressed or only roughly shaped.

Especially finely dressed is the lower, exposed portion of the now displaced lintel which had capped the false door. Here, shallow running punch- or chisel-marks 10 to 15 mm long are overlain and largely obliterated by even shallower multi-tined hammer- or punch-marks 6 to 12 mm long. Vertical grooves about 75 mm long at 35 mm intervals, consisting of contiguous single round punch-marks, define an area of mock board-ends (Figs 230b, 231a).[34] Above the mock boarding this stone is progressively more roughly dressed, with tooling marks up to 49 mm long overlain by single square punch-marks up to 27 mm deep (Figs 228c, 230c).

A free-standing stone dressed on all faces, now in the courtyard in front of the tomb, has a cross-section like a stout letter T and is one of the most finely dressed stones anywhere in the Stelae Park. On it, tooling marks have been almost completely effaced by closely spaced, shallow, multi-tined hammer- or punch-marks (Figs 228e, 230f, 231b). Unlike the variously dressed and considerably worn paving slabs of the courtyard in front of the tomb and the facing blocks of the tomb itself, which are slightly worn, this free-standing stone appears to be completely unweathered: perhaps it had served as a table or bench in one of the chambers.

Several of the main blocks of the tomb have sharply cut square sockets for metal clamps, perhaps inserted to rectify a slippage fault which may have developed after the structure was completed. Only one iron clamp remains in place (Fig. 230e; Munro-Hay 1989: pl. 6.35; D.W.Phillipson 1998: fig. 48): its very close fit is direct evidence of the high quality of stone and iron working.

The Mausoleum and Stela 1

All major exposed stone surfaces of the Mausoleum were well dressed to provide regular, flat surfaces. Tooling marks on the underside of the well trimmed and close-fitting roof-slabs are mainly 44 to 89 mm long. The easternmost roof-slab of the central passage, which extends to form a lintel above the eastern portal, is partly exposed on its upper surface. The vertical edge of this slab is roughly dressed with tooling marks 22 to 49 mm long; its upper surface appears to have been undressed. A larger tool, leaving marks 42 to 64 mm long, was used to finish the regularly shaped rectangular monolithic supports for the brick-arched entrances to each sidechamber (Fig. 231c).

The most finely finished element in this monument is the outer face of the monolithic eastern portal, on which tooling marks only 9 to 17 mm long have been largely effaced by subsequent hammered dressing (Fig. 231d). Above its opening, a shallow horizontal step is defined by a row of contiguous circular punch-marks, each approximately 5 mm in diameter (Fig. 231e). That all surfaces of the portal, including the sill and the edges of the uprights at hand- and shoulder-height, appear to be equally unworn and in pristine or near-pristine condition lends support to the hypothesis that this entrance to the edifice was sealed or abandoned very soon after its erection.

Stela 1 (D.W.Phillipson 1997: 37-43 and references; pp. 161-4, above) was so carefully finished and has become so heavily weathered that few discrete tooling marks can be discerned on it. Those seen measured 21 to 34 mm long. The base, which was much more roughly dressed, retains marks 35 to 44 mm

---

[34] This feature, preserved in wood at Debra Damo (Matthews and Mordini 1959: pl. ivc), is represented in stone on several of the Aksum stelae where it was noted as dentils by earlier investigators (cf. D.W.Phillipson 1997: footnote 33).

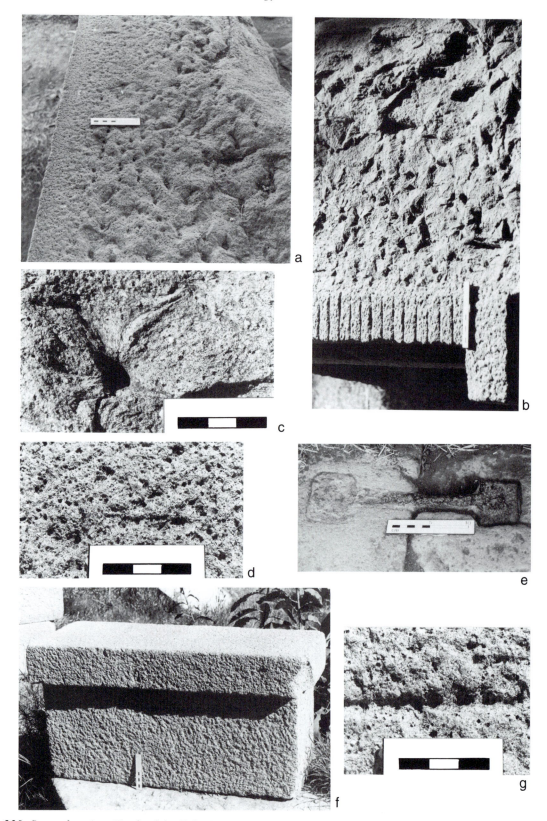

Fig. 230 *Stone-dressing, Tomb of the False Door:* **a** *- punched upper face of the false-door slab;* **b** *- lintel, upper portion of face, regularly spaced single deep punch marks with radiating fracture lines and overly broad chiselling;* **c** *- detail of lintel;* **d** *- detail of lintel;* **e** *- iron clamp, showing the remarkably close fit between stone and metal;* **f** *- T-shaped block, tooled with a 3- or 4-prong punch (not hammered);* **g** *- detail of displaced block.*

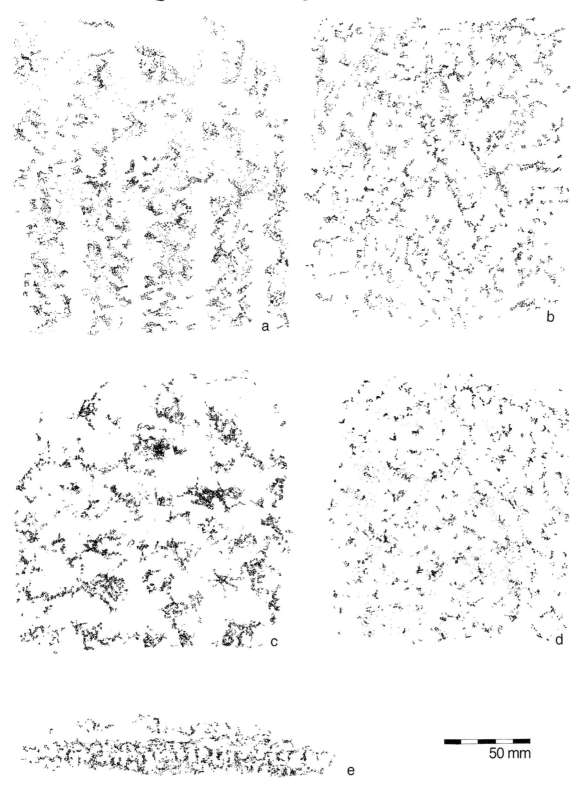

50 mm

Fig. 231 *Rubbings of dressed stones, Tomb of the False Door: **a** - lintel with vertical lines of mock boarding below an area roughly dressed with single punch marks; **b** - fine multi-tined hammer or punch dressing on T-shaped block. Rubbings of dressed stones, Mausoleum: **c** - support of brick arch at the entrance to a sidechamber; **d** - outside of the eastern portal, southern side of vertical at shoulder height; **e** - contiguous single punch-marks defining a shallow horizontal step over the eastern portal's aperture.*

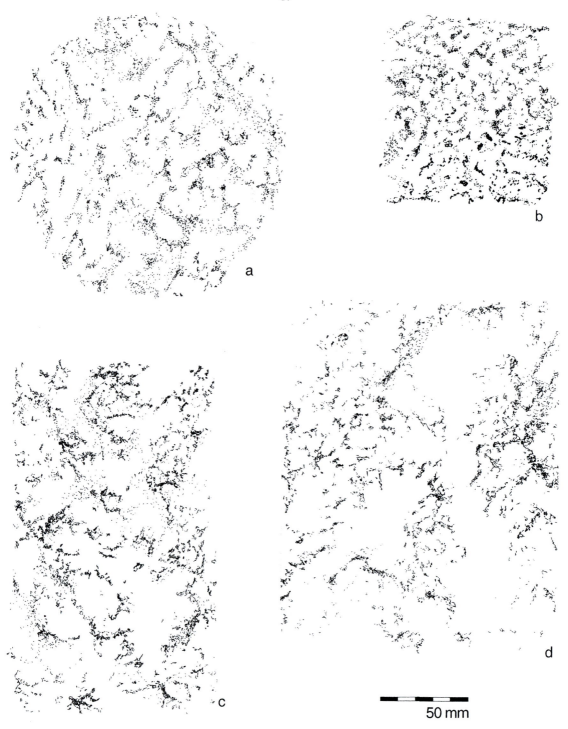

Fig. 232 *Rubbings of dressed stones, Stela 2: **a** - upper part of newly recovered portion; **b** - lower part of newly recovered portion; **c** - weathered southern part of the basal slab (1015); **d** - roughly redressed northern part of the basal slab.*

long, some of which have corners such as might have been left by use of a flat chisel rather than a more pointed tool. There is a clear transitional zone between the roughly shaped base and the finely worked body of the stela (Fig. 233a).

Stela 2

This monument was described by the Deutsche Aksum-Expedition in 1906 (D.W.Phillipson 1997: 33-6 and references), its site being further investigated by the 1993-7 Project (see Chapter 6, above). Three congruent parts of one face and corner at a height slightly above 2.0 m from the top of the base were recovered in the 1997 excavations (pp. 154-5 and Fig. 124, above). On the upper part of this section, a circular monkey-head and the surrounding stone have tooling marks, 28 to 35 mm long and 11 to 15 mm long, which have been only slightly obscured by subsequent hammering (Figs 228f, 232a). A square window-boss in the lower part has been intensively hammered over by means of an instrument with four square teeth, leaving very shallow tooling marks 16 to 20 mm long and effacing evidence of the earlier stages of stone-dressing (Figs 228g, 232b). It would seem that extra effort in the final stage was expended only on those areas which were low enough to be closely viewed when the stela was erect. This variation with altitude in the quality of the final stone-dressing was only visible in this instance because the relevant portion of the stela had been buried and undisturbed for much of its existence.

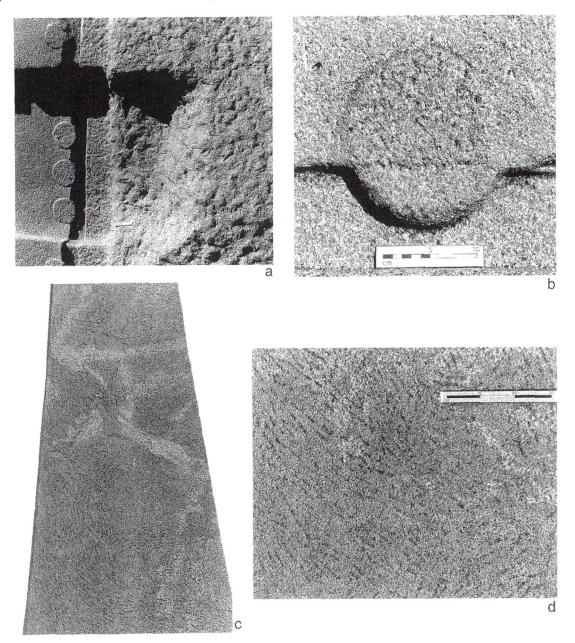

Fig. 233 *Stone-dressing, Stelae 1, 3 and 19:* **a** *- east face of Stela-1 base, showing contrast between the hammer-finished fine chiselled and the roughly chiselled areas;* **b** *- on Stela 3, the rectangles on the face were outlined before the monkey heads were carved;* **c** *- patterned chiselling on Stela 19 emphasises the natural colour-variation of the stone and follows it in several places;* **d** *- decorative use of a toothed chisel or punch on Stela 19.*

Fig. 234 *The south face of Stela 3, showing both its impressive overall symmetry and the variation in detail.*

The basal slab under Stela 2 has a roughly cut transverse step separating the northern and lower portion on which the stela had been erected from the southern portion on which the southern supporting stone is presumed to have stood. The basal slab (1015) itself (p. 143, above) is a natural flat boulder which has only been chisel- and punch-dressed sufficiently to level the central area of its upper surface. The southern portion of this slab (Fig. 232c) is both more finely worked and more weathered than the northern portion

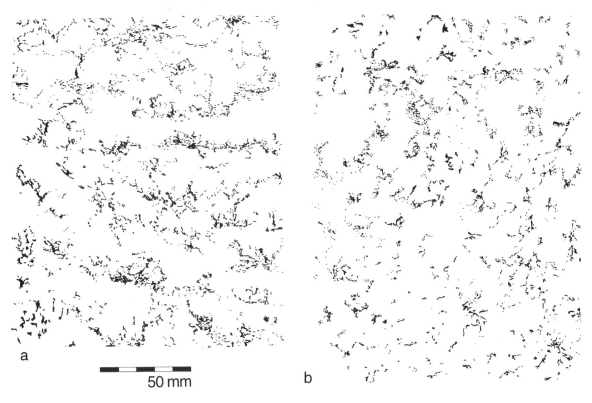

Fig. 235 *Rubbings of dressed stones, Stelae 19 and 21: **a** - Stela 19, running chisel marks in curved rows;*
***b** - Stela 21, finely dressed with possible chisel- and multi-tined hammer-marks.*

(Fig. 232d). It would seem that the slab is a re-used stone - perhaps a capstone or paving slab from an older and abandoned monument - roughly recarved in its northern portion. Tooling marks are 49 to 64 mm long in the northern portion, 25 to 35 mm in the southern portion. Individual punch-marks in both sections vary from *c.* 10 by 10 mm to 11 by 13 mm.

Also associated with the setting of Stela 2 was a slab (1014) which retains clear impressions of the small, square-ended punch used to carve out several quarry wedge-holes and to trim its edge (Fig. 228b). Part of a marble slab, perhaps only fortuitously associated with Stela 2, has a uniform thickness of 74 mm. Its two flat faces have faint parallel striations from polishing, and possible traces of fire-damage.

Stela 3

This stela, which has been standing exposed to the elements for some sixteen centuries, is too worn to permit recognition of discrete tooling marks (Fig. 233b). However, something of the method of organising the sculpted relief carving may be recognised on the front, south, face. That the rectangular areas were delineated before the monkey heads which depend from them is evident from the fact that the lines describing the rectangles continue across the circles. While the entire monument has an impressive overall symmetry, irregularities of the circles and slight variations in the depth and slope of the carved elements suggests that the carving was done freehand by skilled artisans, not guided by precise measurements (Fig. 234). Attention has already been drawn (D.W.Phillipson 1994a: 192, fig. 6; p. 136, above) to the presence on the north face of the stela of clearly divided tooling areas.

Stela 8

On its north face this recumbent, unfinished stela is undressed at its eastern end and roughly dressed but largely unshaped at the western end, which presumably was intended as its base. The main portion of this face has even, regular tooling marks 22 to 34 mm long, some apparently made with a flat chisel rather than with a repeatedly struck punch. The south face is undressed at either end and elsewhere less finely dressed than the north face, with evidence of the use of a broader, blunter tool leaving marks 36 to 85 mm long. A band 30 to 35 mm wide of much finer dressing running along the southern face of the neatly shaped exposed edge perhaps represents the smoothed remains of quarrying scars.

Stela 18

This is a largely natural boulder with very worn quarrying marks visible on one edge and rough dressing by means of individually struck punch marks discernible on its south face only. The rectangular tooling marks are widely spaced and measure from 11 by 21 mm to 20 by 35 mm.

Stela 19

The stone of this stela is unique in having a prominent swirled or marbled pattern of paler colour on its south face, which is emphasised and in part followed or deliberately continued by carefully placed chased tooling-marks 38 to 48 mm long (Figs 228c, h, 235a). The dressing marks are evenly spaced in curved parallel rows, each individual mark itself being slightly curved. With the possible exception of Stela 27, no other dressed stone has received this sophisticated decorative treatment (Figs 233c, d). Dressing on the back of the stela is similar to that on the front, but executed with less care and regularity. On each edge, including the east edge of the north face with its retained quarrying marks, there is a band about 60 mm wide of finer dressing with tooling marks 28 to 34 mm long.

Stela 21

The stone is distinctive in having a somewhat more foliate fracture pattern and a finer texture. The edges and corners of the stela are more finely dressed than the main faces and the bands along the edges are recessed from the north and south face by about 5 mm. The main faces were dressed with small tools, perhaps a chisel and a multi-tined hammer rather than a punch, leaving marks 11 to 19 mm long (Figs 228i, 235b).

Stela 27

This is one of the easternmost stelae in the area of the present Stelae Park. Its regularly spaced rows of tooling marks give the entire surface a rippled appearance. The stone is, however, so weathered that individual tooling marks cannot be discerned.

Stela 107

As on many other stelae, the edges and corners are more finely dressed than the main faces. It has been systematically dressed with neat rows of cuts overlapping one another at approximately right-angles, larger marks being 58 to 67 mm long, the smaller ones 26 to 32 mm. Also noted were a few individual subcircular punch marks with diameters of 6 to 11 mm.

Overview
(D.W.P.)

This chapter offers some preliminary observations and hypotheses on how the ancient Aksumites produced, transported and erected the stupendous monuments for which their civilisation is famous. The largely descriptive material presented here represents only a preliminary stage of research on Aksumite monumental stone-working techniques. It is recognised that the accounts of the quarries are incomplete, and that excavations have not yet been undertaken such as might yield dating evidence or traces of the implements that were employed. Interpretation has been hampered by the scarcity of comparative material: studies of ancient quarrying and stone dressing are remarkably scarce, being virtually non-existant in Africa beyond the Nile Valley. In Egypt, far more attention has been paid to the evidence from the pharaonic period than to that from later times, with the notable exception of the Roman quarries, notably those at Mons Claudianus (Peacock and Maxfield 1997). It is from here, and from more distant areas within the Roman tradition, that most of the comparanda cited in this chapter have been derived. The work serves to emphasise the potential and need for further study both at Aksum and over a much wider area.